HISPANIC CULTURE IN THE SOUTHWEST

UNIVERSITY OF OKLAHOMA PRESS NORMAN

HISPANIC CULTURE IN THE SOUTHWEST

ARTHUR L. CAMPA

By Arthur L. Campa

Spanish Folkpoetry in New Mexico (Albuquerque, 1946)

Treasure of the Sangre de Cristos (Norman, 1962)

The Brand Book (editor, Boulder, 1966)

Hispanic Culture in the Southwest (Norman, 1979)

Library of Congress Cataloging in Publication Data

Campa, Arthur Leon, 1905–1978
  Hispanic culture in the Southwest.

  Bibliography: p. 303
  Includes index.
  1. Southwest, New—Civilization—Spanish influences.
I. Title.
F786.C22   979'.004'68   78–58135

To my wife, Lucille, and to my children:
MARY DEL, ARTHUR, DANIELLE, NITA, AND DAVID

PREFACE

This work deals primarily with the salient manifestations of Hispanic culture in the Southwest, a region that includes the lands that became the northern outposts of the Spanish Empire. Much of the cultural development that took place is implicit in the history of each section of a region, which, over the years of Spanish expansion north and west to the Pacific coast, comprised what is now Colorado, Texas, New Mexico, Arizona, and California. When one looks back over the four centuries of Spanish contact with the land, three periods of history stand out. The nature of the culture introduced by the Spaniards changed during each period, and, although there were some setbacks during the years covered by each successive period, there were also some contributions that made Hispanic culture what it is today.

In order to explain in part the noticeable variations today, I have tried to analyze the contrasts between the two cultures with which the original Spanish civilization has coexisted or merged. The first era extends from Spain's first appearance in the Southwest and ends with the beginning of Mexican independence. Hispanic culture did not cease to exist at this time, but it followed a slightly different trend. The third period begins with the arrival of the Anglo-Americans and the eventual takeover by the United States. This period contrasts sharply with the first two, because in that time the role of the Spanish speakers was reversed. When they first arrived in the country, they became the dominant culture. The Indians who occupied the land would become acculturated to the incoming civilization, primarily through the work of Catholic priests and their missions. And, as might naturally be expected, there was a good deal of racial intermarriage. After 1848 the dominant culture was Anglo-American, a culture that did not establish missions as a vanguard to acculturation but whose basic designs differed little from those of the Spaniards. The Americans were interested in the acquisition of land and the exploitation of natural resources, in which the inhabitants already there played a secondary role.

This reversal of role affected Hispanic culture in various ways. It was the Spanish speaker's turn to become acculturated to another way of life, another language, and another set of traditions and folkways. From a scholar's viewpoint, this cultural phenomenon continues to be a source of investigation and study for social historians, anthropologists, and sociologists. The consequences of this reversal are reflected in the cultural history of the Hispanic Southwest.

Before 1848 the region was not affected by Europe's industrial revolution. It was an agricultural, pastoral culture with a limited amount of trade that was not enough to qualify it as a commercial society. The isolation of the original settlers from the centers from which they had come in the end resulted in the development of the folk society of the Hispanic Southwest. In such a community traditional folkways and practices became important, and they have persisted to a large extent in the entire region. To understand Hispanic culture it is necessary to examine the noteworthy forms of traditional lore. Some of the contrasting behavior patterns that characterize all Spanish speakers, except those who have become so completely Anglicized that they have lost touch with their Hispanic heritage, are an essential factor in a segment of today's population that cannot be treated as a large, uniform civilization.

There are many differences in the various sections that compose the Hispanic Southwest. They have a different history and were settled at different times and for different reasons. The topography, climate, and presence of indigenous tribes differ with each region. The resultant cultures that developed have been conditioned by this variety of circumstances. A brief account of the history of each region is given in order to interpret better the nature of the life that evolved in such contrasting places as the arid part of the Southwest and the fertile valleys of California.

Some features of Hispanic culture are common to all parts of the Southwest, because they stem from the original Spanish civilization that settled the country. Such traits as individualism, the right to be and the right to do, time perspective, and a few residual notions of the medieval honor code are deeply embedded in all the Spanish speakers, regardless of the labels that they use to designate themselves. The same generalization applies to the folk practices that still exist and are observed by many residents of the Southwest, practices inherent in their individualism, *curanderismo*, and maleness and a score of other traditional folkways that are part of the Hispanic personality of the Southwest.

The arrival of American culture, gradual at first and violent shortly thereafter, is also reflected in the cultural makeup of today's Spanish speakers. The degrees of acculturation to American life are an important issue that has not been wholly resolved in many quarters of the region. Finally, the problem of nomenclature reflects many aspects of the cultural formation of more than ten million people whose heritage varies from pure Spanish to Hispanicized Indians, with a vast number of variations between these two poles. The name that each group has chosen for itself reflects its political and social attitudes, colored sometimes with concepts of ethnicity. To cover this myriad of cultural aspects, I thought it best to touch on prominent features fundamental to the life of Hispanos, Mexican Americans, or Chicanos.

The contrasts of the two cultures now coexisting in the Southwest lead to interpretations that are sometimes misunderstood when viewed separately. Some Hispanic traits may appear controversial when viewed exclusively in the light of today's conditions. It is helpful to trace attitudes and practices to their original sources in England and Spain to account for their presence in the Southwest today.

In a survey work such as this, I owe a great deal to the many scholars who have researched the history of the Southwest, many of whom have written about specific areas and periods of history. There are too many of these authors, whose scholarly works I have consulted, to mention them individually. The notes and spot references acknowledge my indebtedness to their valuable contributions.

I am greatly indebted for the helpful assistance provided by Mrs. Sandra York, former Administrative Secretary of the Department of Modern Languages at the University of Denver, who typed and edited the first two drafts of this manuscript. Her patient cooperation greatly facilitated the completion of this book. I also acknowledge my gratitude to my daughter, Mrs. Celia Nita Hamm, who typed and checked the final version. The enthusiastic interest of these two young ladies is particularly appreciated. Grateful acknowledgment is also made to Nathaniel H. Evers, Chairman of the Faculty Research Fund of the University of Denver, who made available funds for the typing of the manuscript.

Denver, Colorado   *Arthur L. Campa*

CONTENTS

ILLUSTRATIONS

MAPS

HISPANIC CULTURE IN THE SOUTHWEST

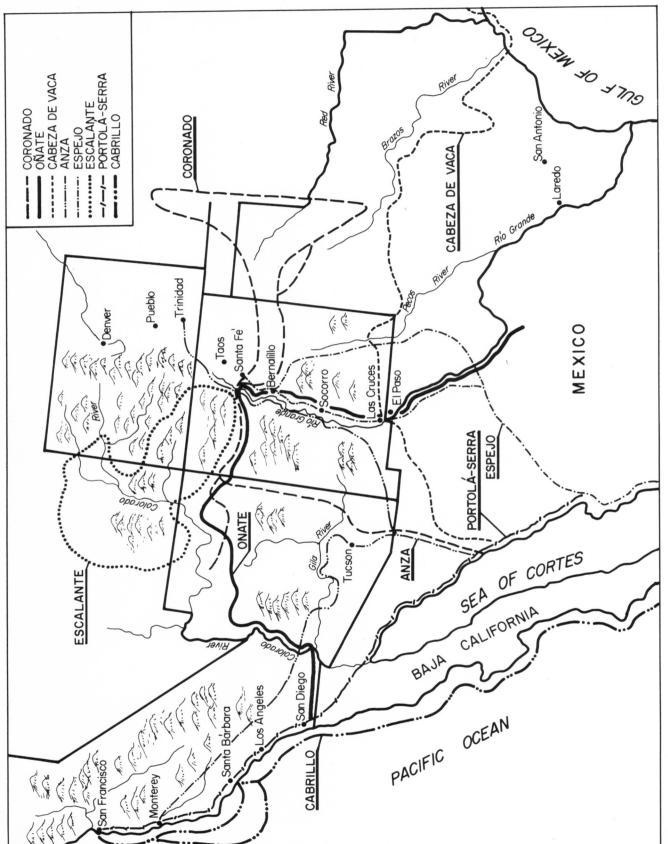

The Hispanic Southwest

One of the difficult problems that confronts anyone making a study of the culture of the American Southwest is the selection of an appropriate term to designate the Spanish-speaking inhabitants from the Gulf of Mexico to the Pacific coast. At different periods of history, and for different reasons, such terms as "native," "Spanish American," "Spanish," "Mexican," "Mexican American," "Hispano," "Californio," and lately the more controversial "Chicano" have been used. Some of these labels are either too restrictive or partly inaccurate.

The varied terminology now in use is often misleading, because it is based on capricious ideas clouded by prejudice and confused by mistaken notions of race and nationality. Thus many of the names applied to the millions of Americans who speak Spanish in the Southwest express an attitude of mind or a political persuasion rather than a clear concept of race, culture, and/or nationality.

Race consciousness was not very significant during Spanish colonial days in the Southwest, first, because the Spaniards had been conditioned to the presence of other racial strains on the Iberian Peninsula, and second, because they tolerated a person's right to be tall, short, black, or white. The Anglo-American knew only two other strains on the continent, the Negro and the Indian, and he had not developed an admiration for either of them. The first was a slave on whom he looked as a useful commodity, and the latter was an enemy whose qualities he admired under the slogan "A good Indian is a dead Indian."

The Anglo-American's concern about race was expressed by traders and travelers coming into contact with the inhabitants of New Mexico. Josiah Gregg estimated the population in the middle of the past century at around 70,000—1,000 creoles, 59,000 *mestizos*, and 10,000 Pueblos. By "creoles" he probably meant the Spanish *criollos*. In 1617 the Spanish priest Alonso de Benavides estimated the Spanish population in New Mexico at 1,500, but Hubert Howe Bancroft reduced that figure to 48, saying that the padre had probably included *mestizos* and Hispanicized Indians in his larger figure. Bancroft could not be accused of prejudice, but his Anglo-American cultural background made him more conscious of cognitive features than the Spanish padre, who in his census based his estimate on cultural attributes.

VARIED LABELS

The Spaniards had a very long list of labels that were used for classification purposes but not necessarily for segregation. For example, a Spaniard born in Spain was a *peninsular*, but if he was born of the same parents in the New World, he was known as a *criollo*. The name *mestizo* was originally applied to a person whose parents were of two different strains, but as time went on it came to mean anyone of mixed ancestry. In the Southwest the name *coyote* is still applied to a person who is half-Anglo and half-Spanish; a *lobo* is one who is only one-fourth a different racial strain (the name *cuarterón* is more common on the Mexican border). There were also names for Negro-white mixtures, such as *mulato* for one half-Negro and half-white and *zambo* for an Indian-Negro mixture.

After the wars of independence in Spanish America, the *criollos* became nationals of whatever country they were living in. In Mexico they naturally became Mexicans. By virtue of this political change, everyone in the Southwest became a Mexican citizen after 1821 and so remained until 1846, when the United States government took over the Southwest. The adjective Mexican is and has always been a national designation, but some ascribe to it a racial meaning. There are Mexicans named O'Gorman, Hayes, Smith, and a host of other names representing every strain in Europe. This error in classification was common until recently, even among some Spanish speakers, who, although they looked no different from many comparable individuals below the border, insisted on being called Spanish American, under the assumption that they were of a different racial stock. Anglo-Americans failed to make the distinction that such individuals were trying to make and referred to them simply as "Mexicans" despite their American citizenship.

Some years ago New Mexicans in particular began objecting to the Anglo-American insistence on referring to them as Mexicans and tried to disassociate themselves from anything that had a Mexican implication. To accomplish this, they insisted on a difference in origin; that is, they were "direct descendants of the Spanish conquerors." This distinction was made on the assumption that the blood of the conquerors had not mixed with the blood of the conquered. "Conqueror" was extended to include anyone who had come into the Southwest before 1848. As descendants of the conquerors, these individuals could claim that they were of "pure Spanish blood." When this line of thought was carried to final conclusion, the deduction was that the New Mexicans were not Mexican, because the latter were not of pure Spanish lineage, and that there was no aboriginal mixture in the former. As American citizens, they could also combine the concept of race and nationality, producing the "Spanish American." Such a name served a triple purpose: It relieved the interested parties of the imaginary opprobrium of being Mexicans, it transformed them into Spaniards, and it expressed their American citizenship. The problem with the name "Spanish American" was that, although it suited them as an abstraction, there was little in their appearance and true origin that could uphold the distinction they were trying so hard to make. Some of this feeling still exists in parts of the Southwest, where they eschew the name "Mexican" in any form.

THE IMPORTANCE OF BEING "SPANISH"

Anglo-Americans, noting the preponderance of aboriginal strains in many of those who insisted on calling themselves "Spanish" or "Spanish American" hesitated to refer to them as such because to them Spanish connoted Spain. Again, most of the *braceros* and laborers who have come to the United States during the past fifty years have been *mestizos* and Hispanicized Indians who do not differ greatly from some individuals in the Southwest whom the Anglo-Americans do not classify as Spanish. Because of the association of "Mexican" with the darker-skinned laborers of the South, this purely national term is applied to all the darker shades and the term "Spanish" to

those who are light-complexioned. Spanish speakers in the Southwest who are of unmixed Spanish heritage do not show much concern for all these classifications.

People in the Southwest, both English- and Spanish-speaking, use the adjective "Castilian" to emphasize the purity of Spanish strain. Oliver LaFarge referred to some individuals in his writings as "half-Castilian." If the other "half" was Indian, the designation should obviously be *mestizo*.

Until recently there was a tendency in restaurants to refer to Mexican food as "Spanish" to make it more acceptable to their clientele. Because the *enchiladas*, *tamales*, and *tacos* that they served have become widely accepted, with no need of linguistic camouflage, the trend is now to advertise Mexican food for what it is. The same changes have occurred with reference to the "Spanish suppers" given by organizations, which today advertise widely their Mexican food, knowing that the general public cannot be deceived any longer. The eyes and the minds of individuals seem to be more ambivalent than their palates.

The preoccupation with not being considered Mexican, being based on the assumption that those north of the Río Grande are different because they are "more Spanish," is half true; that is, the people who have been reared in an English-speaking milieu differ from those who grew up in a Spanish-speaking environment. But the difference is the reverse of what the original advocates intended. The Spanish speakers north of the river have become Anglicized to some extent, while those from the south have preserved the use of the Spanish language, both written and oral, and have a cultural background that is not English.

"NATIVE SONS" AND CALIFORNIOS

Some well-meaning people in the Southwest, mystified by the number of adjectives used, misused, accepted, and rejected, sought to avoid the vexing problem of nomenclature by referring to one and all as "natives." Unfortunately others used the same term in a derogatory sense. Naturally, anyone born on southwestern soil had a legal claim to the distinction of "native," and, when used as an adjective with the noun "son," it produced the very acceptable and proprietary name "native son." It was on the basis of this appellation that the miners in California tried to exclude the Californios from prospecting for gold, because they did not consider them native American sons. In any event, the term "native" is too general to identify a group of people who differ so greatly from the usual "American" that they never call themselves "nosotros los americanos," although they may often express a political concept in English, particularly at election time, by saying: "We Americans."

The term "Californio," used by the colonials on the Pacific coast, was less confusing. The California-born adopted it to avoid being called Spanish or Mexican. The original settlers wished to be known by a name that expressed their independence from two countries whose treatment and political practices they did not approve. Many of the original settlers, however, were *mestizos* and Negroes. The Mexican citizens who immigrated after the rancheros became settled and wealthy were referred to as "Mexicans," and those unfortunates who were sent to California from Mexico because of their misdeeds were called *cholos*. The rest were hostile Indians or converts who lived in the missions for the most part and worked for the rancheros. In the course of time no small number of *mestizos* began to appear, and they either joined their Indian mothers or became absorbed among the *cholos* and the incoming Mexicans, most of whom owned no land and were poor.

When gold was discovered, thousands of Sonorans went to California to impart their mining expertise to the forty-niners. Most of these Sonorenses returned to Sonora, but when they remained in California, they became either Californios or Mexicans, depending on their degree of affluence. After California became part of the Union and the Californios lost their prestigious position, they merged with the masses and were called *pochos*, "faded," by the Mexicans who had preserved their own traditions and language. The term simply meant that, having become Americanized, they had lost their Spanish-Mexican heritage. Mild criticism was implied in picaresque folk songs written about them such as:

Los Pochos de California
no saben comer tortilla
porque solo en la mesa
usan pan con mantequilla

The "pochos" of California
Don't know how to eat tortilla
For at mealtime on the table
All they serve is bread and butter.

The surge of activism among the Spanish speakers in the Southwest has complicated the choice of names by which they are known and has also made it clear that they wish to choose the name by which they are known. In years past the Anglo-Americans used whatever term they chose, depending on the attitude of those who bestowed the name. That is not so today. Some have decided to be known as Mexican Americans, others as Chicanos, and the old colonials in New Mexico as Spanish Americans or as Hispanos.

"MEXICANOS" BUT NOT MEXICANS

About twenty-five years ago, while pursuing phonetic investigations of the Spanish language, I made a cursory survey in central and eastern New Mexico, trying to determine the use of the name that the native New Mexicans preferred to use for themselves. The subjects were bilingual, and the questioning was carried on in either language, but not simultaneously, to keep the answers consistent. The subjects were asked in Spanish what term they used to designate a person who spoke Spanish and was a native of New Mexico. Without exception, they answered, "Mexicano." Later, when being interrogated in English, they were asked the same question in English and invariably they circumvented the name "Mexican" and answered, "Spanish American." When asked in Spanish what name they used for an individual from Mexico they promptly answered, "Mexicano de México." The same question asked in English elicited the answer, "Mexican."

Several inferences were drawn from this investigation, one being that the New Mexicans conceived of two Mexicanos, one living in New Mexico and another below the border. Because both groups have comparable folk heritages, with similar folk songs, folk tales, foods, and customs, it is logical to include them under the same cultural category "Mexicano" when expressed in Spanish. But obviously the English term "Mexican" did not convey the same meaning to the New Mexicans. It became a purely national term, and because the informers were American citizens, they felt that the term did not accurately identify them. They never say, "Nosotros los españoles," or, "Nosotros los americanos," but readily say, "Nosotros los mexicanos." This attitude was somewhat altered by the activist movement.

RECENT TERMINOLOGY

The term "Mexican American," as mentioned earlier, is not entirely accurate. This label is, strictly speaking, a national designation, and so it is reasonable that a person cannot be a Mexican national and an American national at the same time. The term is largely used to designate a person born in Mexico but now an American citizen. When it is insisted that the term must be used for all those of Spanish speech in the Southwest, many native-born Americans of Mexican descent and old Spanish colonials of various parts of the Southwest do not find the term acceptable, and understandably. It would be more accurate to use the term "Americans of Mexican descent." This term would not include the descendants of Spanish families who have been here since colonial days. They prefer to use the term "Spanish American" or "Hispano." Many who live in Texas call themselves "Texanos." The term "Texan" is a translation of the Spanish *texano*, and so Mexicans born in Texas are correct in calling themselves "Texanos."

The term with historical precedence on the continent is the one employed by Diego de Vargas in 1695, when he founded Santa Cruz, New Mexico. He referred to the settlers coming to occupy the village as "españoles mejicanos," that is, Spanish Mexicans. Because they were all subjects of the Spanish crown at a time when Mexican nationality did not exist, it was natural for the old conquistador to use the national term "Spanish" first and then indicate the province where these New World Spaniards originated. Spaniards in the United States follow the same logic today in expressing their American nationality and their original culture. They do not refer to themselves as "Spanish Americans" but as "American Spaniards."

Because a proper designation is sought for American citizens who, like their forebears in Santa Cruz three hundred years ago, need to express nationality and their original culture, they can follow the same logic and use the term "American Mexicans" in good southwestern tradition. "Mexican"—pure and simple—is used for those who are Mexican nationals. American citizens should not accept a dual national designation, because a legal state acquired by birth or by naturalization cannot be dual. The term "American Mexican" has no racial connotation, and it accurately describes a person's cultural background as differing from that of Americans of English descent.

Some people use *la raza* as a descriptive label for Hispanos, but this term has been from its inception a racial term. It is a contradiction for people who constantly charge the "establishment" with racial discrimination to adopt a name for themselves that is based on an inaccurate race label. The term *la raza* is used to identify all Hispanic peoples the world over when celebrating Columbus Day, which in Spanish is called *El Día de la Raza*, the Day of the Race. Mexicans and American Mexicans are part of the same *raza*, but they can hardly claim an exclusive right to the term as a means of identifying themselves.

"HISPANO," A CULTURAL DESIGNATION

Some writers, and many individuals, have selected a name that in a way is a compromise but upon analysis is accurate. The term "Hispano" connotes common cultural characteristics of people from Colorado to Mexico. It does not mean "Spaniard"; it is a purely cultural term with no national or racial overtones. Hispanicized Indians, as well as Mexicans, New Mexicans, colonials, and Californios, are part of the inclusive "Hispano." It means a people having cultural attributes that stem from their Hispanic heritage regardless of nationality. They speak Spanish, they share basically the same cultural values, they have a common philosophy of life, and they have inherited all this from the same source, Spain. It does not mean that they came from Spain or that they do not have any Indian blood or that they have no cultural background of their own. The term simply sets them apart from Anglo-Americans.

"CHICANO," A POLITICAL LABEL

In the last few years the term "Chicano" has gained ascendancy among members of the militant activist "Mexican Americans." It is a term that they believe better characterizes them and their goals and aspirations. "Chicano" is not accepted by the Hispanos who come from the old Southwest but is employed by many people of Mexican descent. Some people prefer this term for valid reasons. First, it begins with the resounding *ch* sound of the strongest Mexican oath, adding strength to the meaning when pronounced vigorously. Because the word "Chicano" was not orig-

6

inally used to designate the highest of Mexican society, the self-deprecatory connotation serves to emphasize the underprivileged status of those who have been the victims of racial, social, and economic prejudice.

Again, the word "Chicano" strengthens their demands from society—Anglo and Spanish, and even from the traditional church groups, as well as from the political establishment—of those rights that have been denied or usurped over the centuries. It is much easier to rally to their cause other members of the underprivileged class by calling for "Chicano power!" than by using the term "Hispano" or even "Mexican American," terms that they consider meaningless and watered down. On page 11 of the January, 1971, issue of *Chicanismo*, a small newspaper published by the Chicano Press at Stanford, appeared a poem by Rosa Elvira Alvarez. In the poem, entitled "Chicano," she stresses the reproach and the challenge inherent in the word "Chicano." This author expresses very clearly and poetically the connotation of the word.

> La palabra Chicano es un reproche,
> Una angustia con algo de esperanza . . .
>
> Es un reto, quizás una bandera,
> El estandarte terco de una raza . . .
>
> La palabra Chicano es una flecha
> Yel arco es el aliento de una raza.
>
> The word Chicano is a reproach
> An anguish with something of a hope . . .
>
> It is a challenge, perhaps a banner
> The stubborn standard of a race . . .
>
> The word Chicano is an arrow
> And the bow is the inspiration of a race.

The word "Chicano" is not new, but it is not found very often, if at all, in historical or popular literature. The *corrido* ballad collections of Rubén Campos, Vicente Mendoza, and Merle Simmons do not mention Chicano in several hundred selections dealing with the Mexican folk. The *Recuento de Vocabulario Español*[1] (a word-frequency study made by a group of leading Hispanic and American scholars under the auspices of UNESCO) did not include the word, though they took sixty thousand samples from newspapers and magazines in the more than a million words included in the study. The Center of Hispanic Linguistics at the National University of Mexico does not recognize the word as a Mexican word in current usage

and declares that it is *pochismo*, that is, a corruption of a Spanish word in the United States. They suggest that it may be an instance of metathesis of the last two syllables of the word *chinaco*, meaning "tramp" or "guttersnipe." A more probable origin comes from the Aztec word *México*, which gave rise to the word *Mexicano*, except that in the Nahuatl tongue the *x* is pronounced *sh*. When the word is apocopated to *xicano*, pronounced *shicano*, the natural result would be to convert the *sh* sound into *ch* because in Spanish the sound *sh* does not exist. This would produce the word *chicano* as it is pronounced in modern Spanish. The Nahuatl-Aztecs adopted the name *México* during their migration from the mythical Aztlán to Mexico. It is also recorded in history that the children of Mexitli transformed the name into Mexicatl by decree of their favorite god. The only dictionary that includes and defines the word *chicano* is *Diccionario Enciclopédico de la Lengua Castellana* by Vastus, published in Buenos Aires in 1941. This dictionary defines the word *chicano* as "liar."

The new feature of the word *chicano* is the use being made today as a name by a limited segment of the Mexican-American minority. They insist that the name Hispano is not acceptable, because it is reminiscent of the brutality of the Spanish conqueror, and that they, the Chicanos, are the children of Aztlán with closer affinity to the Aztecs and other Indians of the Southwest. It is probable that most Chicanos have considerably more Indian than Spanish blood, but when they ask the universities to teach "Chicano studies" and "Chicano history," the meaning of Chicano is extended into the Spanish cultural field, because an exclusive "Chicano culture" simply does not exist.

An interesting sidelight on the use of the name Chicano was provided by a recent survey made by the University of Texas Center for Communication Research. The survey was made for Teletemas, a national project to create cultural and entertainment television programming for Mexican Americans. The research revealed that 43 percent of the persons interviewed in Texas, Arizona, and California preferred the term Mexicanos, while only 6 percent chose Chicanos. There was also a sprinkling of preferences for Mexican American, Latin American, and Texano.

Those who have written on the Mexican-American minority have inevitably begun with the Conquest and carried the story through to the present day. The continuity of southwestern culture is

Hispanic rather than Indian, with no reference to Chicanos, because, to the degree that they have a culture, it must be Spanish Mexican. Those who live in the United States have a culture that is more Anglo-American than anything else. Studies such as those made by Rudolph Acuña, William Madsen, and Julian Nava, as well as the study by the United States Civil Rights Commission, speak of Mexican Americans, begin their story with the Spanish period, and then continue to the present day. No mention is made of the Chicano phase of history or culture in these studies. In his study of the colonials of New Mexico known as Manitos, Munro S. Edmondson does not refer to them as Mexican Americans, much less as Chicanos.

Some proponents of Chicano culture who insist on its Indian background compare pre-Columbian Indian education and culture with what the Spaniards and the English established in America and conclude that they have been sold a bill of goods by both Spaniards and Anglos.

AZTEC CULTURE AND CHICANOS

A *Denver Post* article by an advocate of Chicano culture claimed that in Aztec culture "life revolved around a philosophy whereby education, survival, religion, science, land and the universe were interwoven in the Native American psychology." The author did not give his source for such a comprehensive educational ideology. It must be borne in mind that had it not been for the work of the early Spanish scholars we would have no record of the educational system of the Aztecs. Bernardino de Sahagún, Juan de Torquemada, Andrés de Olmos, Diego Durán, and others spent years transcribing into Spanish the history and culture of the Aztecs from the information given to them by the *tlamatinime*, or wise men. These texts speak not of a utopian state but of a nation girding itself for theocratic imperialism.

The well-known scholar Miguel León-Portilla made a profound study of the Aztecs, summarized in his *Aztec Thought and Culture*. In it he wrote:

The Aztecs oriented themselves toward the path of mystic imperialism. . . . Sacrifice and ceremonial warfare, which was the principal manner of obtaining victims for the sacrificial rites, were their central activities and the very core of their personal, social, military, religious, and national life.[2]

To attribute to the Aztecs an understanding of

the objectives of philosophy and scientific knowledge of artistic intuition would be an anachronism, because the separation of the fields of investigation is the work of modern Western thought.

The writer in the *Denver Post* continues his presentation, speaking of the "rape by the conqueror since 1848" of Chicano education, on the assumption that Indian education continued from the days of the Conquest, but the date given would indicate that he is speaking of the Mexican War. He insists that, in spite of this loss, the Chicanos are now "reaffirming their right to their language, customs, thinking and way of life." The issue becomes confused when people speak of their Chicano culture as aboriginal and then turn to their Hispanic background to reaffirm the former. It is impossible to make a case for Chicano culture, because what the advocates of it seem to be talking about is Hispanic culture of a subcultural group within a minority living in the midst of an Anglo-American society.

In the face of modern civilization, it is hard to conceive of a return to pre-Columbian Indian life as a solution for ills arising in today's society. In a sense the Chicanos are asking to undo the acculturation of the Indian that has taken place since colonial days, a process that has taken more than four and a half centuries to accomplish. Those trying to find a common denominator away from Hispanic cultural history end in a quandary, because there is no corresponding history, literature, or any other attribute of cultural identity for the Chicano. When they attempt to write "Chicano literature," they discover that they need a better knowledge of the Spanish language, an admission of *hispanismo* rather than *chicanismo*.

The history of the Southwest includes Indians, *mestizos*, *criollos*, Spaniards, and Chicanos if you wish. Chicano is simply another name for Mexicans with a different political orientation. To be a Chicano, one must be a Mexican, and if he is born in the United States, he is automatically a Mexican American.

There is no social contract that would enable Chicanos to exist and live as a separate group. The name is a convenient political label but one that is difficult to accept exclusively today, because those who advocate its use find the field preempted by such national appellations as Mexican American, Hispano, and Mexicano, names with a national or cultural significance of long standing. Eventually this insistence on Chicano and *chicanismo* will be replaced by a generic term for which no arbitrary limitations need to be imposed, and which can be acceptable to the entire spectrum of Hispanos in the Southwest. As the socioeconomic conditions of the Hispanos, the Mexican Americans, and the Chicanos attain a proper balance, the search for proper identification will not be as intense and contradictory. It is likely that a more generic and historical designation will be resorted to rather than an activist label. Even now there is a marked ambivalence in the public media, and among writers dealing with news and announcements, about Americans of Mexican descent. The titles of books, monographs, and newspaper accounts use the word Hispano in their headlines, except for militants sponsoring a political cause, whose preference is for Chicano.

The problem of nomenclature is indeed complicated; the members of each group concerned with nationality labels or cultural designations are searching for self-identity, and, depending on their attitude, they will select terms that they consider acceptable for themselves. Some are more interested in selecting a term that is more flattering personally, even though historically or culturally it may be misapplied. When you add to the foregoing categories the pejorative names preferred by those who know nothing about history and less about culture, the public is ultimately at a loss about what name to use for the Hispanos of the Southwest.

The history of Hispanic culture in the Southwest begins with the exploration and conquest of Francisco Vásquez de Coronado in 1540. This important expedition was undertaken by the Spanish crown, through the viceroy of Mexico, as a result of the account given by Alvar Núñez Cabeza de Vaca at the end of his adventure-filled odyssey. That odyssey began in 1528, when Pánfilo de Narváez' ill-fated attempt to explore the Atlantic seaboard to the River Palmas ended disastrously on the shores of Tampa Bay. The resourceful Núñez, better known by his mother's name, Cabeza de Vaca, accompanied Narváez on the Florida expedition and was one of a handful who survived the rigors of the stormy Gulf of Mexico in an improvised shallop that landed them on the Texas shore near what is now Galveston. After eight years of wandering through present-day southern United States and the Southwest, Alvar Núñez reached the Spanish settlement of Culiacán, in western Mexico, in the company of three other shipwrecked companions. One of them, a Moorish servant named Esteban, together with the much-maligned Fray Marcos de Niza, blazed the trail three years later for the impressive *entrada* of Coronado. Esteban was the first Old World man to enter this part of the Southwest, and he also had the dubious honor of being the first Spanish casualty in the long history of the region.

Coronado's expedition officially began its northern journey from the village of Compostela in the state of Sinaloa, where Alvar Núñez ended his long quest for the Spanish settlements. The expeditionary army of three hundred gentlemen, many of them with the rank of captain, and three times that many Indian servants to care for the horses, sheep, swine, and other stock, completed the entourage of the most impressive army ever to enter the Southwest. The trail led north through Sonora and into the Pima Indian country of eastern Arizona and then turned northeast, where the fabled cities of Cíbola lay, according to the accounts heard by Alvar Núñez. The expedition explored the land far and wide along the route for signs of mineral deposits until they reached the cities of Cíbola, a disappointing discovery of mud and stone houses on the rocky cliffs of the Zuñi country inhabited by not-too-friendly aborigines. After hearing fabricated tales about the treasures of Gran Quivira, the general continued eastward to the village of Tiguex[1] on the banks of the Río Grande eighteen miles north of Albuquerque, where he decided to spend the winter and establish his base of operations. From this Indian village Coronado's captains fanned out in all directions, still hoping to find the turquoise-studded walls of cities that lured them on. They discovered the Grand Canyon on the west and were led on a wild-goose chase by an Indian guide through the plains of Kansas and the "wild cow" country in quest of the mythical Quivira. For two years the Spaniards explored a good portion of the Southwest, conquering villages whose inhabitants refused to pledge allegiance to the Spanish sovereign and accept Catholicism. The chronicler of the expedition, Pedro de Castañeda, may have had a premonition of the value of the discovery of the Southwest when he said in the last sentence of his history of the expedition, " . . . may the God Almighty Lord of all things . . . determine for whom this good fortune is preserved." The Indians may not have understood the religion and demands for allegiance to an unknown king, but they did learn that these warriors meant to subject them, use them to provide for their wants, and reduce them all to a vassalage that they were reluctant to accept. They had been suddenly introduced to medieval remnants of Spanish culture and were impressed by mounted warriors, the thunder of their guns, and the sharp edge of Spanish steel. Coronado and his officers were not impressed by what they found, when they compared it with what they had expected to find, but the door was opened through which many from the south would continue to enter: Spaniards, Indians, and a new group called *mestizos*, who would eventually constitute the majority of the population of the Southwest and carry on the culture introduced by Spain.

If the expedition of Coronado did not find the

A dramatic representation, showing sixteenth-century Spanish dress and armor, of Coronado's departure from Compostela, Mexico. Courtesy of Coronado Cuarto Centennial.

Compostela, the village in the state of Sinaloa, Mexico, where the Coronado Expedition of 1540 started on the quest for Cíbola. Courtesy of the Bancroft Library.

The Coronado State Monument, eighteen miles north of Albuquerque on the Río Grande. It is at the site of the old pueblo of Tiguex, which Captain Alvarado used as the base for the explorations of the Coronado Expedition of 1540. Courtesy of the Coronado Cuarto Centennial.

Kuaua Pueblo ruins at the Coronado State Monument. The visitors' center and Sandia Mountains are in the background. Courtesy of the New Mexico Tourist Division.

wondrous sites that the Indians had painted in such glowing colors, it did provide considerable information to the Western world regarding the vast territory that was to become, by the end of the sixteenth century, the northernmost outpost of the Spanish crown. The Indians, on the other hand, were initiated into a European civilization that brought the horse, the sheep, and other important elements of material culture that, together with religion and government, marked the turning point of the Indians' long pre-Columbian history. Despite the disappointment of not finding the Seven Cities of Cíbola and the fabulous treasures of the Gran Quivira, there was enough potential in Coronado's account to arouse further speculation about the "mystery of the north" among imaginative adventurers who could not be easily persuaded that the relatively unknown north was totally devoid of great wealth.

As a result, in the years that followed Coronado's expedition, many official and unofficial attempts to explore the north were made by men who had originally come to the New World in search of a new route to India and continued in this searching frame of mind, looking for gold and silver, new lands to conquer and explore, the fountain of youth, and, among the missionaries who accompanied the military expeditions, souls for the Kingdom of Heaven. This strong impulse drove the restless Spaniards to all cardinal points as far as the Philippine Islands, the Pacific Northwest, Florida, Chesapeake Bay, and, according to seventeenth-century English historian W. Owen, as far as Canada. He quotes a historical account given by Jacques Cartier with reference to the Indians of Terra Nuova in 1533, published in 1545, which he translates:[2]

In April 1534, James Cartier sailed from the port of St. Malo with two ships of 60 tons each, and 120 men. He arrived on the 10th of May following on the coast of Newfoundland; and finding the country covered with ice and snow, sailed to the southward, and entered into a bay which bears at the present the name of Spanish Harbour, where he went on shore. It is reported, that the Spaniards had long before discovered this coast, but were in a hurry to go off again, crying out in their language Aca Nada, that is, there is nothing here; which words the Indians remembering, when the French came on shore, cried out also Aca Nada, Aca Nada! which the French took for the name of the country so that it has ever since been called Canada. This is a strange derivation; but as we find it in the best French authors, it may be worth remarking.

Spanish swords and other armaments of the Conquest. Courtesy of the Arizona Historical Society Museum.

The English, who were the other empire builders of the New World, came a century later to a continent already discovered. Unlike the Spaniards, however, they were initially running away from religious persecution, and after a second attempt they settled on the eastern shores of North America. They did not venture west of the Alleghenies until much later; when they did, it was not to discover and conquer but to acquire more farming land. These tillers of the soil laid the foundation for what was to become the greatest agricultural enterprise of the New World and, unbeknown to them, also laid the base for the economy that made the United States the greatest industrial nation in history.

The Spaniards of the sixteenth century, on the other hand, undertook the settlement and exploitation of the newly discovered lands in a totally different manner. Because they had avowedly come to discover, conquer, and command and not to work, they were not content with a haven where they could settle down to farm peacefully and worship freely. Their quest led them to the land of Moctezuma in Mexico, to El Dorado in South America, and to the Gran Quivira in the Southwest. The quixotic blend of stark reality and the impossible dream urged them on and gave them courage to endure the hardships of conquest. After crossing the continent through uncharted lands peopled with hostile Indians, many simply remarked that "the going was hard." They were not stopped by mountain ranges, rivers, arid deserts, or hostile inhabitants, because they were imbued with the spirit of discovery and ex-

The military dress of Coronado's army reproduced from historical records for the four hundredth anniversary of his expedition. Courtesy of Coronado Cuarto Centennial.

The "mystery of the north" explored by Coronado and his expedition of knights and soldiers. Courtesy of Coronado Cuarto Centennial.

ploration. The vast expanse and uncertainty that was the Southwest appealed to these sons of Castile and Estremadura, kindling their imagination with hopes of another great discovery. When their hopes had run their course, they settled down to consolidate their gains. The Spaniards of the Conquest had become inured to struggle and hardship after several centuries of intermittent wars to drive the Moors from the Iberian Peninsula.[3] There was a unity of effort and belief among all those who came to the New World: one God, one king, and a strong desire to explore and conquer. This trinity lasted for several decades.

The original contact made by Coronado was kept alive by such men as Andrés del Campo, a Portuguese soldier who chose to stay behind with idealistic missionaries. Upon his return to the capital city, he spoke of the marvels he had heard about and seen. (Historians also credit this adventurer with being the first horse thief in the Southwest, for he is said to have run away from the Coronado expedition on a mare that did not belong to him.)

Francisco de Ibarra in 1567 led another, less spectacular expedition through northern Chihuahua and was so impressed with what he saw that

Was this the Gran Quivira? Treasure hunters are still looking for it. Courtesy of Coronado Cuarto Centennial.

he declared the country to be *un nuevo México*, that is, another Mexico. He was followed successively by Francisco del Cano, by Francisco Sánchez Chamuscado, and in 1583 by Antonio de Espejo, an efficient businessman who had the distinction of bringing the first European woman into the Southwest. Casilda Sánchez Valenciano and her three young boys accompanied her soldier husband on the arduous trip but left no evidence that she was the "first white woman" to enter the region. Being first and being white are of greater import to a culture that places a high premium on primacy and pigmentation, that is, on descriptive qualities rather than on substantive being, or what in Spanish is called the *ente*.

The expeditions that followed Espejo's reconnaissance continued to keep alive the embers of hope and expectation and paved the way for succeeding attempts to settle the Southwest. Gaspar Castaño de Sosa in 1590 tried to establish himself in the country but was thwarted by the jealousy of a provincial governor, who accused him of trying to start a rebellion. Antonio Gutiérrez de Humaña and Francisco de Leyva y Bonilla also made an unauthorized attempt to settle five years before Oñate's successful colonizing expedition, but dissension between the two leaders led to the murder of Bonilla and to the eventual annihilation of the party by the Indians.

In the course of nearly half a century, beginning with Coronado, the Indians were intermittently exposed to a culture that found little favor with them because of the excesses of the military and the insistence on introducing a religion whose tenets were inconsistent with the behavior of the men who professed it. These early cultural contacts did not endear the Spaniards to the Indians, and although they yielded reluctantly to the inevitable for several decades, eventually the break came in 1680, when the conquerors were forced from the country for twelve years.

The most successful of all the explorers to visit the Southwest was probably Espejo, who, with an incredibly small group of fourteen soldiers (who never had to fight), accomplished more than Coronado's impressive entry with a colorful entourage of knights and soldiers. This mining man naturally took notice of mining prospects and even explored such ephemeral sites as La Laguna de Oro, the Lake of Gold, but in his final report he did not fail to mention that the land was suitable for farming, with or without irrigation. His information was instrumental in bringing about the permanent settlement of the region by Don Juan de Oñate at the end of the sixteenth century and provided more incentive than all the other explorations put together.

The "unknown north" had become well known by now to the Viceroyalty of New Spain, who felt that the time had come for the Empire to extend its boundaries northward. All that was needed was a leader willing to finance the expedition in exchange for land grants and a title. There was such a man in Zacatecas: Don Juan de Oñate. He was wealthy, adventurous, and willing to undertake the settling of the north, but affairs of state never did move fast, much less in colonial Spain, where jealousies, privileges, and partialities undermined the good will and practical designs of men like Don Juan. His plan was to settle the region that is now New Mexico, but the results of his enterprise extended beyond mere settlement and drove the pivot from which the rest of the

The coat of mail, breastplate, and headpiece worn here were found in a cave in New Mexico in 1940. They date from the Spanish expeditions of the sixteenth and seventeenth centuries.

Southwest was eventually explored and permanently settled.

The expeditions that preceded the Oñate colony of 1598 made known to the Indian inhabitants in the Southwest the coming of another race of men who had great interest in the land and the people of that vast region. Before long a new culture would be introduced by the Spaniards, ushering in customs and ideas that would change the way of life of the inhabitants. Many elements of material culture would benefit the natives, and the combined heritage of both civilizations would produce another culture known as Hispanic rather than exclusively Spanish or Indian.

Nothing was simple in Spanish colonial days, and when the settlement of a new province was at stake, things were made even more complicated by the machinations of influential hopefuls who used their court connections in bidding for the privilege to lead the proposed expedition into the northland. Juan de Oñate had the advantage over the other contenders in that his family was on intimate terms with Viceroy Don Luis de Velasco, and also because he was a wealthy mining man in Zacatecas, an indispensable condition for anyone wishing to lead an expedition into new territory.

Once the contract was signed for the "conquest and pacification" of New Mexico in 1595, the wheels of intrigue and court politics got under way rapidly. Charges, countercharges, and accusations were aired and examined by the crown, but in the end Don Juan won the appointment as captain general to lead the settling expedition to New Mexico after three years of bungling in which the king of Spain, the Council of the Indies, two viceroys and several jealous aspirants became involved. On January 21, 1598, Oñate finally moved his caravan of 43 carts and wagons with a complement of 129 men, 8 Franciscan friars, women, children, Indian servants, and all the necessary supplies and equipment. Because their mission was one of conquest and pacification, they had a good supply of armaments and a considerable amount of trinkets to present as gifts to the Indians.

Had the expedition continued on its way after the first inspection as planned, it would have been better supplied for the long journey, and the full complement of two hundred men would have gone along. A second inspection held back the expedition for a year, resulting in the consumption of supplies and the falling out of many recruits. Despite these drawbacks, the caravan reached the present site of Juárez–El Paso on May 3, 1598, and after a brief ceremony crossed the river and continued north along the Río Grande. The expedition blazed a trail that was substantially the same one followed for centuries with very few changes. On August 18 the main body of the expedition joined the advance party at San Juan de los Caballeros, on the east bank of the Río Grande, northwest of the present site of Santa Fe.

Thus far the expedition had accomplished one important part of its settlement contract, which was to "conquer and pacify" the Indians of the new province. In reality there was very little conquering needed, because of the peaceful and friendly reception given to Oñate and his soldiers as he visited the pueblos along the way to San Juan. The next important mission was the conversion of the empire's new subjects who had sworn allegiance to the crown. The friars who had accompanied the expedition set the entire company to building a church and completed it by September 8, roughly three weeks after the expedition assembled in San Juan. Father Cristóbal de Salazar preached the sermon at the dedication of the first church in the Southwest, and at the conclusion of this event the remaining friars were assigned to various Indian pueblos, where the aborigines would be initiated into a new religion. After a few months the capital was moved to another Indian pueblo at the confluence of the Chama and the Río Grande and rechristened San Gabriel. The permanent settlement was established not by Oñate, however, but by his immediate successor, Governor Don Pedro de Peralta, who moved the settlers to a third site in 1610 and named the new capital La Villa Real de la Santa Fe de San Francisco de Asisi, later shortened to Santa Fe.

San Miguel Chapel, a state and national monument, was the first permanent church established by the Spanish colonists in Santa Fe, New Mexico. It was built shortly after the founding of the city in 1605 and rebuilt in 1710. Photograph by Robert H. Martin Photography.

The interior of San Miguel Chapel, Santa Fe, New Mexico.

The official inspections made before departure and after the expedition was on its way give interesting insights, through their minute inventories, of the culture that was to be established in the Southwest. Mention is made of all the implements taken by the colonists, the large numbers of livestock, foodstuffs, clothing, and articles of trade. Not only are the articles themselves an interesting index to sixteenth-century living but the quantities taken indicate their relative importance. Dozens of knives, scissors, combs, mirrors, and earrings to be used in trading with the Indians point up, to a degree, the European civilization that the Spaniards hoped to introduce. On the other hand, the entry for 88,000 beads sounds like a standard item of Indian trade. There were 750 bushels of wheat for sowing, and a comparable amount of beans and corn, together with 1,000 goats, 4,500 sheep, and 1,200 cattle. That

is a good indication of the Spanish colonists' bill of fare when they settled in the Southwest.

The inclusion of several hundred horseshoes and 140,000 horseshoe nails indicates the reliance on the horse by the equestrian Spaniards. Forty-one reams of paper of twenty quires each indicated that the officials of the colony anticipated a good bit of writing, and the many bolts of fine cloth of every description manifested the desire of the colonists to carry on in the provinces as they were accustomed to do in urban centers. The same may be said for the 413 pairs of single-soled calfskin shoes, 251 pairs of cordovan leather shoes, and many pairs of double-soled boots. The number of medicines is also indicative of the medical practice of the time and explains the origin of certain oils, rubefacients, and draughts common in the Southwest. Such items as rose water, balsam, chamomile, and the time-honored sarsa-

Palace of the Governors, Santa Fe, the first seat of government in the province of New Mexico, now a museum. Photograph by Mark Nohl.

parilla were important in the pharmacopoeia of the Oñate colony.

The extensive correspondence, memorials, *cédulas*, and decrees preparatory to the launching of the expedition speak of regulations, obligations, privileges, and the minutiae attendant on exploration and conquest in colonial days. But all of this voluminous writing makes only a passing reference to mining by declaring that for fifty years only one-twentieth, instead of the customary royal one-fifth, would be turned over to the crown by those who exploited mining deposits. Mining was apparently not an essential part of the expedition, or at least the crown did not give much credence to the alluring tales of Quivira.

The lengthy inventories of supplies taken by Oñate for the future settlement indicate that the future colonists expected to make a living through agriculture and stock raising, despite the mythical treasures they had heard about. Some members of the expedition, to be sure, were greatly disappointed at not having found bars of silver and left the colony at the first opportunity. Mining was a marginal possibility not to be excluded and for which provisions were made by including "four pairs of bellows for mines, in case there should be any."[1] On the other hand, the great number of such farming implements as plowshares, adzes, hoes, and the thousands of head of

livestock is indicative of planned agricultural pursuits.

It is noteworthy that even the soldiers and individual members of the expedition also mention in their personal possessions many farm implements, horses, and mules but seldom are pickaxes, shovels, and other mining tools included in the inventories. In a group of several hundred settlers with many more Indian servants only eleven pickaxes are listed officially, but, again, the number of sheep, swine, and cattle is incredibly large.

These sixteenth-century settlers laid the foundation for a pastoral culture that became characteristic not only of New Mexico but also of a major portion of the Southwest and continued unchanged for several centuries. No mining claims were filed by the members of the Oñate colony except for the report made by Marcos Farfán de los Godos in 1599, when he brought some ore samples that assayed a silver content of eleven ounces to the *quintal*, or hundred weight.[2] There is no record of a follow-up of this discovery, and we hear nothing more of consequence until after the Indian revolt of 1680. On March 26, 1685, a soldier named Pedro de Abalos filed a claim before Don Domingo Gironza Petríz de Cruzate, governor and captain general of New Mexico, for a mine in the Sierrilla de Fray Cristóbal north

21

The original settlers of San Gabriel, New Mexico, in 1598 and a map of Spain showing the localities from which they came. Photograph by José Gonçalves.

of the San Andrés Mountains, to which he gave the resounding name Nuestra Señora del Pilar de Saragossa.[3] A second filing was made in 1709 by Juan de Ulibarrí, who appeared in person before Don Joseph Chacón Medina Salazar y Villaseñor, Marqués de las Peñuelas, governor of New Mexico after the revolt. Perhaps one of the reasons that none of these claims was followed is because of the stipulation, purportedly made by the Indians after the reconquest, that the Spaniards should not engage in mining; they considered it a source of constant dissension. That mining was not exploited until the nineteenth century vitiates the popular notion that the Spaniards went everywhere in search of gold alone.

With no mineral deposits to exploit and no large concentration of Indians such as were found in Mexico and Peru, the colonists could not aspire to *encomiendas* with unlimited local Indian labor. They were forced to become independent farmers with landholdings proportionate to the size of the families. The haciendas mentioned by Diego de Vargas at the end of the seventeenth century were in reality small-acreage allotments for single families to cultivate.[4] This kind of land distribution gave rise to a different form of *patrón* structure with closer interpersonal relationships but without the control of large bodies of people by a single land baron such as those developed in the haciendas of Mexico and South America. In the end, the independent landholder developed a culture that was better able to maintain its identity and to preserve an almost unchanged traditional way of life throughout the colonial period.

Once the new province was consolidated, it became the hub from which further explorations and expansion were undertaken by the Spaniards and also the center from which radiated trade routes to California, to Chihuahua on the Camino Real, to Texas, and eventually to the American

22

The inscription on the rock reads:

Aqui ... ... ernador
Don Francisco ... Anno de Silua Nieto
Quelo ynpucible tiene ya sujeto
Su Braço yndubitable y su Balor
Conlos Carros del Rei Nuestro Señor
Cosa Quesolo el Puso enestE fecro
De Abopsto y Seiscientos Beinte y Nueue
Ques by Ynglcu ñi Pase yla Fe lleue

A part of Inscription Rock in western New Mexico saying that Francisco Silva Nieto led His Majesty's wagons through part of the West in eastern Arizona and western New Mexico in August, 1629. The rock has inscriptions such as this left by the Spanish conquerors as checkpoints for other travelers. Courtesy of Coronado Cuarto Centennial.

frontier through the establishment of the Santa Fe Trail.

Coronado, in his relatively brief contact with the Indians of the Southwest in 1540, left indelible memories among them of Spanish military rule, and the demands inherent in their proposed administration of land and people made them apprehensive of further incursions by the Europeans. The padres also, in their zeal to spread the Gospel, made known to the aborigines that they expected to introduce a substitute for pagan worship. Although the latter acquiesced for practical reasons, they showed their opinion of the new religion by murdering the well-meaning priests as soon as Coronado left.

The many documents dealing with Oñate's expedition reveal the importance that the Spaniards gave to the conversion of the Indians. But despite the freedom of the soul that they were promised, it was not a free enterprise, for the neophytes had to pay tribute and devote a given number of working days to maintaining the institutions of the church, its personnel, and its proposed buildings, the last a major project in itself.

Oñate's colonizers discovered very shortly after their arrival that they could not expect the Indians to provide them with sufficient food supplies, and so they settled in intermountain valleys where soil was more productive and water was accessible in nearby streams. Many of the original villages still stand in the same location where ancestors of today's Hispanos settled in colonial days. The country was suited for stock raising, and for farming along mountain slopes and in the extensive meadows, where the sheep, cattle, and goats that they brought with them in 1598 thrived

23

The portal of the Armijo house in Old Albuquerque, where the original families settled in 1706. Today it houses La Placita Restaurant. Photograph by José Gonçalves.

on the wild grass. The terrain was not unlike that of the Spanish countryside, where a good number of the colonists originated, but there were no cities or villages to frequent. Those they would eventually build.

This complete isolation from their original homes determined to a large extent the nature of the folk culture that eventually evolved. Being thrown on their own resources and having no contact with the outside world meant that they had to preserve what they brought with them: the language, the customs, and whatever knowledge and skills they had when they came. Strictly speaking, these Spanish colonizers were true pioneers who were extending the frontiers of civilization into uncharted territory.

Had the Spaniards been content, while extending the frontiers of Spanish civilization north,

with trading and bartering with their hosts and had not been so insistent on allegiance to the king, and had the missionaries not been so eager to convert the Indians, they would have accomplished much more than they eventually did with the sword and the cross. Antonio de Espejo and his little band of a dozen or so accomplished a good deal more with his friendly approach than many of the conquerors did. After a long reconnaissance he returned to Mexico without having fought a battle or losing a single member of his expedition.

In addition to trading supplies, each member of the expedition brought whatever he considered useful in settling in a new land. One detailed entry lists among a man's personal belongings a few pieces of scrap iron, a hoe, a sword, and twelve horses. Scraps of iron are of little consequence to a man today, but twelve horses are an important consideration affordable by only the most affluent members of society. In colonial days the horse was indispensable to a man who was the product of an equestrian culture, and twelve horses simply ensured a man's way of life even if he came to settle in an unknown land.

In addition to the horse's practical value, a mount marked the difference between a *peón*, a man on foot, and a *caballero*, a man on horseback. Don Juan de Oñate, wishing to recompense the members of his expedition, requested that all be granted the title *hidalgo*, for whom horses were a *sine qua non*.[5] The Spanish horse was a natural means of mobility, more so than the English horse, which meant horsepower, that is, a practical consideration designed for agricultural pursuits that still kept men on the ground. It is not surprising that the viewpoint of both New World cultures should be so different and yet explainable, considering that one was looking at the world at the level of his eyes and the other, mounted on a horse, was looking beyond and down like Don Quixote.

The equestrian has always been the symbol of virility and power throughout the Spanish world whether it be the *charro* of Salamanca, the *huaso* of Chile, the *gaucho* of Argentina, the Mexican *charro*, the Southwestern *vaquero*, or the New Mexican *cibolero*. The emphasis placed on this individual can be judged by the gay trappings with which he and his horse were caparisoned in colonial days. The man so outfitted was hardly prepared to walk behind the plow, and so he took to stock raising in the Southwest and kept his seat on the saddle. The equestrian role in Spanish culture meant much more than a man on a horse. For one thing, it meant that such a man was not close to the soil and therefore not easily given to agricultural pursuits. The Spaniard, however, worked the land successfully when he could have manpower in the form of Indian labor through the *repartimiento*, the *encomienda*, and later under the hacienda system of ownership. To Hispanic people land was more a status symbol, as indicated by the title of *hidalgo* given to the lesser nobility. A man was an *hijo de algo*, a son of something. A *caballero*, or horseman, who had taken part in the conquest of the New World, like the men Oñate brought, was eligible to receive a *caballería*. A direct grant comprising two *caballerías* was awarded to Juan de Oñate by the royal *audiencia* in the name of the king.

The terminology that emerged from the first

The pronghorn, called *berrendo* by Hispanos because of its two-toned color. In the western United States it is called antelope more often than pronghorn because it reminded the original settlers of the antelopes of the Old World. Courtesy of Coronado Cuarto Centennial.

contacts of the land in New Mexico by the Spanish colonists also gave rise to a new nomenclature for the flora and fauna native to the New World. But, unlike land measurements, it is possible to identify meanings definitely, because nature has not changed significantly in the centuries since the Conquest. When no counterpart was found in Spanish for certain species of flora or fauna, the colonists ordinarily used names of similar animals or plants known in Spain. This method was not always accurate, although it became the established usage. For example, when they came across the long-legged jack rabbit, they promptly called it *liebre*, or hare, which, although it belongs to the same genus, *Lepus*, is not the *liebre* found in Spain.

Villagrá referred to the *gallinas de la tierra*, meaning the "chickens of the land," including the turkey, the sage hen, and all other "chickens" native to the Southwest. Today when a good portion of Spanish or "Spanglish" spoken by descendants of Spanish settlers consists of translations from English, or Anglicized words, they assume that by *gallinas de la tierra* the old conquistador meant "ground chickens." For turkey there are a number of words to choose from. The gobbler is called *ganso* in northern New Mexico, which means goose; *cócono* or *güíjalo* is the name used in southern New Mexico and west Texas; *guajolote* from the Aztec in Mexico; *pavo* because it resembled the *pavo real* or peacock of Europe; and, with the coming of the English as the official tongue, the awful bastardized word *torquey*. There was no complete uniformity in the nomenclature of animals, particularly rodents, which differed from one part of the Southwest to the other. In northern New Mexico they still call the beaver *nutria*, the name used for otter in Spanish, instead of its proper name, *castor*. In Mexico the latter word is also applied to the material out of which people make the skirt used by the *china poblana*, the counterpart of the *charro*. In the north *tuza* is used for prairie dog; in the south a *tuza* is a gopher.

An attempt to distinguish between what was Spanish and what was native to the Southwest gave rise to the expression *de Castilla*, used to designate products of Spain. For example, there were *conejos* in the Southwest (which today are called cottontails in English), but the colonists had also introduced the rabbit from Spain, which they called *conejo de Castilla* to indicate that it was the domesticated variety. The same term was applied to gallinaceous fowl known in colonial days as *gallinas de Castilla*. The wild rose was *rosa*, but the domesticated variety from Spain was *rosa de Castilla*. Soap made in the same Spanish province came to be known as *jabón de Castilla*, and so widespread was the acceptance of this product that the name became a trade name, even though "Castile soap" is now produced by American manufacturers. The expression "from Castile," however, eventually became equated with quality in the minds of colonials to such an extent that it developed into a status symbol applicable also to people. Anglo-American writers, taking their cue from Spanish tradition, refer to some of their fictional characters as "Castilian" or "half-Castilian," intimating a person of higher status.

BORROWINGS FROM INDIAN CULTURE

Despite all the preparations made in advance for the occupation of New Mexico, the colonists had to make a number of adjustments and adaptations to the new land. Some topographic features and climatic conditions were not too different from certain regions of Spain, but those members of the colony who had been born and reared in the warmer climes of Mexico had to become accustomed to the harsh winters of the north. Before attempting to Hispanicize the Indians, the colonists had to learn how to survive in a land that was new to them and how to live with people who had already developed a way of life that they must follow, particularly because the first winters were spent in the Indian pueblos. There is no doubt that, by the time they moved the capital to Santa Fe in 1610, the Spanish settlers had picked up a great deal of information from their hosts.

The Indians they first associated with were sedentary agriculturists who knew corn culture and dry-farming methods, were familiar with weather and seasonal changes, and knew also how to supplement their food supply by hunting. The architecture used by the Indians was well adapted to the southwestern climate, and the building materials available made it possible for the Spaniards to build themselves houses that bore a close resemblance to Indian architectural design. With their more extensive knowledge the colonists added a few improvements and a few elements of European architecture that were later adopted by the Indians.

Many of the adaptations and changes that occurred in the culture of the Spanish colonists resulted from their association with the Indians and the use they made of things Indian. A large number of Indian words had already become Hispanicized in Mexico. The names for such well-known commodities as *tomates, patatas, camotes*, or sweet potatoes, *chile, maiz*, and *aguacates*, or avocados, and for hundreds of useful articles were part of the Spanish vocabulary in 1598. There were not as many accretions from the Indian culture of the Southwest, however, because the number of products that the Spaniards could use was comparatively small. Moreover, many of the natural products of the Southwest were also common to

An example of Indian architecture well adapted to the southwestern climate. Courtesy of Coronado Cuarto Centennial.

A scene in Taos Pueblo showing the conical oven adopted by the Indians from the Spanish colonists.

Mexico and were known to the colonists. Botanist Edward Castetter, who made an extensive study of edible plants in the Southwest, found 218 herbs and plants that the Indians used for food, but only a few were ever used by the Spaniards.

The predominant use of corn in various food preparations was continued by the Spanish people in New Mexico and was eventually widely disseminated throughout the Southwest. In most cases the new dishes were also adapted to the more sophisticated European taste. *Atole*, a thin corn gruel made from *masa*, the corn dough used for *tortillas*, was thinned with milk and, with the addition of sugar and cinnamon, used as a drink. The simple *chilaquiles* of the Aztecs were transformed into *enchiladas* by frying the tortilla in oil and adding cheese, onion, and a thick, tasty sauce. These and other changes produced the fare that we know today as Mexican cooking. One dish that bears a Queres or Tewa Indian name is *chaquegüe*, a corn gruel very similar to what is

known as grits in the southern United States. It was served with a meat sauce or with sugar and milk when available.

Another dish of Indian provenience was *mesqui-tamal*, a very nutritious drink prepared from ground-ripened pods of the mesquite tree. The Indians' version was much simpler in that they did not use sugar and pounded the pods instead of grinding them. A variation of the same drink was made from screw beans when mesquite pods were not available. The Pimas of Arizona depended on the mesquite pods during droughts. They ground the pods, seeds and all, and made a sort of bread that the Spaniards found acceptable as a substitute for wheat bread. A few wild herbs used variously as condiments for cooking or as medicinal plants were *pinhué (Hymenosys floribunda* A. Gray Compositae), *oshá (Linguisticum porteri* C. and R.), *chimajá (Aulospernum purpureum* S. Wats.), and *pagué (Dusodia papposa* [vent.] Hitche).[6]

28

The Indians of the Southwest, particularly the women, who wore long hair, used the root of the yucca plant as a shampoo or soap, which they called *amole*. The roots were pounded and then swished in water until a sudsy foam formed. In colonial days, when soft soaps were not easily obtained, *amole* was a good substitute and was extensively used in Spanish households.

An interesting addition to the list of plants adopted by the colonists was a tobacco substitute known as *punche (Nicotiana torreyana* Nels and Mcbr.*)*. This "wild tobacco" was used as far south as Chihuahua when tobacco was a heavily taxed monopoly of the crown. The smoking habit, although acquired from the New World inhabitants, can hardly be attributed to the Indians of the Southwest, but the adaptation of *punche* as a tobacco substitute is truly from the region. The poorer classes in New Mexico continued to smoke the Indian weed until recent times.

Wine, brandy, and rum were the favorite alcoholic beverages of the Spaniards, but in the province of New Mexico they had to wait until vineyards and sugar-cane fields were planted and productive before manufacturing them. Again, there was a substitute in a product that the Tarahumaras of northern Chihuahua and the Yaquis of Sonora called *tesgüino, tiswin,* or *tecuín*. This simple beverage was made from sprouted corn, which was sweetened before it was fermented, when sugar became available. Some Indian tribes went collectively into a *tesgüinada*, or "tiswin bust," as soon as the beverage was ripe. The Spanish colonials learned to make *tesgüino*, and soon the use of it spread into most parts of the Southwest. A similar drink of Aztec origin, known by the name *tepache* (from the Aztec *tepiatl*), became popular farther west. This more varied drink was made from corn, from fruit juices, and from sugar cane. These substitutes began to disappear as soon as the means for making wine and *aguardiente* became available.

Firearms and ammunition were relatively scarce and usually made available to the soldiers of the presidios but not to all the settlers; consequently, many of the soldiers were armed with bows and arrows and lances like their Indian counterparts. One particular use of these weapons was in hunting buffalo, an art that the settlers learned from their Indian neighbors. The Europeans had used both of these weapons for centuries, but in the Southwest they followed the Indian pattern and used comparable processes in manufacturing them.

Another necessity was footgear. The settlers brought a supply of shoes and boots when they entered the province, but in order to replace them, they had to use Indian tanned buckskin and buffalo hides. In many of the larger households the Indian servants turned out the *teguas* needed by members of the family, but the rest of the men had to provide their own by following the Indian pattern and design. It was not necessarily a desire of the Spaniards to become Indianized but simply a way of adopting materials and practical substitutes for use until others were made available.

More supplies arrived from Mexico before long, and more settlers came to increase the colony and replace many who had left. Eventually the colonists adjusted to the land and people around them. There were crops to be raised, stock to care for, and homes to be built as the pattern of southwestern life began to emerge. It was a simple life consisting of only the basic essentials of food and shelter. Anything beyond that was provided by their ingenuity and inventiveness, complemented with a few borrowings from the pueblo and the plains Indians. Nature was not as prodigal as it was in California; weather created additional problems, and distances from the sources of supplies were too great to bring immediate relief when needed.

There was plenty of timber in the nearby mountains, but no lumber mills to turn out building materials. Homes were built of sun-dried adobe, and pine or cottonwood *vigas* were good substitutes for rafters. Spanish settlers were more inclined to adjust to the natural topography than to change their surroundings to suit their needs. If they wanted water for irrigation, they simply farmed along streams from which water could be diverted to their fields. In addition to these handicaps, roaming Indians raided their farms after harvest time. To overcome this danger, the colonists designed their houses with inner patios and barns accessible through a *zaguán*, an opening that gave access to the house built around the patio. For further protection there was a community *torreón*, a medieval-like, thick-walled tower, accessible through subterranean passages leading to each house. This structure was a safe refuge in the event of Indian attacks. The Spanish settlers, like their counterparts on the eastern seaboard years later, wielded a hoe as well as a musket or a lance. Men could be drawn from the fields into the ranks of the militia to repel an attack or to go on a punitive expedition.

A New Mexican *torreón*, or tower, built for protection during Indian attacks. A Spanish adobe oven is on the right. Courtesy of Coronado Cuarto Centennial.

Sheepherders and *pastores* rode modest burros like the one Sancho is riding here.

Despite the drawbacks and handicaps with which all pioneers had to contend, and the first Spanish settlers in New Mexico were no different from others in this respect, the colony finally took hold and began to grow. The settlers developed gradually the design for living that became the way of life for them and for future generations, a way of life that was principally pastoral. Sheep raising became the most successful source of income, and the New Mexicans who eventually accumulated large flocks were often referred to as *ricos*. People who worked for them had a hierarchy of their own, beginning with *borreguero*, or sheepherder, and continuing through *pastor* to *patrón*, the owner of the sheep ranch. The rank depended on the number of sheep under the herder's care. The lowest was the *borreguero*, who was in charge of an *hatajo*, or *hato* at most. He was followed by a *pastor*, who was in charge of a *rebaño*, and the top man was the head of the *partida* on a given range.

Oñate's immediate mission was to pacify and settle the province of New Mexico, but, as an official representative of the Spanish Empire in America, he was also expected to establish the basic pattern of imperial conquest by introducing the three bonds of nationality decreed by the crown: a uniform language for all Indian tribes, which in this case was Spanish; a uniform system of juridical institutions; and the only religion recognized by the Spanish state, Catholicism. The first step in this ambitious program was to persuade the inhabitants of the Southwest to recognize the king as their lord and become subjects of an empire that, according to the message translated into Indian tongues, would protect them against their enemies and also ensure their ultimate salvation through their acceptance of Christianity. The lengthy document read by the secretary of the expedition to each tribe and pueblo spelled out all this to an audience of American Indians who did not understand the Spanish language and to whom the bureaucratic jargon simply meant that they had been overcome by superior arms. The conquerors were careful to warn the Indians of the responsibilities involved in becoming vassals of the Spanish crown: "The governor reminded them that they should realize that by rendering obedience and vassalage to the king our lord they would become subject to his will and laws, and that if they failed to observe them they would be punished as transgressors of the orders of their king and natural master."[1]

Although each Indian village supposedly accepted the conditions set down by the conquistador Oñate, their reactions shortly afterward indicated their unwillingness to submit to the protective arm of the Spaniards by their unsuspected attack on Captain Juan de Zaldívar and his men when he made a peaceful visit to Acoma under orders from Oñate. Under the terms of the "accepted" agreement, this treacherous act was a transgression for which the Indians of Acoma were to be punished. Other tribes suffered the same fate at the hands of their conquerors, in the name of the king, to whom they had rendered homage by accepting the Act of Obedience and Vassalage read to them and presumably translated by an interpreter.

Punishment was not carried out as a reprisal but as due process of law. First Oñate appointed Captain Alonso Gómez Montesinos as an attorney to defend the Acoma Indians when they were brought to trial. At the first hearing evidence that a crime had been committed was established by questioning a number of witnesses. Next the court discussed the requirements of justifiable war, and, after a long review of causes, it declared that war was not justifiable "for mere craving for power, revenge, or greed." The entire company was then assembled in San Juan, where the settlers were provisionally quartered, and orders for the siege of Acoma were given.

The prisoners taken after the successful attack were brought to trial, during which their attorney, Captain Gómez Montesinos, petitioned "that they [Indians] be acquitted and be compensated for the expenses resulting from their arrest." The trial began on December 29, when preparations were made to attack Acoma, and ended on February 12, 1599. In the course of the proceedings several Acoma Indians were questioned by the court, and their testimony was translated by an interpreter. The defending attorney argued in the name of justice that these Indians should not be held responsible because they were *bárbaros*, uncivilized, and his petition was incorporated into the proceedings.

At the end of three days of testimony on both sides Oñate concluded the trial and meted out a cruel sentence for which he had to answer later to the viceroy of New Spain. The trial of Acoma was part of the juridical system that Spain was attempting to institute in the New World, and Don Juan de Oñate, as the representative of that system, was bound to adhere to it. The government organization of all villages in the Southwest was uniformly set up with a nomenclature that has persisted to the present day. Instead of designating

The street in the village of Acoma where Captain Zaldívar of the Oñate Expedition of 1598 met his fate. Courtesy of Coronado Cuarto Centennial.

Acoma Pueblo from a distance. Some of Oñate's soldiers jumped from this mesa when attacked by the Indians and lived to tell the story.

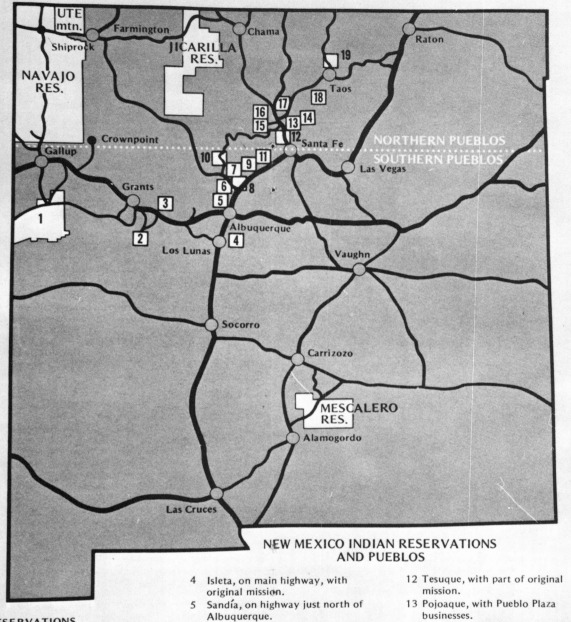

NEW MEXICO INDIAN RESERVATIONS AND PUEBLOS

RESERVATIONS

Ute Mountain
Navajo
Jicarilla Apache
Mescalero Apache

PUEBLOS

1 Zuñi, near point of Coronado's entry.

2 Acoma, the Sky City, with original mission.

3 Laguna, on highway, with original mission.

4 Isleta, on main highway, with original mission.

5 Sandía, on highway just north of Albuquerque.

6 Santa Ana, with original mission still in use.

7 Zía, with strange original mission still in use.

8 San Felipe, with interesting rebuilt mission.

9 Santo Domingo, with unusual rebuilt mission.

10 Jémez, in the beautiful Jémez Mountain region.

11 Cochiti, between Albuquerque and Santa Fe.

12 Tesuque, with part of original mission.

13 Pojoaque, with Pueblo Plaza businesses.

14 Nambé, of the Rio Grande group near Santa Fe.

15 San Ildefonso, famous for its black pottery.

16 Santa Clara, ranks with San Ildefonso for pottery.

17 San Juan, named by Oñate in 1598.

18 Picurís, between Taos and Santa Fe.

19 Taos, with the largest communal dwellings.

Indian villages in New Mexico visited by the first settling expedition of Don Juan de Oñate. Nearly all the original pueblos have continued to the present day. The reservations were set up later during the American occupation.

the head of a tribe or village as "chief," the Spaniards appointed a governor, a lieutenant governor, an interpreter, and a secretary, and these titles became the legal names used in official dealings. The Spanish government presented each village governor with a cane as a staff of office, which was continued centuries later by President Abraham Lincoln, who added a second silver-headed cane to which the Indians refer as the "Lincoln Cane."

The introduction of Castilian as the official language of the Spanish Empire was a slow process because of the limited number of teachers. A handful of missionaries was attempting to teach a totally different culture to various Indian tribes who were not particularly interested in learning the language of conquerors. Moreover, the missionaries spent part of their time trying to learn the dialects of their charges in order to communicate better with them. The communal living of the pueblos facilitated the language-teaching process to some extent, and enough was learned by the Indians that all affairs of church and state were eventually transacted in Castilian.

Things were different, however, among the roaming Apaches, Navajos, and Comanches, who were more hostile to the Spaniards than the pueblo Indians. The most the Spaniards could hope for was to hold the predators in check to protect Spanish and Indian pueblos alike. Although these seminomadic tribes did not become as fluent in the language of the conquerors as the pueblos did, they acquired dialectal adaptations of Spanish for items of material culture that they acquired. The Navajos, who developed a strong taste for coffee, promptly called it *cohueh*, an approximation of the Spanish *café; pan* became *pahj*, meaning bread; *centao* or *cinco* was as common in referring to a five-cent piece as their original *litzu*; and Americans became *Melicano*, patterned after the Spanish *Americano*.

The Hispanicizing of the Indians in the realm was an acculturation process in which both the state and church had a stake, but there was so much overlapping of authority and action that the two institutions were constantly at odds from the very beginning. The church had a closer contact with the Indians through the mission system and profited from neophyte labor to such an extent that, before long, the friars had accumulated considerably more property than the state or the settlers in the way of cattle, sheep, and cultivable land. Jurisdictional lines were difficult to draw.

The governor of the province insisted that his authority superseded that of the pope. This led to a constant state of animosity in which friars were beaten by orders of the military, and accusations were lodged in Mexico City by the church.

Very early in colonial days the friars realized how the Indians' religion was combined with the whole pattern of living. It consisted not only of the observance of a given set of rituals at specific seasons of the year but a relationship with nature and a state of mind that could not be separated from the whole realm of existence. When the aborigines were told that the God of the Christians was a beneficent being, they readily accepted Him and added Him to their own deities. The ritual of the church was interpreted as another form of pageantry to be combined with lustrations and propitiations to which they were accustomed. This combination of pagan and Christian practices made it difficult for the friars to purge the Indians' version of Christianity of much that was considered pagan by orthodox religious worshipers.

Gradually missionaries relaxed their strict and uncompromising attitudes and became content with outward manifestations of conversion so that they could report large numbers of converts to the viceroy, and to the higher echelons of the church, as a measure of their successful work in the mission field. Even the establishment of a mission church within the pueblo did not guarantee that the Indians were Christians in the strict sense of the word. In the end the natives became nominal Catholics, without relinquishing their own ceremonies, so that today they erect a shrine honoring their patron saint and perform their usual dance ceremonials in his honor. But when there was an uprising, as often happened, churches were destroyed, missionaries were put to death, and the Indians reverted to their own forms of worship.

Much of the success of the missionaries in the field was attributable to their practical sense in combining elements of material culture for the well-being of the Indian and religious instruction. Both the churchmen and the state realized the advisability of accelerating the Hispanicizing process by this means. One of the later viceroys of New Spain, Bernardo de Gálvez, was farsighted enough to realize the importance of strengthening the acculturation of the Indian by practical means. He insisted that the Indians be trained in the use of Spanish foods, beverages, clothing, and arms and acquire a desire to own land in the European fashion. This would make them more dependent on Spanish culture and help to wean them from their own separatist and conservative notions that could lead to revolt. To hasten the process, supplies and rations were provided through the Fondo de Aliados, an alliance fund set up for this purpose. What Gálvez was recommending was in essence a guided acculturation.

From the early days of settlement it had been decreed that Spanish villages were to be established near Indian pueblos in order to expose the Indians to the Spanish way of life, hoping that this proximity would eventuate in mutual understanding and voluntary assimilation. The contiguity of Spanish villages to Indian villages was more successful in the assimilation of the Indians than the colonial Spaniards ever imagined. As Edgar L. Hewett points out, the disappearance of some of the pueblos is simply the result of a complete assimilation of such Indian villages as Tomé, Nambé, and Cuyimangué and Socorro and Ysleta in Texas.[2] After World War II, Anglo-Americans seeking pleasanter living conditions moved into these assimilated villages and added the latest layer of contemporary culture. What was an Indian pueblo in the seventeenth century, and a Spanish village before World War II, has become today a typical American town complete with neon signs, filling stations at every crossing, television antennas, and rock and roll. The inhabitants have been so completely assimilated that they have not spoken the Indian dialect of their ancestors for generations and resent any reference to their Indian ancestry. It should be noted that much of the mixing and assimilation of Spaniards and Indians resulted from this early settlement policy.

Some habits and practices had to be modified from the start. The dress habits of the natives were soon changed in the interest of "decency and morality." The *taparrabo*, or G-string, worn by the men on many occasions and the apronlike skirts of the women shocked the sensibilities of the Spaniards, who wore voluminous clothes. The change was readily accomplished, particularly when the Indians were taught to weave in the fashion of the Europeans. Many of the "Indian" garments worn today by members of various tribes consist of articles adapted from the Spanish colonial wardrobe. The white, loose-fitting trousers worn by many pueblo and Apache men are a native version of the Spanish undergarments of colonial vintage. The embroidered shirts on Isleta

The crocheted skirt, the woolen shawl and upper garment, and the silver necklace are dress items adopted by the Indians from the Spaniards. Photograph by Frashers, Pomona, California.

A Zuñi silversmith making silver jewelry in the style learned from Mexican craftsmen in the nineteenth century. Photograph by Frashers, Pomona, California.

and Laguna men are also reminiscent of Spanish shirts similar to the one that Governor Joaquín Alencáster loaned to Zebulon Pike when he was the governor's "guest" at a dinner party given at the Palace of the Governors in Santa Fe.

The Hispanicizing of the Indians of the Southwest was carried out at the onset largely through the efforts of the missions and the friars under the protection of the military, but there was no uniform plan that could be followed throughout all parts of the region. The ideal situation was to have the new Spanish settlements alongside the Indian pueblos, resulting in, as already mentioned, the complete assimilation of the Indians. This was not always possible, because the needs of the colonists required land for raising crops and a constant water supply. When these conditions coincided with the location of the already-established pueblos, it was a simple matter for the Spaniards to build their villages adjacent to their future neighbors.

In more remote areas, where cultivable land was limited and the water supply scant, an additional settlement would have disrupted the life and economy of both Indians and Spaniards. In these places a mission church was built within the pueblo and was manned by a few friars whose living needs could be supplied by the Indian villagers. These pueblos were able to preserve their aboriginal identity by continuing to speak their own language and by preserving their traditional customs, clan and family structures, ceremonial practices, and kinship ties. Such pueblos as Taos, San Ildefonso, Santa Clara, and Santo Domingo and others west of the Río Grande, such as Laguna, Acoma, Zuñi, and Hopi, have had a relatively uninterrupted existence dating back to pre-Spanish days. The inhabitants of these villages made a few practical adaptations to conform with the new order introduced by the conquerors, but they were far enough removed from the Spanish sphere of influence to withstand complete absorption.

In addition to furthering the interests of the church, Oñate also introduced important elements of material culture that before long changed or altered the way of life of the Indians considerably more than the proselyting efforts of the missionaries. The implementation of farming practices, the use of sheep for meat and wool, the adoption of more practical weaving looms, and the eventual use of horses were significant contributions to the Indians, once they got over the urge for reprisal and retaliation resulting from the first impact of

armed conflict. Baked bread, for example, eventually replaced the corn *tortilla* of the pueblos, and Spanish earth-ovens became household necessities in Indian villages where they may be seen today in front yards and are usually referred to as "Indian ovens." The Spanish fireplace built in a corner of the room was another adoption that replaced the original opening in the middle of the roof of an Indian house. The European fireplace, in addition to being cleaner, burned less wood and was a much more practical device for heating and indoor cooking.

On the other hand, the abstractions of Catholic doctrine were not as easily understood and were hardly a substitute for aboriginal forms of traditional worship that the Indians were reluctant to abandon. The exterior forms of Catholic pageantry were generally observed, but as late as World War II some tribes, particularly the Navajos, reduced the abstruse points of Christian theology to the simplest denominator by referring to Protestant ministers as "long coats" and Catholic priests as "long robes."

To ensure the process of conversion, the missionaries tried to check pagan practices that were in direct conflict with their teachings, but whenever they discovered similarities in deities and ritual, the padres found it advantageous to substitute the name of a saint or church holiday to implement an already established custom. The Indians also compromised by having their "idols behind altars," as Anita Brenner would say. It is hardly a coincidence that the Santo Domingo corn dance, an Indian fruition ceremony, should coincide with Saint Dominic's Day. Many Indian ceremonials in the pueblos along the upper Río Grande are held on the village's saint's day, and the villages themselves have been christened with the names of saints as a constant reminder of the faith that they are supposed to profess.

The Indians have gone the sixteenth-century padres one better, however, by including the Virgin Mary in the ritual prayers of today's Native American Church, an official religion built around the peyote cult. This is hardly what the Spanish missionaries had in mind when they introduced Christianity to the Indians in colonial days. In the sixteenth century the peyote cult was already a bone of contention, which the Inquisition tried to eradicate not because the United States outlawed it but because it violated the integrity of Christian worship, which the inquisitors considered heretical perversity and apostasy. United States courts tried

Acoma girls on the way to the water hole with their *tinajas*, wearing dresses woven from wool that was introduced by the Spaniards and necklaces with the Moorish pomegranate bead, misnamed squash blossom. Courtesy of Coronado Cuarto Centennial.

A Navajo spinning wool, a fabric introduced by the Spaniards in the seventeenth century. Before that time there were no sheep in the Southwest. Photograph by Frashers, Pomona, California.

An Indian housewife baking bread in a conical oven of the type introduced by the Spanish colonials. The Indians were taught by the Europeans to make bread from wheat flour. Courtesy of Coronado Cuarto Centennial.

The old and the new: a modern version of the Spanish fireplace introduced in the Indian pueblos in the seventeenth century. Courtesy of Coronado Cuarto Centennial.

to curb the use of peyote because it was considered a mescaline drug.

Anthropologist Omer Stewart, of the University of Colorado, a leading student of and authority on Indian religion, finds a close parallel between the prayers of the Native American Church and Protestant worship. "The Ute meetings," he says, "impress me as similar in spirit and feeling to many Protestant Christian church services. Although the Bible and crucifix are lacking, the confessions, testimonies, prayers, and speeches of the Indians closely resemble manifestations of the religion in which I was reared."[3]

Although the Indians incorporated into their own religious worship and ceremonials many elements of the religion introduced by the Spaniards, the latter have never adopted any of the Indians' religious practices in the Southwest. Observers are often misled by the casual attitude toward Catholicism among some of the Hispanos, but this is largely due to the lack of continuous religious instruction plus the fact that religion, like

41

The Indians of Santo Domingo Pueblo performing the Corn Dance, a fruition ceremony celebrated in August on St. Dominic's Day, combining Indian and Catholic religious ceremonies.

language, customs, and most Spanish behavior in the Southwest, had become a folk culture.[4]

Some writers have insisted that the Penitente *morada* is derived from the Indian kiva or ceremonial chamber, because it is exclusively used by members of the brotherhood during their rituals at Eastertime with a certain amount of secrecy. The possibility of such a parallel is entirely illogical, in view of the zeal with which the Catholic church has tried to maintain its religious worship free from foreign influences for centuries, under the constant vigilance of the Inquisition in colonial days.

The limited resources of the colony could not provide the settlers with sufficient religious ministrations, not by intentional neglect but because conversion of the Indians was a colonization priority included in the contract with Oñate. The Spanish government felt that, as long as the aborigines remained under the influence and tutelage of their own religious leaders, it would be almost impossible to control them and bring them into the cultural fold. It was therefore essential that the missionaries give all their attention to building missions and to converting the Indians in order to hold them responsible for their behavior toward their masters. This made conversion the first step in the "pacification" and acculturation process that would inevitably follow. One of the factors that strongly determined the support given to the outlying provinces by the crown was the number of converts and the progress made in the indoctrination of the Indians.

Mention has been made of the introduction of certain practices that would help improve the economy of the Indians. It followed that increased efficiency and productivity among the native inhabitants would enable them to contribute more toward the welfare of the Spanish settlers. The training of large numbers of artisans throughout the Spanish Empire enabled the colonial Spaniards to build an untold number of churches, cathedrals, and public buildings in Latin America, to say nothing of the crafts that as a result have been handed down to the present time. Had the Indians been segregated and not culturally assimilated, the conquerors would have had to provide themselves with household wares from ordinary clay dishes to elaborately carved furniture and colorful textiles. Indirectly the Spanish colonial arts and crafts for which Mexico is universally known has been made possible by the Hispanicized Indians and *mestizos* who were taught these skills.

In the Southwest, where there was little need for the elaborate products of refined society, most of the crafts consisted of adaptations of products already known to the Indian servants and slaves. They had a basic knowledge of, for example, weaving, pottery making, and curing of buffalo and deer hides, so all they were taught by the Spanish colonial craftsmen was the refinements and adaptations of these skills for production of articles suitable to European taste. The same was true of agricultural practices and the preparation of such staples as corn, dried vegetables, and fruits. As a consequence the colonials eventually turned these chores over to their wards and neglected particularly the textile arts to such an extent that master craftsmen from the textile center of Saltillo were imported toward the end of the Spanish era and the beginning of the Mexican period, short though it was, to train the settlers in lost weaving and textile-production arts.

The Hispanicization process was indirectly furthered by the taking of captives in battle and the purchase of slaves from surrounding Indian tribes. They constituted the bulk of the servant force not only in colonial days but far into the nineteenth century after the American occupation, with a market so well established that there was a standard price for young boys and girls sold in Spanish villages. One of the most welcome wedding presents that a groom could present to his bride was an Indian servant girl to relieve her of menial chores. Male servants and those with no particular skills were used as field hands and also as part of the fighting force of the villages.[5]

The life of Indian slaves was not as afflictive as the name would indicate, because the life they led in Spanish colonial homes did not differ greatly from that of their masters. Living standards were simple, but, compared with the precarious existence led by the roaming tribes to which most slaves had belonged, the security and comforts of a Spanish household were much more desirable. Another factor that ameliorated the lives of these unfortunates who had been sold by enemy tribes or taken in war was the absence of segregation. The more tractable slaves were taught the Spanish way of life, became accustomed to their new surroundings, were treated like members of the household, and eventually blended with the rest of the population by taking the name of the family they served. As late at the 1930's, servants in some larger homes in Ranchos de Taos and in the sheep-raising domains of the Mirabals of western New Mexico were either descendants of Indian slaves or old Indian servants so thoroughly Hispanicized that they were no longer referred to as Indians and were treated no differently from other members of the home.[6] Many of the tasks to which servants and slaves were assigned were not totally new to some of them. The adjustment consisted of performing such chores as corn grinding, called *molienda*, weaving, and preparing food according to the requirements of each household.

Another factor that accelerated the assimilation of Indians into the service of the Spaniards or the Hispanos was the fathering of *mestizos* by the casual relations of a frontier civilization. The familial relationships resulting from this racial crossing accelerated the assimilation process and gave the offspring of such unions kinship rights that their mothers did not enjoy. These instances were much more common than some would like to admit, notwithstanding that the humanistic tendencies of Hispanic people led them to accept the "inevitable" results philosophically.

The contributions of the Spanish settlers in architectural improvements, agricultural methods and products, and the sheep-raising industry were readily accepted by the pueblo Indians and incorporated into their way of life. Instead of depending entirely on wild game for their meat supply, they could now use mutton; wool replaced rabbit skins and wild cotton for their looms. The life of the sedentary Indians was greatly modified by these contributions from Spanish culture, but horses contributed even more to the cultural change of all aborigines, particularly the seminomadic Apaches, Navajos, and Comanches. From the start the Spaniards were understandably reluctant to make horses available to the Indian, because they realized that, as long as the conquerors had superior mobility by controlling horses, they would be better able to hold the hostile tribes in check. Despite the prohibitions against the use of horses by the Indians, the latter lost no time seeking possession of them by raiding Spanish settlements. At first many of the tribes of the Southwest used horses for food, but it is believed that by 1620 the Apaches were riding horses.

Much has been said, even by reputable historians, about the "stray" theory as the means by which horses came into the hands of the Indians. The idea has turned into a legend, because it seems plausible that the early conquistadors would lose some of their horses, which then multiplied as strays over the mesas. Horses are supposed to have strayed from the expeditions of Hernando de Soto, Ponce de León, Coronado, and others. Recent researches, however, have definitely proved that the Indians did not acquire horses until they overcame their fear of them and stole them from permanent settlements; the Southwest was the principal region where horses were raised by Oñate colony descendants.

Cultural changes occasioned by the acquisition of the horse were particularly apparent among the Indians of the plains, who depended largely on buffalo herds for survival. Most historians agree that the Comanche moved into the Southwest not because they were being displaced by the westward move of English settlements but because they wanted to be closer to horses. The ungainly Comanche foot warrior, when mounted, became a formidable centaur whose range of operations both for pillage and for trade extended throughout the Southwest and into Mexico. It was this same mounted tribe that became the settlers' nightmare in Texas many years later. One of the first contacts with Spanish settlements by the Comanches was in Taos at the opening of the eighteenth century, when they camped several thousand strong around the village and invited the Spaniards to trade. This trade developed into the semiannual expeditions to the plains east of the Río Grande known as the "Comanchero trade" and continued until the nineteenth century, when it deteriorated into a fearsome pillage and plunder by the addition of questionable recruits from both Anglo and Spanish elements.[7]

The Spaniards, with their long experience in dealing with the Indians by the time they settled in the Southwest, used trade as a planned enterprise by including items for trading purposes in the inventories of supplies they brought along. Though the conquerors resorted to arms when they met with aggressive resistance, they were cautioned from the start of their expeditions to treat the natives well, and offers to trade often proved successful in initial contacts.

The instructions given Juan de Oñate specifically recommended that they try to encourage friendly association with the Indians: ". . . they must be well treated and regaled and not offended in the least or given occasion to become irritated. In this matter you shall impose the most severe penalties on transgressors."

Many leaders of expeditions into New Mexico had to answer charges of mistreatment of the Indians during the early days of settlement. Coronado himself was brought to trial a few years after returning to Mexico for cruelties against the Indians but was eventually absolved because the charges were not proved.

Very soon after their arrival both settlers and missionaries ran short of supplies that could be obtained only from Mexico City nearly two thousand miles away. First, a request had to be taken to the city outlining the needs of the missionaries, whose expanded activities required expendable supplies with which to minister to their wards. The long inventories requested by the padres was the beginning of a mission supply route that eventually turned into a regular business enterprise.

The first caravan left Mexico City in 1609 with 32 wagons, 500 mules, herds of livestock, and a military escort. In addition to church supplies other articles were added later so that what started as a mission supply train eventually became a trading caravan over a trail from Santa Fe to Mexico called El Camino Real. As other northern settlements of New Spain were established, *caminos* spread into a network that produced the communication routes used later by the Santa Fe trade. California established a comparable route south from San Diego to Mexico City that was also called El Camino Real. On the return south the empty wagons were loaded with merchandise produced in the New Mexican province. After the reconquest by Diego de Vargas in 1692, the caravans, or *conductas*, as these expeditions were called, became one of the most important trading enterprises in the Southwest. When Chihuahua was founded, trade with that city became an annual fair attended by thousands of New Mexican merchants and their families.

All people who planned to attend the Chihuahua fair rendezvoused every year in the village of Sevillita de la Joya, south of Albuquerque, now known simply as La Joya, and made their final preparation for the long trek south. The larger dealers of pelts and wool brought their product in wagons; others loaded *atajos* of pack mules with coarse textiles of homespun materials, buffalo robes, dried fruits, nuts, and anything else that could be bartered through the colonial system of *cambalache*. Historians give varying figures regarding the size of the annual New Mexico–

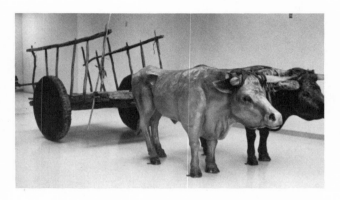

Ox carts carried much of the merchandise to the Chihuahua fairs and later over the Santa Fe Trail to Kansas City. Courtesy of the Arizona Historical Society Museum.

Chihuahua trade, but they all agree that it was one of the largest and most important events in the otherwise prosaic lives of the isolated settlers.

It took several weeks to prepare a *conducta* for the trip. Hundreds of bushels of wheat were

Arrieros loading their mules for the long trip over El Camino Real to Mexico. Strings of these loaded animals constituted the *atajos* that carried merchandise over mountain roads.

A demonstration of Spanish peasant dress of the eighteenth century, showing how a rebozo was worn for different activities in the home or in the fields.

Hispanic women attired in the homespun peasant dress of eighteenth-century New Mexico.

Hispanos in Taos loading their craft products for market as they did in the days of the caravans and *conductas* to Chihuahua and Mexico City.

ground into flour and baked into loaves of bread; corn, beans, garbanzos, and dried meat were packed and loaded; and livestock to take for food and barter was carefully selected. A *mayordomo* was chosen for the caravan, but once the expedition got under way, the commander of the army escort or *conducta* took over the protection and guidance of the overland convoy.

A number of occupations born out of this trade eventually became incorporated in the cattle industry of the Southwest. The *savanero* took charge of the pack animals, the *arrieros* drove the *atajos*, and the *cargadores* packed and secured the load on mules and horses every morning. Pack loading became such a highly developed craft among these future New Mexicans that in the nineteenth century the United States Army in the West learned the art from these experts.

Eighteenth-century Spanish peasant dress for men made from homespun materials, as worn in New Mexico.

As we have seen, a new vocabulary developed during the colonial period as a result of this overland trade, some of which has become obsolete from disuse. For example, a *jornada de recua* was a day's journey with a pack train; the *savanero* continued to ply his trade in the early days of the cattle industry in Texas, and the *tapajos*, used to cover the pack mules' eyes when traveling over shelf roads, continued also during the early period of American occupation. *Cambalache* was replaced by coined currency when the latter became available, although the term is still known by old-timers today. The *jola*, which originally meant one-eighth of a *real*, remained current among the folk around La Joya, New Mexico, where the Chihuahua traders prepared their *conductas* in colonial days, but today *jola* means one cent. *No tengo jolas* also means, "I have no money."

THE CHIHUAHUA TRADE

Despite the volume of the Chihuahua trade, the New Mexicans did not derive the profits they deserved from it, because the *Chihuahuenses* invented a mythical peso value system that worked against the visitors and turned the balance of trade in favor of their hosts. *Pesos de plata*, each worth eight *reales*, were used when selling to the New Mexicans, and *pesos de la tierra*, worth two *reales*, were used in paying for the merchandise brought by the northern traders. The Chihuahua merchants eventually had to be restrained by law to maintain a standard of values, but the visitors had such a hilarious time in the "big city" that they always looked forward to the trip, regardless of profits.

There were also romantic liaisons between New Mexican young men and the girls of Chihuahua, which in many cases culminated in matrimony. Many a young trader who had originally joined the *conducta* to Chihuahua to prove to his prospective father-in-law that he was worthy of his daughter's hand changed his mind after meeting the young *Chihuahuenses*. The girl he had left behind was literally left when the young swain returned home with a brand-new wife. Many families in New Mexico can trace their ancestors on the mother's side directly to families from Chihuahua whose forebears met during the annual fairs. Great enthusiasm was manifested by the northern Mexicans when the long trading caravan approached the city. At the cry of, "¡Ahí vienen los Nuevomexicanos!" "Here come the New Mexicans!" people rushed in carriages and on horseback to meet them and escort them into the city. It was pleasure before business as dances and fiestas opened the annual fair.

The hopes of the original settlers of finding rich mineral deposits that were to make the Southwest "another Mexico," were dispelled very soon after the occupation of the northern land. As mentioned earlier, the Oñate expedition located some diggings that gave promise of good returns, but the assay, ordered by the general, of samples brought by Marcos Farfán de los Godos, apparently was not followed up.

Perhaps it was just as well that the mining fever did not hit the first settlers. Not having developed the prospector's attitude of mind, they had to turn to other sources for a living, such as farming and particularly raising sheep, an important commodity extensively used in trade. Sheep ranching soon became one of the richest enterprises in the Southwest and created the pastoral culture characteristic of most of the region. Some of the original settlers near Santa Fe and Galisteo, such as the Ortiz y Pinos, still graze flocks on the same land apportioned to them in colonial days.

The sheep industry provided the New Mexicans not only with livestock to sell but also with all the by-products to be taken to the markets of Chihuahua, Coahuila, and Sonora. Eventually large flocks of sheep were driven as far west as California, once the Escalante Trail was established. When Josiah Gregg came to the Southwest, he estimated that as many as half a million head of sheep alone were driven to market from the flocks of New Mexico every year, but his estimate may be a little high. A man's wealth was measured in terms of the number of sheep he ran, and some of these ran into six digits. Sheep supplied meat and wool; the latter was turned into blankets, clothing, and rugs for home use and for trade. Very soon after the Southwest became permanently settled, the art of weaving was taught to the pueblo Indians and also to the Indian servants, who wove the large numbers of rugs and yards of homespun wools taken to the trading fairs.

CULTURAL BY-PRODUCTS OF EL CAMINO REAL

As mentioned, the products of colonial settlers in the Southwest were marketed during the fair in Chihuahua and other points south that the trade routes reached. Not only were material benefits accrued from the contacts created by trade, important as profits were to the settlers, but also trade enabled them to keep an unbroken cultural flow that brought them entertainment, information, and interpersonal exchanges through matrimonial alliances that helped keep the country from being completely isolated.

As late as World War I it was customary for troupes of *maromeros*, trapeze artists, actors, singers, troubadours, and clowns to come up the old Camino Real, stopping at every village along the way to perform. During viceregal days these performances were known as *volantines*, but soon thereafter they became known as *maroma*, and under this name they came into the Southwest. In addition to trapeze artists and clowns, companies of comedians traveled as part of itinerant troupes. Many of the plays presented by these traveling companies have found their way into the repertoire of the folk and circulated for decades as folk plays, because people were more

cines for the sick. For the children he always brought toys, dolls, and a species of taffy called *melcocha*, manufactured by his family at home. If he did not have what the customers wanted, they would ask him to bring it on his next trip. These requests he entered in his notebook, and the merchandise arrived without fail with his return trip.

Most of these itinerant dime stores were owned by Spaniards to whom people referred as *gachupines* or *españoles*, though in direct address they called them by their names, Don Tiburcio or Don José. One of the last of these *varilleros ambulantes* was a rotund, florid-faced Spaniard, notorious for his appetite and famous for his singing. In good Spanish tradition his *ambulanza* was pulled by a pair of sturdy little mules to whom he talked as though they were part of the family. His arrival was usually announced by the dogs in the ranch house. The residents from all parts of the ranch gathered in the open patio, filled with anticipation, wondering what Don José would bring this time.

When he was still a distance away, he could be heard talking to his mules: "¡Arre, arre! ¡que ya pronto descansarán!" "Giddap! You'll rest soon enough!" As he drove into a front yard surrounded by spreading cottonwoods, Don José greeted his hosts in the Castilian Spanish he naturally spoke. He alighted from his wagon, mule whip in hand. First the mules were watered and fed by the farmhands, and then the trader went indoors to await his usual Spanish *tortilla*, a thick, omelettelike, oversized pancake filled with potatoes and cheese. As a concession to the Southwest, he had learned to add a touch of roasted green peppers, and to complete his fare he brought along his own bottle of wine.

When he had carefully wiped the last crumbs from the plate with a piece of wheat *tortilla de harina*, the portly Spaniard leaned back, patted his belly contentedly, and exclaimed: "Panza llena, corazón contento," "A full belly makes the heart content." While the trader was eating, several boys were sent on horseback to the surrounding ranchos to spread the word that the *varillero* had arrived and was showing his wares.

For the remainder of the afternoon the front patio was a veritable bazaar for men and housewives arriving on horseback or in buggies, buckboards, and wagons. There were lace and trimmings for a wedding dress, *vestidos de baile* for the girls to wear on Saturday night frolics, assorted straw hats for men who worked in the hot sun, rubefacients and salves for the arthritic, toys and candy for the children, who spent their first *centavos* on the home-made *melcocha* that Don José always brought along. All afternoon silver coins tinkled into the long leather pouch that the vendor closed with visible satisfaction by pulling the drawstring and then stuffing the bulging moneybag into his hip pocket. The paper money he folded neatly and inserted into his money belt, over which he drew a red woolen sash called a *faja*. In New Mexico they have continued to call a belt *faja* instead of *cinturón* or *cinto*.

When everybody's needs had been met, Don José carefully replaced the remaining merchandise in the shelves of his *ambulanza*, to be taken out again at the next stop a few days later. As he emerged from the wagon, this time carrying a guitar, the customers knew that the troubadour-turned-vendor would play and sing not only the regional folk songs he learned in his travels but also those that he labeled *de la madre patria*, "from the mother country," meaning his own country and, by cultural extension, the country of all who spoke Spanish.

The visits of the *varillero* were part of the trading traditions of the Hispanic Southwest, an event that was welcomed three times a year by those who lived in the country. It was a pleasant break that brought together all the neighbors and helped them keep in touch with the outside world through merchandise, conversation, and song. The *varilleros* were said to accrue large earnings from their trade, but people did not begrudge them their profits when they were men like Don José *el gachupín*.

El Camino Real began as a supply route for the first Spanish settlers and later developed into a well-traveled avenue of trade spreading in all directions. It also was the route over which people communicated culture from far-off regions and passed on, by word of mouth, the tradition of the Southwest.

The region that is the present state of Arizona served in the sixteenth century and again in the eighteenth as the corridor for Spanish explorations of New Mexico and for the establishment of the first overland route to California. The initial contact made with the Southwest by Spain was through Arizona in 1539, when Fray Marcos de Niza and the Moorish slave Esteban led the way for the expedition of Don Francisco Vásquez de Coronado. When the Spanish missions and subsequent settlements moved north from Sonora in the late seventeenth century, the beginnings of Arizona began to emerge, although at that time the region was considered an extension of Sonora. After Mexican independence, it became known as part of the greatly extended Free State of the West, El Estado Libre del Occidente, and finally, after the war with Mexico, Arizona became part of the territory of New Mexico. Statehood was not granted to the territory until 1912.

The Spanish crown made its first exploration beyond the Río Grande by sending the expedition of Coronado into northern New Mexico in 1540. Because the Río Grande route was not yet known, the expedition moved north along the Gulf of California coast, with auxiliary support by way of the Gulf of California under the command of Hernando de Alarcón. The territory that Coronado and his army had to cross northward before reaching what is now Arizona was not yet under Spanish control, and he encountered considerable resistance before reaching the land of the Pimas.

The Spaniards did not spend much time trying to convert the Indians along the way, because their objective was to reach the fabled cities of Cíbola and the treasures of the Gran Quivira. They had heard many accounts of these treasures, corroborating the wondrous tales told by Alvar Núñez Cabeza de Vaca at the end of his famous odyssey. Many wonders would be discovered in Arizona by the conqueror before his return to Mexico City in 1542, although at the time these incidental discoveries were of little moment to men searching for fabled treasures.

Coronado moved his army north from Sinaloa and, after crossing the present state of Sonora, reached the Pima country along the San Pedro River of southern Arizona. The padres who accompanied the expedition looked on this promising field with missionary interest, but they realized that on this trip they were emissaries destined to perform a different mission. The expedition continued its march north to the Zuñi villages, the mythical Cíbola of cities paved with gold. The Indians informed them that the treasures they were searching for would be found on the west at the pueblos of Tusayán, the Hopi villages known as Moqui.

DISCOVERY OF THE GRAND CANYON

Coronado dispatched Captain Pedro de Tovar and a detachment of seventeen mounted soldiers to investigate this village beyond the Petrified Forest. The Hopis had heard that Cíbola, where Coronado and his main force remained, had been brutally conquered by warriors who rode man-eating monsters. Fearful of a similar fate, the inhabitants lined up in front of the villages and told the Spaniards not to go beyond their lines. When an Indian warrior, tired of the long parley with the newcomers, struck one of the horses with his mace, the Castilians attacked. Peace was restored after a bloody struggle, and Don Pedro returned from Tusayán with fresh provisions but, more important, with a report that farther west beside a mighty river lived giant people who had great wealth of gold and pearls.

Not wishing to leave any possibility unexplored, Coronado appointed Captain García López de Cárdenas to find this great river and to establish contact with the wealthy Indians who lived on its banks. The captain and twelve men returned to Tusayán, enlisted the services of two volunteer guides, and continued on their way over rocky terrain so thickly covered with twisted pine trees that their progress was greatly hampered. After twenty days of rough travel, short of water for

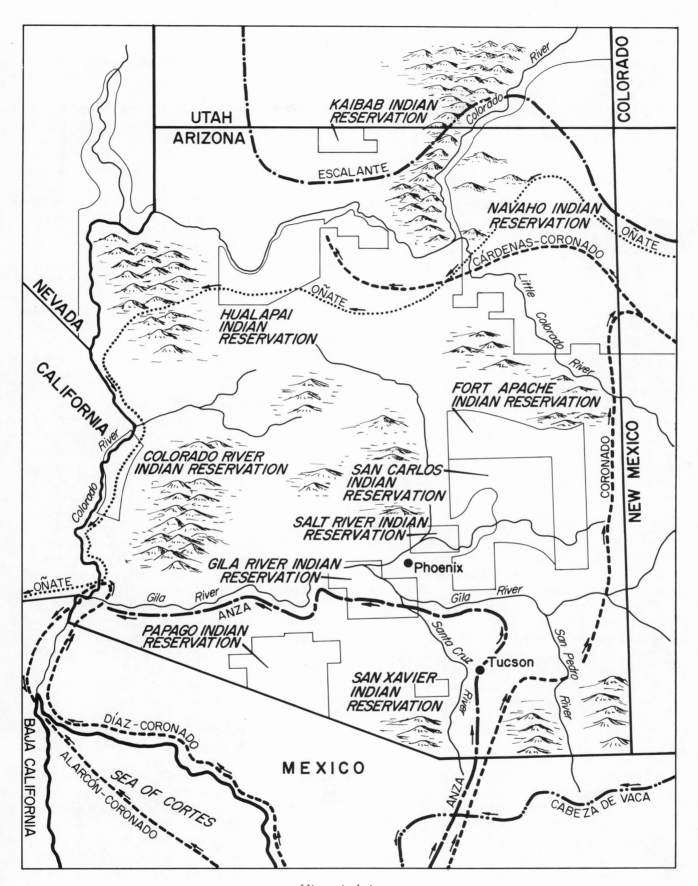

Hispanic Arizona

man and beast, they reached the rim of a deep canyon. The water they expected to reach was at the bottom of a deep gorge two to three leagues wide, according to their estimates, where a river about six feet wide flowed. The captain picked three of his most agile men and sent them down the rocky cliffs to explore the "mighty" river they had come to verify. For several days the men tried to scale the rocky cliffs and returned late in the afternoon of the third day, after having climbed down only one-third of the distance. They encountered boulders "taller than the cathedral of Seville," and the width of the river was as the Indians had said, about half a league, although it looked extremely narrow from the top of the rim. These were the impressions of the first Europeans to see the spectacle of the Grand Canyon of the Colorado.

López de Cárdenas did not know that at the south end of this river the naval arm of the expedition under Alarcón had found the mouth of the Colorado where it empties into the Gulf of California and had sailed up as far as the confluence of the Gila. The naval commander accidentally discovered that Baja California was not an island, but the fact was forgotten until it was reestablished by missionary-cartographer Eusebio Kino in 1702.

The aborigines of the Arizona pueblos made a brief but memorable contact with the Europeans who would eventually conquer their land and who would introduce a new civilization into which many of them would be absorbed. The Spaniards of 1540 were the first to visit them, and they would return a few years later and stay permanently. The advance party coming from New Spain made the Indians apprehensive of things to come, because what they had learned from Coronado's expedition on their first encounter was the mobility of the mounted warriors, the thunder of their guns, and the edge of Toledo steel. Fortunately there would also arrive many years later more peaceful men dedicated to the improvement of the Indians' temporal and spiritual lot.

THE ARRIVAL OF FATHER KINO

A century and a half after Coronado a missionary arrived in Arizona, who introduced the Indians to many practical and useful things that Europeans of the seventeenth century had to offer. His name was Eusebio Francisco Kino. Born in the Austrian Tyrol, educated at the universities of Ingolstadt and Freiburg, he was now a member of the Span-

ish-founded Jesuit order. He had originally planned to become a college professor and had received an appointment to teach at the University of Freiburg, when he fell seriously ill. After he recovered, he decided to become a Jesuit missionary to China. As it turned out, he was sent to Mexico instead and arrived there in 1681. Two years later he was assigned to an expedition to Baja California whose object was to fish for pearls and also to establish a mission at La Paz. Kino was initiated into the mission field, where he was to live an unusual and active life until his death in 1711.

Very early in the conquest of the New World the Spanish crown learned that the best way to hold the conquered land was by acculturating the inhabitants and teaching them the way of life of the conquerors. The medieval mentality of the conquistadors was not prepared to carry out this plan; in many instances they suggested exterminating the Indians in order to take over the country. That was also proposed in Arizona, but there the missionaries prevailed over the military and instituted the mission-pueblo structure in the days when the church was responsible for cultural and educational activities. The trinity of mission, pueblo, and presidio, or fort, was basically used throughout the Southwest with a few variations made necessary by ecological and demographic conditions. This colonization system ensured stability of the Spanish settlement and effected the cultural assimilation of the natives. Eusebio Kino understood this approach better than most missionaries working with the Indians of the Southwest, principally because he emphasized the temporal benefits of his wards while trying to convert them.

In Baja California, Kino had learned the Indians' communal sense of ownership, in contrast to the European concept of personal property. The aborigines expected the Spaniards to share with them everything they had and were very much displeased when they did not give them presents regularly. Having learned this Indian trait, Kino always traveled with a pack animal loaded with trinkets and gifts that he passed out among his Indian friends as an indication that he was willing to share his own property with them. The discontinuance of this gift-giving practice later, during the Mexican period, led to Indian revolts against the new order. The inventories of all expeditions entering the Southwest included large quantities of articles specifically designed for gifts or for trade. (The Anglo-American frontiersman who moved west centuries later became aware of this gift-offering custom, but his deep-seated sense of individual ownership made it difficult for him to part with his property, and often he decried the insatiable "begging" of the Indians.)

After two unsuccessful attempts to establish themselves in lower California, Father Kino and his Jesuit associates moved to the mainland, where they began the mission-founding work that eventually led into present-day Arizona. His first flourishing mission in Pimería Alta, as the land of the Pimas was then called, was Nuestra Señora de Dolores, founded in 1687. From this base of operations Spanish civilization extended north over all of southern Arizona as far as the Gila River. The wise padre realized that the best way to prosper was to have the Indians participate in the construction of quarters for resident priests and in the building of missions. He also taught them to plant and cultivate fields of maize, wheat, melons, and orchards for their support. A good ranchman, he introduced horses, cattle, and other domestic animals to ensure a constant food supply. Kino often said that it was easier to teach a well-fed Indian than a hungry one.

The Pimas along the Santa Cruz and San Pedro rivers raised the usual Indian corn and squashes, but Kino was not content with the meager diet provided by these crops. As early as 1691 he had already established his first missions in Arizona; San Cayetano de Tumacácori, which today is a national monument, and a second one at Güévavi on the banks of the Santa Cruz. By 1700 he had prosperous ranches and missions as far north as San Xavier del Bac, a few minutes out of the city of Tucson, a beautifully restored mission known today as the White Dove of the Desert. He wrote of the successful agriculture over the region he served, mentioning in detail the very fruits and vegetables for which Arizona is famous today. He said in part:

There are good gardens, and in them, vineyards for wine with cane brakes of sweet cane for syrup and panocha, and, with the favor of Heaven, before long for sugar. There are many Castilian fruit trees, such as fig trees, quinces, oranges, pomegranates, peaches, apricots . . . . with all sorts of garden stuff.

The padre listed about everything that a modern menu would include, including flowers, such as "rosas de Castilla y lirios blancos." The most important item in his long list of importations was wheat. The cultivation of this grain spread north to the Gila River Pimas and produced a concate-

San Cayetano de Tumacácori, a mission church founded by the Jesuit missionary Eusebio Francisco Kino in southern Arizona in 1691. It is today a national monument.

nation of changes in Indian culture that had a lasting effect on Indian life and social organization.

Considering all the improvements in agriculture and the products that Kino introduced in the present state of Arizona, it is not surprising that the grateful citizens erected a monument to him and bestowed on him the title "first Arizonan." His

San Xavier del Bac, founded in 1687, one of the principal missions founded by Kino. It is in Arizona, fifteen miles south of Tucson.

The monument to Kino outside the Arizona Historical Society Museum.

Spanish missionaries, as well as some military leaders, who used this region as their base of operations. Kino traveled endlessly on horseback and on foot over all the valleys of Pimería Alta, Papaguería, and the Yuma area. Social worker and missionary, he was also a cartographer and an explorer of no mean proportions. On one of his many visitations down the Colorado to the land of his Yuma friends, his curiosity was aroused when the Indians presented him with seashells that they said came from lands directly west. He made several trips overland to the coast and to his surprise discovered that Baja California was not an island but a peninsula. He jubilantly declared, "¡California no es isla, sino peninsula!" Despite the discovery of Hernando de Alarcón, who sailed to the head of the Gulf of California and continued up the Colorado in 1539, the consensus was that California was detached from the mainland. Kino set the record straight in 1702 and paved the way for a route to the West Coast, which another peripatetic padre was to establish after the death of the venerable Kino.

The settlement of Arizona by the Spaniards was unique in that they did not send an expedition fully equipped and armed cap-a-pie. There was no formal ceremony in which they took possession of the country like the one celebrated by Don Juan de Oñate when he entered the Río Grande Valley. It was unlike the *entrada* of Captain Martín de Alarcón into southern Texas, and it bore no resemblance to the colonization of the lower Río Grande by Don José de Escandón, which historians refer to as the "odyssey of the Río Grande." The occupation of Arizona was simply the extension of Spanish civilization northward, from what is now Sonora, as part of an enterprise in which Jesuit and Franciscan missionaries played a significant role and were supported by the military. This is the reason why so much of the early history of Spanish civilization and culture in this western state revolves around the padres who were sent ahead to establish missions and to introduce a new way of life among the Indians, preparatory to the occupation by settlers. The presidios would follow, and sometimes they were the only outposts that remained on the frontier. Most of the colonial period of Arizona history is so taken up with the work of the missionaries that the reader wonders if anything else happened. Actually there was a good deal of activity by men like Juan Bautista de Anza and by landholders who established the first cattle ranches on their

untiring efforts laid the base for the important industries cattle raising and agriculture, later successfully pursued by Hispanic and Anglo-American residents. Ruth Underhill has summed up the achievements of Eusebio Kino:

Kino was an organizer of the highest ability and he did all that one man could do to put the plan into operation. He established missions; he stocked them with cattle, horses, sheep, goats and poultry, a herd of 500 horses and as many cows being nothing unusual. He taught the natives to build adobe brick churches; to sow and thresh wheat, lentils, and vetch; to plow; and to tend cattle. He made fifty trips throughout the country, baptising and distributing Spanish names to localities and peoples.[1]

The benign winters and extended good weather of southern Arizona seem to have affected the land grants. This activity took place toward the end of the eighteenth century and increased somewhat despite the constant forays of the Apaches.

The work of Kino came to an end with his death in 1711, but although he had toured several times the region below the Gila either by himself or accompanied by Father Juan María Salvatierra or Spanish Captain Juan Mateo Mange, some historians believe that no missions were actually established. There were rancherías, which were only *visitas* in Kino's time. The padre mentions that he had laid the foundations for the mission in Bac, but there is no record that he actually built the church. The effectiveness of his mission work was hampered by the unwise policies of Captain Mange. The Indians resented his harsh measures, and that may have been one of the factors that led to the revolt of the Pimas. When the break did come, the setbacks in the assimilation of the Indians were blamed on the missionaries' strict punishment for minor religious infractions. The missionaries claimed that the taking of the choice land for farming and cattle raising by Spanish farmers aroused the enmity of the Indians; the settlers in turn blamed the soldiers for their arrogant treatment of the neophytes and for taking liberties with Indian women. The chances are that all three accusations were justified in varying degrees. It was characteristic of the way Indians were treated not only in Arizona but throughout the Southwest. The mission-pueblo-presidio system of colonization was successful, but it could also lead to failure and revolt when one of the components overreached itself.

THE POST-KINO ERA

For two decades after the death of Eusebio Kino the only Spaniards who entered Arizona were occasional padres who visited the *rancherías* of the Santa Cruz Valley, or a detachment of soldiers in pursuit of hostile Apaches. Only two priests, Father Campos and Father Joaquín Antonio Velarde, were left in Pimería Alta to carry on some of the work started by Kino. In a few years the Pimas forgot what the missionaries had taught them, and their interest in mission life began to wane. The former vigor of the *rancherías* showed some signs of revival in 1731, when the bishop appointed a group of Spanish-speaking German Jesuits to what Bancroft believed was the first Spanish settlement in Arizona. Father Felipe Segesser was assigned to San Xavier del Bac, whose foundations were laid by Kino in 1700. Juan Bautista Grashoffer went to San Miguel de Güévavi, on the banks of the Santa Cruz River near the present international line, and Ignacio Javier Keller began visiting what once had been flourishing *rancherías* along the Gila.

The only excitement was the silver strike of Bolas de Plata at Arizonac in 1736, but this bonanza lasted only until 1741. One of the surface nuggets weighed 2,700 pounds, and others of lesser size convinced the discoverers that they had found a *criadero de plata*, a field where silver literally grew like plants. This unparalleled wealthy deposit of almost solid silver was a sensation while it lasted, but was closed down by royal decree when the miners failed to pay the royal one-fifth to the crown. Arizonac gave the name to the state, an almost prophetic name associated with the future mining state that was to emerge.[2] That this rich strike was made in the shadow of the Jesuit mission field may have given rise to the folk tradition that this order left buried treasures when they were banished from Mexico by Charles III in 1767. Many legends of Jesuit buried treasures persist from lower Sinaloa through Arizona, but the churchmen contend that their overnight expulsion gave them no time to bury anything, certainly not treasures of gold and silver that they did not have.

The Spaniards had tried to bring the Moquis into the Spanish cultural fold since the days of Juan de Oñate in New Mexico. That included not only religious conversion but also the adoption of cultural habits that would make them more dependent on the conquerors and thereby easier to manage. The Hopis, who in reality were an independent, peaceful people, were particularly averse to accepting the religious teachings of the padres and any of their ministrations. They had been contacted by the Spaniards since the days of Coronado and Tovar, whose memory they did not cherish. García de Cárdenas also passed through the village known as Tusayán in those days, and later Espejo searched for information about mineral deposits. After the settlement of New Mexico, the Franciscans succeeded in establishing three missions at Awatobi, Oraibi, and Shongopovi and two *visitas* at Walpi and Mishongnovi, which lasted from 1629 until the Indian revolt of 1680. That brought to an end the Spanish missions among the Hopis for a long time to come. The churches were destroyed, two friars were put to death, and two were thrown over the cliff.

Many years later the Jesuits from Arizona also made several attempts to gain a religious foothold among the Hopis but met with little success. Father Ignacio Javier Keller tried to preach to them in 1741, as did Father Jacobo Sedelmain three years later. Rodríguez de la Torre, about the same time as trailblazer Silvestre de Escalante, tried to enlist the cooperation of the Hopis, but he too met with resistance resulting from the memories of the 1680 revolt, which still rankled their minds. When Father Garcés, the peripatetic Franciscan, tried to establish a New Mexico–California route through the land of the Hopis, they refused his gifts and did not open their doors to him. The strongest opposition came from the Hopi religious leaders, who vehemently opposed interlopers threatening to wrest from them control of their people by teaching a new doctrine. That apparently did not extend to those material benefits that Spanish culture could provide. Escalante reported in 1775 that the Hopis had accumulated over 30,000 sheep, many horses, and other stock.

Three projects, which unfortunately did not materialize, interested the Jesuits from the time they arrived in Arizona until the arrival of the Franciscans. First, they had been attempting since Kino's day to extend their work beyond the Gila, but in doing so they purposely underestimated the distance to the Hopi villages from southern Arizona. Both the Franciscans in New Mexico and the Jesuits in Arizona vied for control of the Hopi mission field, resulting in a sort of feud that lasted for almost fifty years. Second, the Jesuits realized that the Gila basin was a natural route for an overland communication with California, whose occupation was imminent. The third project that generated greater effort to establish their missions in the Hopi villages was the possibility of linking the two mission fields, New Mexico and Arizona, and eventually California. Some historians claim that the rich silver deposits that were said to exist at Cerro Azul along this route may have been a factor in this interest. The bishop of Durango and the king himself became involved in the controversy and changed sides several times as "evidence" was presented by each party "proving" that their order was preferred by the Hopis and that the other was greatly despised. The king settled the rivalry in favor of the Franciscans, and thus was the Hopi contest laid to rest until the arrival of the first Franciscan friar in Arizona, who replaced the Jesuits after their banishment in 1767.

Father Francisco Tomás Hermenegildo Garcés, a native of Aragón, Spain, was the worthy successor of Kino after an interim of fifty-eight years. Garcés was immediately assigned to San Xavier del Bac on his arrival in Guaymas in 1768, and he began visitations. He made two trips to the Gila, visited the Pápagos, and by 1771 had gone down the Colorado to the land of the Yumas. Like the Jesuits who had preceded him, Garcés was also interested in linking the missions of Arizona with California with an overland route that he envisioned while on those southern trips.

In 1774 the young padre's dream became a reality. He was instructed to accompany Captain Don Juan Bautista de Anza on an expedition to the new settlement of Monterey, on the California coast. Garcés' experience across the Colorado in Yuma convinced Anza that a new route was feasible through southern Arizona. They went together with a small party of thirty-four men early in January and a month later crossed into California at the Gila-Colorado junction. The Yuma Indians at the junction received them well and helped them ford the river. The route was established, and at the same time the possibility of working with the Yumas aroused the interest of the energetic padre. The party returned to Tubac, where Anza was stationed, but Garcés, who was interested in linking New Mexico with California, continued to the Hopi villages, where he spent two nights camped in the patio of an inhospitable pueblo and then returned to Tubac. In 1775 he accompanied Lieutenant Colonel Anza once again on an expedition to San Francisco Bay, where they were to plant a colony. A group of 240 people and over a thousand animals left the presidio of Tubac in late October, and again Anza left Garcés at the Colorado junction. Anza continued to San Francisco and established the site for that great metropolis by using Arizona as a springboard for exploration and settlement.

Meanwhile, Garcés continued his visitations, first to the Yumas, to whom he promised a mission that never materialized. His extensive travel reports resulting from these extended trips give considerable information about Arizona; the locations of the various tribes, his suggestions for their conversion, and the establishment of presidios. But the war against the Apaches, bureaucratic procrastination in Mexico City, and lack of funds prevented the carrying out of the promised plans at the Yuma villages. When Garcés visited them in 1781, the dissatisfied Yumas rose against the Spaniards, killed fifty of them, including Gar-cés, the padre who had engineered the route to California through the region and who had walked thousands of miles in the interest of the Arizona Indians and the Spanish crown.

ACCULTURATION OF THE PIMAS

As we look back at the work done by the early padres and by the few settlers who joined them at the missions, pueblos, and presidios, greater accomplishments of church and crown objectives are evinced than would seem at first glance. In 1961, in *Acculturation of the Gila River Pimas*, Paul H. Ezell appraised the degree and forms of acculturation of the Gila River Pimas after two and a half centuries of nondirected Hispanic acculturation. The process in the Gila River settlements differs from that along the Santa Cruz and San Pedro rivers, where the Indians became converted and lived under the aegis of the missions, exposed to persuasive, directed, and even coercive acculturation. It was not accepted acculturation because the neophytes had but one choice, the one selected by the missionaries. In the case of the Gila Indians it was more like dealing between equals. The Spaniards, and later the Mexicans, were happy to maintain this relationship because it caused less friction, and the Gila settlements became a sort of buffer state between Hispanic people and the hostile Apaches.

One of the factors that brought about a number of modifications in the life of the Gila River Pimas was the introduction of wheat. The same may be said for the other Piman peoples along the Santa Cruz and San Pedro rivers, today called Sobaipuris. The settlement pattern of the northern Pimas consisted of widely separated houses and villages. With the introduction of wheat the Pimas grouped their houses closer in order to cultivate their fields and also to protect their harvest from marauding Apaches. The acquisition of more efficient iron farming tools and the ox-drawn plow enabled them to increase their production, thereby providing additional marketable products. A marked rise in the standard of living resulted from new crops, more efficient food production, and a varied diet. The addition of beef, poultry, fruits, and vegetables hitherto unknown to the Pimas changed their eating habits and also made it necessary for them to specialize what once had been a relatively simple life.

Another important change brought about by

Eighteenth-century grist mills used in the Southwest for corn and wheat. Comparable mills can be found in Texas, New Mexico, and Arizona. Courtesy of Arizona Historical Society Museum.

contact with Hispanic culture was an elementary concept of commerce in place of gift trading. Manufactured goods and food surpluses were marketed, and as a result the Pimas began to acquire a sense of relative values for trading purposes. The mission Indians accepted most of the elements of Hispanic culture that the missionaries considered good for them, but the Gila River Pimas, who were free agents, accepted Hispanic culture on their own terms. In contrast to the New Mexico Indians, who a century earlier had accepted other barnyard stock, such as swine, sheep, and goats, the Gila Pimans rejected these meat- and wool-producing animals. They accepted horses as mounts

A group of Apaches performing the Devil Dance. The introduction of wheat in the seventeenth century encouraged fixed settlements for its cultivation and caused the population to be more susceptible to the attacks of these Indians. Courtesy of Coronado Cuarto Centennial.

and also as prestige animals. Underhill's statement that Eusebio Kino taught the Pimans the manufacture and use of adobes did not include the Gilas, because they continued to use their own structures, albeit with one concession to their Hispanic neighbors: they replaced the usual mats that covered the roofs with thatching and dirt topping, which the Spaniards introduced very early in their contacts in Pimería Alta.

Aside from the purely material products derived from this undirected acculturation, the Gila Pimas made social-organization changes by reinforcing their cooperative defense efforts. To keep the Apaches in check, they joined forces with the Spaniards in punitive expeditions against these

seminomadic tribes. The increased density of their population also brought about more complex institutional organization beyond the simple community by creating a supravillage council with a top official comparable with a governor. In reality all the changes extant today are, according to Ezell, the realization of Spanish and Mexican objectives that the Gila River Pimas assimilated by their own choice.

The introduction and dissemination of Hispanic culture throughout the southern part of Arizona to the Gila River was an enterprise that began when Niza passed through the state in 1539 on his way to the mythical land of Quivira. Kino crisscrossed the southern half of the state to the Gulf of California, establishing missions, or *visitas*, among the Indians. Garcés continued the work of Kino and was instrumental in the establishment of additional Spanish settlements, as well as Indian missions. In 1776, during the days of Garcés, the pueblo Tucson took its name from the adjoining Pima *ranchería* Tucson and continued a more or less precarious existence until the American occupation.

SPAIN'S LAST EFFORT AGAINST THE APACHES

Despite the efforts of Kino and Garcés to establish a church-centered Spanish civilization in Arizona, by the end of the third quarter of the eighteenth century very little of their efforts could be called stable. The crown tried to hold the Indians in check to allow settlers to move in and exploit the resources of the region, but even that proved almost impossible until the Apaches were defeated. Conditions had deteriorated before the death of Garcés, although the optimistic padre felt that great progress was being made. The reports of the missionaries gave a false sense of security and accomplishment, because they were based on the performance of the few converts around the missions or those who congregated at the *visitas* from time to time. Most of the Indians lived outside the sphere of influence of the missions and consequently were very hostile. Even the so-called peaceful Pimas and Yumas rebelled several times and put to death the very missionaries who had worked so long and hard in their behalf.

King Charles III was apprised of the deteriorated conditions in the northern frontier and made several administrative changes by which temporary progress was made. At the end of the Seven Years' War in Europe, France ceded to Spain the Louisiana Territory west of the Mississippi and thus removed the threat of infiltration on the Texas frontier. The resources from that eastern area were used in the northern frontier to bolster the insufficient defenses of Arizona against the marauding Apaches. The northern provinces were eventually separated into an independent unit, the Provincias Internas, and the policy of gentle persuasion was replaced by aggressive action against all tribes that were hostile to Spain. That enabled the settlers to occupy lands around the presidios and to begin to exploit natural resources through mining, ranching, and agriculture.

Toward the last quarter of the eighteenth century the military began to take the initiative in the pacification of Arizona. The King's Royal Regulations of 1772 called for more effective administration of the frontier, increased efficiency of the army, and more independence for the commanders who were to implement the regulations. Admittedly the military was to do by forceful means what the missions were unable to accomplish by religious and peaceful means. The first commandant vested with the responsibility of carrying out the provisions of the king's wishes was Colonel Hugo O'Connor, an Irish mercenary with a distinguished record as a campaigner in the Spanish army. He is credited with having moved the presidio from Tubac to Tucson and thereby helping establish the Spanish settlement in 1776. Several able inspectors and military engineers appraised the situation in Arizona and appointed some of the ablest men to defend the presidios and to undertake offensive campaigns against the Apaches.

The Apaches did not yield readily. There were too many of them and too few soldiers during the late 1770's. Spain was having additional expenses because of the support she was giving to the American Revolution, but by 1786 she was able to wage a vigorous war against the Indians. In 1790 they sued for peace. Instead of being settled within the shadow of the missions, the Indians were settled around the military presidios, where they became more or less dependent on the Spaniards for rations and arms. Their good will was courted peacefully, now that they were subdued, with presents, drink, and defective arms that would force them to apply to the conquerors for help in repairing them. These peaceful settlements were referred to as *establecimientos de paz*, much to the displeasure of the missionaries, who complained that the Indians were being corrupted by Spanish vices and were not taught any of the Spanish virtues.

Despite the criticism of the missionaries the military policy instituted by Viceroy Bernardo de Gálvez produced results. For thirty years, from 1790 to 1820, the Apaches were at peace, and settlers began to locate in and near Tubac and at Tucson. There was no rush to occupy lands made available by the new land grants of Sonoita and Canoa, but the San Bernardino Grant did show a considerable increase in stock raising. By the end of the Spanish period Ignacio Pérez, who had purchased this large grant, was running cattle on a six-digit scale. Mining activities and extended farming around Tubac and Tucson increased progressively as the Mexican era began. Several thousand head of cattle, sheep, and horses were added to the usual crops of corn, beans, and vegetables. The formerly abandoned sites of Tucson and Tubac could boast a population of over one hundred, in addition to the garrison at the presidio.

THE MEXICAN PERIOD

The transition from Spanish to Mexican nationality did not affect the Arizona region uniformly; neither was the time schedule observed. The people of this far-off frontier were vaguely aware of the struggle for independence but did not begin to feel the effects of it until conditions began to deteriorate once again. Some of the Spanish officials in Arizona simply took the oath of allegiance to the new government and continued in office through the first part of the Mexican period. Civil government and institutions did not change; the local *alcalde*, or mayor of Spanish tradition, continued throughout the Free State of the West, of which Arizona was part; and the presidios whose personnel had taken the oath of allegiance to the Republic of Mexico stayed at their posts. Their pay, supplies, and equipment became woefully inadequate to repel the reopened hostility of the Apaches.

Ten years after Mexican independence the Apaches began their depredations once more. They assumed that the new regime would change the Spanish policy of distributing presents to which they had become accustomed during the long period of amnesty. The answer to this uprising was the invoking of the Royal Regulations of 1772, which had been successful earlier in bringing the Apaches to terms. The northern frontier was Mexican politically, but the cultural heritage of Spain still hovered over the land. When the regulations were published in 1834, the Mexicans forgot to delete the signature of the king that appeared at the bottom of the document. "Yo el Rey," "I the King," was the apparent authority under which the edict was published.

The frontier seemed to be more concerned with the removal of personalities than with the abolishment of Spanish institutions. Very soon after independence, the missions received the *coup de grâce* when they were secularized. Through that change Governor Gándara of Sonora purchased the 52,000 acres of the mission Tumacácori for the paltry sum of $500 and turned it into a successful cattle ranch. From then on the missions were gradually abandoned and continued to decay until their reconstruction in the late nineteenth century. The only two structures that resisted the erosion of time and the elements were San Xavier del Bac and Tumacácori. The missionaries who had kept these structures in good repair were banished from Mexico when they refused to take the oath of allegiance to Mexico, and their departure hastened the neglect that caused their ruin.

With the disappearance of the missions and the inability to reinstate the king's regulations of 1772, the Mexican authorities resorted to the scalp-bounty system. Each Indian male's scalp brought fifty dollars; a woman's or a child's, twenty-five dollars. The problem was the difficulty in differentiating between a friendly Indian's scalp and that of a hostile one. It was also impossible to tell whether a scalp was that of a Mexican citizen whose hair was similar to that of an Indian. The bounty system led to many abuses by scalp hunters, who literally depopulated some of the villages. Even some Americans who began to enter the Arizona region went into scalp hunting as a business. James Johnson took a sack of "presents" to an Indian village in which he included a plugged and primed cannon bomb. When his Indian friends gathered around the sack, he touched the fuse with his lighted cigar and walked nonchalantly away. The explosion provided him with a number of scalps. He failed to collect that of Mangas Coloradas, who got away and lived to take revenge by killing scores of American settlers later on. James Kircher and his mountain-men associates are said to have gone into the scalp-hunting business on a wholesale scale and in one year alone reaped a bounty of over $100,000.

At the end of the war with Mexico, there were only two principal villages in Arizona: Tubac and Tucson with the army presidio. The work of the missionaries with the Pima peoples along the Gila, San Pedro, and Santa Cruz rivers familiarized these Indians with Europeans and indirectly was of great help to the United States military expeditions that crossed Arizona. The Arizona corridor established by Spanish padres and by commanders like Anza and others during the Mexican period continued to be used by military men of a third nationality who crossed through it on their way to California. First, General José Castro, coming from California during the Mexican War, crossed over into Sonora in 1846, and Kit Carson followed in the same direction when he was a dispatch bearer for Commodore John F. Stockton, announcing prematurely the United States victory in California. Shortly after the taking of New Mexico, Brigadier General Stephen W. Kearny followed the Gila River trail to California to the Colorado junction. He was followed by the Mormon battalion under Lieutenant Colonel Philip St. George Cooke who opened the wagon route, which proved greatly useful to the gold-seeking forty-niners on their way to California. The Arizona corridor continued to be used by United States military men on different missions, but it was not until the Gadsden Purchase was consummated that any of those who traveled through Arizona remained to settle it. It was crossed by Major Lawrence P. Graham in 1848 and by Captain L. Sitgraves in 1851, who followed pretty closely the old trail pioneered by Fray Garcés in 1776. Finally, the Arizona corridor was explored by Lieutenant A. W. Whipple and his party in 1853 in what was known as the "Pacific Railroad survey." This would eventuate into a permanent route when the last spike was driven.

The long Hispanic period of Arizona came to an end in 1855, when the boundary commission determined the limits of the two nations. For another year, however, Tucson and that part of Arizona which had been settled by ranchmen and farmers after Spanish days would still be under the protection of the Mexican garrison at the presidio in Tucson. Eight years after cessation of hostilities, in March, 1856, Captain Hilarión García withdrew the Mexican garrison from Tucson, much to the consternation of resident Americans and Hispanic settlers who were left exposed to the terror of Apache raids. Not until November did the United States First Dragoons take over the fort, and the Stars and Stripes flew over Tucson for the first time. Arizona has always been one of the most peaceful regions in the United States, insofar as wars are concerned, though it was one of the most active in Indian warfare. The transition from Spain to Mexico was almost unnoticed, and the occupation by the United States had to wait until the Gadsden Purchase was engineered, the international line agreed upon, and the Mexican garrison withdrawn. As already pointed out, Arizona was a very busy corridor, beginning in 1540 with Coronado, and crisscrossed by explorers, missionaries, military leaders, and, last, gold seekers and settlers.

As was to be expected, life in Tucson after 1848

Estevan Ochoa, head of one of the Southwest's leading freighting businesses and a cultural leader in Arizona in the middle of the nineteenth century. Courtesy of Arizona Historical Society Museum.

centered principally around Anglo-Americans; news, events, and personalities bore English names with an occasional sprinkling of Spanish-named citizens. Hispanic culture did not disappear; it simply fell into the background. Businessmen like Jesús and José Redondo made a good living by raising cattle near Yuma and driving them to the California gold fields, where they sold them to butchers for a handsome profit. Estevan Ochoa, a native of Chihuahua, became prominent in New Mexico and in Arizona, not only in the mercantile business but in public administration as well. He chaired the convention in Las Cruces where the Arizona Territory was proposed and also where the candidacy of his friend Sylvester Mowry was announced as Arizona's representative to Congress. Later, as a member of the state territorial legislature, he introduced the Education Bill at the request of the governor, and when he was mayor of Tucson, he presented the silver spike to President Crocker of the Southern Pacific Railroad when the terminal was reached. As early as 1863 he formed the Tully and Ochoa freighting firm over the Santa Fe Trail; he and his partner, Carlos Tully, came to be, according to one author, "the merchant princes of their day in the far Southwest." When Tully was married to Adela Barón, it was considered the event of the season, in both duration and elegance, according to the press reports.

Arizona Hispanos were to be found in all walks of life. There were brave frontier wagonmasters, like Santa Cruz Castañeda, who refused to turn over his cargo to a band of two hundred Apaches and defended his charge until the arrival of the United States Cavalry. The famous story of Vicente Hernández and his beautiful young wife continues to be retold in the press even today, almost a century after their tragic death. Historian Frank Lockwood of Tucson wrote in 1932: "Never before in Tucson had so many people assembled for a burial service. All places of business were closed including saloons and gambling places."

One of the industries that has been part of the heritage of Hispanic people in the Southwest is cattle raising. In Arizona ranching had been extensive since Spanish days, but after Mexican independence the new government was unable to protect the stock raisers from Indian depredations, and the cattle industry declined. After the Gadsden Purchase many Sonoran cattle raisers who had abandoned their ranches renewed their former industry and were considerably successful.

Sidney B. Brinkerhoff, in his Introduction to Yjinio Aguirre's article "The Last of the Dons," states: "The contribution of Spanish and Mexican cattle ranchers to the development of the Southwest is well known. . . . Unfortunately for the student of history, information about the life and accomplishments of these families has not always been ready available."[3] We do know that rancheros like the Oteros and the Robles ran herds of 20,000 head, with large remudas of horses for tending the cattle. Well-known ranchers in nineteenth-century Arizona included the Pachecos, the Robledos, the Aros, and the Aguirre family, who have continued their interests to the present day. In the last three generations of Aguirres in Arizona, Pedro, Epifanio, and Yjinio, cattle interests have been consistently cultivated, with herds numbering five-digit figures. Smaller cattlemen, called *poquiteros*, "small fry," ran herds of around 5,000. Today the descendants of many of these cattle barons constitute some of Arizona's leading families, many of them intermarried and completely assimilated.

Another indication of the Hispanic population's participation in the life of the new territory was a

Yjinio Aguirre, proud descendant of the Aguirre family of Arizona and one of the last of the dons. He publishes regularly in the *Journal of Arizona History*. His family's cattle ranches have covered as much as twenty-seven sections of the state. Courtesy of Yjinio Aguirre Collection.

problem reported by some schoolteachers in 1872. They said that it was difficult to teach because such a large proportion of the students spoke no English, and the teachers spoke no Spanish. Bilingual education was already a problem in territorial Arizona.

There were instances, some not particularly praiseworthy, when Anglo-Americans, Mexicans, and Indians cooperated as they did in the Camp Grant Massacre. Led by William Saunders Oury and Jesús M. Elías, the citizens' army, composed of 6 Anglos, 48 Mexicans, and 94 Papagos, attacked the Camp Grant Indians at dawn and killed 128 men, women, and children.

Pedro Aguirre, pioneer cattle rancher in Arizona in the 1880's. Courtesy of Yjinio Aguirre Collection.

Pedro Aguirre at work, ca. 1900. Courtesy of the Arizona Historical Society Library.

More worthy contributions have been pointed out by historian Odie B. Faulk:

In Arizona the frontiersman found a fully developed legal structure in the European sense, a heritage of three centuries of Spanish exploration, settlement and development, a legal system based on Roman Law, as opposed to the common law of England, but which had been modified to fit the necessities of life in arid Arizona.[4]

There is no question that the Spanish heritage was particularly pervasive in mining, ranching, and agriculture. Many of the laws that Arizona included in its constitution were drawn almost verbatim from the Spanish code, and many of the practices in the life of early Arizona were those of the Spanish-Mexican settlers. Mexican food is no novelty today, but it is interesting to note what the Juni-

per House, the first hotel in Prescott, Arizona, offered in 1864:

BREAKFAST
Fried Venison and Chili
Bread and Coffee with milk

DINNER
Roast Venison and Chili
Chili Baked Beans
Chili on Tortillas
Tea and Coffee with milk

SUPPER
Chili, from 4 O'clock on[5]

One aspect of Arizona history that should not be overlooked is the contribution made by Hispanic women to the life of the territory and state.

Antonio Soza, head of a well-known Hispanic pioneer family in Arizona, with his wife and child. Courtesy of the Arizona Historical Society Library.

Beatriz Aguirre, daughter of Pedro Aguirre, later Mrs. Robert L. Wood, one of the many Hispanic ladies who helped build Arizona. Courtesy of the Arizona Pioneers' Historical Museum.

Many frontiersmen from the East, and some from across the sea, found Mexican women unusually attractive—so much so that writers of the early days of Arizona speak of the "civilizing influence and the cultural contribution" of Spanish women. Arizona's early life revolved almost entirely around Tucson, and most of the important personalities were residents of the historic city. Famous frontiersmen and businessmen married young Spanish women in Arizona, and some went down into Sonora to find wives to share their successful lives. Frank Lockwood mentions a number of prominent frontiersmen who married Mexican girls: Hiram S. Stevens married a Santa Cruz girl, and Samuel Hughes, a native of Wales well known in western history, married Atanacia Santa Cruz. Mark Aldrich, the *alcalde*, as the mayor of Tucson was called at the beginning of the American era, married Teófila León. Pete Kitchen married one Doña Rosa, and Louis J. F. Jaeger married a beautiful Mexican girl from Sonora, Cleofas Saiz.

Solomon Warner, Tucson's wealthiest businessman, also took a Mexican wife. Peter R. Brady, a member of the boundary commission and elected four times to the territorial legislature, married Juanita Mendibles. Fritz Contzen, a government employee in Tucson, married Margarita Ferrer, from Mexico, and in 1873 took her to Germany, where he became chief forester to the prince of Waldeck. Margarita learned German as well as English and toured Europe with her husband. The well-known William S. Oury, a good friend of the Mexican population, married Inez García, of Du-

70

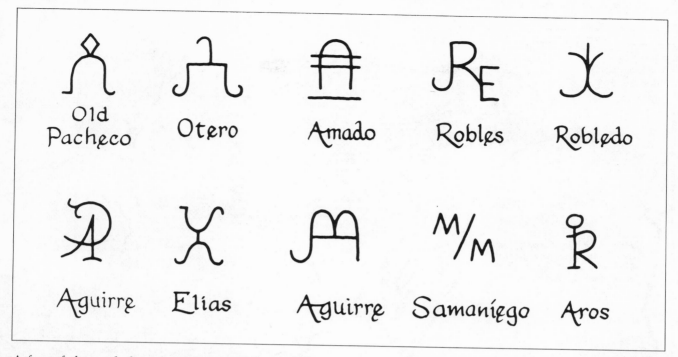

A few of the cattle brands of Spanish-Mexican families in Arizona. All these brands date from the eighteenth century, and some are still in use today. Courtesy of the Yjinio Aguirre Collection.

rango, and became a leading soldier and politician. There are but a few of Arizona's leading Hispanic women who adjusted well to their new nationality and joined in building the state of Arizona.

Arizona did not have the large population of Texas, New Mexico, or California, but it was the first state in which official contact was made with the land we now call the Southwest. It was the site of Coronado's entry, the region walked by the imagination-rich Fray Marcos de Niza, and the land where Esteban, the ambitious Moor, met his doom. Arizona was the region where two missionaries made history: Kino and later Garcés, who helped pave the way for the settlement of California. And Arizona is the border state that has established practical ties with northern Mexico's progressive businessmen through in-service training provided by Arizona State University.

Today Arizona has a Spanish-speaking population of roughly half a million, most of whom are second- and third-generation Americans of Mexican descent, with a few descendants of the old families who were living in Arizona before the advent of the Anglo-American era. The industries introduced by the early Spaniards today constitute the mainstays of Arizona's income-producing endeavors. Mexican-Americans are active in every level of government (for example, Governor Raúl Castro, native of Sonora, lawyer, and diplomat).

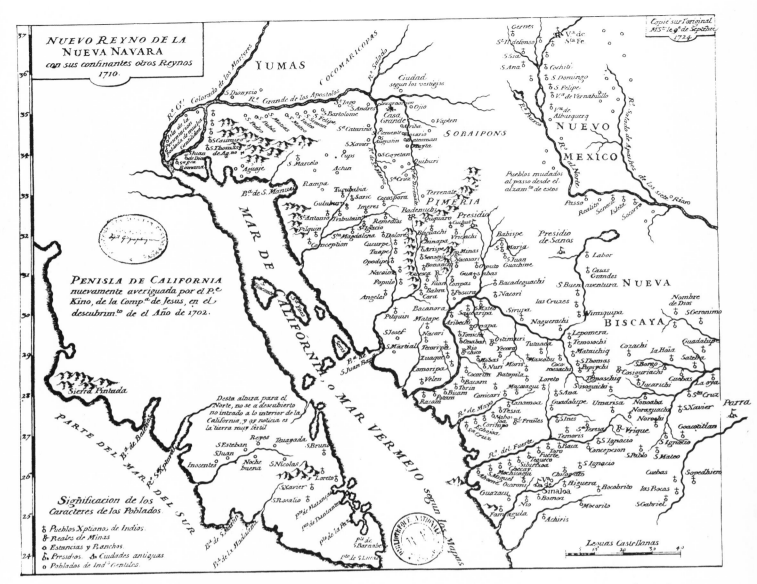

A map of northern Mexico and the Southwest prepared by Eusebio Kino in 1710. Baja California is not here shown as a peninsula, which it had been thought to be for almost two centuries. The key indicates Christian Indian pueblos, mines, ranches, presidios, and old Indian villages. Courtesy of Charles W. Palzer, S. J., University of Arizona Museum.

The last region in America to be occupied by Spain was for a long time what Bancroft calls a "cosmographic conjecture," bounded by land masses that were known as early as the sixteenth century but whose exact geographic position had not been established. The chain of events leading to the discovery of California and the early history of this fascinating region place in focus the functioning of Spanish institutions and the internal struggles that plagued so much of Spain's empire in America. The long period of exploration, the events that led to eventual occupation, the establishment of the mission-pueblo-presidio trinity, and the struggle of church and state among the colonizers in California provide an interesting thumbnail sketch of what took place throughout the Spanish empire. The Spanish period was relatively short, the Mexican period even shorter; but those eras are among the most interesting chapters in the history of the Southwest.

DISCOVERY AND EXPLORATION

Hernán Cortés, the conqueror of Mexico, and Nuño de Guzmán, president of the Royal Audiencia, were interested in probing the Northwest for reported treasures. Their rivalry kept Cortés from undertaking an overland search, but the seasoned conquistador was not easily discouraged. His first attempt, by sea in 1532, was thwarted by the undercover work of his ambitious rival Guzmán, or so it was rumored. The second attempt a year later came to grief with the desertion of one of his naval commanders, Hernando de Grijalva, and a mutiny in the second ship. Mutineer Fortún Jiménez went ahead toward the California coast and discovered a bay to which he gave the name La Paz, "The Peace." The beginning of Hispanic culture in California got off to a bloody start, notwithstanding the peaceful name of the first landfall. The ill-fated mutineer was killed with most of his crew by the Indians on the mainland.

Word reached Cortés through the survivors of Jiménez' expedition that the "island" they had discovered was rich in pearls. This news encouraged him to lead a third expedition to the Northwest. His ship reached the "island" after a difficult passage, and once on land, he found additional problems. The unproductive land was barren, the Indians were hostile, and the pearls were not easily obtained by his men, who were starving to death. By 1536 the remaining members of the expedition had returned to the mainland, and Santa Cruz, as Cortés named the "island," was left for later adventurers to explore.

One of Nuño de Guzmán's captains, Diego de Alcaraz, met Alvar Núñez Cabeza de Vaca and his companions at the end of the latter's eight-year odyssey in Bamoa, a village by the Sinaloa River. The tale of Cíbola, which Núñez embellished with accounts of cities paved with gold, rekindled interest in the "Unknown North." Some believed that this treasure could be reached by sea. Cortés lost his bid to search for Quivira by land to Vásquez de Coronado, but he decided once more to search by sea for another Mexico. In 1539 he sent three ships under Francisco de Ulloa, who sailed past Santa Cruz and up the Gulf of California and discovered that the "island" that Cortés had named was a peninsula, a fact verified, as mentioned before, by Eusebio Kino in 1702.

According to Bancroft, Ulloa named the land California: "Ulloa sailed down the coast in 1539, and the name California first appears in Preciado's diary of that voyage."[1] John W. Caughey is more inclined to give the credit to Francisco de Bolaños, who explored the same peninsula in 1541: "[Bolaños] is . . . the most likely candidate for the honor of having named California."[2]

The name California was known to the Spaniards long before the discovery of the California coast. In 1508, Garcí Rodríguez de Montalvo (known in later editions of his works as Garcí-Ordóñez de Montalvo) edited the first four books of the well-known novel of chivalry, *Amadís de Gaula*. He claimed to have corrected *(enmendado)*

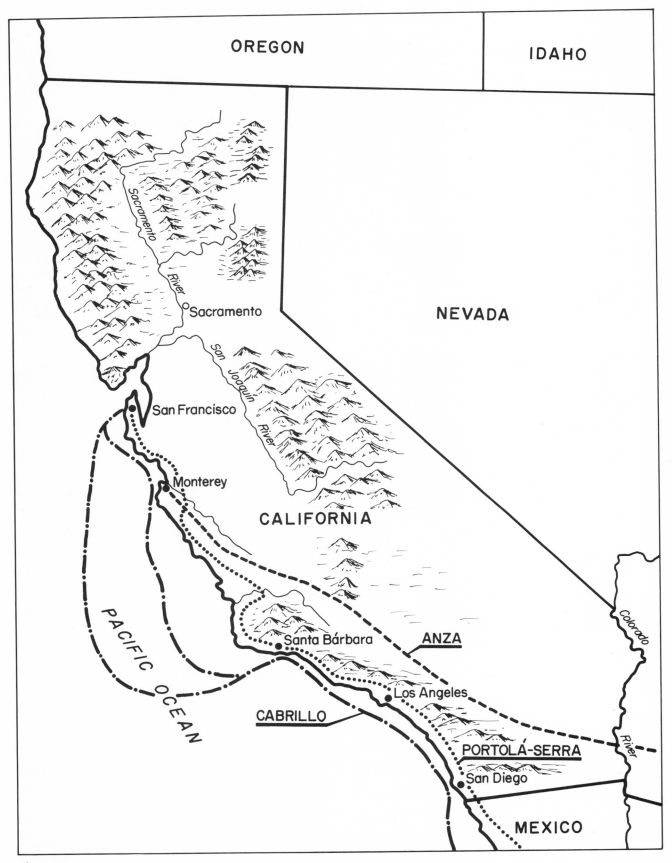

OREGON

IDAHO

NEVADA

Sacramento

San Francisco

Monterey

CALIFORNIA

PACIFIC OCEAN

Santa Bárbara

ANZA

Los Angeles

CABRILLO

PORTOLÁ-SERRA

San Diego

MEXICO

Colorado River

Hispanic California

the first four books and added a fifth, entitled *Sergas de Esplandián*, narrating the exploits of the son of Amadís. The author mentions in this additional book that the Christians of Constantinople were opposed by Queen Calafía and her Amazons of the Island of California "at the right hand of the Indies." The *Libros de Caballerías*, as these fantasies were called, were well known to the conquistadors, who were involved in comparable chivalric adventures. It is therefore logically surmised that, if Ulloa named California the land he observed from the deck of his ship, he had in mind the island of Queen Calafía. Moreover, Ulloa had been sent by Cortés, who was convinced that there was an Amazon Island. Bolton quotes from the *Colección* of Pacheco and Cárdenas the instructions that Cortés gave to his relative, Francisco Cortés, advising him of the great wealth to be found in the northern provinces, "one which is inhabited by women, with no men, who procreate in the way which the ancient histories ascribe to the Amazons."[3]

During the sixteenth century the Spaniards skirted the coast of California, sailing around the peninsula and up the head of the gulf, but they did not establish a settlement. Hernando de Alarcón followed Ulloa's route in 1540 in support of Coronado's land expedition and penetrated beyond the gulf by sailing up the Colorado River for two hundred miles, according to his calculations. Bancroft believed that he probably sailed only fifteen miles upriver.

THE CALIFORNIA COAST

The first navigator to sail up the California coast was Juan Rodríguez Cabrillo, who in 1542 left the port of Navidad twenty miles north of Manzanillo. At San Quintín, about two hundred miles south of the international border, he took formal possession of the land and continued north to "a port enclosed and very good." He named it San Miguel but the name was changed later to San Diego. Further north they discovered Santa Catalina and San Clemente islands and continued to Point Concepción above Santa Bárbara, where luck turned against the great navigator. A strong wind drove the ships west to the islands of Santa Rosa and San Miguel, which they named Las Islas San Lucas after taking formal possession of them. On November 6, 1542, Cabrillo's flagship, the *San Salvador*, and the *Victoria* rounded Point Concepción and sailed beyond Monterey Bay,

where the two vessels became separated. They were reunited ten days later at Bahía de los Pinos, on the thirty-eighth parallel, and christened it Bay of Pines because the shores were covered with pine trees. Thirty years later Francis Drake sailed into the same bay, the location now known as Drake's Bay.

Cabrillo died on the expedition but left orders insisting that Bartolomé Ferrelo, the second in command, continue exploring the coast of California. They encountered such strong winds that they were unable to land anywhere beyond Point Concepción, but they reached north of the present boundary of Oregon at 42 1/2° latitude before turning back.

PIRATES AND FREEBOOTERS

One of the serious problems of the last half of the sixteenth century was the constant threat of English and Dutch pirates who preyed on merchant ships on the way to Spain and on those sailing along the Pacific coast. This freebooting is now enveloped in an aura of maritime romance. At the time when Cavendish, Drake, and the Dutchman Pieter Heyn were plundering the galleons from Peru and from Manila, piracy was recognized as a patriotic endeavor. Spain (and to some degree Portugal) was concerned in attempts to discover, conquer, and colonize the new lands and was sorely affected when the economic returns were stolen by daring foreign pirates. The westward thrust across the Pacific to the Philippines and the Orient was another highly profitable commerce, and the returning Manila galleon laden with rich cargo had to be protected. On the Spanish Main some protection was afforded by escort ships, but on the West Coast such escorts were not altogether successful.

One of the English freebooters who regularly plundered the shipping lines along the Pacific coast was Sir Francis Drake. He intercepted many merchant ships, attacked defenseless coastal towns, and looted homes and business houses. He has been given more than his share of credit for the discovery of San Francisco Bay, however. Drake's Bay has also become a point of reference when writing about Spanish explorers such as Cabrillo, who sighted the same bay decades before Drake did. The persistence of the Drake legend is based on a single happening unrelated to exploration.

In 1579, Drake was trying to find the long-sought "Strait of Anian" to be able to return home without risk of being intercepted in the Strait of Magellan. Discouraged by the cold weather of the northern latitudes, he decided to find a port in which to make repairs to his famous *Golden Hind*. He sailed south along the California coast, where he found a "conuenient and fit harborough," faint praise for the Golden Gate, as Caughey wrote. After adjusting Drake's latitude calculation of 38°30', some historians believe that he had discovered San Francisco Bay; others doubt that he was ever near it. The narrative written by a crew member was not a naval log, but it mentioned that in order to claim the land for the English crown the men placed "a plate of brasse, fast nailed to a piece of sixpence currant English monie."[4]

After refitting his ship, Drake sailed around the Cape with a heavy load of Spanish silver and gold taken from the treasure galleon *Cacafuego*. Because of these losses, the Spanish crown ordered the viceroy to find a suitable port of call where the Manila galleon crews could have a short respite from the ravages of scurvy and obtain provisions. Such a port could also give intelligence of roaming pirates and provide protection for the rest of the trip to Acapulco. The search for a safe port on the California coast is another adventure-filled account, including the story of an incredible feat of survival after a Manila galleon and her valuable cargo were lost near today's location of Drake's Bay above the Golden Gate.

SEBASTIAN VIZCAINO

In 1595, after the severe loss of a galleon under the command of Sebastián Rodríguez Cermeño, the king ordered an exploration of the California coast. The man commissioned for this undertaking was no newcomer to Pacific sailing. Sebastián Vizcaíno was a successful merchant who was on the Manila galleon *Santa Ana* when the freebooter Thomas Cavendish plundered it in 1588. He had also tried unsuccessfully to tap the pearl fisheries of Lower California and was planning a second attempt when he was appointed by the viceroy to lead an expedition up the Pacific coast.

Vizcaíno set sail on May 5, 1602, from Acapulco in command of three ships, the *San Diego*, the *Santo Tomás*, and the *Tres Reyes*. The route along the coast was the same one taken by Cabrillo and by Cermeño, but Vizcaíno ignored the explorations of his predecessors by renaming many of the known landmarks. Most of the names

that he gave the bays where he stopped and the islands that he explored became the permanent names.

Like Cermeño, Vizcaíno was a careful observer and a good judge of the new land and its possibilities. In addition to bestowing such names as San Diego, Santa Bárbara, San Pedro, and the islands San Clemente and Santa Catalina, he gave detailed accounts in his diary of the flora and fauna of the coast. At the port of Monterey, which he named after the viceroy, he detailed the topography and the wildlife:

The land is fertile, with a climate and soil like those of Castile; there is much wild game, such as harts, like young bulls, deer, buffalo, very large bears, rabbits, hares and many other animals and many game birds such as geese, partridges, quail, . . . and many others which I will not mention lest it be wearisome.[5]

To show where he had been, he took the customary readings of the land and prepared maps that, in the main, were relatively accurate by modern calculations. He was greatly impressed by Monterey as a suitable port for the Manila galleon, and declared, "We found ourselves to be in the best port that could be desired."

The crew of the flagship suffered from scurvy and other afflictions, and Vizcaíno decided to continue north from Monterey Bay after sending back the *Santo Tomás* with the disabled sailors. According to his calculations he entered San Francisco Bay, as Drake's Bay was then called by the Spaniards. Fog prevented the explorers from making further observations beyond Point Reyes and so, after eight months of difficult seafaring, they turned back, to face a harrowing voyage in which a good part of the crew perished. The *Tres Reyes*, which had become separated from the flagship, was carried north to Cape Blanco at latitude 43°, where the cold was so intense that the men nearly froze. They turned back and fared no better than Vizcaíno did on the return trip. Commander Martín de Aguilar and pilot Antonio Flores died in the northern latitudes, and only five of the original crew returned to Acapulco.

Bancroft believed that Vizcaíno "had accomplished no more, and indeed in several respects less, than had Cabrillo sixty years before." Caughey gave the colorful explorer more credit for his accomplishments:

Denied thus the opportunity to establish the first settlement of Alta California, Vizcaíno nevertheless deserves full recognition for his exhaustive survey of the coast from the tip of the peninsula to beyond Monterey, for his permanent contributions to the nomenclature of the coast, and for the glamor he bestowed upon California through his praise of the Port of Monterey. His work was a fitting climax to the revival of interest in exploration which characterized the latter part of the sixteenth century.[6]

SETTLEMENT OF ALTA CALIFORNIA

The establishment of Spanish civilization in Alta California was a gradual process that began with the explorations of Baja California commencing with Jiménez' discovery of the lower end of the peninsula in 1533. The settlement of Alta California was 236 years away, but the eventual establishment of missions, ports, and garrisons in the semiarid peninsula, provided many of the supplies and personnel for the expeditions of 1769. The first incentive that led to the intermittent arrival of Spaniards in what they first described as the "Island of California" was the pearl fisheries discovered by Cortés and Vizcaíno. For a century and a half there were expeditions of pearl fishermen, both adventurers and under legal contract. They reaped profits from this industry, but no settlements were established until Governor Isidro Atondo y Antillón of Sinaloa landed officially in 1683. Kino accompanied Atondo and was indirectly instrumental in starting the first phase of an enterprise that led to the settlement of first cities in Alta California.

The second incentive was by no means secondary to the Jesuit missionaries, whose interest in converting the Indians was awakened and encouraged by Kino after he spent two years with Atondo trying to establish a foothold on the California "island." Although this first attempt had to be abandoned in 1685, Kino considered the primitive natives a fruitful field for carrying on the Christianizing and civilizing program to which the priests were dedicated. He convinced the Jesuit order and his good friend Father Juan María de Salvatierra that missionary work should be begun. Salvatierra founded Loreto, about two hundred miles north of La Paz, and was joined in the first few years by Francisco María Pícolo, Juan de Ugarte, and Jayme Bravo. Together they established six missions.

After Salvatierra died in 1717, the Jesuits continued as missionaries and military commanders under an unusual arrangement made by the crown, but the small numbers of troops assigned to them were not enough to hold the Indians in check when they revolted. Contrary to the optimistic appraisal given by Kino when he returned from the peninsula, the natives were not docile, simple creatures waiting to be Christianized. They showed no interest in conversion, rebelled when the rations handed out to them were reduced, and went so far as to attack the Manila galleon when it touched at Cabo San Lucas in 1735. It is to the credit of the Jesuits that they had established missions two-thirds of the distance north on the peninsula by the time they were banished in 1767. Constant turmoil with the Indians, the barrenness of the soil, and sickness among the settlers led to the poverty and decline that Visitador Gálvez noted during his visit in 1768. Despite these adverse circumstances, Baja California had a good share of the responsibility in the expansion of the northern frontier to the "other" California.

Several fortuitous circumstances led to the official settlement of Alta California. To begin with, one of Spain's ablest monarchs had been on the throne long enough to acquaint himself with conditions that needed action and change. Charles III was particularly interested in expanding the empire to the Northwest because of the maritime trade with the East. Second, he was greatly concerned over Russian encroachment from the north and was also disturbed by the possibility of an English fleet crossing over the Strait of Anian to attack the Pacific coast as the pirates customarily did. The missionaries too were interested in a northward expansion that would provide them additional aborigines to convert.

When Charles III ordered the occupation of San Diego and Monterey, he was echoing the favorite enterprise of his visitador general, José de Gálvez. Viceroy Marqués de Croix in Mexico not only was receptive to the plan but gave Gálvez the cooperation he needed to carry out this important expedition. All he needed was able military leaders, experienced naval commanders, and dedicated missionaries with whom to establish the missions. This was the third set of circumstances that enabled Gálvez to undertake the occupation of the two important bays that had been discovered and highly recommended by Cabrillo and Vizcaíno.

It was necessary to have good leaders for the three institutions mission, pueblo, and presidio when occupying an important location for the first time. These three institutions used by Spain throughout her New World empire may appear like separate entities at times, particularly those where authority overlapped. As components of a centralized enterprise whose objectives were eventually achieved, the crown used such offices as that of the visitador general to consolidate the efforts and activities of the church, civil, and military authorities. Theoretically all three institutions worked harmoniously, but in reality dissension arose from institutional and personal jealousies. At the onset of the California project, however, the naval commanders, the military leaders, and the Franciscan fathers were united in the plan to settle California. Gálvez, Viceroy Croix, and the king, who represented the high command, worked together from the start. Captain Fernando Javier de Rivera y Moncada, Captain Gaspar de Portolá, and Commanders Vicente Vila and Juan Pérez, both experienced pilots of the royal navy, constituted the military phase of the expedition. The missionaries were none others than the experienced Mallorcan Father Junípero Serra and Fray Juan Crespi, who acted as diarist. Priest and cosmographer Miguel de Costansó and Lieutenant Pedro Fagues, commanding twenty-five Catalonian soldiers, were also an important part of the expedition to San Diego. The military and religious leaders constituted the distinguished representatives of two agencies that made possible the settlement of San Diego and Monterey.

The preparation for the founding of the California missions was a well-conceived plan that took a year from the time it was first proposed until the expedition reached San Diego. The move northward was a four-pronged approach resembling a military pincers movement. Gálvez took two troop-transport vessels with which to send two detachments of the expedition by sea under the command of Vila and Pérez. Portolá and Rivera were to lead two groups by land and meet the naval part of the expedition in San Diego. Serra accompanied the Portolá band, and Crespi went with Rivera, making a total of three priests by sea and by land. Considering the size of the sailing vessels, they carried a surprisingly large assortment of supplies, people, and stock. The land parties too were well equipped with a pack train and driven stock for the establishment of the first presidio and mission. The pueblo would come later.

The *San Carlos*, under the command of Vila, put to sea on January 9, 1769, followed by the *San Antonio*, under Pérez, on February 15. The land parties in Lower California gathered three-fourths of the way north on the peninsula and founded the first mission of the expedition at a midpoint supply village named Velicatá. The new mission was christened San Fernando and was left in charge of Father Miguel de la Campa, who joined the Alta California party later. The *San Antonio* dropped anchor in San Diego Bay on April 11, 1769, after a relatively safe and uneventful cruise, but the flagship *San Carlos* did not fare as well. All hands were stricken with scurvy and were unable to lower a boat. The first activity of the expeditioners consisted of taking care of each other and waiting for the arrival of the land parties. They were not afflicted badly by the scourge, particularly the Portolá party, which took longer to arrive after a comparatively easy journey. Rivera's party ran short of supplies along the way, and both captains were troubled by Indian deserters. Of the 219 who started from Lower California, only 126 arrived at their destination, but before long many of these succumbed to scurvy, the usual affliction of sailors in those days. On July 1 all four branches of the expedition were united at San Diego Bay, one year after they began preparations in Lower California under Gálvez, and on July 16, 1769, Serra founded the mission San Diego de Alcalá. The port had been dedicated by Vizcaíno many years before.

The California coast had no Indian villages where the missions could be founded. It was open territory with convenient harbors but not always with potable water supplies and fields that could be cultivated. When the Spaniards started on an expedition to establish a mission, a pueblo, and a presidio, they had to carry all their supplies, equipment, and personnel. From San Diego, Portolá took the few people who had survived hunger, scurvy, and thirst and headed north to find the Port of Monterey, the main objective of the original expedition. The two land commanders, Costansó, two missionaries, a small detachment of soldiers, and a few Indian auxiliaries, making a total of sixty-four persons, constituted the personnel of the expedition that set out to find the Bay of Monterey. All necessary equipment and supplies were taken by a hundred-mule pack train.

They did not recognize Monterey Bay on this trip, although they were actually in it, and continued north to San Francisco. The Bay Area was thoroughly explored from all vantage points, and as a result San Francisco Bay proper was discovered. Sergeant Ortega tried to reach Point

V. R. DEL V. P. F. JUNIPERO SERRA

hijo de la S.ta Prov.a de N. P. S. Fran.co de la Isla de Mallorca. D.r y Exc.do de Theol.a Comis.o del S.to Of.o Mis.r del Ap.co Col.o de S. Fern.do de Mex.co Fund.r y Presid.te de las Miss.es de la Calif.a Septentr.l Murió con gr.de fama de sant.d en la Mis.n de S. Carlos del P.to del N.vo Monte-Rey á 28. de Ag.to del 84. de edad de 70. a.s 9 m.s 4 d.s hab.do gastado la mit.d de su vida en el exerci.o de Mision.o Apost.co

Fray Junípero Serra, from Palou's *Life of Junípero Serra*, printed in Mexico City in 1787. Courtesy of the Bancroft Library.

San Diego de Alcalá Mission, founded July 16, 1769, on San Diego Bay in California, the first mission founded by Junípero Serra.

San Carlos Borromeo Mission in Monterey, California, founded June 2, 1770, by Junípero Serra.

Reyes, got as far as the estuary, and was blocked by what is now the Golden Gate. A second attempt to find Monterey Bay was made on April 16, 1770. Portolá again headed the overland party and arrived a few days before the supply ship *San Antonio* hove in sight at the beach where they had planted a cross on their first visit. On closer examination they realized that this was indeed the bay they had been looking for. On the last day of May the ship arrived, and on June 3, Portolá took possession of the country again. The mission of San Carlos and the presidio were formally established not far from where Father Antonio de la Ascención had said mass on December 17, 1602, during Vizcaíno's visit to Monterey.

The frontier was moved three hundred miles north with the founding of Monterey, but it did not remain static very long. San Antonio, San Gabriel, and San Luis Obispo soon followed. The Franciscans, under President Junípero Serra, and Viceroy Antonio Bucareli were of one accord that a sixth important location should be settled with a mission, a pueblo, and a presidio at San Francisco. The Bay Area had been reconnoitered by other explorers, but the site for the actual settlement was left to Juan Bautista de Anza, who had been advanced to lieutenant colonel and was to lead the expedition.

The viceroy was unusually liberal with the crown's funds in outfitting the enterprise to San Francisco. There were four mule trains, over three hundred head of cattle, and all the personnel necessary for an expedition of this magnitude. Anza was supplied in Mexico City with horses, arms, and complete equipment so that he could begin recruiting immediately. In addition each family was to be clothed from head to foot, with pay and rations from the day of enlistment. At San Felipe de Sinaloa, Anza opened a recruiting station and had no difficulty enlisting men and families. They rendezvoused at the presidio of Horcasitas and continued to Tubac leaving there on October 23,

Juan Bautista de Anza: pathfinder, founder, pacifier of Indians, and administrator. Anza led the expedition that founded San Francisco in 1776.

Diego. The expedition was delayed by crossings, drought, and a stopover in San Diego, where the Indians had been giving trouble. Governor Rivera of Alta California was a jealous obstructionist who hindered Anza to the point that he had to turn back to Mexico City after choosing the locations for the presidio and the mission for San Francisco. Fray Pedro Font, the diarist of the expedition, and Anza were enthusiastic about the new location. Font wrote in his diary that it was "a marvel of nature, and might as well be called the harbor of harbors." The infantile tantrums of Governor Rivera prevented Anza from leading the settlers to San Francisco, but Lieutenant José Moraga, who succeeded Anza, followed the recommendations of his superior, and the presidio was founded on September 17, 1776, followed by the dedication of the mission on October 9. The arrival of the *San Carlos* provided materials for the artisans, who built the first houses and palisades for the fort and also augmented the celebration taking possession of the land by firing the ship's guns. The Indians were so terrified by the explosions that they did not come back for four days.

Unlike other provinces in the Southwest, California began as a clerical province first and as a military frontier second. Each succeeding mission up the coast was founded in much the same manner. Each expedition was organized with the combined efforts of a military escort and missionaries, who founded a presidio and a mission. This order of occupation was the result of the manner in which ownership of the new land was determined. It was not possible for a party of Spanish settlers to undertake on their own the establishment of a town or the taking of land even if it was not occupied. Ownership of the land was vested in the crown, and the king determined the manner in which it was to be parceled out.

In California land was given out in the form of a grant either for settlement or for cultivation and stock-raising purposes, but those who occupied the land were not given title to it. They were simply entitled to usufructuary benefits as tenants. The only persons the crown recognized as landowners were the Indians, once they complied with certain provisions and conditions. Anyone holding a land grant or a rancho understood that, while he could enjoy the benefits and products of the soil, he could not alienate any part of it. Moreover, if the land was not used productively or if it was abandoned, title to it was lost.

1775. By that time the party had increased to 240 persons, including soldiers, families, muleteers, and servants, not including 8 infants born along the way. The San Francisco expedition must have been an impressive caravan on the march. One historian wrote that, "the cavalcade was equivalent to a ranch on the move, and every night the camp looked like a good-sized town."

It was a long, "slow, tedious, and difficult" journey from Arizona down the Gila River to the junction of the Colorado and northwest to San

To ensure successful results, the settlers were given land to till in the manner described, in addition to the four square leagues to which each village was entitled, together with a liberal section set aside for the commons. For ranchos where extensive property was needed for grazing, the sizes of the grants were in thousands of acres. Depending on the manner in which the land was to be utilized, the grantees were provided with stock, mules, horses, and seed to give them a start. In some settlements, such as San Francisco, the settlers were paid wages and given rations. These were repaid to the crown, amortized over a period of several years, in exchange for which men were expected to bear arms during enemy attacks.

An important factor in Spain's successful colonization was the stress the administrators and leaders placed on material and nonmaterial culture. The missionaries themselves did not limit their activities to preaching and catechizing the Indians. The process of conversion was accelerated by bringing the natives to the mission, where they were taught Spanish and were introduced to the fundamentals of Christianity. As soon as it was practical, they were also introduced to ways of living that were appropriate to the conditions of the country, and to the understanding of the prospective converts. In addition they were taught useful arts and crafts, such as weaving, tanning, and leatherwork. These skills made the Indians more productive and useful to the Spaniards at the pueblos and at the presidios. At the same time that the wards of the church were being trained in the spiritual tenets of Spanish civilization, they were automatically turned into artisans who could fit into the new way of life. This process may not have been altogether altruistic. The missionaries, who did most of the teaching, had one eye on the Kingdom of Heaven and another on the comforts and profits that skilled converts could provide.

It has often been said that the California Indians were very docile, thereby making the work of the missionaries and settlers comparatively easy. This was true on first contact with the natives and during the first stages of settlement. But when the novelty of the newcomers wore off, the Indians grew bolder and committed the usual depredations, burning down the missions and killing anyone who resisted, as they did in San Diego in 1775. Unlike the Apaches in Arizona and other tribes in the Southwest they did not organize offensive campaigns, but their uprisings could be

very costly. The missionaries noticed that even those Indians who came to the missions for hand-outs and stayed were apathetic about learning and were not really in great need of the protection and facilities the missions had to offer. At first they even refused the food offered to them; they thought that it caused the sailors' scurvy. They would not eat cheese because they thought it was made from human brains, and they turned down brown sugar because they thought it was the Spaniards' excrement. They mistrusted the Spaniards in other ways: after five years of contact with the missionaries only four hundred children had been baptized, and not a single adult had accepted the religious rites of the church. The Indians' passive resistance to the new religion slowed the development of the colony because, not being converts, they could not be forced to work for the missions. It was difficult to persuade them that they were in danger of losing their souls and in need of salvation. The Spaniards had, in a sense, created for the Indians a spiritual malady of which they were not aware and at the same time offered the treatment and cure for it. Throughout America it often happened that the Indians accepted the benefits of material culture but were reluctant to trust their souls to the invaders. This was usually due to the examples set by the soldiers, whose behavior was not consistent with the religious faith they professed.

It was not expected that the missions would continue indefinitely as the homes of the Indians or that they would remain entirely dependent on the direction and guidance of the missionaries. The missions were planned as a transitional step between the primitive state of the Indian and his incorporation into Spanish society. When the missions were secularized, it was hoped that the mission Indians would become part of the pueblos or constitute their own villages, becoming useful citizens of the empire. Costansó, the priest-cosmographer who accompanied Portolá in the founding of Monterey, recommended that Spanish families "should be settled near the missions and mingle with the natives. Thus the missions will become towns in twenty-five or thirty years."[7] In New Mexico this plan had been carried out successfully in the early seventeenth century.

PERMANENT SETTLEMENTS BY CHURCH AND STATE

From the crown's viewpoint the ultimate objective

was to establish permanent settlements along the coast of the newly explored region in order to hold it and to keep it from falling into the hands of the Russians or the English. The explorers and colony leaders named by the crown were usually eager to assume the responsibility of these enterprises and share some of the cost of the expeditions in exchange for titles, appointments, and other perquisites derived from mining, stock raising, and trade. The army was the only arm of the service that was employed and paid by the crown, despite the fact that the payroll was slow in arriving. Presidial soldiers were allowed to augment their salaries by farming and stock raising when they were permanently stationed. They received land allotments and other privileges like the settlers.

The church had subsidies for the maintenance of the missionaries and for the upkeep of the missions. The missions were also alloted land, which was put under cultivation as soon as enough converts were living at the missions. By the end of the Spanish period the mission lands were the most productive and had the largest herds of cattle. Additional income was earned for the church by Indian craftsmen, who, after learning a trade, turned out items to be sold at the presidios, pueblos, and ranchos. In fact, all manufacturing was done by mission Indians. Since there were not enough settlers to run the ranchos, Indians were hired from the missions to work with the stock, on the farms, and in the households of the wealthier settlers. This practice provided the missions with additional income.

LEADERSHIP AND GROWTH

By 1785 the pattern for the growth of California was beginning to emerge. The province was very fortunate to have had from the outset a number of able men who planned, directed, and carried out the work. First, Charles III, one of Spain's most enlightened monarchs, gathered around him men like Viceroy Bucareli in Mexico and Visitador General José de Gálvez, who not only saw that the king's wishes were carried out but also added much sound advice by being in the field personally. For the difficult task of blazing trails from Mexico to California, there were men like Don Juan Bautista de Anza, Fernando de Rivera y Moncada, and Gaspar de Portolá. The sea lanes were sailed by the ablest of Pacific coast seamen, Juan Pérez, and among the missionary explorers

were such dedicated men as Junípero Serra and Francisco Garcés.

The next step was growth. This was accomplished by two appointees, one a churchman, the other an administrator of the crown. At the death of Serra, Fray Fermín Francisco de Lasuén, a man of considerable experience in Baja California, replaced him. The second appointee was Felipe de Neve, governor of the province. These two men were interested in making California less dependent on Mexico for supplies and thereby eliminate the transportation problem. To accomplish this, Lasuén did not discourage Serra's interest in founding additional missions; in fact, in the eighteen years he spent in California, Lasuén doubled the number of missions. More important, however, he brought about the economic growth that eventually put the missions at the head in grain, vegetable, and cattle production. The missions were no longer exclusively agricultural centers; artisans imported from Mexico taught the Indians such skills as carpentry, masonry, textile weaving, and ironwork. This training made vocational people from pastoral ones, a development that would prove valuable a few years later.

Governor Neve turned out to be far more than a mere bureaucrat. Instead of sitting at his desk, he traveled up and down the province acquainting himself with conditions and recommending improvements and changes to the viceroy. When he was aware of need for reform, he made his own decisions and got approval from the viceroy after the work was finished. His study of water sources and arable land resulted in a new emphasis on farming and irrigation. He also imported a variety of farm stock, including swine and fowl, which was necessary for the maintenance of the population. Not only did he recommend the importation of supplies but also he set down some important recommendations for the administration of the pueblos: the land they were to receive and the manner in which irrigation water was to be distributed.

Once the pattern was established for the continued growth of the province, Neve sent for more settlers. It was not easy to find settlers for the new pueblos, in spite of the determined efforts of the governor. He realized that, to have stability and to utilize the land's resources advantageously, he needed more civilian villages and permanent settlements. Time proved him right. Some of the villages had very unpretentious beginnings. Los Angeles, today a metropolis with a large Hispanic

Santa Barbara, one of the best-known missions in California. It was founded in 1786 by Fray Fermín de Lasuén, successor to Fray Junípero Serra.

population, began modestly with two Spaniards, a few *mestizos*, a Negro, and some Indians. Yet within four years Los Angeles had become one of the leading agricultural regions of the province.

EDUCATION

Traditional culture passed from one generation to another, and the provinces maintained the practices and mores generally inherent in a folk culture. To complement this culture of custom, it was necessary to institute formal education, what the folk liked to call "book learning." The authorities in Mexico City and the governor's office in California were naturally interested in perpetuating the useful material culture, and, as already mentioned, that was accomplished to some extent by bringing artisan teachers to the province. The second step was the establishment of a school

system to provide the necessary training for children and adults at the pueblos and presidios. In 1793 the count of Revilla Gigedo, viceroy of Mexico, ordered the establishment of schools in California for the *gente de razón*, converts and their children. The Indians were to be discouraged from speaking their own languages and urged to adopt Spanish to become assimilated more quickly into the culture of the settlers who shared the land with them. When Diego de Borica became governor of the province, he too manifested the same interest in education and began to inquire at the presidios about potential teachers. No formal training was required of them; they simply needed to know how to read and write and to have some familiarity with arithmetic. Even so, it was not easy to find men with the necessary qualifications. A few of the children of the well-to-do were sometimes taught by a padre. A housewife might gather

84

a few family friends and teach them from time to time. These women volunteers were called *amigas.*

Because the early settlers were recruited from the humbler ranks of Spanish colonial society, men who could read and write were rare. The life they led in the provinces did not demand skills other than those directly concerned with subsistence. The missionaries, on the other hand, were usually educated men, trained abroad or in Mexico before being assigned to the mission field. They were not much interested in teaching their charges anything beyond *doctrina cristiana* and the prayers necessary to participate in church worship. They were so busy overseeing all the business affairs of the missions that they had no time to impart learning to the settlers. Literate people were so scarce that the army was hard put to find someone in the ranks who could act as an amanuensis. An officer or soldier who could read and write was transferred from one presidio to another to keep records.

Governor Borica's quest for schoolteachers yielded some interesting results. By December, 1794, he had found a retired sergeant named Manuel de Vargas who was to open the first school in California. He taught at San José first and then transferred to San Diego, where he was offered $250 a year. Ramón Lasso, an ensign, succeeded Vargas in San José with the meager salary of two and a half reales a year for each student. The third teacher to join the education system of California was a *grumete*, or cabin boy, named José Manuel Toca, who was assigned to Santa Bárbara in the fall of 1795. Teachers were to be paid through voluntary contributions. When this arrangement failed, Governor Borica levied a tax on married men and bachelors alike, to be paid in currency or in kind. Attendance was obligatory for children over seven and under ten. Noncommissioned officers who could not read or write were also ordered to enroll in the new schools. To ensure compliance with regulations, Borica had regular reports and examination copybooks sent to him from time to time. Used notebooks were turned in to be used in the manufacture of cartridges. Despite the enthusiasm of Governor Borica, public schools did not prosper. The low salaries were no incentive to prospective teachers, and the apathy of students and parents soon reduced attendance to few or none. To make matters worse, Arrillaga, the governor who succeeded Borica, was also apathetic about education. As a result the incipient school system of the province was blighted.

Don Pablo Vicente de Sola, the next governor, used not only his office but also his own means to raise the cultural level of Californians. When he learned from one of the teachers that the accomplishments of his charges consisted of being able to sing well in church and take part in the weekly processions of the rosary, he was not favorably impressed. The governor sensed that something was amiss. He summoned the students to his office and gave them a copy of the Spanish constitution of 1812, several numbers of the *Gaceta de México*, and a copy of *Don Quixote*. His selections were indicative of the way he thought education should proceed for enlightment of the subjects of the crown. He founded separate schools for boys and girls in the capital and insisted that the progress of the state depended on the education of its youth—very progressive ideas for a Spanish provincial governor at the beginning of the nineteenth century.

Instead of relying entirely on semiliterates for teachers, he was careful to choose men of good character to reopen the schools. The retired sergeant Vargas continued to teach in the new school system. Sola himself founded a high school and imported two Spanish professors to teach there. He felt that, to accelerate the mission work, it was necessary to train Indians to take their place in the church program. He had envisioned practical educational programs for California. Unfortunately the viceroy in Mexico was not as progressive as the governor. Sola's ambitious program came to nought for lack of interest and the funds with which to implement it. Bancroft quoted a significant part of a letter Sola wrote to Comandante Argüello of San Francisco: "Do not accept any excuse from parents who refuse to send their children to school because if the youth is not educated, the country, instead of progressing, will retrogress, something that the authorities should avoid at all risks." This is an indication of the thinking of some of the higher officials in California who held the best interests of the province at heart.

RACIAL STRAINS OF COLONIAL DAYS

Many writers have underscored the variety of racial strains that settled California, particularly the principal pueblos, Los Angeles, San Diego, Monterey, and San Francisco. This heterogeneity has been pointed out to refute the often-stated claims that speak of "Spanish California." It is true that there were from the beginning of settlement *mestizos*, *criollos*, mulattoes, and Spaniards. But what is probably meant by "Spanish California" is its cultural heritage. There was considerably more uniformity on this score than the variegated racial strains might indicate. They all spoke Spanish, were governed by the same laws, belonged to the same church, shared a comparable traditional heritage, and were engaged in the same enterprises.

A glance at such officeholders as governors, *alcaldes*, army officers, and presidio commanders shows that they could be, and were, anything from native-born Spaniards to *mestizos*. Moreover, the record of their performance was not based on their ethnic strain. The only institutions with a preponderance of Spaniards were the missions, but that is understandable because of the specific training that the padres had been given elsewhere before arriving to assume their posts in the provinces. What they all had in common was their acquired heritage, a heritage born of custom and strengthened by the rules that governed their society.

The only segment of the population of the West Coast that was totally different racially and culturally was the Indian. It was the express duty of the missionaries to integrate the aborigines into Hispanic society as quickly as possible. To accomplish this task, the Indians had to be induced to live in the missions, where the acculturation process usually began. Once they were converted, they were at first given responsibilities assigned to them because of their ancestral heritage. In the process of assimilation, however, they contributed the labor that enriched the missions, raising cattle, harvesting crops, and manufacturing articles sold to the settlers and the presidial soldiers.

SPANISH HERITAGE

The Spanish heritage of the Californians included the traditions and customs inherent in Hispanic culture. Marriage customs, folk dances, folk music, and all the folkways transmitted from generation to generation were part of the life of the inhabitants, whether *mestizos*, *criollos*, or Spaniards. The formal elements of culture, however, were not as easily transmitted, because they depended on study and learning that were not readily available in California for many decades.

As the settlers became more affluent, they tried to emulate the niceties of cultivated society by acquiring things that would make their lives more interesting and enjoyable. Such material things were made available through trade with other nations and through free commerce with the internal provinces. This was accelerated after the province became free of the restrictions of the Spanish Empire.

By the first decade of the nineteenth century the province of California not only had been successfully settled but had developed a distinctive culture, different in many respects from that of other provinces in the Southwest. It was more of a clerical province than New Mexico or Texas, where the missions did not flourish to the same extent economically and culturally. Moreover, there was a closer working relationship between the settlers and the missions in that the latter controlled the labor force of converts under their care. The viceroyalty in Mexico City provided the missions with teachers to train the Indians in the various occupations needed for the production of useful articles. No such working conditions existed in New Mexico, and in Texas only San Antonio Mission offered this training.

In the end this arrangement accelerated the establishment of Hispanic culture in California on a much broader basis than elsewhere in the Southwest. The objectives of the founders had been carried out to the extent that the restrictive regulations of the crown allowed. The dream of Junípero Serra had been realized by the founding of twenty-one missions from San Diego to San Francisco. The efforts of José de Gálvez to occupy California through the establishment of presidios and pueblos had also been successful, although not with the same thoroughness of the mission work. The settlers and the soldiers were mostly humble, untrained folk who were not always willing to work and who lacked the dedication and enthusiasm of the padres. The missionaries, on the other hand, had a definite plan of action for which they had been well indoctrinated and trained. Also, they had more say in transacting their affairs and enjoyed greater privileges than the settlers.

When the Indians were induced to live in the missions, they were converted and baptized as first steps toward becoming acculturated to Spanish life as useful subjects of the crown. They were taught Spanish and weaned from their aboriginal lives and tongues. Since the government recog-

nized the Indians as the only owners of the land, once they were civilized, they were given land to cultivate and cattle to raise.

The missionaries became more interested in the services that the neophytes could provide than in preparing them to become subjects of the crown when the missions were secularized. The Indians were subjected to many restrictions and were severely punished when they failed to carry out the duties assigned to them. In addition to the usual religious responsibilities of attending mass and learning prayers, they were trained in manual skills or assigned to work with the large herds of cattle of the missions and to work in the fields from sunup to sundown. Many of the mission Indians were also hired out to the ranchos and to pueblo households as domestics. Their salaries were paid to the mission, and they were given *sarapes* and loincloths and were fed *pozole*.

A by-product of the missions' economic control was the acquisition of the choicest lands, which in turn produced larger and better crops and increased the size of their cattle and horse herds. This situation created constant friction between the settlers and the missions. The presidial soldiers acquiesced, because they received many of their supplies from the missionaries. Some rancheros were denied land grants when the missions insisted that the land to be distributed was needed by them in order to provide for the Indians under their care.

Although this policy furthered the interests of the church, it slowed the progress of the pueblos and gave little encouragement to free enterprise. The greatest restriction, however, was the mercantile policy of Spain, which prohibited international commerce and allowed trade with the internal provinces only under special arrangements. Eventually the increased production of cattle and horses and the large crops of grain demanded foreign trade, but it was not allowed, and so a good deal of clandestine trading and contraband running took place. Even some of the missionaries participated in this lucrative undercover business.

Map of the missions in California established by Junípero Serra and Fermín de Lasuén. Courtesy of the Wyman Company, San Francisco, California.

The Americans, like the Russians, were interested in sea-otter pelts, but unless they were willing to run the risk of coastal cannon, they had to use their own means for acquiring a cargo to take home. The great number of hides and tons of tallow produced at the ranchos could provide the ranchers with the means to acquire the household wares, fabrics, and utensils lacking in California. Because commerce could not be freely carried on, the productiveness of the land did not benefit the people and in the end stultified the growth and progress of the country.

One of the drawbacks of Spain's policies was her attempt to ensure progress by negative means. The church was to be strengthened by allowing no other faiths to enter the Spanish realm. Economic stability was to be achieved by closing the ports to trading vessels of other countries. This state of affairs during the Spanish era in California led one historian to comment that "the Spanish heritage—creaked with decrepitude."

Despite the shortcomings of the government, by the end of the Spanish period in 1822, California had ensured the continuity of Hispanic culture on the western coast of North America. The missions had made a special effort to convert the Indians in sufficient numbers to turn them away from indigenous practices. They were being trained to become assimilated in the society of colonial Spain by learning Spanish and becoming useful artisans. This practice was to become effective with the eventual secularization of the missions, a plan that the crown had had in mind from the outset. The missionaries were lukewarm to this idea; they were not overly willing to give the Indians a secular education. The economic benefits of their large Indian labor force and monopoly of manufactured products were a potent argument in favor of keeping the missions under their control.

The Spanish material culture of the empire was ensured in part by the artisans who were sent to California to teach their trades. It was cheaper and much more practical to manufacture useful articles from wool, leather, and wood in California than to ship them by sailing ships from Mexico or from Spain. The viceroyalty and the provincial governors also encouraged the production of hemp and linen in California. The abundance of cattle, sheep, and agricultural products provided the necessary raw materials with which to manufacture products for local consumption. This policy introduced all the fruits and other agricultural products for which California would eventually become famous. Oranges, grapes, and other fruits grew in abundance and made possible the distillation of brandies and wine making. The fortuitous circumstances of fertile soil and a long growing season with no extremes of cold and heat enabled the Californians to duplicate to a large extent the life of southern Spain. There was some prospecting and mining during the Spanish period, but as the cattle industry increased and the land was cultivated by Indian labor from the missions at very little expense, there was no great incentive to take to the streams and mountains to look for minerals. Life was much more enjoyable at the ranchos and was not too difficult at the pueblos and presidios. A certain amount of geographic determinism was involved in a country that was already as far west as anyone could go on land. The first Anglo-Americans who landed on the eastern shores had had a strong desire to keep moving west, so much so that "westering" became an obsession. The allure of the West made easterners restless. The Californians were already in the West, and so they were more relaxed.

The Mexican period lasted for twenty-five years, an interlude as history goes. But despite its short duration it ushered in a number of important cultural and economic changes. This was the period that Bancroft described as the "halcyon days," but it was also the precursor to the decline that the Californios suffered after the American occupation.

The struggle for Mexican independence began in 1810, but California was not aware of it until word was received in 1822 that all residents of the province were to swear allegiance to Emperor Agustín Iturbide. Within a year they were asked to support the new republic when the empire fell. Not having taken part in the armed conflict, they had no time to develop the animosities that accompany a struggle of such magnitude. As a consequence there was no immediate interruption of the cultural and social life of the province.

POLITICAL CHANGES

The first change was political. The last Spanish governor, Sola, the presidios, the pueblos, and the missions swore allegiance as a matter of course and continued in office until the official agent of the Mexican government, Agustín Fernández de San Vicente, arrived to oversee the election of a new governor. The Californians wanted to elect a Spaniard named José de la Guerra, unmindful that they were now citizens of Mexico. Fernández, who understood the climate in the Mexican capital, suggested that a California-born Spaniard would be more acceptable at a time when the Mexicans were shouting, "Down with the Gachupines!"

The Californians were happy with some of the changes instituted by the Mexican government but were disillusioned by the way the province, now turned into a territory, was looked upon by the new regime. No one seemed to know just how this far-off land was to function politically, although many of the residents began to aspire for power once the heavy hand of Spain was removed. Sectionalism began to develop when the northern pueblos became convinced that the *abajeños*, "southerners," were too influential. The capital was moved from San Diego to Monterey and then to Los Angeles almost at the whim of the factional governors. Before long California had become one of the most turbulent provinces politically. Bloodless revolutions, consisting mostly of fiery oratory, parades, and threats, took place. The local citizenry were so divided over the appointees sent from Mexico that they began to talk about being independent not only from Spain but also from Mexico. With the help of some of the Americans who had already become assimilated into Californian society, a native son by the name of Juan Bautista Alvarado revolted against Mexican appointee governor Gutiérrez and set up his own administration with the full support of his friends. California was now to be a free and sovereign state until Mexico abolished its centralist tendencies and restored the federal constitution of 1824.

The same struggle that eventuated in the separation of Texas and the temporary alienation of New Mexico took place in California. The former provinces wanted more independence to carry on their own affairs instead of being dictated to by a centralist government. Spain had left a rich cultural legacy in the New World, but it did not prepare the former colonists for self-government. This blind spot in the Spanish heritage created a political problem that plagued many Latin American countries for decades.

The tenuous hold that Mexico had over California became further strained by the practice of using it as a kind of penal colony. Many of the colonists sent from Mexico were convicts. They went to California to expiate their sins, so to speak, and were not inclined to work and contribute to the life of the country. Culturally, few of these individuals had much to recommend them, and the Californians, who were already dissatisfied with the political practices of Mexico, looked on them with skepticism. To differentiate the convicts from other Mexicans, they referred to them as *cholos*. Within the same territory five names

José de la Guerra, a native-born Spaniard and prominent Californio at the time of the Mexican War of Independence. His house in Santa Barbara is preserved as he left it. Courtesy of the Santa Barbara Historical Society Museum.

might have produced salutary economic and cultural results if political conditions had been less complicated and also if the imminent benefits of secularization of the missions had not hung in the balance. The Californios had valid reasons for their apprehensiveness about the proposed colonization project of José María Padrés and José María Hijar. But much could be said in favor of the enterprise when the potential contributions of the coming settlers were considered. Both sides of the controversy that arose have been appraised by historians from Bancroft to C. Alan Hutchinson, but there seems to be no consensus about the merits of the project.

Padrés had proposed the utilization of mission lands for a large settlement of Mexican colonists brought in under proper arrangements financed by Mexico. When he lived in California, political differences that arose from this proposal led Governor José Figueroa to banish Padrés in 1831 (banishment was an effective weapon frequently used by those in power to get rid of their opposition). Back in Mexico, Padrés persuaded José María Hijar, a wealthy landowner of considerable influence, to join him in the projected colonization enterprise. Both had the backing of Acting President Valentín Gómez Farías, who took office during the leave taken by President Antonio López de Santa Anna. The colonization party consisted of three hundred men, women, and children, whose expenses were paid from Mexico to northern California where, it was hoped, they would be allotted land, farming implements, and mission Indians to work for them. Padrés was to replace the ailing Figueroa as comandante general, and Hijar was appointed director of colonization. Both had official papers spelling out all their duties and responsibilities, but soon after the departure of the colonists Santa Anna returned to the presidency and canceled the appointments. A messenger was sent by land to inform Governor Figueroa and the Padrés-Hijar directors that their orders had been rescinded.

Figueroa had no intention of carrying out the provisions contained in the orders, and the change of orders that reached him before Hijar and Padrés arrived saved him the trouble of refusing. The two leaders remained as directors of a colonization that did not materialize. Nevertheless, over two hundred of the colonists chose to stay in California.

Among other things, Californios were not willing to accept the twenty-one administrators Hijar

were used to designate the various groups: Spaniards, *criollos*, Mexicans, *cholos*, and Californios. The last, a term that was neither Spanish nor Mexican, the settlers chose for themselves. They were no longer subjects of the crown, and so they were not Spaniards. Because of their dissatisfaction with the policies of Mexico they shunned Mexicans. The name Californio had much to commend it.

THE PADRES AND HIJAR COLONIZATION ATTEMPT

Not all the colonists sent to California were convicts and undesirables. One project in particular had brought to occupy posts that had been promised to natives of the territory. Moreover, they felt that the colonists were about to become owners of mission lands and cattle that they were planning to take over after secularization of the missions.

The colonists were not necessarily farmers and cattlemen, but, because they expected to hire Indians to do the work, that was no obstacle. In the groups there were a number of well-prepared teachers, craftsmen, and professionals, who were badly needed in California. They would have made a great contribution to the life of California. Not everything was lost, however; many of the colonists stayed to found some of the leading families of California.

SECULARIZATION OF THE MISSIONS

Secularization of the missions meant that they would become simple parish churches and that the Indians would be free at last from the control of the padres. The process was carried out surprisingly well, insofar as the church was concerned, although the missionaries were not in favor of it. The secularization process began in 1826 and extended over a period of ten years, during which time the rich land of the missions passed into private hands. Land grants were made to almost anyone who applied for them, and in the end over ten million acres were allotted to around eight hundred rancheros who otherwise would have become laborers instead of wealthy stockmen. The already thriving cattle industry continued its upward climb after the newly created class learned the art of converting cattle into hides and tallow, two items in great demand at the time.

The Indians' dreams of freedom from the control of the padres soon turned into nightmares for many of them. They had become so accustomed to living under the tutelage of the church missions that they were not prepared to venture out on their own. Some found employment on the ranchos, others returned to the secularized missions; many tried to go back to their former *rancherías* and lifeways. A few were able to live on the lands allotted to them, but most of them simply disappeared from the scene.

ARRIVAL OF FOREIGNERS

Many foreigners, principally Americans, had heard wondrous tales about California's eternal spring,

farming land, and countryside of unsurpassed beauty. They had arrived at first by sea as early as 1814, when the Englishman John Gilroy landed on the coast, married a Spanish girl, and became a prosperous rancher. Thomas Doakes arrived in Monterey in 1816, the same year that Daniel Call went to Santa Barbara, where he married and settled down. By the end of the Spanish period there were already a couple of dozen Americans settled and assimilated in California. Bancroft gives the names of three hundred Anglo-Americans who entered California, took up residence, and married into native families.

Anglo-American infiltration by land began early with the trappers, as it did elsewhere in the Southwest, sometimes the same men who had exhausted the streams of New Mexico and Colorado. Such well-known characters as James Ohio Pattie, Thomas L. "Peg-leg" Smith, Timothy Flynn, and the Bible-reading Jedediah Smith tried their luck in California streams with little success and considerable hardship. Those who followed the mountain men found farming and ranching much more profitable along the Sacramento Valley. There the Swiss-born American John Sutter had set up a permanent base of operations, which by 1846 had attracted over a thousand Anglo-American land seekers to California valleys. Many more would follow when gold was discovered.

California has always drawn people of all nations like a magnet. First it was the traders along the coast, followed by the trappers, the land seekers, and the gold miners. The English were the first to obtain permission, soon after the settlement of the province, in order to initiate trade. Shortly thereafter the Yankees followed suit more successfully and traded gold for supplies badly needed by the Spanish Californians, who managed to trade despite the restrictions of the crown. Once the ranchos began to thrive, the settlers had inexhaustible supplies of hides and tallow, which clippers took around the globe and sold along the South American coast as well as back at their eastern bases on the Atlantic seaboard. These seafarers were more welcome than the intruders in the north, who took up land without benefit of legal process, hoping that the restrictive policy of the Mexican government would change and allow them to stay.

The cotton goods, household necessities, tools, and luxuries brought by the enterprising Anglo-American traders on the coast helped make the life of the rancheros more enjoyable. International trade familiarized the Californios with a wide variety of articles and inadvertently helped pave the way for the arrival of another culture. The trading lanes of the Southwest, whether by land or by sea, have always served as a cultural bridge between the Hispanic provinces and the Anglo-Americans. In California the mutual trade between rancheros and merchants established very amicable mutual relations, which soon led to liaisons between the Anglo-Americans and the daughters of the leading families. Thus was the assimilation of the two nationalities begun that would be reflected years later in politics and government.

In the ensuing years the names of Apheus B. Thompson, William Goodwin Dana (who fathered twenty-one children), Abel Stearns, and the Englishman Hartnell became so well entrenched in the commerce of the province that they became part of the "Mexicanized gringos" who inhabited the Southwest successfully before it became part of the United States. The cultural life of California began to take on an inter-American color and lose some of the restrictiveness that had characterized it during the Spanish regime. Spain, as an experienced trading nation, perhaps realized that opening the western coast to foreign trade would result in changes that would alter her own hold on the subjects of the crown.

The assimilation on the Pacific coast was the reverse of what occurred regularly in the eastern United States. English speakers formed a cultural minority, adjusted to Spanish-Mexican life, became Mexican citizens, and were given land grants. The adoption of a new life was voluntary and without incident because it was not a circumstance of war. It usually began when a budding or successful businessman joined hands with a charming señorita, who helped her Anglo husband adjust to a life that he found good, financially remunerative, and happy. His sons and their many offspring became part of the California population.

The liberalizing of trade by the Mexican regime opened the door to infiltration from all sides: from east to west, along the Spanish Trail; by the sea lanes of the West Coast; from the north by Russia, a less welcome nation reaching over Alaska and south to the Spanish settlements. California seaports were visited by trading vessels from countries all over the world. Between 1825 and 1830 ships from Germany, England, Latin America, France, and Mexico came to trade with the Californios. The Russians came too, although they were not as well received because of their deplet-

ing sea-otter trapping in Mexican waters and because Spain and Mexico sensed their interest in expansion south into their domains.

RUSSIAN-SPANISH ROMANCE

When the famine-stricken Russian colony in Alaska was in need of supplies, a young commander named Nikolai Rezanov sailed south to the Spanish settlements, not knowing that the mercy mission on which he was embarking would lead to one of the best-known love stories of California. In San Francisco he met and successfully courted the daughter of Spanish Commandant José Darío Argüello, who promised his beautiful daughter's hand in marriage to the handsome Russian officer. Duty bound, Rezanov sailed back to Russia in 1806, never to return to his beloved Concepción (or Concha) Argüello, who, believing herself abandoned, entered a Dominican convent after a long and painful wait, only to learn thirty-six years later that her lover had died in Siberia in 1807 on his return trip.

PROSPERITY IN THE PROVINCE

California was the last of the Spanish internal provinces to be settled, almost two centuries after the settlement of New Mexico and a century after that of Texas. Yet in the short space of five decades the Californians had more functioning missions, and the population, although small, was able to enjoy a more abundant life with less effort than that of either the Texan or the New Mexican colonials. This prosperity was not attributable as much to the diligence of the Californians as to fertile soil and favorable weather.

Not long after the missions were established, there developed two ways of living, so to speak, one led by the rancheros, who acquired large tracts of land where cattle grew and multiplied, despite the large numbers slaughtered for hides and tallow. The second group of Californians consisted of pueblo residents and presidial soldiers of more modest means. The missionaries and their many converts, who also farmed large tracts of land with the unlimited manpower provided by the converts, outnumbered the Spanish colonials almost twenty to one.

The political and economic importance of the missions grew in proportion to the number of laborers and workers they provided the rancheros for agriculture, cattle tending, and household chores, not to mention the missions' extensive holdings and many cattle herds. The rancheros were left to enjoy the mounting profits, and lead a life such as has never been known elsewhere on this continent. Their homes were amply provided with wines and food supplied by their own land and with luxuries brought in by the traders all year around.

DIFFERING OPINIONS OF CALIFORNIOS

Many writers have expounded on the paradisiacal life of the Californios, whose long hours of leisure were spent in constant merrymaking and enjoying their equestrian hobbies, for which they owned unlimited numbers of fine horses. Travelers fared well on the California coast, stopping at the hospitable ranchos or at the missions where food, shelter, and new mounts were provided without charge to strangers as well as friends. Even enemies were offered the hospitality of the large homes, and once being guests, they were treated with the courtesy befitting the traditional Spanish honor code.

The seafarers and traders who married into the Californian families became adjusted to this life and expressed a yearning desire for its return after the coming of other Anglo-Americans to whom leisure and its accompanying enjoyment seemed like a waste of valuable time. Alfred Robinson referred to the Californios as "generally indolent, and addicted to many vices, caring little for the welfare of their children, who like themselves, grow up unworthy of society."

Richard Henry Dana (to whom Bancroft refers as "the sailor boy"), in his book *Two Years Before the Mast*, expressed his puzzlement at the ways of the Californios, first because he did not understand the Spanish love for equitation, being himself more of a sea rover, and second because he judged them by his own standards. The Californios were like all Spaniards, the products of an equestrian culture evinced by the *vaqueros* of Texas, the *charros* of Mexico, the *ciboleros*, or buffalo hunters, of New Mexico, and the gaily caparisoned rancheros of California. The men in Monterey seemed to Dana to be always on horseback, and he was probably right. Said he: "They get on a horse when only five years old . . . and may almost be said to keep on him until they have grown to him. They can hardly go from one house to another without getting on a horse."

Bancroft ascribes to John Bidwell, the hardy traveler who reached California after months of hardships on the trail from Missouri, the follow-ing remark: "It is a proverb here that a Spaniard will not do anything which cannot be done on horseback." Although that may have been generally true of the more affluent settlers, many others were responsible for the thousands of bushels of corn, wheat, chick peas, and barley that were harvested every year in California. The same may be said of the vineyards and fruit orchards, which were part of the country's material culture, passed on to future generations.

Dana, who was more impressionistic than he was scholarly, was greatly amazed by the sight of a man who impressed him as being a gentleman, although he did not have a cent in his pocket: "I have often seen a man with a fine figure and courteous manners, dressed in broadcloth and velvet, with a noble horse completely covered with trappings, without a *real* in his pocket . . ."[1] Such a man was no different in many ways from the hidalgo gentleman of the Middle Ages described in *Lazarillo de Tormes*, a Spanish picaresque novel of 1554. The Californio was perhaps the nineteenth-century version of this historical prototype. Had Dana been better acquainted with Spanish culture, he would have recognized the Californio's ancestor.

Unlike the hard-working New Mexicans, who had to eke out a living by dry farming under the constant threat of marauding Apaches, the Californios had the independence of landholders who could afford to employ converts from the missions at very low wages to work for them. This kind of living did not develop the *patrón* system of New Mexico, but neither did the Californios establish the closely knit settlements able to withstand Anglo-American influence after 1848. When the former lost their land to aggressive newcomers, few centers of resistance remained besides the main cities, where many of the leading families blended with the incoming Anglo-Americans.

The Spanish period from 1769 to 1821 has been hailed by many writers as the greatest and most romantic in California. Early historians such as Bancroft do not commit themselves outright, although he goes into great detail in describing the outdated customs of the Californios at the end of the Spanish period. The Mexican women who arrived with the Hijar colony introduced the styles of the capital, which the *provincianas* of California admired and promptly adopted. The Californios were more likely to accept the newer Mexican taste because, though they may not have cherished the politics of the capital, they did not eschew the

The Mexican *jinete*, prototype of the California ranchero, whose trappings were described by Richard Henry Dana.

cultural contributions made by Mexico. Caughey, looking at the economic history of California, feels that the zenith of pastoral life was reached during the short Mexican period.

No other province of the Spanish empire has elicited as many contradictory opinions as California. Some claim that there never has existed a veritable paradise anywhere on earth comparable with eighteenth-century California. The manner of the West Coast inhabitants was considered the acme of hospitality, gentility, and generosity. Others could see very little to recommend in the people, even in the women. Dana, with his proclivity for passing judgment on the Californios, aroused resentment among his own compatriots by declaring that the women had but little virtue and then added the ordinary stereotype, "The jealousy of their husbands is extreme, and revenge deadly and almost certain." Anglo-Americans who were happily wedded to California women, such as the like-named William Goodwin Dana, would have taken

exception to his remarks. James Clyman, coming to California from Oregon in 1845, went further, by saying that the Californios, particularly the army personnel, were "weak, imbecile and poorly organized and still less respected."[2] The further removed the writers from the Californio days, the higher their praise of the paradisiacal life and the more virtuous and attractive the women.

SOCIAL CASTES OF THE CALIFORNIOS

Many accounts have been given by Americans of all classes regarding the nature and cultural attainments of the Californios. Trappers, land seekers, traders, soldiers, and travelers have commented on every phase of life in California from 1825 to 1847. There is no consensus regarding the society that existed at the end of the Mexican period. One of the reasons for the divergence of opinion is that the writers did not explain what they meant by "natives," "Mexicans," "Spaniards," and "Californians." There was great difference in the cultural level and living habits among the wealthy class, the missionaries, the *mestizos*, the converts, the Indians in the *rancherías*, and those whom the resident Californians designated as *cholos*. There was also a great difference in the proportion of these various classes at the time when the various reports, accounts, and travelogues were written.

The wealthy classes, consisting of prosperous rancheros, merchants, and government officials, set the pace for the high living often spoken of. They celebrated lavishly all holidays, birthdays, weddings, and saint's days with a largesse seldom seen in early America. Scores of cattle were roasted and served to invited guests, who sometimes numbered into the hundreds at the large ranchos. Brandies and wines flowed as the celebrants danced Spanish *fandangos*, *jotas*, *contradanzas*, and all manner of folk dances invented by the Californios. The women, always the center of interest, dressed in silks and laces brought by the sea merchants from Spain, France, and Mexico. The *caballeros*, dressed with the rare elegance of the Californian horsemen, always mounted on feast days on horses festooned with silver trim and decorated saddles. They could afford to be hospitable to friends and strangers alike when they set a well-provided table and offered travelers a change of mount, a usual courtesy to the *forasteros*, as strangers were then called. This was the affluent Californio to whom writers ascribe the halcyon days of the pre-American era.

The *mestizo* was very much in evidence, despite the belief of many writers that after the secularization of the missions they "disappeared into the pale." The blood of the conquerors mixed freely with the blood of the conquered, as it did elsewhere in the Southwest, and produced the large body of the Hispanic population that survives to the present day. The dark skin and black hair of the Hispano attests to his dual heritage. In California some members of this group attained the same level of affluence and importance as that of their Spanish forebears, when they became fully acculturated to Hispanic society.

The *mestizos* participated in many of the social activities of the wealthier class, but not at the same level of entertainment, because it was beyond their means. They became the laboring class of California, even before the American occupation. Despite greater freedom under the Mexican regime, a freedom that was born out of unconcern, there continued a very marked class distinction.

The Indians belonged to one of two groups, the converts at the missions or the Indians of the *rancherías*, who were "pagans" and led a simpler, more primitive life. The latter came to the missions and the presidios for supplies and handouts, but mainly they lived off the land, fishing, hunting, and gathering fruits. They were not as well organized for hostile incursions as were the Apaches and other tribes farther east. Their forays were mostly uprisings, sometimes with the participation of discontented converts from the missions, but they did not wage constant warfare. The Indians who roamed freely did not form part of California society at any level, whereas the Indians who were born and reared at the missions eventually became part of the general population, particularly those who married *mestizos* in the pueblos or soldiers in the presidios.

The missionaries were mostly of Spanish or *criollo* origin. They were better educated and trained than the rest of the population and lived with their wards, busily directing the activities of the missions. A good deal of their work was devoted to animal husbandry, farming, and supervision of arts-and-crafts industry. The missions introduced agricultural products, such as oranges, figs, grapes, berries, and cereals, that were later cultivated by the settlers who did not engage in cattle raising. The intellectual and cultural level of these padres was higher than that of the rest of the population, whose schooling was meager at best.

Each class in the society of early California had different rights and privileges under the Spanish social system. These inequities led to constant dissatisfaction and internal struggle. The objection to a ruling class from Mexico gave rise to adverse criticism by the natives, who felt oppressed. All kinds of vices were ascribed to the Mexicans by the original Californios and later by the Anglo-Americans, who felt that the affluence of the territory had been brought about solely by the virtues of the Californios. Many Mexicans, on the other hand, considered the Californios a backward lot of *mestizos* and rundown inhabitants of a far-flung penal colony. The Hijar colony members were critical of Californian women's manner of dress and considered them backward and provincial.

CULTURAL DIFFERENCES

The culture that developed in California from the

Spanish-Mexican heritage differed from that in other parts of the Southwest because of economic and climatic conditions. In New Mexico there were fewer land grants, and much of the land in the grants was arid with no accessible water for irrigation. Also, many of the haciendas mentioned in the records of Diego de Vargas' day were one- or two-family tracts. By contrast the California rancheros were given extensive tracts of land, where they ran unlimited herds of cattle whose totals they did not know even after the annual rodeos. Horses became so numerous that they had to be killed in large numbers to conserve the pastures for grazing cattle.

The social life led by the affluent rancheros was an earthy relationship of family and friends, where all enjoyed bull baiting, horse racing, cock fights, and *fandangos* accompanied by singing and guitar playing. The folk traditions of the Californians included those of their Spanish heritage and also those brought from Mexico by the constant flow of welcome (and unwelcome) colonists. Anglo-American visitors with a literary bent, such as Charles Lummis, published large collections of California Spanish folk songs and other folklore material. Eventually the Mexican tradition took up where the colonial Spanish left off, giving present-day California a much stronger Mexican flavor. The Spanish heritage has not been allowed to die, however. The old missions have been reconstructed in an effort to preserve the continuity of the state's historic past. Today fiestas and pageants, such as the Santa Barbara Fiesta, highlight the more spectacular aspects of Spanish tradition.

In addition to the parties given by each household in California, other occasions, such as the village's patron saint's day, birthdays, and *días de santo* for members of well-to-do families, always called for fiestas. When all these festivities were added to church holidays, Christmas celebrations, and carnivals, the Californios had no dearth of entertainment. These same occasions were celebrated in New Mexico and in Texas in a more moderate form, with greater emphasis on the religious aspect of the fiesta. The Californios, particularly the men, did not observe the religious amenities of their *compañeros* back in New Mexico. This is reflected in the presentation of religious folk plays, such as the "Shepherds' Plays," popularly known as *pastorelas*. Juan B. Rael, formerly of Stanford University, in studying the diffusion of these folk plays in the Southwest, found in California only eight of seventy-seven versions from Mexico and the southwestern states.

The cultural life of the Californios, more informal than that of the Southwesterners, was given to gaiety and enjoyment. There were several reasons. First, they had acquired greater affluence in a shorter time; the land was more productive and the climate more favorable than that of a large part of Texas and New Mexico. These favorable factors released more time that could be used for personal enjoyment. Moreover, the California settlers did not have to wait centuries for traders to come from other lands to purchase their products and in exchange provide them with household wares, hardware, and luxuries for gracious living. As early as 1790, only fourteen years after the first missions were established, the English were sailed into California ports. Another economic factor that influenced the cultural life of the province was the accessibility of Indian labor. The missionaries trained and prepared the labor force that performed most of the work for the rancheros and their households. Elsewhere in the Southwest the larger portion of Indian labor was secured by buying slaves from other Indian tribes or by taking prisoners of war.

When all these conditions are added up, it is not surprising that so many observers referred to the province as "Romantic California."

The occupation of California did not begin with a military invasion. It was a gradual process impelled by hopes of financial profit and moved by the restlessness that characterized the American of the nineteenth century. The tales he heard about the wonders of California aroused in him man's insatiable desire to improve himself, which in the case of the middle westerners and some easterners meant setting off to the West Coast. Some of these hardy frontiersmen had vague notions of distance and were not sure of the location of the land of milk and honey, but they kept going over partial trails, crossed the snow-covered sierras, and finally entered the fertile valleys of California.

The first to move overland were trappers, or mountain men, followed soon after by tillers of the soil in search of more fertile land. The trappers did better as trail blazers and guides than they did as trappers, but the farmers found what they were looking for. All they needed, once having arrived, was legal residence and patented ownership for the foreign land they occupied. But those could wait.

The sea lanes brought traders and merchants to the coastal cities, where they traded for the hides and tallow that the Californians had in great quantities. They in turn brought articles and products that made the lives of the Spanish settlers more comfortable and enjoyable. These merchants, while not as large in numbers as the land seekers, became better adjusted to Spanish life and were generally well received by the California settlers. Their greater commerce know-how and their thrift philosophy, both indispensable to merchants, helped them build their fortunes in a relatively short time. Unfortunately for the Californians, there were not as many of these Americans in Mexican California as there were squatters and gold seekers later on in the northern part of the territory.

MILITARY OCCUPATION

The United States cast covetous eyes on California long before instigating the war with Mexico in order to acquire it. The hundreds of Americans who settled in California before 1846 were essentially precursors of the squatters who followed in their footsteps. This movement of population clearly presaged the plans that the United States had in store for the occupation of the West Coast. In addition to the attraction that the land had for American agriculturists, the apparent interest that the English manifested in acquiring California helped expedite the ultimate American takeover.

It was evident to the United States that England had long wanted to occupy California. To begin with, Sir Francis Drake had claimed the region for England in 1579. In 1774, after the settlement of the province Juan Pérez, one of Spain's greatest seamen, sailed to the southern boundary of Alaska and into Nootka Sound. Bruno Heceta formally claimed the California coast for the Spanish crown, but four years later, in 1778, that claim was challenged by England's Captain James Cook on his third voyage. Later the United States entered the controversy with England over the Oregon Territory and almost brought the two nations to war again in 1843. The conflict was finally settled by Secretary of State James Buchanan through a compromise on the forty-ninth parallel, to which Lord Aberdeen agreed in 1846. With these antecedents still hovering over the scene and rumors of an English fleet on Pacific waters, Washington would not be superseded by a sea power still claiming the land north of California. Moreover, President James Polk had set in motion operations for the acquisition of the California Territory that were evident even before hostilities erupted between Mexico and the United States.

THE BEAR FLAGGERS

The Californios were not too apprehensive about what was in the offing, first, because they were ambivalent about Mexico's policies, and, second, because they had become accustomed to Anglo-

Americans in their midst as traders, merchants, or intermarried members of their families. Consequently, the first overt acts of cattle and horse stealing by Americans were not considered rebellious acts but simply thefts and lawlessness.

The American takeover began on June 14, 1846, when a band of unkempt rebels already living in California, led by William Knight, Robert Semple, and others, and calling themselves the California Battalion of Volunteers, surrounded the home of General Mariano Vallejo in Sonoma and demanded his surrender. The general invited the besiegers to come in and have a drink of wine, as was the custom when visitors called on the mannerly Californios. It was ironic that the Bear Flaggers, as this band of "patriots" was known, had picked a man who was a good friend of the Yankees. He had showed a disposition to make an independent state with the help of the United States, but the turn of events did not allow his idea to materialize. In justice to Vallejo, whatever his politics may have been, he conducted himself bravely on this occasion and with the dignity of a *caballero*.

General Vallejo was probably selected as the victim because he was a wealthy upper-class landholder who could be used as the symbol of the "oppressor" from whom the California Battalion of Volunteers was going to "liberate" the unfortunate Californians. He and members of his family were held incommunicado for four months, during which time Don Mariano may have reflected on the recompense he received from the very people whom he had helped so often. The incident was duplicated throughout the territory, where ranchos were devastated, cattle killed, and crops destroyed as a prelude to the war the Americans were trying to incite. Unlike the Texans ten years earlier, these rebels had no pretext under which to attack and kill innocent people like the aged José de los Reyes Berreyesa and his two nephews, Francisco and Ramón de Haro, as they beached their boat after a fishing trip. They would justify their rebellious depredations if they could force the Californians to retaliate. The loud declarations promising to liberate the "Spaniards" and civilize them puzzled the Californians who considered themselves quite civilized and humanistic.

FIESTA IN MONTEREY

Down the coast, in the harbor of Monterey, another scene was unfolding in contrast to the epi-

Mariano Vallejo, wealthy landholder and general during the period of Mexican rule in California. He was imprisoned by the Bear Flaggers, who attempted to "liberate" the Californios. Courtesy of the Bancroft Library.

sode of the Bear Flaggers (who had meanwhile set up a republic, flag and all, with the aid of the enigmatic spy, John C. Frémont, who apparently was working under the aegis of President Polk). Commodore John Drake Sloat entered Monterey harbor and announced that he was taking possession of the land for the United States, which was now at war with Mexico. He advised the surprised residents that they were to carry on as usual, with all the guarantees of free citizens, and that the country was now American soil. The courteous commodore and his guarantees impressed the people of Monterey so well that they treated the entire fleet to a fiesta, even though it was on a war mission. This event moved Chaplain Walter Colton to write later that the Californios, even in war, observed all the amenities and made a person as secure as by his own fire-

The Battle of San Pascual, where General Kearny was defeated by the Californio horsemen. From a painting by Walter Francis. Courtesy of the Bancroft Library.

side when he was their guest. "He may fight you in the field, but in his family you may dance with his daughters," he added. By tradition the Californios were following the Spanish honor code that stated, "Hospitalidad antes que parentela," "Hospitality before relatives." The chaplain's appraisal of California's Spanish culture is worthy of contrast to the performance of the rebels in Sonoma.

The military occupation was not without incident, as had been expected by some of the American troops when Kit Carson informed General Stephen Watts Kearny that the "Spaniards" would run rather than fight. He mistook the Californians' easy-going ways for cowardice. The people were dissatisfied with Mexico's policy of using California as a penal colony and by its general neglect of the territory. This was a family affair, but when their soil was invaded by a foreign army, they rallied to their country's banner and gave a good account of themselves. They overcame American troops in San Pascual and ran General Kearny through with two lance thrusts after defeating him on the pass. The California lancers outmaneuvered American regulars in this encounter and inflicted many casualties without suffering any losses. The experienced horsemanship of the Californios stood them in good stead several times during the short war. As wars go, however, the battles in Alta California were not as bloody as those in Baja California and other parts of Mexico where the regular armies of both countries met in formal combat. The losses for the Californios were not on the field of battle but in the events that followed the war.

LAND LOSSES

The sparsely populated California of Mexican days had enabled the settlers to own almost unlimited land on which to raise the thousands of cattle and horses basic to their way of life. The *modus vivendi* of a pastoral people had created a cycle of life over the years that included rodeos when the natural increase of their herds was branded. It also included cultivation of gardens, orchards, and wheat fields and the making of wine with which to entertain their friends on festive occasions. The life of the Californios revolved around the ranchos, not the cities. The agrarian, pastoral life these people had developed made land tenure necessary.

Even before the Treaty of Cahuenga, signed on January 13, 1847, signaled the end of armed hostilities, American land seekers had already staked out claims on the land grants of the settlers. The size of the Spanish and Mexican land grants irked the newcomers. Eager to acquire property, they insisted that no men had a right to as much land as the Californians held. The term "vacant" or the more lenient "apparently vacant" was the pretext used by squatters to move in and fence large tracts of land within the property of the California rancheros.

The squatters dispossessed many of the original grantees, particularly in the north. The land law and complex and lengthy court litigations meant defeat for the Californians. Long delays caused many of the claimants to become bankrupt before cases were settled. This loss of land meant the termination of a way of life to which the rancheros had become accustomed over the years. Historians have been critical of the manner in which the land law was applied and less than happy with the high-handedness of the American squatters. Bancroft, who consulted all documents available on the subject, wrote: "It was the Californios own-

ing land grants under genuine and valid titles, seven eighths of all claimants, before the Commission, that the greatest wrong was done. They were virtually robbed by the government that was bound to protect them."[1] According to one historian, it would have been less detrimental to the owners if all grants had been temporarily approved and then the false ones selected. Seven hundred genuine claims came up for review, but no distinction was made between genuine and fraudulent. Bancroft further adds: "Land monopoly in California is due less to the original extent of the Mexican grants than to the iniquitous method adopted by the government."

Fraudulent claims were concocted with "proofs" of forgery and perjury—these were the most successful. One of the problems was that the members of the United States commission were unfamiliar with the people, the customs, and the language in which the grants were written. Some of the translations used in court were ludicrous. Had they employed old Californios like David Spence, William Hartnell, and Abel Stearns and a few natives like Pablo de la Guerra, who had bicultural backgrounds, a more equitable settlement would have been made with greater dispatch. One historian summed up the handling of the grants by saying that it was a "history of greed, of perjury, of corruption, of spoilation and highway robbery."

HISPANO-MEXICAN LAND TENURE

Added to the ills of the land settlements was the fact that the rancheros did not understand the American concept of land tenure. When they were asked for documents and written proof of ownership, they were surprised that anyone should question their ownership; they had become accustomed to living on the land, and no one had ever challenged their rights to it. True, sometimes the boundaries of the land grants were vague and overlapping, but since there were no fences, a few acres more or less in adjacent properties did not matter. The original settlers relied on traditional occupancy and common knowledge, but this sort of proof did not hold up in an American court. Moreover, many of the Californios did not understand English, much less the legal nuances with which their claims were denied. Adjustment to the American judicial system was part of the "culture shock" suffered by the Californios.

As the Californios lost their land to the Americans, the cultural effects began to be felt. The old settlers could no longer live in the gracious manner to which they had been accustomed in the days of Mexican rule. In the southern part of the state old families were able to hold their land longer. They continued the practice of living today and enjoying their fiestas, weddings, and birthday celebrations, unmindful of the diminishing resources that would soon reduce them to poverty. Fiestas, quantities of beef roasted on the spit, *vinos del país* to enliven the celebrants, and lively *fandangos* for young and old were soon to end. The south was spared for a few years much of the grief suffered by the northern landowners, because the grazing land of the southern ranchos was not as fertile and desirable as that in the northern valleys and because there were no fabulous gold strikes in the sunnier south.

THE GOLD STRIKE

The discovery of gold at Sutter's Mill on January 24, 1848, brought a number of events that in the end proved disastrous to the Californios and their culture. The circumstance of war, the gradual but inexorable loss of their land, followed by greed, envy, and the racial chauvinism that came to the surface with the insatiable search for gold disillusioned many of the old settlers. Their hopes that the American regime would bring them the guarantees and the pursuit of their own way of life promised by Commodore Sloat when he entered Monterey harbor never materialized.

The human tidal wave that hit California was too large and arrived too suddenly to provide a period of adjustment and adaptation that would temper the attitudes of the miners in their enthusiasm for quick wealth. Coming in the wake of conquest and imbued with the feeling of manifest destiny, they did not realize that the discoverers and settlers of the West Coast were native sons entitled to the same privileges they claimed as American citizens. It is a long story, well told by many historians. The concatenation of illegal "laws," armed sorties against "greasers" and "foreigners," and many other violent incidents forced most of the Californios who had gone north to return to their homes in the south.

The search for gold was aggravated by the multitude of foreign arrivals and by the invidious practice of classifying the natives as foreigners in order to displace them. Prospectors came from Chile, Peru, Hawaii, the Philippines, France, China,

Mexico, and as far as Australia. Romanticists look today at the gold rush through glasses tinted with romance and adventure, but the Californios who were at the scene would hardly have called it romance as they were subjected to indignities and ousted from the mining fields of their own country. To have to pay a miner's tax arbitrarily levied was an affront and a violation of the Treaty of Guadalupe Hidalgo, which exempted Mexicans and Californios from any charge or tax not paid by American citizens.

The Californios were not inactive observers during the gold rush. They, together with thousands of Sonorans who came up from Mexico, probably mined as much gold as the Anglo-American argonauts, but they spent it, gambled it away, living today with little thought of tomorrow. The southern rancheros also earned good profits from the high price of beef transported over the sierras by reliable muleskinners, or *arrieros*, whose reputation for honesty and efficiency became proverbial. They also packed in other supplies and tools to the mining fields, where gold seekers paid high prices for scarce merchandise.

The resentment of American prospectors, aroused by the "luck" of the more experienced Sonoran miners, led to the usual prejudices resulting from fear of competition. The Sonoran Mexicans had been mining gold for centuries before the arrival of the forty-niners and were more successful in finding bonanzas. They introduced the Americans to the *batea*, or miner's pan, for placer washing, taught them the patio process for gold recovery, introduced the *arrastra* for crushing gold-bearing quartz, and in the end were ousted as "foreigners."[2] Other Latins, such as Peruvians, Chileans, Frenchmen, and Californios, were included in this category of unwanted competitors. When the southern Californios and the Sonorans left the mining fields, Anglo-American merchants saw their profits plummet because their own kind were not as liberal spenders as the departed Latins had been.

REPRISALS OF THE CALIFORNIOS

The excesses committed in the mine fields and resentment about the loss of land aroused many native Californians against the newcomers. The ensuing belligerency of ordinarily easygoing people led to reprisals and personal revenge. Fuel was added to the fires of hate when a man was unjustly hanged, a woman despoiled, or a family evicted

An ore crusher of Spanish days used in Arizona, a variation of the *arrastra* introduced to the forty-niners by miners from Sonora, Mexico. Courtesy of the Arizona Historical Society Museum.

from its land. According to Spanish tradition, a person's honor could be restored only by shedding the enemy's blood. This violent reaction was part of the honor-code legacy of medieval Spain that persisted, though not necessarily as a code, throughout the Spanish Southwest. In a time of crisis the Californios, guided by this tradition, fell back on practices that were part of an inherited value system. Many aspects of Hispano-Mexican behavior parallel portions of the Spanish honor code, though the code was originally meant for noblemen and the court. It was an instance of vertical and horizontal transmission, a not-uncommon development in traditional lore. (Many of the folk dances of Hispanic people in the Southwest are of courtly provenience. *La varsoviana*, a well-known folk dance, was originally a dance of the court of Varsovia, in Warsaw, Poland.)

The indignities suffered during the occupation of California and the subsequent injustices in the gold fields left a number of Californios embittered, or, more explicitly expressed, *agraviados*. Their sense of being was denied to them when they were ousted from the gold fields as foreigners, and their *amor propio* was wounded when they were unjustly treated simply because they were "Mexicans." In retaliation they resorted to personal interpretations of justice. This is what produced the Murrietas, a name that identified many Californios attacking on the highways and on Anglo-American ranches. American highwaymen

also helped complicate the problem of banditry during this era. The difference between Hispanic and American outlaws was that the *bandidos* were impelled by revenge, whereas the Americanos went out for profit and gain.

The upsurge of *bandidos*, folk heroes in the eyes of the Californios, brought out an extralegal counterpart with the Spanish-derived name vigilantes, who meted out their own brand of justice to those whom they considered deviants. In San Francisco they achieved a modicum of respectability under the name Vigilance Committee. Elsewhere they became lynch mobs whose a priori notions of guilt condemned the culprits before they were apprehended. In many cases, being a "greaser" was reason enough for the Anglo-American vigilantes to swing a man from the limb of the nearest tree, after "due process of law."

DEPRESSION, FLOODS, AND DROUGHT

The succession of setbacks suffered by the Californios with the arrival of gold seekers and the aggressive squatters were not over when the depression that followed the gold rush drove down land and cattle prices with disastrous results for the pastoral Californios. The foresighted had acquired enough resources in affluent days to weather this succession of misfortunes. Many more could have survived the economic crisis if nature had not lent a hand to aggravate their troubles.

It almost seemed as though the vagaries of the weather had conspired against the rancheros, north and south, by alternately drenching their lands with torrential rains and subjecting them to a devastating drought. These conditions continued from 1861 to 1863. When the sky opened in November, 1861, it did not close until it had deposited fifty inches of rain on Los Angeles and Santa Barbara. Houses were washed away, fields were ruined, and crops were destroyed. In northern California the havoc caused by rain followed by years of drought produced the same effects. The succession of these extremes in weather ruined more than three-fourths of the rancheros' cattle holdings.

The disaster diminished production, while taxes continued to accumulate unpaid. Land values fell so low that properties could not yield enough to pay the taxes in arrears. Entire ranchos sold for a fraction of what they were worth. The standard of living of the original owners fell so low that many never regained their former affluence.

103

REPUBLICAN EXPERIENCE

The short Mexican period conditioned, or somewhat prepared, the Californios for a republican government, although they did not participate in it as long as they might have. For the first year after the signing of the peace treaty, many local officials, such as the *alcaldes*, continued to function as they had done in Spanish-Mexican days. Americans, who believed that the United States Constitution covered them like an umbrella wherever they went, objected to the continuity of Mexican offices and chafed even more under the provisional military government set up by the United States. The Californios were happy with the military government because it served as a buffer to the excesses of the Anglo-Americans, whose prejudices soon began to surface.

When the Constitutional Convention convened in 1849, a few native Californians, Pablo de la Guerra, José A. Carrillo, Mariano Vallejo, and four others, were elected delegates to represent around 13,000 of their people. Among the other forty delegated were many old-timers friendly to the Californians, with whom they shared opinions as well as problems. The number of Hispano delegates was larger in proportion to the native population. Together they made their voices heard in the chamber, even when they were voted down, which was often. After the state was admitted to the Union, many Californios became disenchanted with the manner in which business was conducted in the legislature. It was expensive for them to serve away from home in an atmosphere that was overtly hostile to them and to which they were not accustomed.

The bitterness and incomprehensibility of the lawmaking process was too strong a contrast to the friendly, easy way of handling affairs of state to which the Californios were accustomed. The result was eventually a virtual withdrawal with no Hispanic leadership left at the state level. Locally the old settlers continued to be a strong force, particularly in the cattle-raising south, where they were more highly concentrated. Santa Barbara and Los Angeles were strongholds of Hispanic political influence, and most of the offices were held by Californios. It is to the credit of men like Senator Andrés Pico, Assemblyman José Covarrubias, Pablo and Antonio María de la Guerra, and José Sepúlveda, as well as wealthy old dons like Antonio Coronel and Don Mariano Vallejo that the Californios continued in impor-

José Sepúlveda, a member of an important Californio family who had a varied career during the period of the American occupation. Courtesy of the Bancroft Library.

tant offices for several years, despite the odds against which they had to struggle. Even so, Vallejo in the north and Juan Bandini in the south, who thought that by becoming Americanized they would be supported by the Americans, were disillusioned to find that many of their former Anglo friends let them down in the end.

One outstanding individual who was spectacularly successful in politics was Romualdo Pacheco, a member of the second generation of Californians. Pacheco, who entered politics at an early age, combined the glamour of the past with an enviable civic and military record and an unusual education in the Sandwich Islands. When he was thirty years old, this aristocratic native son, married to an American girl, became lieutenant governor, and when Governor Newton Booth went to the United States Senate in 1875, Pacheco served as governor of California until the end of the term. This was a circumstance that politicos were careful to avoid thereafter.

A NEW CATHOLICISM

The Californios, who had lived so leisurely during Mexican days, were facing problems of land tenure, political intrigue, ethnic discrimination, and many others that they had not anticipated. Life among the gringos was a complicated and sometimes incomprehensible affair. Roman Catholic Californios, accustomed to the friendly and casual manner of the parish churches of Spanish and Mexican days, were shocked at the businesslike manner of Baltimore Catholicism, which demanded strict adherence to the tenets of the church, including financial support. The separation of church and state in the United States placed more responsibility on the members. This was part of the adjustment that the change in church administration introduced. The Californios reacted to the new order in much the same manner in which the Hispanos of New Mexico did when Bishop John Lamy and his French associates entered Santa Fe in 1850 and instituted reforms.

In colonial days the Spanish Catholic church had been an effective acculturation agent through which the Indians changed to a more or less European way of life, or as close to this desideratum as pioneer conditions would allow. Now Hispanic Californians were being Anglicized with the help of the same institution they had used in mission days, within the memory of some of the older Californios. The difference between the Indians and the Californios was that for the latter the adjustment was internal because they were already Catholics. Nevertheless, it was difficult to break traditional attitudes and habits of long standing.

In Indian indoctrination there was little choice of the language that was used in teaching church doctrine; part of the acculturation process consisted of learning Spanish. In 1850 the problem was not that simple, because the Californios spoke a European language that was difficult to ignore, much less forget. When language became a factor in school teaching in a society that spoke either English or Spanish, the question arose what language was to be used in teaching in private, church-affiliated, and public schools. The Spanish-speak-

ing members of the church hierarchy, such as Bishop Tadeo Amat and Father Bernardo Raho, took a middle position by trying to institute bilingual education in church-supported schools. Some Anglo-Americans, particularly those who had been living in California for many years before the American occupation, endorsed bilingual education—they were bilingual themselves. Most were unwilling to consider the Spanish language as the medium of instruction in the public schools. Bilingual or all-Spanish teaching was attempted in private schools, but it did not thrive for lack of financial support. Since most of these efforts were organized by the Catholic church, they could not receive public funds. Eventually the problem was solved by ignoring the second language and teaching exclusively in English. The Spanish language continued to be used by both Californios and Mexicans as the language of the hearth, and so it has continued to the present day.

SPANISH-LANGUAGE PUBLICATIONS

Formal and cultivated Spanish was used by educated Californios in writing histories and memoirs, as well as in editing newspapers. Most of the historical records made by Californios in the Spanish language are found today in the Bancroft Library of the University of California in Berkeley. They are listed under such designations as *Relaciones*, *Historias*, *Acontecimientos*, *Documentos*, and *Memoriales*; some are informally labeled *Cosas de California*, such as the extensive collection left by Antonio Coronel.

Newspaper editorials and news accounts shed considerable light on the history of the Mexican period in particular. The most important of the Spanish-language newspapers were *El Clamor Púbico*, *La Crónica*, and *El Eco del Pacífico*. The first was edited by Francisco P. Ramírez, a young enthusiast who covered every problem and every happening affecting the welfare of the Latin Americans. In his book *The Decline of the Californios*,[3] Leonard Pitt devotes an entire chapter to this publisher, detailing the role the twenty-two-year-old crusader played in the lives of his compatriots. Ramírez was an educated man, fluent in French, Spanish, and English. In addition to his linguistic achievements, he was well versed in American history and in Mexican current events. This versatile newspaperman could editorialize on the importance of education for the Hispanos, on the evils of prostitution, on the virtues of the United

States Constitution, and on Thomas Jefferson, whom he greatly admired. Ramírez' editorial policy was not unilateral; he knew the shortcomings of his own people, and he understood the rascality of the Anglo-Americans. Above all, he expressed deep concern for the improvement of the Hispanos and recommended that they implement the advantages available to them as citizens of an affluent nation. He also brought to the attention of his readers the failure of the United States to live up to the promises and guarantees implicit in the peace treaty. Much of what he wrote more than a century ago would be endorsed by American citizens today.

TRANSITION TO MODERN TIMES

As the end of the nineteenth century approached, the California known to Spanish speakers since they founded it in 1769 began to disappear through a transformation brought about by economic changes, politics, industrial technology, and to some extent Providence. The fatalistic Californios liked to believe that Providence had taken a hand and tipped the scales against them. Part of this fate was the arrival of the Yankees, whose acquisitiveness had deprived them of their land through crafty speculation and schemes. The younger generation, twice removed from its pioneer forefathers, was not so sure that an unbenign fate or the Anglo-American invasion alone was responsible for the blight of its ancestors' fortunes. Nevertheless, it did not exonerate altogether the conquering Americanos, who took the best part of its heritage.

Many circumstances brought about the changes with which traditional ways could not cope. First, the military occupation by the United States wrested the initiative and the authority from the former citizens of Mexico. The gold rush that followed on the heels of conquest was of short duration, but it was an intensive, dehumanizing experience that showed the materialistic phase of American culture. The political intrigues that accompanied the establishment of state government soon pushed most Californios to the periphery of effective participation, partly because of their lack of enthusiasm for government at the state level. Next, the tardy and unjust legalization of many of the land grants forced them into costly litigation, complicated by bureaucratic red tape that rancheros did not understand. Then, nature's meteorological vagaries, which alternated floods and drought, had catastrophic effects on the land

and property of the already beleaguered Californios. Finally came the railroad, a great advantage to society as a whole, but to the Californios signaling another invasion of Americans bent on land speculation that broke up large ranchos into farms where truck gardening and wheat fields replaced roaming herds of cattle.

Not all the Californios suffered from the land partition. Those who still owned large tracts profited by these new developments. But when capital is something to spend rather than to speculate with, it is enjoyed for a short time, and then depression follows. The Californio's penchant for enjoying the good life while it lasted soon consumed the wealth earned from the sale of their properties. Many landowners could have recouped their losses, joining in the new agricultural industry that was mushrooming around them, but they did not change from cattle raising to sheep raising and truck farming, despite the demand for these commodities. They resisted the new industrial culture by clinging tenaciously to their traditional way of living. The Bandinis, the Sepúlvedas, the Coronels, the Argüellos, the Vallejos, and the Verdugos still enjoyed their fiestas, although on a less prodigal scale. They sang the popular folk songs of the day, such as *La Hamaca*, *A la Orilla de un Palmar*, *El Zapatero*, and a Chilean *canción*, *Asómate a la Ventana*. They danced to the tunes of the *fandango*, the *contradanza*, and the *jota* of bygone days. Cockfights, bull baiting, and other diversions were held until the frowning authorities outlawed them. Members of the younger generation, already interspersed with the many Mexicans who continued to come to California, were more adaptable. They became *agringados*, *pochos*, just as the early Anglo-Americans had become Hispanicized and later Mexicanized in the affluent days of Hispanic California.

HISPANIC CULTURAL LEGACIES

Despite the changes resulting from a new dominant culture, the Californios left a legacy for posterity. The names of cities, towns, mountain ranges, rivers, and coastal prominences given by the early voyagers and by settlers of the eighteenth century are reminders of a culture that laid the bases for modern California. The names of such sea captains of the Spanish empire as Sebastián Vizcaíno, Rodríguez Cabrillo, and Juan Pérez still remind Californians of the men who pioneered the coast in Spanish days. The history of the West Coast is not complete without the names of the first

Antonio Coronel dressed as a Californio of Mexican days with his wife. Courtesy of the Bancroft Library.

settlers and builders like Juan Bautista de Anza, Fray Junípero Serra, Gaspar de Portolá, and Fermín Francisco Lasuén. The Spanish heritage is also evident in the architecture that is characteristic of California. The missions of colonial days have been rebuilt as monuments to the efforts of dedicated men who tried to acculturate the Indians rather than decimate them with gunfire.

The influence of the former sovereigns, Spain and Mexico, is also felt in the municipal and state codes of law. When the California constitution was drawn up in 1849, many of the laws regarding water rights, property rights, inheritance, mining, and riparian rights were incorporated into that document. The community-property system placed the wife as an equal factor in the accumulation of property. The rights of appropriation in mining became the custom during the gold rush, and were legalized in 1851 by the adoption of Section 651 of the Practice Act. The California legislature recognized and sanctioned "customs, uses and regulations of miners" when not in conflict with the constitution, making them "as much a part of the law of the land as the common law itself."[4] American judges and legislators declared time and again that British common law was often inapplicable to conditions that obtained in the West. The United States Supreme Court held that the doctrine of riparian rights contained in common law was inadequate for the protection of miners. It was a practical decision taken with regard to water rights, because Spanish law was designed for a region short of water, whereas British common law was designed to serve a country with an excess of water.

HISPANO-MEXICAN CULTURE

Today's Hispanic culture in California is essentially Mexican, with a basic Spanish heritage characteristic throughout Latin America. Spanish culture underwent a gradual change through the large influx of Mexican nationals and the decline of the original Californios. The phenomenal industrial growth that took place at the turn of the century attracted Mexican laborers in agriculture, fruit harvesting, mining, and railroad maintenance. The newcomers were not absorbed into manufacturing industries at the outset because they were rural folk with no industrial skills. A couple of generations later their descendants, who had attended school and become adjusted to "American" life, made their way into packing and canning industries. Mexicans were also successfully em-

ployed in mining, work in which they had had centuries of experience. After the railroads were built, the maintenance crews throughout the state were manned by Mexican labor. Railroad foremen were strongly in favor of hiring Mexican workers because, not being nationals, they could live with their families away from the cities. This was convenient for the railroad companies, but the isolation alongside the railroad tracks deprived children of school and precluded the benefits of urban life.

Mexicans coming to California did not have to break with the pastoral traditions to which the Californios held so strongly. The newcomers from Mexico were thus more adaptable to other industries. Living in barrios on the periphery of the large cities, the Mexicans were able to carry on their own cultural traditions, kept current by a constant stream of arrivals from south of the border. The barrio centers were instrumental in perpetuating Mexican nationalism through clubs, associations, and the parish Catholic churches, which provided them with a strong cultural bond. The Anglo world around them was where most Mexicans earned their living, but within their little Mexicos life went on with all the traditions of their heritage. The Mexican community eventually absorbed most of the Californios who, being landless, had to accept urban employment. The Mexican milieu was not in reality a totally different cultural experience for them. It was a culture with a slightly different orientation but was not essentially different from their own of pre-American days.

After the turn of the century, and increasingly so during the Revolution of 1910, Mexicans began to arrive in California in greater numbers than ever before. During both world wars, contractual groups under the *bracero* program were brought in to replace the men who had joined the armed forces. In addition to these three historical periods, during which the Mexican immigration movement peaked, laborers continued to enter the United States by whatever means they could improvise. The largest concentration of Mexican immigrants and also permanent settlers centered in and about the city of Los Angeles.

Mexican workers went to California for the same reason that everyone had gone since it was settled by the Spaniards. People went to find employment and to improve their financial condition. Large numbers of the Mexican immigrants were absorbed into agricultural industries from the Mexican to the Canadian border. A few with professional and academic training followed their specialties in cities, but they were not a significant number until post–World War II benefits became available.

AFTER WORLD WAR II

World War II produced a number of interesting changes among the Mexican Americans who were in the armed forces, and those changes were reflected in their immediate families and close friends. The intensive association with other Americans, under conditions that tended to neutralize individual attitudes on both sides, enabled them to work together on an equal basis. In this more or less neutral atmosphere the Mexican Americans became more easily assimilated to a life that some had observed as outsiders at home but in which they were now participants without overtones of social and racial discrimination. They shared life with the same advantages and inconveniences, the same dangers and frustrations, and they shared assignments under impersonal authority. They celebrated successes together and also griped together the way soldiers usually complain. That Mexican Americans won their proportionate number of awards and medals and that they advanced to company and field grades, including that of general, gave them a source of confidence unknown in prewar days.

These successes also raised some pertinent questions about the life they had led in their respective home towns, the restrictions that American society had placed on them, and the adverse conditions resulting from limited opportunities. The experience in the armed forces changed the traditional folk fatalism into an aggressive desire in many of the more ambitious to lift themselves to a higher plane of accomplishment. For many the opportunity to realize this was made possible by the G.I. Bill. With the implementation of this new legislation a new era dawned. In California where many institutions of higher learning were established, Mexican-American students enrolled in numbers never known before. What was more important, however, was that many children of that generation of veterans carried on where their parents left off. The tradition of going to college, unknown to most Mexican Americans before the war, became accepted though not always practiced. Members of the postwar generation were even more restless than their parents, and in some respects more demanding. Their restlessness coincided with the upheaval of Anglo-American

activists who had become disillusioned with the "establishment." The Spanish speakers joined the chorus of voices demanding change. What they wanted was more attention and official recognition of their neglected Hispano-Mexican culture. This meant special courses in the college curriculum with more relevance to them as members of the American community of Mexican descent. As a result many colleges and universities instituted new curricula called Mexican-American Studies and Chicano Studies, with special courses never before taught in universities throughout the Southwest.

MEXICAN-AMERICAN MOVEMENT

As this movement progressed for the West Coast to Colorado and southern Texas, many problems of identification, nomenclature, rationale, and objectives arose. The philosophy underlying the movement lacked consensus, because the ideas of the leaders had not coalesced. In California two groups developed, with the adoption of the term Mexican American in the south generally and the term Chicano in the north. The Californios had completely disappeared by this time, but the term Hispano was still preferred by those who considered themselves descendants of the Spanish settlers of the Southwest. Some young people, aware of their Indian origin, advocated a return to Indian culture. Such symbols as Aztlán, Quinto Sol, and others with the same connotation became popular. They went back to the court of Moctezuma for their inspiration, assuming that all Mexicans in California had descended from the imperial court of this Aztec emperor (though in reality the California Mexicans came from all parts of the republic, particularly Baja California, Sinaloa, and Sonora; quite a few were Hispanicized during colonial days). According to the United States Immigration Service, a relatively small number of Mexicans came from the central plateau, because most immigrants were seeking the agricultural work in which they were experienced. Urban Mexicans, unused to farm work, had a difficult time finding employment.

CULTURAL FORMATION OF SPANISH-SPEAKING CALIFORNIA

Regardless of the labels that Spanish-speaking Californians use today, the fact remains that their cultural formation has been for the most part

109

Hispanic—and Anglo-American to a lesser degree. One would be hard put to select the Indian cultural attributes of Mexican Americans, even among those who prefer to be closely identified with their Indian background. All of them speak Spanish, have been baptized in Christian churches, bear Spanish names, follow traditional practices and folkways of Hispano-Mexican provenance, and in the main are guided by a value system that is basically Hispanic. As they inevitably became Anglicized through living in the United States and being educated in American schools, the Indian remnants of their culture disappeared. Naturally their physical appearance reveals the characteristics of the *mestizo*, a human type that has been in the making since the arrival of Cortés.

Mexican Americans, like all Spanish speakers in the Southwest, do not want to lose their cultural identity. Words "acculturation" or "assimilation" sound to them like imprecations, because they are synonymous with cultural decapitation. To prevent this, a good deal of thought is given by Mexican-American Californians to those cultural elements that they wish to preserve and those that they are willing to discard. On the other hand, they must also decide what cultural content to adopt from American civilization. The movement has to make some decisions when setting up a school curriculum that is adequate to their needs.

From a practical viewpoint, the concern of the Spanish speakers in California, as elsewhere, is how to become integrated into American life and enjoy a proportional participation in public, cultural, and economic affairs with corresponding benefits accrued to them and their families. A good deal of progress has already been made. The results are evident and measurable. Spanish-surnamed individuals are found today in all segments of the economic, professional, and cultural life of the West Coast. The numbers are not yet proportionate to population, but the direction in which their concerted efforts, with the effective participation of institutions of higher learning, is taking them will change many adverse conditions of long standing. They seem restless because they must catch up.

The large majority of Mexican-American Californians are agricultural workers who follow the crops into Oregon and Washington. The most active and vocal are those who attend colleges and universities throughout the state. In their attempts to find solutions to their social and economic problems, they carry on consistent research whose results are published in magazines and professional journals. Mexican-American scholars with doctorates in the social sciences, pure science and mathematics, such as Octavio Romano, Feliciano Rivera, Fernando Peñalosa, Julián Nava, Uvaldo Palomares, Herminio Ríos, and many others, have already made their mark in their respective fields. There are also men in public life: jurists Manuel Ruiz and Carlos Terán, U.S. Congressman Edward Roybal, Assemblyman Alex García, attorneys, medical men, publishers, and businessmen cover the spectrum of American professional life. All these, together with labor leaders like César Chávez and his followers, attest to the profound interest that Mexican-American leaders have in entering the American scene on all fronts, but without losing their cultural heritage.

The fields of art, music, and literature have not been neglected by the present generation of Spanish-speaking people. Just now there seems to be a very strong tendency to turn inward for artistic inspiration in an effort to explain their own Mexican culture. As their experience broadens, so will their artistic expression. One look at the list of publications by them from leading publishing houses reveals the widespread search for self-expression and creativity. As more Spanish speakers become qualified, the legacies of their heritage together with their present experience will provide them with a fuller field from which to draw for a broader artistic and literary expression. The full participation in all realms of American life augurs well for a segment of the California population whose dual heritage supports and strengthens their bid for a brighter future.

For almost two centuries the Spaniards devoted time and effort to the discovery, exploration, and settlement of the Southwest, from the time Alvar Núñez inflamed their imaginations with the wondrous tales of treasure-laden lands in the unknown north. Their concern during this long period was primarily the founding of settlements enduring enough to establish a permanent and indisputable claim to that part of North America. New Spain, the viceregal province that centuries later was to become the basic culture center for the Southwest, was hard put to provide enough funds and personnel to develop the vast territory fast enough to check the infiltration by other nations eager to acquire a foothold. Spain's borderland frontiers became very extended ones that had to be protected against the attacks of hostile Indians and the encroachments of Europeans who believed that within those borderlands lay treasures like those of Mexico and Peru.

Even though both the French and the English hoped to find mineral wealth in the Spanish provinces, their immediate treasure lay in the fur trade and in trapping. Spain's mercantilistic practices prevented free access to the beaver-rich streams west of the Mississippi, but many English and French trappers found their way into the region either officially or on their own. The lives led by these hardy trappers were adventurous and primitive. Because they lived in the mountains where the streams were, they came to be known as "mountain men." They were the first Anglo-Americans with whom the Spanish colonials came in contact in northern New Mexico, where they rendezvoused with their annual catch of furs. Some settled in Taos, and those with more urban inclinations married and, in the latter part of the eighteenth century and the beginning of the nineteenth, became the pivot for much of the western trade that brought the Anglo-Americans and the Spanish colonials together.

The adventures of Kit Carson, Charles Bent, Antoine Robidoux, Lucien Maxwell, Carlos Beaubien, Ceran St. Vrain, and Jedediah Smith have filled the pages of history. They were the vanguard of the flood that would soon follow the trails to the Southwest in quest of furs, trade, and land. The impression they created on first contact was not very favorable. They were unkempt, many were illiterate, and, because of their lack of social contact (save with the Indians of the trail), they were looked on by the colonials as crude and uncultured. After living alone along the mountain streams, trapping and skinning beaver and muskrat, they arrived in Taos thirsty for liquor popularly known as "Taos lightning" and eager for feminine companionship. It can hardly be said that these men were pioneers, that is, men who brought into uncharted wilderness the fruits of civilization. First, it was not a wilderness they entered but a country that had been inhabited by Europeans for more than two centuries. Second, their brand of civilization would hardly be considered by Americans east of the Mississippi as representative of the best they had to offer, although one historian has said that this breed of men was "typical of those who had steadily pushed the fringes of civilization westward from the Atlantic seaboard."[1] Somewhere along the line that author completely ignored Spanish civilization. Other writers have expressed a similar attitude in dealing with the Southwest, perhaps, because of the differences in motivation and interests of the two cultures.

With few exceptions, the New Mexican colonials never became interested in trapping. That trade was left to the French and the English, who took advantage of the vagaries of fashion to supply furs for beaver hats that had become so popular in Europe and the United States. The Spaniards in Europe and in the New World followed their own mode of dress, and tall beaver hats were not part of their fashion, and so they did not take the interest in trapping that other Europeans did. The Spaniards and the colonials were more interested in buffalo hides, used extensively in their trade with the Indians and with other colonials in the internal provinces. The trade that eventually became important in bringing together the two cultures in the Southwest was the one that flourished over the well-known Santa Fe Trail.

SPANISH BORDERLANDS INFILTRATED

The infiltration of the internal provinces of Spain was first attempted by the French along the Mississippi after Canada was ceded to England under the Treaty of Paris in 1763. They trapped along the riverways from Canada to the Gulf of Mexico and were even more active in trading with the Indians than the English were. When the latter entered the trade, they joined the French, and together they moved over the west to the coast of California. That movement brought into the Southwest many Frenchmen whose names have figured prominently in the history of the region. Being a people who, like the Spaniards, spoke a Romance tongue, they had little difficulty becoming completely acculturated and assimilated into Spanish colonial life, and they succeeded to such an extent that many of the Spanish-speaking families in New Mexico today are of paternal French ancestry. The prejudices and national animosities between the English and the Spaniards were not as strong between the French and Spanish colonials. The threat of French infiltration on Spain's eastern frontier was accompanied by all sorts of intrigue and connivance in which the French citizens changed their allegiance whenever it was to their advantage to do so.

The French founded such important centers as St. Louis and New Orleans during this period and thus participated in the building of the West and the Southwest through their commercial and military activities. In 1763 the region became the frontier between England and Spain when France ceded the Louisiana Territory to Spain to keep it from falling into English hands. Very soon thereafter this frontier became important when the newly formed United States of America took over what once had been English territory. The interests of the new nation had already been manifested, and now under their own flag they were even more eager to move west under the conviction that theirs was a manifest destiny. They too needed furs, but, unlike the French, they were more interested in extending their land holdings beyond the Mississippi to the Pacific Ocean.

Some historians of the period were so imbued with the spirit of the "inevitable law of the frontier" that they evolved a frontier hypothesis, whereby they imagined that Anglo-Americans from the eastern seaboard advanced westward across the Middle West and the Southwest all the way to California, as though there were nothing in between but uninhabited wilderness. This thinking led to the application of the term "pioneer" to every American who went west, even after the Civil War. John Francis Bannon disagrees with this designation when he says: "The Anglo-Americans who came into Texas with Stephen F. Austin were not in the true sense pioneers; they found not a wilderness, but a society already in existence, and a foreign power in possession. Neither were the traders who came across the Great Plains to traffic at Santa Fe."[2] It has been characteristic of Anglo-Americans to consider themselves pioneers wherever they go and to refer to the residents as "natives" (or even a less flattering designation). Because they were successful in building a great nation, even though many of the great builders were not necessarily of English stock, in that sense they did "pioneer" the land and its resources. This attitude has set apart from the start the "Anglos" in the Southwest and the "natives" who preceded them by centuries. The cultural dichotomy becomes greatly intensified when a group of latecomers arrives that is large enough to develop its own social life.

In the early nineteenth century, when the traders began to probe the commercial possibilities of the Southwest, they had to associate with the Hispanos of the region and did so successfully. The attitude of the Hispanos toward the Anglo-Americans has not entirely changed since the coming of those early traders; that is, they accepted them individually even though they distrusted them as a group. Today one hears the expression among New Mexicans: "Es un americano muy bueno," which in a sense means that the person in question is a good American—it also intimates that there are others who are not. This reaction to the latecomers is based largely on the differences between Spanish and Anglo-American orientations. Anglo-Americans, given to institutional thinking, look on a culture as a social entity with an inherent set of characteristics and habits that may or may not be acceptable to them. Anyone belonging to this culture is supposed to have the characteristics, habits, and appearance with which the Anglo-American has endowed him as a member of a group. Therefore, any individual variation is viewed with suspicion. This practice has produced a number of stereotyped judgments, which the Hispanos have had difficulty in overcoming and which have resulted in much of today's prejudiced thinking.

FIRST IMPRESSIONS OF THE PEOPLE

When the first traders came into New Mexico at the beginning of the Santa Fe trade, many classified the settlers as untutored Indians, and even their Christian background was questioned. Bannon says: "To the newcomers, however, Christian or not, these Borderlanders were just Indians. Even the brand of Christianity to which they had been exposed rendered them suspect, for the Anglo-American frontiersman, in general, considered Roman Catholicism as something non-American."[3]

This negative attitude made it difficult if not impossible for a person to be considered as an individual. All Hispanic peoples were dark, unprogressive, untrustworthy, lazy, and unpredictable. Thus any individual in this cultural group automatically possessed all those characteristics. If a Hispano did not conform to the stereotyped characteristics by which he had been identified and was light-complexioned, trustworthy, and ambitious, he was considered to be so *in spite* of belonging to the group in question.

On the other hand, the individualistic nature of Hispanic people puzzled those Anglo-Americans who knew little about the culture. The Anglos were accustomed to a sort of conveyor-belt psychology, and any exception to their own misconceptions was upsetting—their assembly-line concept was broken. This cultural predestination has been very apparent until lately in the minds of some Anglo-Americans. Years ago it was generally accepted that railroad attendants and porters were black, Greeks ran restaurants and candy stores, Irishmen were policemen, Jews were naturally merchants (and so to be kept out of law and medicine), Mexicans were laborers, and Indians had no business being anything but primitive and picturesque for tourists.

Each of these ethnic groups has fought an uphill battle to break through the stereotype barrier created by the Anglo-American mind, and today's blacks and Mexican-Americans, or Hispanos (depending on the national or cultural classification used) are the latest to try to break through the barrier.

The tendency to generalize arose from the very first contact between Anglo-Americans and Hispanos, but the degree of understanding was in direct ratio to the close contact established with the old settlers. The prisoners of the abortive Texas expedition, for example, who willy-nilly became closely associated with their captors, noticed the marked individual differences among many of the men with whom they had dealings. Some Mexican officers were characterized by the Texans as gentlemen of the highest order, and the Texans had nothing but praise for the humaneness of the women they met on the road south to Mexican imprisonment. Lieutenant Zebulon Pike was even more deeply impressed by individual commanders who escorted him and his party and often spoke of them as men of great integrity and merit. Josiah Gregg likewise mentioned all the failings that he noticed on his trading expeditions, but he seldom generalized on the character or conditions of the Southwest. The same may be said of men like Colonel James Magoffin and other Kentuckians who went west, married into Spanish families, and became Mexican citizens.

FIRST ATTEMPTS TO TRADE

The first attempts to open trade routes between the Louisiana Territory and the internal provinces were made under the Spanish government. After the Louisiana Territory was ceded to Spain, Spanish traders sailed up the Mississippi to St. Louis and thence by mule pack across the internal provinces. Pierre Vial, who became a Spanish subject and changed his name to Pedro Vial, was successful in opening a trail from San Antonio to Santa Fe in 1786, and the following year the governor of New Mexico sent José Mares over the same trail to San Antonio from Santa Fe.

The French who had joined Anglo-Americans in trapping took part in the commercial infiltration of the Southwest. In fact, French traders were the *avant garde* of the Santa Fe Trail. In 1804, Laurenz Durocher and Jean Batiste Leland arrived in Santa Fe with a pack train of merchandise. Instead of returning east, they remained in the Southwest and enjoyed the profits of the merchandise they had brought on consignment from another businessman in St. Louis. Trade possibilities continued to beckon Anglo-American traders who were willing to risk the hardships of the trail and the red tape of Spanish-Mexican government regulations to make good profits derived from a trade that extended deep into Mexico.

After Mexican independence the willingness of

the colonists to engage in trade was reflected in the protection and welcome given by the Mexican army to the trading caravans when they reached the borderland of the Spanish Southwest. Thomas James and John McKnight made the trip to Santa Fe at the head of a party of nine traders, but the losses along the road were too great to be compensated for by the sale of goods in Santa Fe. The first successful trader of the Santa Fe Trail had the same effect on the merchants in Missouri of the fisherman who makes a good catch on a mountain stream. William Becknell, loaded with $15,000 worth of merchandise, not only completed the trip but was pleasantly surprised to find that Spain's mercantilist policies had been lifted. The soldiers he met along the way actually welcomed him to what was now Mexican territory and encouraged him to drive his pack train to Santa Fe, where he sold his entire cargo for over $90,000. He went back to tell of his success, a commercial success that led to commerce over the prairies after 1821.

One important factor in the Santa Fe trade was acquisition of Mexican pesos by the St. Louis merchants, who preferred that currency; the Mexican peso contained 374 grains of silver, whereas the United States dollar had only 371.25 grains. The pesos, together with other precious metals taken in trade, helped stabilize the Missouri monetary system by selling at par and even higher, and the trade the coins represented helped the Missourians to make a good living and at the same time provided the Hispanos of the Southwest with such needed commodities as cotton and woolen goods, cutlery, silks and velvets, feminine toiletries, and hardware. On the return trip the merchants did not go empty-handed; they took mules, horses, furs, buffalo robes and hides, and not-inconsiderable quantities of gold and silver with a total value of around $130,000 annually, and even more, according to Josiah Gregg.

THE FIRST MULES

One item that grew out of the trade into the Southwest was the draft animal usually referred to as the "Missouri mule." It resulted from the cross breeding of the mare from Missouri and the Sonoran jackass.[4] The Spanish mule was a small animal used for the saddle as well as for pack trains, but the mule developed in Missouri was a very large animal later adopted by the army and hence popularly called "government mule." The Sonoran

jackass was a large, short-haired burro with a black line running down the spine from the base of the neck to the rump and an intersecting line crossing the withers. Legend has it that most burros have this marking because a donkey carried Jesus into Jerusalem. Unlike the jackasses used by prospectors, the Sonoran breeding jack was at least three spans taller, and with a correspondingly large frame. Many rancheros in the Southwest used these burros as mounts because of their surefootedness and their endurance.

According to Glenn R. Vernam, in his comprehensive study *Man on Horseback*[5], in 1783 the king of Spain, through the Marquis de Lafayette, gave George Washington a couple of donkeys, and from them came the first mules on the eastern seaboard. The Marquis entered into the gift because all help from Spain to the Thirteen Colonies, including the supplies and funds provided during the Revolutionary War, was given through France.

ANGLOS AND HISPANOS MEET

Before trade over the trail to St. Louis was initiated, the southwesterners were unfamiliar with the Anglo-American culture that was to engulf them. Trappers and fur traders had made their appearance, but as long as the country was part of the Spanish Empire, the newcomers were looked on as interlopers rather than tradesmen. Spain was well aware of the United States' interest in expanding westward, and it was doing everything possible, short of force of arms, to keep the intruders away. The southwestern provinces were also interested in initiating trade relations with the easterners but could not foresee the political implications. Some, particularly the officials of the crown, were reluctant to allow Anglo-Americans to enter, because they sensed in the maneuvers of the easterners an interest beyond trade.

The Spanish authorities had experienced the incident in which Zebulon Pike had become "lost" and had set up a fort flying the United States flag. It was not an impressive expedition that the Spaniards met, but it was not difficult to infer the object of the Americans' presence. The soldiers who accompanied Pike fared badly because of inclement weather and a lack of supplies, and so when they arrived in Santa Fe, they were objects of pity and were treated with the hospitality for which the New Mexicans were well known. Many of the Pike party were hatless and were asked if it was the custom for Anglo-Americans to wear no hat. Lieutenant Pike himself was lacking proper clothes, and he was promptly accommodated by the Spanish governor at the palace in Santa Fe. The soldiers were taken in by the Spanish colonials and were so well provided with merrymaking during the celebration in progress that they were a bit worse for wear the following day. This early contact between the two cultures was considerably more cordial than meetings that were to follow. The Americanos spoke well of the New Mexican colonials, and Lieutenant Pike was more than lavish in his praises. The young American officer may have been more observing and more practical-minded than he has been given credit for. Some historians feel that it was because of his favorable reports that trade with Santa Fe was proposed when he returned.

It is difficult to reconcile some of the opinions expressed by early nineteenth-century travelers and traders, who came to the Southwest and reported that people were so backward and so poverty-stricken that they had little to recommend them. At the same time, the traders endured the hardships and dangers of the trail in their eagerness to reach Santa Fe, where they disposed of their merchandise among the same people of whom they spoke so contemptuously. If the Hispanos were so destitute and backward, where did they acquire a taste for the luxuries they bought, and, more important, how were they able to pay for them?

Anglo-Americans came from a relatively classless society, and on arriving in the Southwest they were unprepared to judge the people they encountered in a class-structured situation. The part of the population that was primarily in evidence was not affluent colonials but *mestizos* and Hispanicized aborigines along the roads and around the plazas. These were the people on whom Americans at first based their generalizations. Had they waited longer to understand better what they saw, they might have judged more accurately. Even the poet Walt Whitman declared at first that the mission of peopling the New World with a noble race was America's and that Mexicans should not be allowed to have a part in it. Years later he changed his mind and wrote eloquently of the Latin contribution to the American people.

Those Anglo-American frontiersmen who stayed and looked beyond exteriors found courtesy and other virtues to respect. They spoke admiringly of feminine attractiveness and established close relations that led to a good number of liaisons with the leading families. Eventually the Mendelhalls, Smiths, Charleses, Leopolds, and Fosters joined the Chavezes, Salazars, Oteros, Ortizes, and Bergeres in Santa Fe. Further south, the names Barncastle, Griggs, McKinney, and Fountain blended into the Hispano population of the Mesilla Valley, where their descendants became Spanish speakers first and then bilingual. These names, and scores of others who could not resist the charm of the young ladies they so often spoke of, became the hyphen of English-Spanish cultures more than a century ago.

THE SANTA FE TRAIL—AN INTERCULTURAL ROUTE

The trail of the Santa Fe trade played a role on the southwestern plains comparable with that of the great rivers in other parts of the world. In the beginning, goods moved over the land connecting two population masses with two different cultures, but the people who moved these goods in trade also brought new standards of living, other habits, different ideas, and a religious persuasion that had separated the two cultures many centuries before in Europe. The newcomers, repelled at first by much of what they saw, wrote many commentaries that revealed their likes and dislikes, approbations and prejudices of people accustomed to a way of life they thought superior because it was their own and gave first impressions rather than calculated judgments. Those who had not yet gone through the sod-house era referred to the adobe houses as "mudhuts" and divided the population of the province into two categories based on the degree of pigmentation. The light-complexioned Mexicans were "Castilians," and the darker shades were "natives" or "Indians." It was not easy for these sons of a Puritan tradition to divest themselves of their imagined virtues and standards—imagined because these same critics plied themselves with hard liquor and established red-light districts, saloons, and gambling houses when they settled in parts of the Southwest unoccupied by Spanish colonials.

The trade that had begun between Missouri and Santa Fe soon became an international commerce extending into Chihuahua, Aguas Calientes, and even Mexico City. Santa Fe was merely a port of entry that pack trains and wagon caravans went through with merchandise consigned to merchants in the interior provinces. Traders came all the way from New York and Philadelphia. In fact, many of the sources of supply were in New York, and eventually the trade was carried on directly with the East by twenty-one trading companies through the Spanish firm Peter Harmony, Nephews and Company in New York, by-passing Santa Fe entirely by a more southerly route into Chihuahua through Texas. The importance of this trade was emphasized by Charles Bent, a well-known trader who on July 1, 1843, wrote to the United States consul residing in Santa Fe:

> The trade of this country is of some importance to the United States, and particularly to Missouri—there is annually taken to the U.S. in precious metals, about half a million dollars, besides other property—this would have increased to a larger amount if traders to Mexico received protection from the U.S.[6]

The Santa Fe Trail, born out of the trade incentive between the people of the Southwest and the merchants of Missouri, developed into a supply line when the Anglo-Americans moved permanently into the West. It was a freighting enterprise linking the Middle West and the Southwest with plodding oxen, pack mules, and wagons until the region was permanently united to the rest of the United States with the coming of the railroad in the 1880's.

The Santa Fe trade was not exclusively an Anglo-American venture, as is often implied by the accounts written in subsequent years. Like all arteries of commerce, such as the Tigris, the Euphrates, the Nile, and the Mississippi, the traffic moved both ways, carried on by the two peoples concerned in it, the Anglo-Americans and the Hispano Mexicans. Members of merchant families from Mexico and the Southwest moved freely from west to east like their counterparts coming west. The residents of the Southwest had traded over longer routes and in greater numbers at the beginning of the seventeenth century, long before the English settled on the eastern shores, and continued trading, as one of the principal occupations, with the Indians and with the internal provinces. The last phase of their trading expeditions was the Santa Fe trade. Once the restrictions imposed by Spain's mercantilistic practices were removed, the colonists, now Mexican nationals, entered the trade with as much vigor as the merchants from the east. In fact, they were better suited to travel over the plains; they knew the country better, were acquainted with many of the Indian tribes, and were inured to hardships and privations of

the open country. The Romeros of Las Vegas, the Chavezes, Ortizes, and Armijos of Santa Fe, the Ochoas and the Aguirres of Arizona and Las Cruces freighted over the trail and even formed some of the most important companies in the Southwest. These names are mentioned from time to time in the accounts written by eastern merchants, but the impression gathered from such casual references is that the Hispanos of the Southwest did not participate in the trade.

It never occurred to the Hispanos to write about something they had been doing for centuries, whereas the Anglo-Americans who were coming into contact with the West for the first time were impressed by everything they saw, negatively or positively. The narratives of Pattie, Fremont, Dana, Davis, Gregg, and a host of others are very informative, but they have a tendency to exaggerate their accomplishments and omit the scores of names of people engaged in comparable enterprises. Even the military enlarged an Indian attack or an encounter into an event worthy of Waterloo. If the "battle" was lost, it became an "Indian massacre"; if defenseless women, old men, and children were wiped out by a surprise attack, it became a "glorious victory" for the United States Army.

The participation by Hispanic merchants in the Santa Fe trade was an outgrowth of the trade itself. Many eastern merchants, once having sold their goods in the Southwest, did not wish to be encumbered by a long caravan of empty wagons when they did not have a heavy cargo to take home, and so they disposed of their wagons readily. Thus the carrier wagon itself became an important item in trade. Often it was profitable for the traders to take horses back to Missouri; in such cases wagons were traded for stock. Interest in the Santa Fe trade spread east and across the Atlantic to Europe, which sent many fortune seekers eager to try their fortune in the new land. As the eastern population began its westward movement, after the Southwest was acquired by the United States, the role of traveling merchants changed to that of "merchant-colonists," as Milton W. Callon calls them in an interesting study made of this second phase of the Santa Fe trade.

THE MERCHANT-COLONISTS

The new territory became a Mecca for adventurous men, particularly for those who sought to improve their financial lot. Trappers and mountain

A part of a seven-train caravan of the Aguirre freighting company leaving Wilcox, Arizona, in 1889. There were twenty-seven wagons pulled by ninety-eight mules. Hispanos in the Southwest began freighting over El Camino Real as early as 1606 and continued until displaced by the railroads. Courtesy of the Yjinio Aguirre Collection.

men had come on a different mission, but those who stayed were part of the group that Callon calls "merchant-colonists":

The first merchant-colonists came from among the trappers who preceded the opening of the Santa Fe Trail. The earliest trappers opened the trade channels for those to come later. By the time Charles Beaubien, Lucien Maxwell, Ceran St. Vrain, Kit Carson, Charles and William Bent came to New Mexico, the pattern was set.[7]

They learned the Spanish language, became acculturated to the life in the Southwest, and married into the local families, indicating that they had decided to settle down permanently. Some not only gained wives but became Mexican citizens and later acquired large tracts of land. Callon follows the fortunes of most of the merchant-colonists in northern New Mexico, who helped develop the country by providing avenues of sup-

ply even to not easily accessible mountain villages.

The Santa Fe Trail had spawned a secondary trade through these eastern colonists, who spanned out in all directions wherever commercial profit was available. Through these supply centers the Hispanos began the process of acculturation to Anglo-American life, even though they had little contact with the people personally. The foods, tools, furniture, and household goods from eastern markets created different living habits among New Mexican folk and gradually made necessities out of articles that at the outset were considered luxuries. House interiors replaced their simple handmade chairs, stools, and tables with mail-order furniture, and walls were soon resplendent with photographic enlargements made from small daguerreotypes in gaudy gilt frames provided by the Cruver Manufacturing Company of Chicago. The flat-roofed adobe houses that for centuries had been part of the landscape now appeared

117

with gabled roofs of galvanized tin. Eventually homespun shawls and cloth disappeared, and American-made products brought in by the merchant-colonists replaced most of the necessities of the home. The trade that only a few decades before had started with pack mules over the prairies had become an instrument of culture change.

The products that the merchants introduced—tools for farming, means of communication, conveyances, foodstuffs, household goods, building materials, and many other commodities—soon became indispensable to the colonists, and, in adopting these new products, they were adopting a *modus vivendi* comparable with that of their purveyors. There was no resistance to this process of acculturation, and in the end the newcomers made comfortable profits, acquired land, and settled down to enjoy the fruits of their endeavors, unaware of the cultural change that they had brought about so painlessly.

Many of the business houses of the Southwest date back to this merchant-colonist era. The Kroenigs, Ilfelds, Hahns, Hunings, Staabs, Spieglebergers, Rosenwalds, and Bibos, to name a few, established business enterprises that thrived and have continued active to the present. There is hardly a city, a town, or a village of any consequence in the Southwest, with the possible exception of California, where at least one of these names is not known. From Taos to El Paso, and from Arizona to southwest Texas, these merchants operated stores and wholesale houses. In addition to selling their own imports, they also purchased native products that could be marketed either at home or in eastern markets. The Ilfeld company, for example, was responsible for introducing a food that in the East was known as "Indian nuts" and in the Southwest as *piñón* nuts. This company bought the *piñón* nuts from Indians and Hispanos after the autumn gathering, and, although the crop was not as productive then as it is now, it was an item worth handling. As late as 1930, 140 carloads of *piñón* nuts were shipped east, mostly to New York, representing a total of 5 million pounds.[8] At that time the price paid by the merchants was ten cents a pound. Today the same product retails for two dollars a pound.

The story of the Santa Fe merchants has countless implications, among which may be included the effect of their merchandising enterprise on the lives of the Hispanic population. Some were content to constitute the buying public, while others joined the Anglo-American businessmen and even-

tually became independent merchants themselves. One local merchant who learned his trade well from the eastern newcomers was Juan de los Reyes Santiestevan, whose descendants still live in Taos. He was born in Truchas, the highest mountain village in New Mexico (so high indeed that the residents always speak of "going down" whenever they leave on a trip). Santiestevan entered the Wooton and Williams store in 1840 and after a series of changes from one merchant to another, including a successful venture into freighting over the Santa Fe Trail, became an independent merchant and founded the first bank in Taos. The Santiestevan family has continued to be prominent in educational and civic affairs. Members of the family have been school superintendents and county sheriffs and even a Methodist preacher.

Unlike Anglo-American traders, Hispanic participants in this trade did not write about their experiences on the road. Except for the occasional mention of Spanish names or the recorded transactions of trading activities, the impression remains that they took very little part in this important enterprise. The reason is simple: The Hispanos of the Southwest had been on the trade trails as early as 1609, and by the middle of the nineteenth century it was no novelty to them to transport merchandise over the trail, meeting hostile Indians, living outdoors exposed to blizzards, rain, and waterless land. These were realities to which they had become accustomed since colonial days. The same was true of the cattle drives from Texas after the Civil War. Untold numbers of pages have been written about the Chisholm Trail and other famous or infamous drives across the plains. The saga of the cattle drives continues unabated on television, telling of the hardy men who withstood the rigors of nature to provide meat for eastern tables.

Brownie McNeil, who grew up on King Ranch, in Texas, wondered what ever happened to the many vaqueros employed in these drives. On inquiring, he found a good number of ballads in Spanish telling about the same happenings in eight-syllable verse. Again, little has been written about the Mexicans of the cattle industry by the Mexicans themselves because they too considered this occupation an everyday affair, nothing extraordinary or exciting because it was second nature to men raised in an equestrian culture. Moreover, material things were taken for granted by realists such as the southwestern Hispanos.

The traders and merchants who came from the

East over the Santa Fe Trail paved the way for the large business houses that were eventually established in the Southwest. Many of these houses are still operated by descendants of the early traders; they no longer consist of a few wagons around the plazas but are now large warehouses and establishments with branch houses in principal cities from Las Vegas to Santa Fe, Albuquerque, and El Paso. A by-product of this trade was the gradual introduction of manufactured merchandise to a region that subsisted largely on homegrown products. The increased variety of supplies included not only foodstuffs but also drugs, tools, and implements that helped increase local production. These larger business houses also supplied retail outlets in remote areas and provided Hispanos with an opportunity to engage in commerce by opening small stores supplied by the large warehouses. Small businessmen, particularly those in remote villages and towns, did not have the capital or the means of obtaining merchandise with which to go into retail business.

The Hispanos were introduced to merchandise of Anglo-American origin, and they gradually became accustomed to different tastes and habits that brought them a little closer to the dominant culture. The merchants and the traders, who were increasing their avenues of trade and finding new customers, thus became effective instruments of culture change without knowing it. While historians have often said that these merchants and traders paved the way for eventual envelopment of the Southwest, it should be also noted that the Hispanos reaped great benefits from the commercial enterprises introduced by the Anglo-Americans.

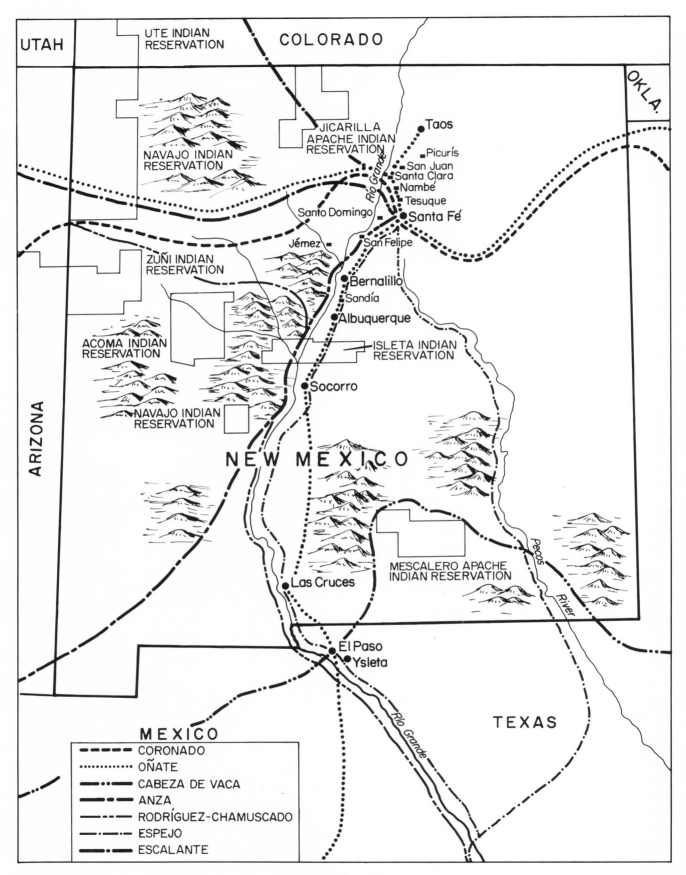

| UTAH | UTE INDIAN RESERVATION | COLORADO | OKLA. |

NAVAJO INDIAN RESERVATION

JICARILLA APACHE INDIAN RESERVATION

• Taos

■ Picurís

■ San Juan
■ Santa Clara
■ Nambé
■ Tesuque

Rio Grande

Santo Domingo

● Santa Fé

Jémez ■

San Felipe

ZUÑI INDIAN RESERVATION

● Bernalillo

Sandía

ARIZONA

ACOMA INDIAN RESERVATION

● Albuquerque

ISLETA INDIAN RESERVATION

● Socorro

NAVAJO INDIAN RESERVATION

NEW MEXICO

Pecos

MESCALERO APACHE INDIAN RESERVATION

River

● Las Cruces

TEXAS

● El Paso
● Ysleta

Rio Grande

MEXICO

- - - - -	CORONADO
・・・・・	OÑATE
-・・-・・-	CABEZA DE VACA
-・-・-	ANZA
-・-・-	RODRÍGUEZ-CHAMUSCADO
-・-・-	ESPEJO
-・・-・・-	ESCALANTE

Hispanic New Mexico

It is axiomatic that when two cultures meet they tend to reject each other, and when they are at different stages of development certain aspects of their initial rejection often become endemic and chronic. Moreover, the rejection results in a number of stereotyped concepts accepted thereafter as faithful and accurate descriptions of each other. These generalizations create biases and prejudices that are difficult to eradicate and constitute barriers to mutual understanding. Many of these prejudices in American society have a long history and can be summoned by nothing more than a label that brings them to mind. An experiment reported in the *Journal of Abnormal Psychology* entitled "Ethnic Dislike and Stereotypes" showed how perception can be changed, or modified, by cultural definitions only.[1] A group of 150 persons, 100 of whom were college students, rated 30 photographs of young women for beauty, intelligence, acceptance, and the like on a five-point scale. Months later the same photos were assigned names such as Finkenstein, O'Shaugnessy, and Donizetti. The original choices were greatly changed, once the traditionally established prejudices were recalled by the names.

Over the past two centuries misinterpretations of Anglo-American and Hispanic cultures have resulted from the westward movement of Anglo-Americans into the Southwest, particularly along the nascent waters of the Río Grande from southern Colorado to northern New Mexico. At the time when these cultures met, there was a great dissimilarity in their development. More than that, a different spirit guided their respective orientations. The opening of the nineteenth century heralded the imminent fall of the Spanish Empire in America; for the United States the same century was a period when the young country was gathering momentum for tremendous growth and development.

THE LOUISIANA PURCHASE—OPENING WEDGE

The Louisiana Purchase was the opening wedge for westward expansion, an expansion that would double the territory of the United States by mid-century. President Polk himself stated on May 30, 1846, that he had declared it his purpose "to acquire for the United States, California, New Mexico and perhaps some of the provinces of Mexico when peace was made."[2] The war with Mexico was his means of realizing this objective. The people of the Southwest were descendants of a breed of men called conquistadors, who centuries before had occupied the country with a comparable impetus under the expanding force of the Spanish Empire. But, by the middle of the nineteenth century, these same people were witnessing the last rays of a sun that was setting on the once proud empire that brought them to the upper Río Grande.

The meeting of the two main cultures of the New World was inevitable after Spain left the scene. Trappers, traders, and prospectors had been denied entry into New Mexico until 1821, but after Mexican independence they were free to come under more liberal conditions specified by the new government. Mexico was trying to stand on its unsteady legs as a new republic, burdened with several centuries of historical conflict, trying now to find its own identity, trying to find a symbol around which to rally its people and fuse them into a nation. It was a difficult feat, complicated by a population consisting of Europeans, Indians, and *mestizos*.

The Anglo-Americans, who saw their day dawning brighter and brighter, were imbued with the assuredness of success. Their absolute faith in their moral and social institutions convinced the standard bearers of American culture in the Southwest that they not only were right but were superior to anyone else in the world. W. W. H. Davis, bearing an appointment as United States attorney, arrived in New Mexico in 1853, and was so convinced of this that, after cataloging the deficiencies of the Hispanos whom he came to serve, declared that they lacked "the stability of character and soundness of intelligence that give such vast superiority to the Anglo-Saxon race over every other people."[3] In his patriotic enthusiasm Davis, a typical Victorian American, as Harvey Fergusson describes him, included the rest of the world when singing the praises of the Anglo-Saxon race, of which no doubt he considered himself a worthy representative.

Davis was representing a culture that was on the ascendancy, while New Mexico, a far-flung and neglected frontier of the now defunct Spanish Empire, was uncertain about its future and ambivalent about the people who now governed them. Those who had resources on which to draw made the best of it and prospered, but most of the people, with little to build upon, had no alternative but to remain indifferent or become fatalistic. The trappers and traders who entered the Southwest by way of the northern frontier along the Río Grande were determined to make their fortune in the new land. As John Francis Bannon says in *Spanish Borderlands Frontier:* "The Anglo-American was aggressive and acquisitive—He was rarely motivated by anything other than individual aggrandizement."[4] They trapped beaver along the streams of Colorado and New Mexico and penetrated the Gila River into northern Mexico.

As mentioned earlier, the New Mexicans, who had been living for centuries in the midst of potential wealth, did not trap the fur bearers. When they needed pelts, they obtained them from the Indians and sold them to Anglo-American traders. Hispanos were more interested in buffalo robes, and in buffalo meat, which tided them over the winter months and could also be traded at the Chihuahua annual fairs. They served as guides and camp tenders to the expeditions of trappers from St. Louis, Canada, and the middle western states. Some of the groups leaving Council Bluffs had as many as 116 men at one time, bound for the streams of northern New Mexico, where they rendezvoused in Taos and Santa Fe. The Hispanos were not subservient, but the fire that had propelled them over uncharted territory and made them fight and hold the land under the banner of Spain for 250 years had died down considerably. It would be many decades before the embers of these fires would glow anew and burst into flame.

The adjustment made to the newcomers was not as violent as it was in Texas, first, because the contact with Anglo-Americans was gradual, and, second, because there were not manifest any of those heroic bloody struggles in which the national epic of Mexico abounds, as some historians

put it. In addition, the region was more heavily populated with original colonials who had been on the land for a long time. The small landholders were not important enough for the Anglo-Americans to bother, and the *patrones* who owned large land grants were not easily displaced. Except for Santa Fe, most of the small villages were far removed from the trade routes, which the newcomers seldom left. Many remote mountain towns have continued to the present very much the same as they were when the Anglo-Americans arrived.

AMERICANS ON SEVERAL FRONTS

In addition to the upper Río Grande, the Anglo-Americans moved on two other fronts but under different conditions. In Texas they were invited, first by the Spanish government and then by Mexico, to settle north of the Río Grande to check the infringement of Spanish territory by nationalistic Americans. Most of these new settlers came from farming communities, knew how to make the most of fertile land, and knew how to implement the cattle-raising industry they encountered in Texas. In California it was altogether different. The Californios had great ranchos with large herds of cattle and horses. Although distant from the approaching westward movement, they established contact by sea with merchants who did not have to fight the plundering Indians of the plains or drive through heavy snows and over rough roads to reach their customers. Had there been no gold discovery in California, it is doubtful that the country would have been taken over as soon by the incoming Anglo-Americans. It is likely that a new nation might have emerged with the combined strength of the Anglo-American merchants who had settled comfortably on the West Coast and the Californios. The tide of gold seekers overwhelmed the Californios by their sudden arrival, by the great numbers who moved into the mining areas, and by the brashness with which they took over the land.

In New Mexico the attraction of trade and profit was uppermost among the incoming Anglo-Americans. The reports of forerunners, such as Pike, were very encouraging for adventurous men of that era. The trappers, who in a sense were the vanguard on the Santa Fe Trail, went west to make their fortune and were joined by experienced trappers from Canada and from French Louisiana. These men had trapped and carried on trade with the Indians since their arrival in the Middle West, and, now that they were detached from their own country, they swelled the numbers of trappers who emptied the streams of beaver and muskrat.

Spain realized from the start what these hardy men were after and, when they sought to enter the internal provinces, kept them out successfully. Later the Hispanos of New Mexico also foresaw the danger of allowing the mountain men to enter the territory indiscriminately. In 1812, when Don Pedro Pino attended a meeting of the Cortes in Spain, as a delegate from New Mexico to that congress, he mentioned the "imminent danger of being seized" by the Anglo-Americans. Shortly after Mexican independence, the same alarm was sounded in a letter to the federal government in Mexico City in April, 1831, which said in part: "Beaver skins is a branch productive for Anglo-Americans alone who make hunts and even camps which last many months, the result of which will be the extinction of the species. They take enormous quantities without limit or consideration."[5]

NEW MEXICANS' FAILURE TO EXPLOIT RESOURCES

The failure of the New Mexicans to exploit one of their important natural resources was part of the pattern throughout the Southwest. The first official report by an inspector of the Mexican government on the progress made by the Anglo-Mexicans in their newly acquired Texas lands, spoke glowingly of the agricultural accomplishments of these new citizens, but he decried the lack of land utilization by the Spanish Mexicans. The willingness of the newcomers to exploit whatever natural resources were at hand was part of the adventurous spirit of a new culture on the upswing. The Mexican *mestizos*, who constituted most of the population, were apathetic because life did not hold for them the rewards or the privileges of the more fortunate. Theirs was a roulette-wheel philosophy, as Gamio points out, "A ver que Dios nos da,"[6] "We'll see what God gives us." Anglo-Americans who came into New Mexico spoke of the lack of initiative of the *peones* but did little to improve their lot.

One of the tragedies of this segment of the population, the *mestizos*, was the lack of self-identity. Being products of two peoples and of two cultures, they were unable to choose those elements of their dual heritage that would enable them to compete with the *patrones*, much less with the enterprising

Mountain men, Indians, and Hispanos meet in Taos during the San Gerónimo Fiesta as they did in the early nineteenth century.

Anglo-Americans, who had no cultural ties with them. The declarations of the incoming dominant culture manifested, from the day the Anglo-Americans entered the Southwest, how they had charted their future course, and with no problems arising from a dual heritage their minds were free to decide their own destiny.

Governor Antonio Narbona, who arrived in New Mexico when the Anglo-Americans were first appearing in the territory, was an energetic Mexican of European ancestry who had little sympathy for the lack of enterprise and for the poor state of civilization that he observed in New Mexico. His administration was noted for his improvements in the defenses of the country, his insistence on the honest accounting of revenue, and his enforcement of law. When trade with the United States came to his attention, he said in part: "Trade with the United States would help to civilize the New Mexicans, giving them ideas of culture which they need to improve considering the disgraceful condition that characterizes the remote country where they live detached from other peoples of the Republic."[7] The difference between his attitude and that of the incoming Anglo-Americans was that the governor tried to do something to remedy the situation.

FIRST CONTACTS BY MOUNTAIN MEN

The first contacts between the newcomers and the Hispanos were made by the mountain men who came in great numbers to the upper Río Grande.

These men, although not highly cultured, were representative of the spirit of enterprise and expansion that filled all Anglo-Americans coming into the Spanish Southwest. They fought Indians if need be and also took their women as wives on a temporary or permanent basis. They fought the weather and all the obstacles of nature to reach their objective, which at first was beaver and other furs. They went to the Spanish settlements and enjoyed the comforts they had to offer. If they found girls willing to have them, they married and settled down to farm after the fur trade gave out. The French Americans were of the same persuasion, and, because of their cultural affinity with the Hispanos, they settled down readily, especially when the wives brought the dowry of a land grant. All these men were true to their objectives, and in order to achieve them, they changed their political allegiance by becoming Spanish subjects at first and Mexican citizens after 1821. Such names as Carlos Beaubien, Antoine Leroux, Bergere, and many others are still known among Hispanic families of New Mexico, not as French or English, but as Spanish speakers.

These Frenchmen, together with their Anglo-American companions, were not highly trained individuals who would raise the level of culture in the Southwest by their presence, but they did help acquaint the settlers with the civilization that was to engulf them within a few years. The traders and merchants to whom Governor Narbona referred in his dispatches were greater instruments of cultural change than the trappers, because their enterprise was more lasting and contributed material things that helped raise the standard of living of everyone. Moreover, they became permanent settlers, because their business depended on continuity, whereas the trapper, like the miner, exploited the resources of the land and moved on.

One of the early trappers who applied for a license to take fur wrote to Governor Bartolomé Baca acknowledging receipt of his license: "His excelance govirnor of New Mexico Barola Marie Barker, I rcvd the licance you granted me by the onrabel prest of Santa Cruse Manuel Radar and will comply with your order and obey them punctaly."[8] It was signed "Wm. Becknell." This was a good rendition of French and English by the old trapper and trader. As for obeying "punctaly" the laws, many of these trappers bootlegged furs out of the country to avoid paying taxes, and they imported goods used in trade by the same method.

NEW SETTLEMENT PATTERN

One interesting development that took place in New Mexico with the coming of Anglo-Americans was the settlement patterns that they introduced. They did not alter the original Spanish pattern, but the business and commercial center of the city or village was shifted by the establishment of new towns within the borders of the original villages. As a result, the newer parts of cities like Las Vegas and Albuquerque completely overshadowed the older settlement, and in time the latter came to be known as "Old Las Vegas" and "Old Town," respectively. The tacit implication was that the Anglo-Americans wanted to be a separate part of the same city and were unwilling to participate in the life of the original settlers. This set the pattern for coexistence of both cultures, one Anglo-American, and the other Hispano.

Fifty years later came the Mexican Americans, who also settled in the Spanish-speaking sections of the cities. The members of the well-to-do Hispano families, as well as cultured Mexicans who occasionally moved into New Mexico, usually lived in the new cities, unless their business interests required otherwise. Eventually the old and new parts of the same city became linked together by the extension of the main street, but they persisted as separate social and cultural communities whose boundaries were crossed for business reasons. They were bound as an economic entity, but the lines of social contact were mutually separated. In contrast to these dual towns, Santa Fe remained a single city on the surface, largely because it was the capital of the state where both cultures came together from the beginning.

CULTURAL MIDDLEMEN

One element of the population that brought the two cultures closer was the Jewish merchants, who, as members of a minority catering to both groups, could stand aloof from the animosities that separated Hispanos and Anglo-Americans. Traditionally the Jews have been closer to Hispanic peoples all over the world because many of them, particularly the Sephardics, had a past that linked them with the Spanish speakers in Europe. Even though they had been forced to leave Spain in the sixteenth century, they had reached a zenith of their cultural development there. In Spain they had been the leading merchants during the Middle Ages, and now they met the same civilization in the New World as merchants once again, although not necessarily Sephardics. The roster of merchants in New Mexico today includes many Jewish names among the leading businessmen whose ancestors arrived during the past century from central Europe.

Another group that contributed to better intercultural understanding was the artists and writers who went to Taos and Santa Fe toward the end of the nineteenth century. These Anglo-Americans had a greater historical and artistic perception with which to gauge and judge Indian and Spanish civilizations. Cultured and educated individuals, they showed great concern for the traditions of the country. They were instrumental in restoring historical sites in northern New Mexico, and they wrote about what they saw with greater artistic discrimination. Painters saw the same things that had prompted earlier commentators to say that "the minds of people are as barren as the land with as little hope of being cultivated" or to report that Las Vegas was nothing but a "dirty mud town." But these artists and writers saw other values than had been seen by the men who said that New Mexicans had "inherited all the vices of their ancestors," that they had a natural depravity because "such have been the habits of the Spanish race since time immemorial."

The recognition of the values found in Hispanic culture led not only to the reconstruction of historical buildings but also to the conversion of the modest adobe houses, which the first comers saw, into artistic architectural designs known today variously as Santa Fe houses, Spanish-Indian architecture, and lately simply "southwestern style." The artists put on canvas scenes and landscapes emphasizing beauty rather than desolation. The Hispanos who had become indifferent to their own culture were inspired by what they read and saw and began to recover pride in their past.

Some Hispanos who misunderstood the motives that led men to write about the region, scholars to delve into history, and painters to record on canvas the story of Hispanic culture in the Southwest interpreted these efforts as one more form of exploitation. It is true that many jumped on the bandwagon and wrote inaccurately and with bad taste about the country and its people while others viewed the subject in the same light as a scientist considers an epidemic or a geological formation. As an artist in Taos once said: "In a group of one hundred artists 50 percent are bound to be cock-eyed."

THE TRIETHNIC TRAP

Anthropologist John J. Bodine believes that the situation in Taos militated against the Hispanos, who were caught in a triethnic trap. According to him, the Taos Anglo-Americans,

have consistently placed the Spanish Americans on the lowest rung of the ladder. . . . From the Anglo point of view one can legitimately speak of the mystique of Taos. In its creation the Anglos have glorified Indian culture and relegated the Spanish American to the bottom of the prestige structure.[9]

Even those Anglo-Americans who entered New Mexico during the early days of the Santa Fe Trail and who married Hispano girls are suspect in their motives. Warren A. Beck believes that men like Colonel James Magoffin, of Kentucky, who became a Mexican citizen and accepted the ways of the land, provided a "welcome group around which the ultimate seizure of Mexico's territory in the Southwest could be effected."[10] Many of the scouts, trappers, and traders who lived in Taos and Santa Fe proved quite useful to the American army during the Mexican War, even though they had sworn allegiance to the country that had given them a home, land, and the opportunity to make a livelihood. Magoffin and Kit Carson, who were married to Spanish-speaking women, made no effort to hide their national preference. On the whole it would seem that the initial contact of Hispanic and Anglo-American culture through trade routes was only part of a sequence in the acquisition of the territory by the United States.

One of the social graces that surprised most Anglo-Americans who came into the Southwest for the first time was the brand of courtesy that they observed among the people in all walks of life. When Governor Baca of New Mexico announced a 50 percent increase in duty for imports to the province, Senator Benton of Missouri asked Augustus Storrs about the New Mexicans' attitude toward the United States. The old trader answered by saying that the respect, friendliness, and hospitality with which Anglo-Americans were received was in indication of the way the New Mexicans felt:

The door of hospitality is opened with a cheerful welcome, and every office of friendship and kindness which might be expected from intimate acquaintances is voluntarily proferred by a stranger. . . . In all the principal towns the arrival of the Americans is a source of pleasure, and the evening is dedicated to dancing and festivity.[11]

Storrs appears to have been the kind of person who would elicit this sort of welcome anywhere. His diplomatic manner in dealing with the people of New Mexico was no doubt the reason that he became the first American consul in Santa Fe in 1825.

HISPANIC SOCIAL GRACES

Anglo-Americans always noted and commented on the courtesy of the Hispanos partly because they did not expect people "so far away from civilization" to possess such fine social graces. Imbued with the belief that they were pioneers opening uncharted territory, they forgot that the Southwest had been occupied by another culture for two centuries before their arrival.

As time wore on and the prejudices of their Elizabethan ancestors began to come to the surface, many Anglo-Americans pictured the Mexicans as superficially polite and generous but below that social veneer treacherous, dishonest, and promiscuous. The Hispanos and the Mexicans who were aware of the Anglo-Americans' ulterior motives looked on them as political expansionists, economic materialists, religious heretics, and cultural barbarians. These contradictory attitudes existed at a time when both sides were already suspicious of each other because they were meeting on a sort of battlefield of competitive industry. The object of each party to this meeting was to best the other by any means possible. This was hardly a time of cooperative understanding and was certainly not the most tolerant. As one author put it, "It was a cut-throat enterprise in which no hold was barred."

Before the Anglo-Americans and the Hispanos of the Southwest went to war, they courted each other with phrases couched in diplomatic speech, but after the end of the war with Mexico, when the ultimate issue was decided, Anglo-Americans, now treading on their own national soil, reverted to the standards of social behavior to which they had been conditioned. They began to shun close association with those of darker skin color, and in those who came from the American South these prejudices were accentuated. The constant reference to the color of the Hispano population in the Southwest was indicative of an inherent preoccupation with color shades that would not have bothered other travelers.

APARTHEID MENTALITY

In order not to be considered deviants from standards of acceptance, Anglo-Americans set their villages, or sections of the towns where they lived, apart from the rest of the population. Their choice was not always premeditated; it was simply the observance of a way of doing and a way of thinking to which they had become conditioned because they equated lightness of skin with superiority. Those who decided to marry Hispano girls were said to have "gone native," and if they married Indian girls, they were called "squaw men." The Anglo-Americans may not have been traditional in their thinking, but they were psychologically conditioned to think like the rest of their society.

In writing about their first experiences in the social life of the New Mexicans, Anglo-Americans, who were supposed to be profound believers in the noncaste structure of society, always were profuse in their descriptions of the upper classes. They enjoyed the company of the *ricos* and were very willing to receive an *abrazo* from "Castilian" girls because they were as "white-complexioned as our own Anglo-Saxon daughters." Davis was shocked when he came across a group of 150 *ciboleros*, or buffalo hunters, just as they were setting out from Santa Fe. They had 500 pack animals and 50 *carretas* in which to bring back the already dried *charqui* six months later for sale. Said he: "They made as mottled an uncivilized appearance as can well be imagined; no two of the same costume, and, upon the whole, they looked not unlike a party of gipsies."[12]

The comments on the folkways and appearances of the Hispanos and the Mexicans were a way of looking at other nationalities. When Anglo-Americans described the common people, it was more of a critical appraisal showing disapproval of their habits and appearance. The national dress of other people was usually referred to as "costumes," because most Anglo-Americans considered their style of dress the norm. The same person who described the buffalo hunters as "mottled and uncivilized," because of the way they were dressed took two pages to describe how a "Spanish *caballero*" was dressed in New Mexico. He mentioned every item from the buttons on his trousers to the rowel of his spurs and gave an itemized account of what it cost a mounted gentleman to dress.

A Spanish-Mexican girl models a homespun dress of the kind worn by Spanish settlers of the peasant class.

More than a description, it was an economic appraisal.

The people of the upper Río Grande may have been equally surprised by the attire of the trappers, but one is put hard to find a Spanish description of these men, and particularly what they wore, because the Hispanos were concerned more with the behavior of the Anglo-Americans when they arrived in Taos and in Santa Fe than with their manner of dress. The Hispanos, as products of a culture concerned with being, noticed particularly the nature of Anglo-Americans and in their initial contacts with them were courteous, regardless of how these trappers were outfitted.

The energetic Anglo-Americans, obsessed with change, growth, and development, could not tolerate the casual manner of the Hispanos in New Mexico. This did not mean that the latter could not rise to the occasion when necessary; it simply meant that, until the occasion arose, they did not waste effort by being restless. The suggestion made by some writers that association with the trappers made people in the upper Río Grande more hardy and resistant is another misinterpretation of character when we consider that the New Mexicans had been hardened by two and a half centuries of pioneer existence in a virtually isolated land. Anglo-Americans, coming into a country that was new to them, felt that a change was necessary and that they should be the ones to introduce the change. This is to some degree the attitude of a conquering culture. The Spaniards had earlier tried to change the Indian to conform to their own standards.

After the newcomers had been in northern New Mexico for a while, much of their original zest died down, and, if they remained, they tended to blend and adapt themselves. There never was a complete adjustment, however, because Anglo-Americans continued to arrive and renew the spirit that had brought them in the first place. The Hispanos, on the other hand, had arrived long before the Anglo-Americans, and what changes were needed had been made in colonial days, so that their living patterns were thereafter repetitive from one generation to another. It was not a matter of choice as much as one of custom and tradition. The tendency of the Hispanos after 1848 was to continue as they had always lived, even though they were constantly harassed by those who felt they had a better way of doing. Until Anglo-Americans could overwhelm the original settlers with numbers, they could either adapt, as some

did, or set up their own communities. That is what led to the dual towns throughout the Southwest.

THE PRIMACY SYNDROME

Many of the changes that Anglo-Americans made in the upper Río Grande consisted of the introduction of materials and products to which they were accustomed. Some writers have been misled by the extensive use that the Hispanic settlers made of such staples as beans, chile, and corn, assuming that that was their exclusive fare and that fruits and vegetables were introduced by the first Anglo-Americans of the trade era. True, many useful items were introduced by the Santa Fe Trail merchants, but when the Spaniards entered New Mexico, they brought with them all the edible products known to Mediterranean peoples. As a matter of fact, the northern Europeans did not add a single product to the European menu before they came to the New World.

The reason that men like Josiah Gregg, W. W. H. Davis, and others insisted that the frontiersmen introduced a number of products into the Southwest for the first time is that Americans seem to be unduly concerned with primacy. Unless they are first in everything, they tend to feel inferior. When they went west, they made a note of all the "firsts" and placed placards to commemorate the achievements. When the gallant Colonel Pike went to Colorado, he is said to have been the first to discover the peak that now bears his name, although it had been known to the Spaniards for over two centuries before him as El Capitán.

NEW MEXICANS GO EAST

Although most New Mexicans were not familiar with Anglo-American culture to any great extent before the opening of the Santa Fe trade, a large number of wealthy settlers had traveled east as far as New York. Some of the leading families such as the Pereas, Chávezes, Oteros, Sisneros, Gutiérrezes, and Lunas sent members of their families to private schools in St. Louis and New York City. Schooling in New Mexico consisted for the most part of individual tutoring by itinerant teachers from Mexico for the few who could afford it. There was no school system. In 1837, a Captain Sena from Mexico had a small school in Santa Fe, which was attended by Francisco Perea, Francisco Chávez, and Nestor Armijo, members of families who were active in politics and army life after the province became a territory of the United States.

The experiences their sons had in Yankeeland were comparable with those of any well-to-do Anglo-American young man. Juan and Leandro Perea, together with José Chávez, went to New York City, where they enrolled in Bank Street School, a well-known private school. One of their teachers was a refugee Spaniard, Mariano Velázquez, who, although a member of the Columbia University faculty, devoted his spare time to Bank Street, where a number of leading New Mexicans studied under him. These young men were only three New Mexicans who had the opportunity to receive an education. The few young men from far-off New Mexico who went east to school roomed with Anglo-American students and learned a way of life that the trappers who came to Taos and Santa Fe never could have taught them on the frontier. Instead of waiting for the culture that would eventually assimilate them, they went out to meet it at the source under much more favorable circumstances. Other young students, such as the Oteros and the Lunas, studied in St. Louis and then went on to visit Philadelphia, Baltimore, and other eastern cities. They usually returned by way of the Erie Canal to Chicago, after stopping to sightsee in Washington. Francisco Perea was presented by his father to President Zachary Taylor on one of these trips, and fifteen years later, as a colonel in the United States Army, he was presented to President Abraham Lincoln.

Many of the wealthy stock raisers of northern New Mexico traveled on business caravans to California, where they toured such cities as San Francisco and Los Angeles. On the return trip some continued south to Mexico City before returning home. By the slow means of transportation these trips extended over the better part of a year.

At the beginning of the Civil War bearers of most of these names appear on the record as officers in the Union army, where they performed creditably. A larger percentage of Hispanos enlisted in the army from New Mexico than from any other state, in proportion to population, according to historical records. During the war Colonel Perea was placed in command of four battalions of volunteers from New Mexico Territory. A few decades later their descendants made up a sizable portion of Teddy Roosevelt's Rough Riders in the Spanish-American War.

It was an impressive record by men whom the Anglo-Americans of the 1840's characterized as devoid of initiative, because they appeared too casual and easygoing. Colonel Perea was elected to the United States Congress and also served four terms in the territorial legislature. He was present at Ford's Theater the night Lincoln was assassinated. His eventful life included two marriages and eighteen children by each wife.

Tomás Gutiérrez, a companion of Perea's school days in New York, learned English so well that he stayed in the East for a time and made a number of speeches in New England during Lincoln's presidential campaign. According to those who heard him, he "spoke impeccable English." The New Mexicans' interest in politics was an acculturation product that began early and has continued as a way of life in the state from the largest city to the humblest pueblo.

The meeting of Hispanic and Anglo-American cultures at the beginning of the past century did not always result in the total domination of the cultural minority, as it is sometimes supposed. There were always enough Pereas, Oteros, Chávezes, and others with the same drive and motivation to dispel the idea that all Hispanos were unable to perform at the same level as "enlightened" citizens. The meeting of the two cultures in the upper Río Grande was also made more viable by the participation of such men as Bent, Magoffin, Carson, and others who joined the Pereas, the Jaramillos, and the Bacas during the early and critical period of intercultural adjustment. Much of the behavior pattern that continues in New Mexico evolved from those beginnings.

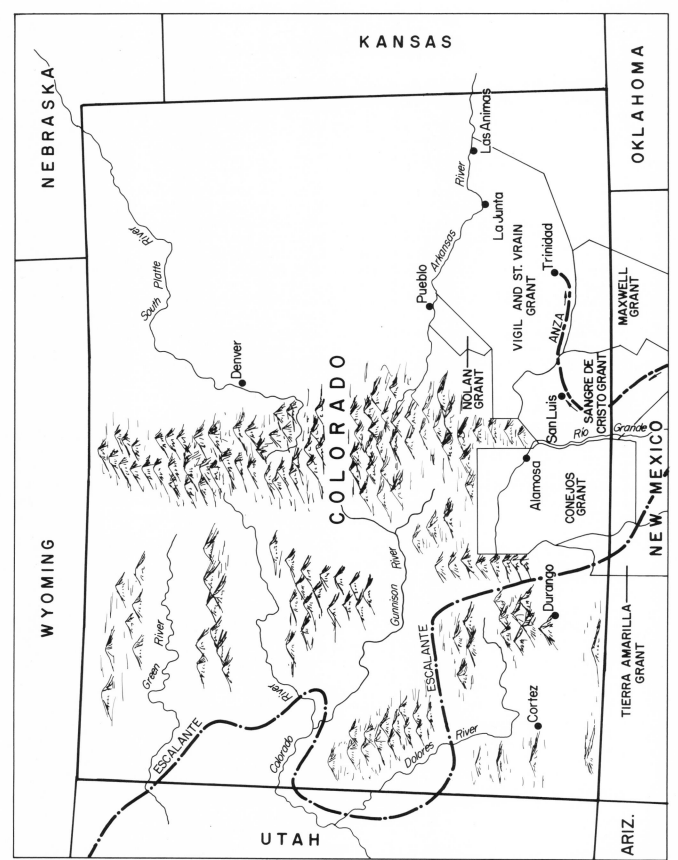

KANSAS

NEBRASKA

OKLAHOMA

WYOMING

UTAH

ARIZ.

NEW MEXICO

COLORADO

Las Animas

La Junta

Trinidad

Pueblo

Denver

San Luis

Alamosa

Durango

Cortez

South Platte River

Arkansas River

Green River

Gunnison River

Colorado River

Dolores River

Rio Grande

NOLAN GRANT

VIGIL AND ST. VRAIN GRANT

ANZA

SANGRE DE CRISTO GRANT

MAXWELL GRANT

CONEJOS GRANT

ESCALANTE

ESCALANTE

TIERRA AMARILLA GRANT

Hispanic Colorado

Trading, mining, and agriculture were the basic interests that kept Spanish, French, and English settlers on the move in the Southwest during the era of discovery and also in succeeding periods. During the first two and a half centuries that followed the settlement of New Mexico, no significant mineral discoveries were made to initiate large-scale population movements. The Spaniards of the seventeenth century had all the cultivable land in the upper Río Grande they needed for a relatively small number of colonists that was spread over the intermountain valleys in the early stages of expansion.

The Spanish conquistadors were not content, however, with establishing a colony and settling down. Juan de Oñate, who led the settlement vanguard into the northernmost province of the Spanish Empire in 1598, undertook the first exploration expedition scarcely a month after his colony had been established in San Juan. In the months that followed, he explored hundreds of miles west, east, and north, seeking information about the surrounding tribes and looking for mineral deposits. The conquest and settlement of the New World were enterprises carried out by a vast military and political structure in which the army, the church, and the settlers took active parts.

The mining possibilities, and the rich farming land of what is now Colorado, did not escape the observation of the early Spanish explorers. They named the rivers, valleys, and mountains beyond Pike's Peak, known to them as El Capitán, and took careful note of the flora and fauna of the region. The Anglo-American frontiersmen who arrived 250 years later found a country from Kansas to California that had been crisscrossed by Spanish armies, by explorers, and by missionaries. The topographical landmarks had names that the newcomers translated into English whenever possible, even if they came up with such approximations as Wolfano for Huérfano and Picketwire for Purgatorio. The Arkansas River, which was to become the international boundary between Spain and the United States after the Adams-Onís Treaty of 1819, was known as the Napestle, although Ulibarrí christened it Río Grande de San Francisco when he crossed it in 1706. The Canadian River was originally Río Colorado, the Red was Río Rojo, the North Platte was San Lorenzo, and the South Platte was Río de Jesús María. The Platte farther east had the unaesthetic name Río Chato, for reasons known to the Spaniards alone. The Purgatoire of southern Colorado was known as Las Animas, and the Saint Charles was San Carlos. Many of the principal mountain ranges, such as Sangre de Cristo and San Juan, retained their original Spanish names, except Pike's Peak, which became rechristened with the American explorer's name.

The expansion of Hispanic civilization into Colorado was a process that took place in three stages, beginning with the long period of reconnaissance and exploration from the sixteenth through the eighteenth centuries. The second period began with the Mexican land-grants era and with the first attempts by Taos families to settle in the Conejos River valley. The third stage of Hispanic expansion began after the American occupation, particularly when rapid industrialization took place in Colorado.

The first Spanish contacts in Colorado are not generally well known, because most people assume that the founding of San Luis in the south in 1852 constitutes the first entry of Hispanic people into the state. Historians and other informed individuals are well aware, however, of the events that took place beginning after the middle of the sixteenth century. Leo Grebler has offered this explanation for the lack of information about the Southwest:

Because so many Americans have a limited knowledge of their country's history, they are only dimly conscious of the early colonization of parts of the Southwest by people of Hispanic-Mexican origin. Or, if they know about it, they are inclined to shrug it off as a quaint accident of history without consequence.[1]

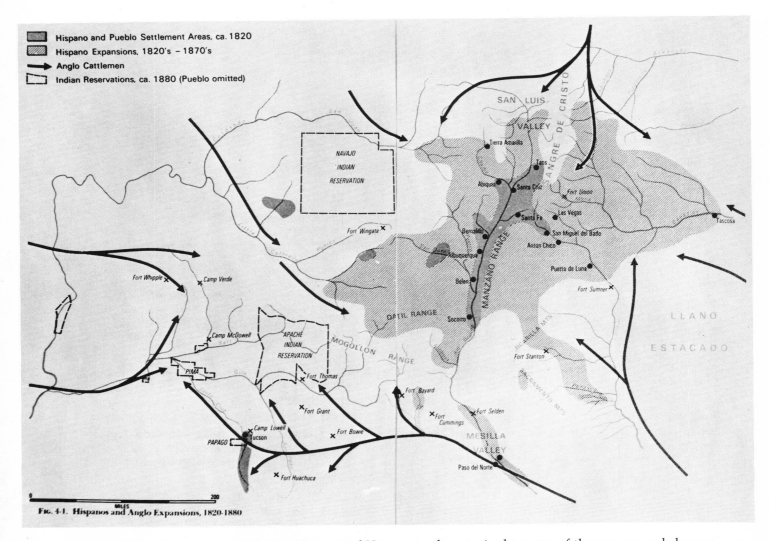

Legend:
- Hispano and Pueblo Settlement Areas, ca. 1820
- Hispano Expansions, 1820's – 1870's
- Anglo Cattlemen
- Indian Reservations, ca. 1880 (Pueblo omitted)

FIG. 4-1. Hispanos and Anglo Expansions, 1820-1880

Hispano and Anglo expansion, 1820–80. The original Hispano settlements in the center of the map expanded many times over into west Texas, eastern Arizona, and southern California. Reproduced from D. W. Meinig, *Southwest: Three Peoples in Geographical Change, 1600–1970* (New York: Oxford University Press, 1971).

The story of the West from an eastern viewpoint naturally begins with the exploits of men like Lewis, Clark, and Pike and other forerunners of the American westward movement. This leaves a gap of more than two centuries between the modern Anglo-American period and the Spanish explorations of Vásquez de Coronado, Juan de Oñate, Diego de Vargas, Juan Bautista de Anza, and others who reconnoitered and explored much of what is now the state of Colorado. Many topographical features were named by these early explorers as they opened the trails that others followed centuries later. The Spaniards traveled north from outposts in the province of New Mexico, while the Anglo-Americans pushed from the Middle West on trapping and fur-trading expeditions that eventually extended into the Spanish settlements. Because Anglo-Americans are usually more interested in the westward movement of their own frontiersmen, readers are more concerned with the exploits of these men than with the history that predates the American occupation of the Southwest. The resulting impression is that the American frontiersmen, known variously as mountain men, traders, and trappers, discovered an unknown land. Such expressions as "the first white man to cross the Rocky Mountains" and "the first white baby born in the West" overlook the long period of Spanish history of the Southwest.

CORONADO CROSSES COLORADO

Francisco Vásquez de Coronado was the first Spanish explorer to cross part of the territory from which Colorado was formed. When this conquistador and a detachment of his army marched along the Cimarron in quest of the mythical Quivira in 1540, he was opening the way for many others who became more familiar with the eastern portion of the state in the years that followed. As Alfred Barnaby Thomas says: "His Odyssey to Quivira initiated on the plains a long procession of Spanish explorers. Their history furnishes the needed perspective with which to view the activity of the Anglo-American—i.e., the last phase of western plains exploration."[2]

The failed dream of fabulously rich cities and the treasures of Quivira that led Coronado's expedition over the Southwest was a disappointment that produced a lull in northern exploration for four decades. The Spanish frontier moved north from Mexico, however, as new mining sites, such as Zacatecas, Durango, and Parral, were discovered. By 1580 the northern settlements had reached the headwaters of the Conchos River and had opened a much shorter approach to the New Mexico region than the one Coronado used in 1540. One of the first aspirants to plan an expedition into the "unknown north" was Agustín Rodríguez, a Franciscan missionary. He obtained permission in Mexico City to form a party with which to explore the land of the Pueblos mentioned by Indian captives taken in punitive campaigns. Fray Rodríguez and two other Franciscans were escorted by a squad of soldiers and their commander, Francisco Sánchez Chamuscado. The small party journeyed down the Conchos into the Río Grande and then followed it north as far as the Manzano Mountains of central New Mexico, east of present Albuquerque. Their enthusiastic report of the country that they had visited was an incentive to larger expeditions that penetrated deeper into the new land and reached closer to what is now Colorado. The explorers of each succeeding attempt used the experience of preceding expeditions as a springboard to further explorations. The Spaniards arrived in what is now Colorado in gradual stages.

THE PURGATORY IS BORN

"A short cut to glory," as one historian put it, was taken by Gaspar Castaño de Sosa in 1590 with an expedition of 170 people, including women and children. He traveled up the Pecos River and went as far as Taos, where he was arrested and brought back to the Spanish settlements. This thwarted attempt was headed north and, had it not been stopped, would have reached Colorado.

The expedition that followed Castaño de Sosa's interrupted attempt started as an official raid against rebellious Indians in 1594, but the leaders, Francisco Leyba de Bonilla and Antonio Gutiérrez de Humaña, moved by reports of northeastern wealth, decided to do some explorations of their own northeast of New Mexico. They reached the Arkansas and continued probably as far as the Platte. A quarrel between the two leaders led to the death of Captain Leyba de Bonilla at the hands of Gutiérrez Humaña. No journal was kept of this expedition because it was unauthorized and, more important, because of the tragic end of the entire party, with the exception of an Indian named Jusepe, who fled and was held captive by the Apaches for a year. He escaped and made his way to one of the Pecos pueblos, where Oñate found him in 1599.[3]

Gutiérrez de Humaña had gone beyond New Mexico into Kansas along the Arkansas, but whether or not he touched on what is now Colorado soil is a matter of conjecture. The tragic ending of this expedition has given rise to the idea that, because these Spaniards died without benefit of clergy, they were souls lost in Purgatory, a theological error that produced the name of a river in southern Colorado, Las Animas Perdidas de Purgatorio. Whether Leyba de Bonilla and Gutiérrez de Humaña crossed this river or not, the folklore that surrounds it did cross it and produced not only the name Purgatorio for the stream but also Las Animas for a county and for a city in Colorado. If we consider that Colorado was until 1861 a part of the Kansas Territory, it can be safely asserted that some of these expeditions did cross the state at that time.

JUAN DE ONATE IN COLORADO

Juan de Oñate, settler and governor of the province of New Mexico, was another early Spaniard who touched on lands of which Colorado was a part during the first decade of its existence.

Remnants of the apple orchard planted by Spanish settlers in the eighteenth century in a mountain town east of Albuquerque. The Manzano Mountains took their name from this orchard, literally "apple mountains."

In 1601, Don Juan led an expedition consisting of "more than seventy men, . . . all very well equipped, more than seven hundred horses and mules, six mule carts, and two carts drawn by oxen conveying four pieces of artillery, and with servants to carry the necessary baggage, . . ." according to the "true account of the expedition."[4] The army crossed the Pecos River and the Canadian farther east, following a northeastern direction until they reached the Arkansas. This seemed to be the usual travel route used by early explorers who still were guided by thoughts of Quivira. Oñate also passed through the land out of which Colorado was carved centuries later, following a route closer to the southeast corner of the state.

FIRST EXPEDITION TO COLORADO

The first expedition to penetrate what is now Colorado was led by Juan de Archuleta in 1664, when he was sent to retrieve a group of malcontent Taos Indians who had run away to El Cuartelejo in eastern Colorado. Archuleta took with him twenty soldiers and a force of Indian auxiliaries and brought back the Indians. This brief statement is all the description given of a perilous trip over mountains and plains where the Apaches roamed, a trip that probably took about a month and a half. In all probability the Archuleta party went north from Santa Fe by way of Taos, entered the plains by way of Trinidad or Walsenburg, and crossed the Arkansas near the present site of Pueblo. This can be adduced from other expeditions and from a study of the terrain. From there Archuleta and his party probably turned east to the Cuartelejo in the Apache country and found the Indians that he had been sent to retrieve. From then on, Colorado's streams, mountains, and peaks became familiar sites for the exploring Spaniards.

VARGAS IN COSTILLA COUNTY

By the middle of the seventeenth century the Spanish settlers of northern New Mexico had become well acquainted with the territory north of Taos and with southern Colorado. When Diego de Vargas led an expedition in 1694 into what is now Costilla County, he spoke of rivers and mountains by names that were familiar to him and his army. Spanish expedition leaders entering unknown country usually named the topographical features as they crossed them, but that Vargas

did not bother to name the rivers, mountains, and peaks that he used as landmarks for his route clearly indicates how familiar he must have been with the terrain.

After the reconquest of 1692, the Spaniards in Santa Fe were hedged in by surrounding hostile Indians who had thoughts of attacking the garrison and destroying the colony as they had done in 1680. Two years after the reconquest the supplies that the colonists had brought from the south, and those they had gleaned from abandoned granaries, were at dangerously low levels, with no immediate relief in sight. Vargas, after conferring with some experienced natives of the land, decided to search for food among the abandoned Tano and Tewa pueblos. In his roundabout journey, trying to avoid contact with the hostiles who surrounded him, he went by way of the "Yuttas" (Utes), a friendly nation from which he could come out on the Chama River and find buffalo. He placed the train between a vanguard of forty soldiers, and a rear guard of thirty more well-armed veterans. His route carried him north to Arroyo Hondo, past San Juan, where he crossed the Río Grande, and followed the Chama to Caliente Creek and San Antonio Creek. He was attacked by a combined party of Taos and Picuris Indians, but they were no match for the army. They camped along the Culebra River in present-day Costilla County, where the Utes mistook them for Tewas and attacked. The mistake was rectified, and the Utes explained that they had attacked Vargas because the Tewas and Picuris went into Ute country disguised as Spaniards and even carried a bugle. On the return trip the Vargas expedition found a large herd of buffalo that supplied them well with needed meat. They also hunted elk and other game before returning to Santa Fe on July 23, 1694, after having been gone for seventeen days and having traveled around 350 miles. Don Diego José de Vargas Zapata Luján Ponce de León y Contreras, governor and captain general of New Mexico, had journeyed to southern Colorado eighty-two years before the United States had come into being.[5]

ULIBARRI TAKES POSSESSION

Governor Francisco Cuervo y Valdez of the province of New Mexico received word from Don Lorenzo, the Picuris chief, who had fled to El Cuartelejo in 1696, stating his people's desire to return to Picuris. In 1706 the Spanish governor sent Juan

The annual reenactment at Santa Fe of the entry of Diego de Vargas into New Mexico as he reconquered the territory after the Indian Revolt of 1680. Photograph by Mark Nohl.

de Ulibarrí, a seasoned veteran, with forty soldiers and one hundred Indian allies to retrieve the fugitives. Unlike his predecessors, he did not go to El Cuartelejo by way of the Canadian River but traveled north to Taos and thence to the location of present-day Trinidad, crossed the Purgatoire (which he named the Santa Ana River), and reached the Arkansas after naming every stream and river along the way. He crossed the Arkansas, christened it Río Grande de San Francisco, about fifteen miles from the site of present-day Pueblo, and was so impressed by the valley that he made an entry in his journal describing it: "The plain on our side is a strand of a long league

of level land and extremely fertile as is shown by the many plums, cherries, and wild grapes which there are on it. . . . It bathes the best and broadest valley discovered in New Spain. . . ." Twenty days after leaving Santa Fe, Ulibarrí reached his goal on August 2, 1706. The Apaches were not hesitant in returning the Picuris, and within ten more days they were ready to return.

Before beginning the long journey south, at a time of the year when they were certain to run into early winter snows, "General Juan de Ulibarrí, sergeant-major of this kingdom," as he called himself officially, decided to take formal possession of the land that he named "the broad

136

new province of San Luis." His journal entry reads in part:

The Reverend Father Fray Domínguez de Aranz . . . intoned the *Te Deum Laudamus*. . . . After these holy ceremonies were over, the royal Ensign Don Francisco de Váldez drew his sword, and I [Ulibarrí], after making note of the events of the day and hour on which we arrived, said in a clear, intelligible voice: "Knights, Companions and Friends: Let the broad new province of San Luis and the great settlement of Santo Domingo of El Cuartelejo be pacified by the arms of us who are the vassals of our monarch, king and natural lord, Don Phillip V—may he live forever." The royal Ensign said: "Is there anyone to contradict?" All responded, "No." Then he said, "Long live the king! Long live the king! Long live the king!" and cutting the air in all four directions with his sword the Ensign signaled for the discharge of guns. After throwing up our hats and making other signs of rejoicing, the ceremony came to an end.[6]

With this colorful ceremony the region that is now Colorado became part of the Spanish Empire in America, seventy years before the new republic of the United States was born. Both the name San Luis, now transferred to southwestern Colorado, and the Ulibarrí family name have come down to the present day as a continuance of the state's Hispanic origin.

VALVERDE RENAMES THE PURGATORY

The Spaniards of the seventeenth and eighteenth centuries made long expeditions into Colorado for three reasons: first, to punish Indian raiders or to bring back fugitives and captives from El Cuartelejo; second, to scout for indications of French incursions into Spanish territory; third, to search for possible mines. They looked on the French traders as intruders who were trying to occupy the territory of Spain by inciting the Pawnees and the Comanches, who entered the Spanish domains for the first time in 1704 to attack the Spanish settlements.

In carrying out the above objectives, the Spaniards used three routes into Colorado. When they went to El Cuartelejo after fugitives or to repulse the incursion of the French, they headed north from Santa Fe and then east to the Culebra Mountains. They turned northeast to the Purgatoire and thence to the eastern plains. When they were prospecting for minerals, they usually went north to La Plata Mountains, sometimes as far as present-day Gunnison, and into the Great Basin past

the present state line. The third route they used was a more direct route north to Taos through the present San Luis Valley, Vargas' route in 1694.

The expedition of Governor Antonio Valverde Cosío in 1719 against the Comanches was a much larger force than the one taken by Ulibarrí thirteen years earlier, but it was directed toward the same Cuartelejo, where the Comanches usually attacked the Apache tribes, such as Jicarillas, who were friendly to the Spaniards. Valverde started from the presidio of Santa Fe on September 15, 1719, with 60 presidials. In Taos he opened ranks for volunteers to join the expedition and increased his force by 45 settlers and 465 Indian allies. He enlisted 196 more Indians from the Jicarilla Apaches along the Cimarron, bringing his command to around 800, including regulars, militia, and Indian allies. He also had a combined total of over 1,000 horses, not including pack animals. With this strong force Valverde marched north, crossed the Purgatoire, and renamed it Las Animas. By this last name the river was known for over 70 years. It appears on Escalante's map, undoubtedly prepared by his cartographer, Bernardo de Miera y Pacheco, in 1778, and again the name Las Animas is used by Juan López in his map of 1795.

Valverde did not follow the difficult trail of Ulibarrí because he had a large enough force to repulse any attack by the Comanches and the Utes. He moved northward through the location of present-day Trinidad, crossed the Huérfano River and proceeded to a point below the Arkansas southeast of Pueblo. For several days Valverde followed cold Comanche trails and campfires until he met the messengers from El Cuartelejo announcing the coming of the Apaches, who were eager to talk to him about protection from the hostile Comanches and Pawnees. After a long meeting several miles east of La Junta, he decided to start back before winter set in. The Apaches told the governor about the alliance of the Pawnees and the Jumanos with the French, the armaments they used, and the imminent danger of attack.

Valverde's journal is an interesting and valuable document filled with human interest and with details of what they did en route. It reveals a great deal about Spanish culture and Indian life. He mentions coming to an Apache camp where the fields of corn and squashes were growing and cautioning his men not to tread on the fields and damage the growing crops. When he met with

Indians, he always shared his food with them, even to the point of offering his own plate of mutton when Chief Carlana arrived at dinnertime.

Valverde's diary is interspersed with anecdotes about meeting with bears, lions, and other fauna of the region. He was impressed by the abundance of game, fish, and plants along the trail, although the men's experience with poison ivy and the painful reactions to it were not exactly pleasant. The governor's proclivity for naming every stream he crossed, even renaming those that had already been named, and the exclusive use he made of saints' names are somewhat tiring. He must have been a very religious man, to judge by the number of masses that were held along the way, even when the party was pressed for time. Unfortunately, the part of the diary that tells of his return trip has been lost, and historians have to conjecture the route he followed. Valverde did mention that he did not return by the plains, which meant that he could return by the only alternate route: following the Arkansas to the Huérfano River and then crossing over the Sangre de Cristos to Taos. The inference is well taken by Thomas, who concluded that the governor returned by way of Taos and then south to Santa Fe.

Valverde's report to the viceroy in Mexico City that there were French establishments on the South Platte was very disquieting. The viceroy sent orders to establish a presidio at El Cuartelejo with a complement of twenty-five soldiers and some missionaries. The purpose of this fort was to hold back the advance of the French from the Platte to the Arkansas and possibly even to the Río Grande. Governor Valverde preferred to establish an outpost on the Canadian in the *rancherías* of the friendly Jicarilla Apaches one hundred miles from Taos. In the meanwhile, the governor sent a reconnaissance expedition that would also be able to attack the French and their allies if it met them.

VILLASUR AT THE PLATTE

Pedro de Villasur left Santa Fe in July, 1720, with a well-equipped army of forty-two soldiers, three settlers, and sixty Indians. The now-familiar route to Taos was followed by the expedition to the Cimarron and northward to Trinidad and Walsenburg. They crossed the Arkansas below Pueblo and continued to El Cuartelejo. They did not tarry there, because their object was to contact the French who were beyond Colorado in Nebraska. The army came to the South Platte and found no Frenchmen there, and so they crossed over to the North Platte and decided to look for the Pawnees who were allies of the French. Not far above the junction of the North and the South Platte they found a large encampment of hostile Pawnees who rejected all overtures made by Villasur. The following morning, before sunrise, Villasur and his expedition were encircled by Pawnees, who poured a deadly fire into the Spanish camp and almost wiped out the expedition. The amount of gunfire, in addition to the Pawnee arrows, convinced those who escaped that there were Frenchmen in the attack. It was a setback to Spanish arms that at the time seemed almost fatal. The Spaniards had not only reached Colorado again but had crossed it from south to northeast, albeit with disastrous results.

EXPLORATION OF THE GUNNISON COUNTRY

Governor Tomas Vélez Cachupín of New Mexico was greatly interested in exploiting the mineral resources of the province. Rumored mineral deposits in the region northwest of Santa Fe led him to send several expeditions into what is now southwestern Colorado. In 1765 he sent Juan María de Rivera into the San Juan and Gunnison country with a prospecting party and, encouraged by Rivera's reports, sent two more parties, the last one in 1775. After several months of prospecting along the San Juan River and its tributaries, Rivera reported promising gold and silver discoveries. He crossed the La Plata Mountains to the Dolores River and penetrated north to the Gunnison River, where he carved the date and his name on a cottonwood at the mouth of the Uncompahgre.

Historians assume that not only Rivera but also other Spaniards must have prospected throughout the southwestern Colorado region, to judge by the names they gave to the mountains and streams, names that have been retained. La Plata, which means "silver," was given to both mountain and stream because silver was found there. Such river names as Animas, Mancos, Florida, Los Pinos, and the San Juan itself date back to the Spanish period of exploration around the time that Washington was fighting the British. These excursions also served to prepare men like Andrés Muñiz and Joaquín Laín, who later served as guides to the Escalante party in 1776.

THE DOMINGUEZ AND ESCALANTE TRAIL

The next explorer to penetrate into Colorado on the way to California was Fray Silvestre Vélez de Escalante, who came to New Mexico in 1768 and became interested in a joint project that Father Garcés had proposed when he was working in Arizona. Actually the Escalante expedition grew out of the interest that the Jesuits had manifested in joining the province of New Mexico with California. Garcés had accompanied Juan Bautista de Anza when he pioneered the first overland route to California from Tubac, Arizona.

The Escalante expedition consisted of the nominal head, Fray Francisco Atanasio Domínguez, Escalante, and eight horsemen, including mapmaker Don Bernardo de Miera y Pacheco, who was "to make a map of the land they might go through." Escalante's plan was to avoid crossing the chasm of the Grand Canyon by traveling through the friendly Ute territory. He left Santa Fe on July 29, 1776, and went directly to Chama, crossed what is now the Colorado–New Mexico border on August 5, in the vicinity of the Navajo River. He followed the Navajo to the junction of the San Juan near Pagosa Junction, describing that country as having "leafy forests of white poplars, low oaks, cherry trees, apple trees, citron [lemon] trees and cacti." He was in Colorado from August 5 to September 11, entering north of Dulce, New Mexico, and arriving in present-day Utah below Dinosaur National Monument on U.S. Highway 40. As was customary when Spaniards traveled over uncharted territory, Escalante named a few places along the way. Like his predecessor Ulibarrí he gave a complete description of the country he traversed and pointed out various locations where he felt that settlements could be established and farming could be successfully undertaken, observations that materialized years later. Coloradoans may derive great satisfaction from knowing that the scenic beauty of the state did not escape the observant eye of nature-loving Spaniards like Father Escalante, long before tourism became a significant economic factor in the state.

ANZA SOUTH OF PUEBLO

A man who deserves to be remembered in the history of Colorado is Juan Bautista de Anza, governor of New Mexico from 1777 to 1788. He was a second-generation *criollo* from a distinguished Spanish family in Sonora. Among other things, he pacified the Indians of that state and later founded San Francisco, according to Bolton. One of the first problems that he faced in New Mexico was the constant forays of the Apaches, the Utes, and particularly the powerful Comanche nation, who attacked the weaker tribes and wiped out Indian pueblos and Spanish settlements alike when they needed horses and slaves for trading.

When he became governor of New Mexico, Anza gave the utmost priority to the Comanche problem. After training an army of six hundred mounted soldiers, Governor Anza moved north through the San Luis Valley, defeated the rear guard of the Comanches, and engaged the main body of warriors south of Pueblo at the foot of Greenhorn Mountain. The Spanish army retrieved a considerable amount of property—more than one hundred horses could carry, according to Anza—and routed the Comanches. Most of the important chiefs were taken as prisoners, and the leader, the vaunted Cuerno Verde, or Green Horn, whose depredations had been the scourge of the Southwest, perished in the encounter. As a reminder of Anza's successful expedition, a town, a river, and a mountain peak in Colorado bear the name of his Comanche adversary, whom Anza admired for his daring and valor. The irony of fate is such that Anza's name has been reserved for motels instead. The confrontation of the Southwest's leading Indian chief and the Spanish commander was also reported by the popular muse in a historical play entitled *Los Comanches*, where the encounter is still reenacted and the final battle recorded in heroic verse. For almost two centuries the play resulting from this battle and three landmarks in Colorado have attested to the struggle of Indian and European for the hegemony of the Southwest.

ANZA RESETTLES THE COMANCHES

Governor Anza understood the Indian problem in the Southwest better than most Spanish commanders who came in contact with the aborigines. He realized that the way to solve the problem was not simply by waging war, although he first had to gain their respect by conquest, a pattern common among the Indians. Once having done this, he set out to make peace not only between Indians and Spaniards but also among the Indians who were constantly warring with each other. First, he managed to bring the Utes and the Comanches to terms. Knowing that the Comanches were the most powerful and most able fighters, he brought the principal chiefs to Santa Fe after the battle and received them with great honors and a fiesta. A few years later he brought together the Comanches in Pecos, north of Santa Fe, and entrusted the successor of Cuerno Verde with keeping the peace in the Southwest, an honor that Ecueracapa readily accepted. A trading fair followed, during which a schedule of prices was set to protect Indians who did not have a strong sense of material values. The next step in removing the constant threat of the plains, was to resettle this warring tribe by making agriculturists from seminomads. Unlike his predecessors, Anza did not set out to punish his adversaries by executing them or by enslaving them. He was one of the few Spanish commanders—perhaps the first—who tried to help the Indians and the settlers by ensuring peace among them.

To resettle this warring nation, Anza set aside some land on the Arkansas, provided the Indians with seed, plows, and all the necessary farming implements, as well as people who could teach them how to farm. Later, at the request of the Jupe Comanches, he sent thirty Spaniards from New Mexico to help them build houses for their new village, San Carlos. It was the first resettlement project in Colorado and was, in a sense, the first unrestricted Indian reservation. Unfortunately, when Don Juan returned to his hacienda in Sonora, the Comanches also left the village, fearing that they could not enjoy the same guarantees under other Spanish leaders. They were probably right, for Colonel Anza was unique among the Spanish conquistadors. That Anza was a second-generation Spaniard, a *criollo* who was not planning to return to Spain, where he might live in the splendor of his conquistador laurels, but an American who was willing to share with the original inhabitants the land and its resources may have been the reason for his success in dealing with the Indians. If we add to these characteristics his great integrity and courage, his unusual leadership may be better understood. Colorado does well in claiming as part of its history an early American who left such a positive record for posterity.

Soon after American independence was won, the Anglo-Americans began to "cast covetous eyes," as one writer puts it, toward the West. The incentives were many: riches in gold and silver extracted from mines by Spaniards, trapping for pelts along the virgin streams, trading with

the citizens of far-off Santa Fe, and the acquisition of land were motivating drives in the Yankees. The land along the Mississippi had been ceded to Spain by the French in 1763, and so those living within the boundaries of the Louisiana Territory were already in Spanish land. If they continued to move west into New Mexico and Texas, they were not entering a different country. That changed, of course, in 1800, when Louisiana was ceded back to France.

In 1773 the relatively easy journey to Santa Fe by John Rozee Peyton, the first Anglo-American to enter the city from the east, would not have been so easy if it had been attempted thirty years later. One difficult barrier that stood in the way of trade and travel was the large number of Indian tribes that inhabited and roamed the prairies between United States territory and the Spanish frontier. In the struggle for supremacy along this frontier the Indian was often a pawn whose interests could be served by the quality and quantity of gifts bestowed on him by the French, the Anglo-Americans, and the Spaniards.

The official expeditions sent by the United States government, such as those led by Lewis and Clark and by Zebulon Pike, indicated to the Spaniards the ultimate intentions of the newly formed republic. What they failed to grasp was the degree of aggressiveness of the Americans moving on the western frontier. In an effort to sound out the intentions of the French and of the Anglo-Americans, Spain sent expeditions north and east into Colorado and Texas. All military parties were ordered to enlist the cooperation of such tribes as the Comanches, the Pawnees, and the Kiowas. To accomplish this alliance, large quantities of presents and medals were to be distributed among the tribal chiefs. The Anglo-Americans and the French gave arms and ammunition to the Indians, tactfully strengthening their relations with tribes who were ambivalent about the Spaniards.

PATHFINDERS OF SPANISH DAYS

One pioneer pathfinder employed by the Spanish governor in Santa Fe was a French interpreter and gunsmith named Pedro Vial, whose first mission was the opening of a trail from San Antonio to Santa Fe in 1786. For two decades Vial—who usually traveled alone and wrote his reports and diaries in poor French that had to be translated into Spanish—crossed over uncharted territory to Natchitoches, St. Louis, and the rest of the

Spanish Southwest, including Colorado. He was at home with Utes, Comanches, Sioux, and Pawnees and particularly with all tribes with which he had to deal in carrying out his missions for the Spanish government.

On October 14, 1805, Governor Joaquín del Real Alencáster of New Mexico sent Vial on an expedition to the Pawnees with a set of detailed instructions. Vial was to spend the winter with the Pawnees and to "inform himself of the progress of the Anglo-Americans in Missouri. . . ."[7] Vial was to learn all he could about the Lewis and Clark Expedition and also win the friendship of the Pawnees and other Indians of the region.

Vial's party left Santa Fe in October, 1805, and traveled north by way of Taos, where he enlisted fifty more recruits. He continued northeastward and crossed the Vermejo River and the Colorado, which today is called the Canadian. The men penetrated what is now Colorado and followed Las Animas River (as the Purgatoire was called by the Spaniards) until they reached the junction with the Arkansas near the location of present-day Las Animas (had Vial been a Spaniard, he would have referred to the Arkansas by its Indian name, Napestle, or by the Spanish appellation, Río Grande de San Francisco).

They were met on the north side of the Arkansas by a band of over one hundred unidentified Indians, who rejected the expedition's peaceful overtures. The Indians attacked at midnight and pillaged their provisions and the implements that they had destined for presents. After a series of running attacks the Indians withdrew, and the Spanish party decided to return to Santa Fe because they were running low on ammunition. Several significant features about these Indians were mentioned by Vial. They were heavily dressed, they had no arrows, they were mounted in battle,

and they all used firearms. Loomis and Nasatir conclude from these data that the affair had "all the earmarks of an American-instigated attack!" The Vial party sustained only one casualty, a soldier wounded in the leg. There seems to be a discrepancy in the report of the battle: Vial speaks of the enemy having one hundred men when they first met, but after the battle he says that, "notwithstanding the fact that their force was three times the size of ours, started to withdraw." This would mean that the Indians had three hundred warriors to his one hundred soldiers.

Pedro Vial and his men were among the last to enter Colorado on official business of the Spanish government. His associate, Juan Lucero, of Santa Fe, continued successfully on many solo expeditions at the suggestion of Governor Alencáster, who was well pleased with his performance. In 1806, Lucero and his interpreter, Martín, were sent to meet with the Comanches at the confluence of the Almagre, the Fountain River today, and the Arkansas. His mission was to win the cooperation of the Comanches and also to enquire about the activities of the Anglo-Americans who were moving into Spanish territory. He continued his travels into Indian country as an emissary of the Spanish government and was probably the last person of the colonial period to make official Spanish contact with what is now Colorado.

The first period of Hispanic history in the state ended with the activities of Carabineer Lucero and Pedro Vial, the Frenchman who was in the service of the Spanish crown the last twenty years of his life. Together they opened new trails to Santa Fe, fought Indians defensively, and unintentionally helped open the way for the commerce of the prairies that eventually became a connecting link between the settled Hispano Mexicans of the Southwest and incoming Anglo-Americans.

The movement of Hispanos into Colorado coincided with the westward movement of Anglo-American traders and French trappers even before Mexican independence. The first attempt of New Mexicans to settle into what is now southern Colorado in the San Luis Valley was made in 1842, but the resistance of the Utes and Navajos drove the farmers back to the Colorado–New Mexico line. Ten years before that they had participated in trading enterprises with Anglo-Americans and Frenchmen along the Huérfano River and in the headwaters of the Purgatoire, when the Bent brothers built Bent Fort in 1842 near present-day Pueblo.

Anglo-American and French trappers had been working the Colorado streams since the 1820's but had not penetrated south into Spanish territory because of Spain's restrictive policies. After Mexican independence was won, the cooperative attitude of the Mexican government brought the mountain men to Taos, and eventually the combined efforts of the Anglo-American frontiersmen and the Spanish-Mexican pioneers began the second stage of Colorado history. As long as the fur trappers lived along the streams and away from centers of civilization, the need for social life was negligible. But as the fur trade declined and they began to establish trading posts and farms, the settled way of life demanded some of the basic amenities of home life.

The only social pattern available in the territory was provided by the Spanish settlers, who had been in the Southwest for over two centuries and had adapted themselves to frontier life. They led a simple life, which over the centuries had lost the restlessness and acquisitiveness of the Anglo-American newcomers. The early conquistadors had been motivated by the same spirit of adventure that brought the mountain men into Colorado and New Mexico. The differences in their achievements were conditioned by the period in which they lived, and so the social order they established was characteristic of the culture that they represented.

During the first stage of the Anglo-American period in Colorado, the new arrivals, including the French, followed closely the social pattern of the Spanish settlers. They built the first houses and forts with the help of New Mexican builders and adobe makers, whose experience in the Southwest had taught them the kind of housing that was practical in the land. Only when the prospectors and miners lived alone in the mountains of northern Colorado did they erect log cabins in traditional Swedish style. The more intimate details of home life, such as cooking and sewing, were provided by the New Mexican women from Mora and Taos whom the frontiersmen married. In the main, life in the middle of the past century was Hispanic, with an overlay of Anglo-American frontier culture. Years later, when the territory passed into United States hands, it was the dominant Anglo-American culture that modified the Spanish way of life and caused it to assume a lesser role.

A Spanish-Mexican institution that was instrumental in bringing Anglo, French, and Hispanic settlers together in Colorado was the granting of land to be developed and settled. Land grants were not designed with this intercultural effect in mind; they were used as a buffer to keep foreigners from occupying Mexican territory at a time when it was evident to the Mexican government that United States citizens were encroaching on its territory. Although formal possession of the land north of what is now New Mexico was taken by Ulibarrí in 1706, Spanish and, later, Mexican families did not move north. The Indian barrier, and to some extent the mountain ranges that separated the unoccupied territory, were deterrents to settlement that were not easily overcome.

In the late 1840's, Governor Manuel Armijo of New Mexico made a total of 197 grants, ranging from small parcels to the giant Vigil and St. Vrain range comprising 4 million acres south of Trinidad and extending to the Arkansas River. Cornelio Vigil was a judge in Taos, and Ceran St. Vrain was a naturalized Mexican citizen of French descent. When Vigil was killed in the Taos uprising, his partner, St. Vrain, and Vigil's heirs presented their claim to the United States surveyor general, who recommended to Congress that the original grant be confirmed. The grant was reduced to 97,390.95 acres, based on the Mexican Congressional Act of 1824, which decreed that no person should be granted more than 11 square leagues.

Few Mexican land grants in Colorado and New Mexico were confirmed by Congress, because most of the grantees did not bother to file claims or because they had not fulfilled the conditions laid down by the Mexican government. The most important (and the largest) of the grants in Colorado that was not confirmed was the Conejos grant in the southwestern part of the state. In 1833 a group of citizens from Taos petitioned for land along the Conejos River but failed to occupy the land because of Navajo attacks. In 1842 a group of families led by Seledón Valdez, José María Martínez, and Julián Gallegos petitioned for a renewal of the grant. The Mexican government apprised them of the conditions for approval of a grant and, after reminding them that they had failed to fulfill the conditions, gave them a second chance. Again they were unable to hold the land of the Conejos grant, though eighty-three heads of families had done some plowing and sowing. When the claim was filed for the third time, this time before the American authorities in 1861, it was turned down because of the lapse of time, during which most of the original claimants had passed away, and the legal conditions had not been met.

The Nolan grant, originally made in 1843, included more than half a million acres from southwest of Pueblo on the Arkansas to the Wet Mountains adjoining the Vigil and St. Vrain grants. After the death of Gervasio Noland, a naturalized citizen of Mexico, his widow petitioned the surveyor general's office, but the case was delayed and was not settled until 1870, when Congress again applied the Mexican Congressional Act of 1824 and allowed Nolan's widow only eleven square leagues.

Three of the grants that were confirmed wholly or in part by Congress after long periods of litigation were situated partly in Colorado and partly in New Mexico, although at the time when the grants were made the entire region was known as New Mexico. The Beaubien and Miranda grant was formally made in 1843, although the petitioners, Guadalupe Miranda and Charles Beaubien, had filed for the contract in 1841. Beaubien was a French Canadian who had renounced his British citizenship to become a citizen of Mexico and who through this change of allegiance ultimately became the largest landholder in Colorado. Part of the grant extended into Colorado south of Trinidad, with the Sangre de Cristo Range as the western border, running as far south as Taos. It was one of the largest grants confirmed by Congress in its entirety, consisting of over one million acres. Upon Beaubien's death the grant passed into the hands of his son-in-law, Lucien Maxwell, and since then the grant has been known as the Maxwell grant.

One of the earliest petitions for a land grant was made in 1832 by a number of New Mexicans led by Manuel Martínez and his eight sons. The land requested was situated in the upper Chama River west of the San Juan Mountains, extending north along the Navajo River into Colorado. Congress confirmed the entire tract without reducing the original grant, and since then it has been known as the Tierra Amarilla grant.

The late Governor Ralph Carr of Colorado, an eminent attorney before entering politics, directed research into the title of the Sangre de Cristo grant and wrote of it:

The record of the Sangre de Cristo Grant, constitutes a veritable "Who's Who in the West" from the day a 13 year old boy and the Sheriff of Taos County rode away from the Governor's Palace across the Plaza of Santa Fe sometime during the New Year revels of 1844 with a paper in their saddle bags which identified them as joint owners of the Grant.[1]

The Taos sheriff referred to by Governor Carr was Stephen Luis Lee, and the boy was Narciso, the young son of Charles Beaubien. In 1843 Lee and young Beaubien were granted by Governor Armijo over 1 million acres of land adjacent to the Vigil and St. Vrain grant, embracing the valleys of the Costilla, Culebra, and Trinchera rivers —the region known today as the San Luis Valley west of the Sangre de Cristo range. When Lee and young Beaubien were killed in the Taos Rebellion of 1847, Charles Beaubien inherited his son's half of the grant and bought Lee's half for $100. The grant of this valuable and colorful piece of real estate was confirmed by Congress in 1860. Beaubien invited settlers to his land, and from this invitation resulted Colorado's first town, San Luis. One of the interesting features about this town is the 860-acre commons that it still holds.

Before long Colorado became a potpourri of

San Luis, the first town established in Colorado, as it appeared in 1899. Today it is a good-sized town serving the surrounding countryside. Courtesy of the State Historical Society of Colorado Library.

Anglo-Americans, French Canadians, New Mexicans, and Indians. Unlike the orderly occupation of New Mexico by Juan de Oñate, Colorado was settled in a series of sorties and probings for possession of land that was by legal precedent Spanish, was exploited by Canadians and Anglo-Americans, was disputed later by Mexico, and was harassed by the roaming Comanches, Utes, Pawnees, and Apaches. By this time the religious zeal of the Spanish had been lost. The Hispanos were not interested in converting the Indians as their ancestors had been, nor did they try to establish Indian missions.

The meeting point of all cultures of Colorado was Fort Bent, built with the help of a group of Taos adobe makers. All four races occupied the fort at various times—some helped and some hindered the development of early Colorado until the fur trade disappeared. Some writers do not consider this stage of Colorado history very important, but culturally it cannot be overlooked because it brought together the peoples of the Southwest and placed in sharp focus many intercultural relations under conditions that were more liberal than they have been at any other time in the history of Colorado.

In Colorado's early days Anglo-Americans and Frenchmen married or simply lived with Indian women (the Hispanos had no need to take Indian wives, because they had been established in the

land for centuries before the coming of these new settlers). The more conservative of the new arrivals married Spanish girls from Taos and brought them to live in the trading posts and farms of Colorado. The pattern of life for these newcomers had to be that of the land into which they had come. They lived in adobe houses and included in their daily fare such staples as *frijoles, chile, tortillas, sopaipillas,* and various dishes prepared with mutton and lamb. The Hispanic pattern was complete when they learned the Spanish language and spoke to their own children in the language of the Spanish settler. Many practical-minded Anglos and Frenchmen were selective in choosing brides from leading families who could be useful in acquiring land grants and thus ensure the legal acquisition of property. Because the madonnas of the trail had not yet arrived in Colorado, many men took Indian wives, some of whom also became prominent in the life of the West.

The adaptation to the life of the Southwest was complete when Anglo-Americans and Frenchmen alike became Mexican citizens. As citizens of the new republic, they were able to file for land grants, and their requests were honored by the Mexican authorities, as already mentioned. This would be significant for the state of Colorado, because the Bents, St. Vrain, and Kit Carson were part of those transactions. Many well-known travelers, such as Rufus B. Sage and John C. Frémont, who

Taos, New Mexico, where the trappers and mountain men rendezvoused and where "Taos lightning" originated. This photograph was taken in 1928, before fires destroyed the old plaza.

visited Fort Pueblo in the middle of the last century, mentioned as a matter of course the wives of the Anglo-American frontiersmen who entertained them during their visits. The Englishman George F. Ruxton stopped at Pueblo Fort in 1847 and was hospitably entertained by John Hawkins, a trader who lived at the fort. Ruxton did not fail to mention that Mrs. Hawkins, a Mexican from New Mexico, did the honors during his short visit. Governor Bent of New Mexico, who was killed during the reprisals of 1847, was married to Ignacia Jaramillo, of Taos, and her sister Josefita was Kit Carson's wife until his death.

Today many Colorado Spanish speakers bearing English names are descendants of these early marriages. In some cases part of the family became English-speaking, depending on which line of the family they followed; others became Spanish speakers by the same process. The Bent family might have followed a more natural descendancy if Governor Bent had not been killed.

The Bent episode is generally referred to as a "revolt," but technically it was a continuation of the war that was then in progress between Mexico

and the United States. Because New Mexico was part of the Mexican nation, one could hardly expect the citizens of a country at war to be loyal to the enemy, with whom hostilities continued for another year until the signing of the Treaty of Guadalupe Hidalgo in 1848. A provisional government, such as was set up in part of the occupied territory, was not binding to the conquered until the last shot was fired. (As a parallel, history books usually teach that the French who fought back the conquering Germans during the occupation of France during World War II are considered patriots for their resistance to occupation by today's standards, but the New Mexicans who tried to recapture their own land during the war are referred to as traitors.) Bancroft was of the opinion that General Kearny had overstepped his authority in New Mexico by arrogating to himself powers that he did not have and that belonged to the nation. On this point he said:

He [Kearny] had no power to make New Mexico a territory of the United States, of the people citizens, or non-submissive enemies traitors, nor could he in

145

a sense exact an oath of allegiance to the United States. All these matters would be settled by the final treaty closing the war.[2]

As pointed out previously, the French who numbered among the mountain men as traders and trappers were more readily assimilated by Hispanic culture, because contact with their own civilization was more remote, and France had lost the race for the acquisition of territory in America. Moreover, there was a close affinity between French and Spanish cultures through a common religion and through the similarity of Romance languages. Most of the French traders and trappers who remained in Colorado married into Spanish families and became absorbed by the Hispano population. Autobees, Beaubien, Choury, Charlefou, and many other southern Colorado Hispanic families no longer speak French and consider themselves Hispanos. The same is true of a number of English names borne by families who are considered Spanish-speaking. Shannons, Ewings, Deus, and Bentons in southern Colorado have ancestors who came both from the East and from New Mexico.

The annexation of the Southwest to the United States and the gold discoveries that followed on the heels of the Mexican War were perhaps the two most significant events that tipped the cultural scales and ushered in the change from Spanish to Anglo-American culture. For centuries the Indian had to adjust to Spanish civilization and adopt much of the material and nonmaterial culture that the Spaniards had to offer. Now the Hispanos became a subculture overnight and began the slow and arduous process of acculturation, sometimes willingly, at other times under protest. It was a mutual acceptance during the first stages. The existence of another European culture, albeit a folk culture, helped establish the incoming Anglo-American civilization by providing the newcomers with a foothold and with the impetus provided by trade. The Santa Fe trade, spreading like a net over the Southwest and into Mexico, was made possible by the presence of customers.

The arrival of Anglo-American settlers after the Mexican War meant additional defenses against the Utes and Apaches, who had waged constant war against the Spanish settlements. Had it not been for this threat, the people from New Mexico would have spread northward earlier and in greater numbers. In 1842 several families from New Mexico tried to establish themselves in the San Luis Valley but had to abandon their efforts to farm the fertile land because of the Utes who ravaged the territory.

Because of the threat of Indian attacks, most of the plazas built in southern Colorado when the Spanish settlers moved in were medieval defense structures. Individual homes were built around a central patio with a high wall, accessible only through a single opening called a *zaguán*. Over each flat-roofed adobe house rose a *pretil* to serve as battlements when attacked by the Indians. Anglo-Americans who settled in Colorado soon saw the practical value of this architecture and built their houses in the same fashion. Early American travelers who visited the Southwest were critical of "sun-baked brick" construction but

soon discovered that adobe houses and fortifications could not be set on fire when besieged by attackers. Bent's Fort and El Pueblo Fort in Colorado used this same Spanish architectural design, and the military posts that followed utilized the comparable presidio plan throughout the Southwest. Zebulon Pike, who was not accustomed to southwestern tactics, erected a palisade fort of pine timbers. In an attack the highly inflammable pine would have gone up in flames, leaving his troops exposed to Indian arrows and Spanish firearms.

Other adaptations to Hispanic ways of life were reflected in the foods used by the Anglo-American settlers. Chief among them were the staples *chile*, *frijoles*, and *tortillas*. Along the upper Greenhorn Valley, Zan Hickman served a *chile con carne* dish in which the *carne* was bear meat; and, according to eminent Colorado historian LeRoy Hafen, *chile* was a specialty in pioneer days and was served on state occasions. It was served to Kit Carson at Bent's Fort whenever he chanced to journey by. The *Denver News* reported in 1863 that *atole*, made form ground parched corn and corn *masa*, was a palatable drink served in the absence of coffee. This drink continues to be a daily beverage for the poor in Mexico, and many people today drink it by choice rather than for economic reasons. *Atole blanco* was particularly liked with *carne seca*, grilled, dried meat, or with mutton in colonial days in southern Colorado.

Hispanic influence was particularly evident in the homes of Anglo-Americans who married women from New Mexico. They prepared the food that their ancestors had prepared for centuries. No trapper, trader, or farmer would turn down hot *sopaipillas* served with a dish of *chile con carne* and *frijoles* with hot coffee when the weather dipped below the zero mark. These frontier commodities caused Pike to glow when speaking of the food he ate when he meandered into Spanish territory and was waited on by Spanish girls. The first wave of Anglo-American settlers to settle in the Southwest adapted themselves to the life of

The house in Trinidad, Colorado, of Felipe Baca, one of the first Hispanic pioneers in southern Colorado. The house is now the Baca House Pioneer Museum. Courtesy of the State Historical Society of Colorado Library.

the country and took up ways of life that were essentially the same as those of their hosts.

When history is written by Anglo-Americans, from an Anglo-American vantage point, it tells of the men who went West and were successful. It seldom mentions those men who were already there, which in a way is understandable. A few Spanish names figure in the records throughout Colorado history, particularly in those sections of the state where there was a concentration of Spanish families. Pedro Valdez and Felipe Baca hauled flour from Mora, New Mexico, to the Denver gold fields, and as they passed by the Purgatoire Valley, they were very favorably impressed by the land they saw. In the return trip they took some melons and vegetables back to Mora and convinced their friends that the Purgatoire held greater promise than the cold valley of Mora. In 1860, twelve families loaded their possessions in twenty wagons and, after arming themselves well for the usual eventualities of the road, traveled safely over Raton Pass and to the present site of Trinidad. They founded a number of plazas, the usual fortified homes. In this manner Madrid, San Miguel, Trinchera, San Francisco, Apodaca, Los Baros, Medina, and other towns were born.

The expansion into Colorado from the original settlements in New Mexico was a small part of the vast population movement that took place from the upper Río Grande in all directions, quadrupling the territory occupied in Spanish colonial

days. After the Comanche threat ended, the Hispanos moved more vigorously into the fertile valleys of Colorado. An agricultural and pastoral culture, they sought land where water for irrigation was accessible. The Purgatoire, Huérfano, Greenhorn, and San Luis valleys, with all their tributaries, were dotted with the Spanish-named *placitas* of farmers and sheep raisers, whose descendants occupy them today.

Some Hispano settlers in Colorado participated in public affairs and engaged in trade and freighting, though not organized to the same degree as that of the Anglo-Americans. One outstanding businessman in southwestern Colorado was Miguel Otero, a well-educated lawyer and businessman from the leading Spanish family in New Mexico. Otero was a different class of trader, more in the order of a modern businessman, and stamped his activities in the state by giving his name to one of Colorado's counties and also by founding La Junta, known for the first three years as Otero until the name was transferred to the county.

Other Spanish speakers participated in the life of Colorado's southern cities. In 1867, Trinidad elected Juan Gutiérrez, Sr., probate judge and his son, Juan, Jr., as sheriff. Jesús María García was elected assessor, and Ramón Vigil was made coroner. In the early days of Trinidad, Spanish influence was predominant. Of the seventy-two county and precinct officers, only eleven understood English, because most of the population as late as 1873 was still Spanish-speaking.

The Hispanos also took part in the business life of Trinidad. As already mentioned, the founders of the city were engaged in freighting flour to the Denver gold fields. The Trinidad directory of 1871 lists Federico Benítez as a jeweler and dealer in ivory; there were two Mexican musicians and one Anglo in town, but there were three Mexican silversmiths. It is difficult to tell whether the people referred to in the records of the time were actually Mexicans or Hispanos (that is, descendants of the Spanish colonials). Anglo-Americans who went to Colorado after the Mexican War referred to all Spanish speakers as "Mexican," sometimes not as a mere designation but as a pejorative. One does not know, for example, whether Juan Ignacio Alires, the county treasurer and Trinidad's first merchant, was indeed a citizen of Mexico or a Hispano from northern New Mexico. He is listed as a "prosperous purveyor of food and liquor" in the 1870's.[1]

The Hispanos who went into Colorado after

the mid-1850's brought with them their traditions and practices, both religious and secular. The first Spanish church was Our Lady of Guadalupe, built in 1858 in Conejos. The religious folk plays, *Los Pastores*, and others composed around biblical themes, were performed in Trinidad and in the San Luis Valley just as they were presented in New Mexico and other parts of the Southwest. The folk dances, folk songs, and traditional games were part of Spanish life in Colorado. The isolation of some of the mountain villages helped preserve many customs and practices that disappeared in centers crossed by Anglo-American culture.

The records of Trinidad show that *la corrida del gallo*, or rooster pull, was enjoyed by both Spanish and Anglo audiences in 1867. Ralph C. Taylor has written that until a quarter of a century ago the people of the upper Purgatoire presented the pageant *Los Comanches* celebrating victory of the Spaniards over Chief Cuerno Verde who was defeated by Anza at the foot of Greenhorn Mountain in 1779. This historical play is still well known in New Mexico. The flavor of life in Trinidad was so markedly Hispanic that William A. Bell, a surveyor on the Kansas Pacific Railway Company, once said it was the only Mexican town north of Raton Mountain. But he added, "My horse is safer in a Trinidad corral than in Fort Union."

To judge from its name, one would hardly know that Walsenburg was a Spanish town when it was founded. Don Miguel Antonio León was responsible for the first plaza built on the site where the present city now stands. Don Miguel, according to a contemporary writer, ran an idyllic settlement then known as La Plaza de los Leones. Spanish traditional customs prevailed among the inhabitants; young children doffed their hats in the presence of their elders and behaved with a courtesy scarcely in evidence today.

Although history records little of what went on among Hispanic people, enough references are made from time to time to indicate the presence of the Southwest's original European civilization. Some writers, however, have said outright that the city of Pueblo was neither Spanish nor Mexican. Yet there are historical references indicating that it was more Spanish than it was English, as attested by the name of the city today. A prosperous rancher who lived not far from Fort Pueblo and was involved in the life and activities of the fort was Marcelino Baca. When the fort was attacked by Utes, not a single English name appears on the record, but seventeen Spanish surnames,

such as Valencia, Cisneros, País, Medina, Vigil, Sandoval, Martín, and Miera are mentioned. And when a punitive expedition was sent against the Utes under the command of Kit Carson, Dewitt C. Peters, the army surgeon, said of the Mexican volunteers:

Soon after their enrollment they purchased woolen shirts and felt hats, the color of which, in each company, was similar; this fact with a little drilling, gave them quite a military appearance. Never were men prouder of the position they now held than the volunteers under consideration; and a more daring and expert band of horsemen has been seldom collected.[2]

Even though the history of Colorado to date has been told generally from an Anglo-American viewpoint by Anglo-American writers, Hispanic names are mentioned in connection with the state's activities. That Trinidad's first newspaper, the *Enterprise*, was published in English and Spanish in 1870 indicates that there must have been at least an equal number of readers of both languages. That may have been what led Casimiro Barela, a delegate to the constitutional convention of 1875, to introduce a provision whereby all laws would be published in English and Spanish. The provision was adopted by the convention, which added German as well, with the stipulation that the practice was to be followed until 1900 (the delegates must have felt that by that date everyone would be conversant in English).

Because so much of the activity in southern Colorado consisted of trading, trapping, and farming, all of which extended into northern New Mexico, it was natural that the Hispanos in New Mexico would move north to find better land or to work at the trading forts such as Bent's Fort and Fort Pueblo. Travelers passing through the region spoke of the Hispano sheep raisers and farmers, as well as of the people who lived at the forts. Chávez and Avila were hired to build houses in Pueblo when the city began to develop, and many families settled there. Most of the traders, as already mentioned, had Spanish or Indian wives. At one time there was only one Anglo-American housewife in Bent's Fort, a fact that was of little consequence in the days when the mixture of all races of the region was accepted by the settlers.

Writer Albert Richardson looked askance, however, at the international mixing in the fort, and in his book *Beyond the Mississippi* he derided the Spanish inhabitants, saying that they were as low as the human race could get and that their behavior was at the same level as that of animals. The book had a very wide circulation in the East, and a second edition was published in 1867. It may well be that Richardson's appraisal caused some of the newcomers to Colorado and the Southwest to have preconceived notions regarding the cultural nature of the Spanish population. Governor Bent and Kit Carson probably had a much different opinion of the Hispanos in the region, married as they were to Mexican sisters. Carson had become so Hispanicized and accustomed to the Spanish language, which he spoke fluently, that when he realized he was dying he called to Dr. Tilton, his attending physician, "Doctor, compadre, adiós."

Carson's death did not pass unnoticed by his Hispano friends in Taos. In 1929 a number of old letters, some of which bore the Pony Express seal, were found at Ojo Caliente in an abandoned shack that had been a post office in territorial days. Among these there was a ten-stanza poem written in a literary-quality Spanish. It is a eulogy entitled "En la Muerte del Finado Kit Carson," "On the Death of the Late Kit Carson." It is signed, "Por un amigo. Fernando de Taos, N. Méjico, Mayo 23 de 1869." A photostat of the original poem is in the Kit Carson Museum in Taos.

One of the colorful trappers who became thoroughly Hispanicized in Colorado was the much-married Frenchman Charles Autobees, who took Indian wives without benefit of clergy and finally settled down when he married Serafina Avila. She bore him five surviving children whose names have undergone a number of Hispanicized variations. One of Autobees' many activities was a partnership with Simeon Turley, the enterprising citizen who created a beverage regularly consumed by the Anglo-American frontiersman, particularly the trappers and traders who had their rendezvous in Taos. Turley grew the corn in Arroyo Hondo from which he manufactured "Taos lightning" in his own distillery, and Autobees, the salesman, distributed it in casks throughout Colorado and shipped it east by way of Fort Pueblo. Some writers blame the Ute massacre at Fort Pueblo during Christmas, 1854, to drunkenness caused by this beverage.

Autobees also participated in more worthy causes among his adopted Spanish-speaking confreres. In 1899 he joined other settlers in the construction of the Huérfano Valley Catholic Church and contributed a statue of San Isidro, patron saint of the farmers. This same statue of the saint is taken out on Saint Isidore's Day processions on

May 15. In one of the recent processions Autobees' great-grandson carried the statue, which his ancestor brought into the territory more than a century ago, according to Ralph C. Taylor.[3]

The Hispanic settlers of southern Colorado, like the early Spaniards, built churches shortly after a village was established. This building was normally the principal structure around which the *placitas* grew, and much of the village social life centered around church activities, fund-raising fiestas, religious celebrations, and patron-saint festivities. The first church built in Colorado was Our Lady of Guadalupe, erected in Conejos in 1858. Not only did the church building bring together the people in the village but it also provided a feeling of security and permanence. The belfry or church tower is the characteristic landmark seen in the distance when one approaches a Spanish Mexican village, much as the water tank against the skyline is the symbol of Anglo-American towns in the Southwest. Hispanic churches have also been indispensable sources of vital statistics for researchers, because, in the absence of government records, usually available in county seats, the church recorded the births, marriages, and deaths in the village.

Hispanic people have been conditioned by tradition to look on the church and the padres as counselors on temporal as well as religious matters. In the early days of settlement the priests were usually the most literate persons in the villages, and because confession is part of the Catholic ritual, the padres were well informed about the problems of their congregation. In early Anglo-American Colorado communities where there were no Spanish churches, some Hispanos attended Protestant services. When the Protestant Reverend John L. Dyer preached on Sunday in Trinidad in 1865, one-third of the congregation was composed of Hispanos.

As the Anglo-American population increased, proportionately fewer Hispanos participated in public life; nevertheless, names of the original Spanish settlers appear in the records from time to time. A very unusual post was held by a Mexican named Mariano, who was Chief Ouray's private secretary during the last four years of that famous Ute chief's life. Another little-known item of interest was the state's first school roster. A colorful schoolmaster named Goldrick opened the first school in Denver in October, 1859. His class consisted of four *mestizos*, four Mexicans, and five children from Missouri. The proportion of pupils

Kit Carson's home in Taos, New Mexico, now a museum.

was clearly not in line with the total population.

A few Anglo-Americans were conscious of the state's Hispanic background and either named or renamed some locations in the state by changing the English into Spanish names. After a visit to Mexico, Governor Hunt was so intrigued by Spanish names that he changed the original name for Salida, because the name more properly described the gateway through the mountains. Colonel John M. Francisco, who despite his name was not Spanish, settled at the site of what is now La Veta and gave it that name because of a vein of metal or gypsum nearby. The trend of using Spanish names for some Colorado villages and landmarks would indicate that the Anglo-American settlers were conscious of the region's early culture. They usually chose euphonious names, such as Rosita and Querida—two mining towns below Pueblo. Captain Craig named Las Animas and also changed the name Catlin, a good historical name, to Manzanola.

Although the number of Spanish names among public servants is proportionately few, there are enough to show that the Hispanos kept their hand in politics from the very beginning of the state. Of the thirty-nine members of the Colorado Constitutional Convention of 1875, three had Spanish surnames: Agapito Vigil, Jesús María García, and the well-known Casimiro Barela took a very active part in this convention for seventy-two ses-

sions. Vigil, a native of Taos, was a seasoned veteran of political life—he had served in the territorial legislature of New Mexico in 1859. García also had some experience in public life, having served as Las Animas county assessor in 1867, as county judge, and as county clerk. When he died in 1896 the *Daily News* said of him that "his money and time were always at the command of his friends and he knew no enemies, but regarded all as friends."

Casimiro Barela came to the convention with a good record as a former sheriff and assessor. After Colorado was admitted to the Union, he served seven consecutive four-year terms as senator. This earned him the sobriquet of "perpetual senator." All three of the convention delegates were prosperous ranchers in Las Animas County, and historian Frank Hall, in his *History of the State of Colorado*, wrote that, "taken together, the Mexican delegation won the confidence and regard of all, as well as their lasting friendship." Barela's public-service career in Colorado covered half a century, in addition to which he was a successful cattleman and horse breeder. In recognition of his accomplishments he was included as one of sixteen prominent men in the state to have his portrait in stained glass placed in a window of the rotunda of the capitol building. He is described in the manual of the Fifteenth General Assembly as "keen, fearless, and capable in argument without

Casimiro Barela was born either in Spain or in Mexico. He was active in politics and in farming and cattle raising in southern Colorado. He was a member of the Colorado Constitutional Convention in 1875 and served seven consecutive terms in the United States Senate; hence his sobriquet, "the perpetual senator." This is a 1915 photograph.

a superior as a parliamentarian." Other Hispano members of the Colorado legislature served in the first meeting of this body. Víctor García and Jesús Barela, in addition to their regular duties as legislators, also served as the first legislature's official translators.

ADJUSTMENT OF HISPANIC CULTURE

The experience of men like Casimiro Barela has not been altogether lost in Colorado; the Hispanos

of the southern part of the state continued to participate in public life, though not in commensurate proportion with the total population. With the coming of Mexican labor during World War I and World War II, the number increased with a second group of Spanish speakers, who eventually became the present-day Mexican Americans. The Hispanos who moved into Colorado during Spanish-Mexican days began to acculturate and assimilate with the Anglo-Americans when they arrived. Consequently, the Hispano settlers of Colorado adjusted to American life earlier and were better able to participate in the life of the state.

The Mexican American, with closer family and cultural ties in Mexico, did not consider himself at the outset as part of the population; he was less familiar with the English language and was ignorant of the social and legal institutions under which he would have to live. Most of these immigrants found it more convenient to live in neighborhood clusters on the periphery of the larger cities.

Very soon after the middle of the nineteenth century the traders and trappers receded into history and became interesting figures in the history of the state. The colorful mountain men were superseded by the feverish miners, who skyrocketed the state into national prominence and brought great numbers of Anglo-Americans and other non-Spanish peoples into the country. Some Hispanos from southern Colorado continued their trading operations by freighting supplies to the mining camps in much the same fashion that the Californios provided the mining camps of the West Coast with beef and other necessaries by mule train.

Mining, like fur trading, in turn gave way to permanent industry, such as agriculture, sugar-beet culture, cattle raising, railroad building, manufacturing, and allied occupations that increased demands for labor. Then the Hispanos began to move north from southern Colorado and New Mexico in search of work. The steel mills in Pueblo, the coal-mining operations around Walsenburg, the agricultural fields throughout the state, and railroad construction provided employment for thousands of Hispanos and Mexicans from the south. In the first half of the twentieth century immigrants from Mexico remained in the state and greatly increased the population of Spanish speakers. This period of expansion moved large numbers of the original settlers from the San Luis Valley and from Trinidad into the larger cities, such as Denver and Pueblo, where employment was more readily available. Most of the Hispano residents in the state still have family ties in southern Colorado and New Mexico, and those who are classified as Mexican Americans have theirs in the parts of Mexico where their grandparents and parents originated. When moving into the larger cities, Hispanos tended to settle on the periphery, where they continued to a large extent the traditional way of life to which they were accustomed. This voluntary segregation was responsible for the delayed acculturation of Hispanic residents in the state.

The Mexican and Hispanic labor force was drawn into Colorado's sugar industry and railroad building very early. Large numbers were employed in the Grand Junction area in 1899, as were German-Russians who had emigrated from Russia, where they had gone during the reign of Catherine the Great. They were employed in the Colorado beet industry because of their extensive experience in this work from 1870 when they immigrated to Pennsylvania. In 1901, fifty-six German-Russian families had already moved to Greeley. The sugar refineries reported in the same period that Mexicans were more productive workers in the beet industry than any other ethnic group. The labor commissioner of the Great Western Sugar Company said in 1925 that Mexicans in the Colorado district of the company produced approximately a half ton more per acre than the German-Russians, who were then the second class of beet laborers. This record has continued to the present, according to the public relations officer of the same company, who said recently that it wanted Mexican labor because they had the highest man-hour production of any group of workers in the field.

The same was true of workers on the Santa Fe Railroad. One of the foremen declared, during the height of railroad traffic years ago, that they employed Mexicans on the tracks because they usually came to this country to work and were therefore more desirable. They were not interested in politics, and, having fewer social and family ties than the Hispanos, they never took time from work to visit relatives in New Mexico or Colorado. On the other hand, this isolation also made Mexican workers more vulnerable to exploitation by their employers. Sociologist E. S. Bogardus said in a 1933 study that, "the Mexican peon arrives poor and he is not equipped to climb out of the slough of poverty. Conditions in the United States do not give him the stimuli or the essential opportunities for developing the necessary momentum." This applied also to the beet worker

and to the railroad worker, who lived with his family in a railroad-car "apartment" alongside the track.

For a long time a distinction was made between the Mexican labor force and the Hispanos of Colorado and New Mexico. Although they both often worked in the same beet fields, the latter had more mobility and would work for an entire season to build up enough economic resources to tide them over when the *ranchitos* were unproductive or when families wanted extra cash. Many young men of school age also joined the sugar-beet forces for a season and then continued their usual lives outside the beet camps. Many Hispanos employed today in gainful occupations or in responsible administrative positions in industry and in public schools can remember the days when they spent a summer or a season doing back-breaking labor in the Colorado beet fields. Their attitude differs from that of the Mexican peasant who, as Bogardus pointed out forty years ago, lacked the essential opportunities and the necessary momentum to develop.

Not being as tied down to menial labor as was the Mexican immigrant, the Hispano adjusted earlier to American life. And although he had to face many of the prejudices that the Mexican faced, he was not troubled by the same problems that beset the Mexicans of those days, and even the Mexican Americans of later years, the native-born American citizens. The Hispanos naturally had a stronger sense of belonging and therefore did not seek redress by harking back to Indian culture or to a mythical Aztlán. The Indian was an individual whom he had to fight to protect his crops and family, and he had never heard of Aztlán until the Mexican Americans brought up the subject.

On the other hand, the Hispano of Colorado and New Mexico shows greater concern, and has always complained, about his lost land grants and the loss of grazing rights traditionally granted him under the *mesta* system of Spanish days. Like the Indians of Taos Pueblo, he wants to recover the use of land that has been set aside as national forests. The Hispano is concerned about discriminatory practices of which he has been the victim and which have retarded his advancement and his earning power. But he is not thinking about setting up a new nation in the Southwest, nor is he involved in nativistic movements for a return to Aztec days. His experience with Indian culture has been the reverse of that of the Mexican. He Hispanicized many Indian villages in the Southwest and established a better working relationship with his neighbors by making "Spanish" folk out of what once were purely Indian.

In a way the Hispano is able to understand the assimilation and the acculturation process now under way, by which it is the Hispano's turn to modify his culture. In this struggle he is joined by the Mexican American, who has introduced a good proportion of Mexican-Spanish culture with which to make the Anglo-American more receptive to the mutual process of acculturation. The dominant culture no longer insists that the subculture give up its total personality in order to become acculturated. Historically the great cultures of the world have always taken a good amount from the conquered, even though the latter were overwhelmed. As a result the world has been peopled by cultural hybrids since the beginning of time.

Colorado, like other southwestern states, is going through an interesting period of acculturation, and inevitably there is going to be a lot of give and take. The problem of the Mexican American and the Hispano is to determine what to take from their own culture that will not be excess baggage and what to accept from the dominant culture that will not give them cultural indigestion. There are today a few professional Hispanos in Colorado who occupy positions of responsibility and importance in public life. Although their numbers are not proportionately large, they are significant in that they have demonstrated that the field is open to anyone who is willing to obtain the training necessary to become a teacher, a doctor, a lawyer, and so on. Lately a number of students have taken advantage of programs in law opened to Hispanos or Mexican Americans in two leading schools of law, the University of Colorado and the University of Denver. Many of these students will soon swell the ranks of those now listed in the directory. One of the leading lawyers in Denver and a former attorney general is Charles S. Vigil, whose son joined him after graduating from the University of Colorado. The number of Hispano medical doctors now in Denver and in other principal cities of the state continues to increase with each medical school graduating class. Among them is a leading plastic surgeon.

The teaching profession has enlisted large numbers of men and women in Denver, as well as in other cities throughout the country. The significant increase from year to year is indicative of the interest shown by Mexican Americans and His-

panos in the advancement of their own people. In Denver the number of Mexican American and Hispano teachers employed in 1964 was 72, and there were 4 administrators. By 1971 the number of teachers had increased to 156 and administrators to 15, according to figures provided by Dr. Roscoe Davidson, assistant school superintendent. At the college, university, and doctoral level more Spanish names appear from year to year.

In government service, both state and national, the increase of Mexican Americans and Hispanos has been more dramatic, according to administrators of federal agencies. Reasons for this increase include better understanding of government structure, knowledge of requirements for positions in various agencies, and, finally, knowledge about how to apply for these positions. Many young Hispanos and Mexican Americans now enter college with better oriented objectives, aiming for positions that just a few years ago they did not know were within their reach or even existed.

Not all these increases of Spanish-speaking personnel in government agencies and in schools are the result of a natural or normal evolution. Many programs have been instituted for minorities all over the country, and many administrators and employees are taken from the same minorities that they serve. Creating these programs and staffing them with members of ethnic groups for whom they were designed is in a sense an aberrant situation. If the programs are discontinued for economy reasons, or because they have outgrown their usefulness, it will be interesting to see how much of this personnel will be absorbed by the normal market, and also how well prepared they will be to assume responsibilities other than those designed for a given group. One positive result of these programs in Colorado has been the opportunity that some individuals have had to demonstrate their ability to perform on a par with other members of society. Those who have developed substantial and useful skills will eventually fill positions in the normal course of events.

Meanwhile, there is still a good deal of dissatisfaction among militant Mexican Americans and Chicanos, who feel that industry, business, and education have been too slow in according them a proportionate share of benefits and opportunities. To provide for some of the often-voiced requests, various programs have been instituted in municipal schools and state colleges and universities. To accelerate the progress of those who are deficient in language, some municipalities have organized bilingual programs. Colleges and universities have added such new offerings as Chicano and Mexican-American studies. So far these measures have not produced the improvement and progress envisioned by proponents, but they have helped assuage the feelings of critics. No course offerings or new programs are any better than the effort put forth by the participants. In the last analysis the success of these programs will be gauged by the improvement and advances of the students for which they were designed. It must be understood that thus far not enough time has elapsed to provide a basis for a meaningful judgment of the program's efficacy. It does indicate consciousness in the educational system that something must be done to remedy a long-standing problem.

Tales of the fabulous treasures of Quivira and of the Seven Cities of Cíbola led to the occupation of the upper Río Grande at the end of the sixteenth century. No such incentive for expansion existed in the lands that the great river coursed as it turned abruptly southeast from where El Paso now stands and continued to the Gulf of Mexico. Nevertheless, during colonial days the Río Grande became the bastion of Hispanic culture for the northern provinces of the Spanish empire. As the Spaniards moved northeast on exploring expeditions, on trading sorties, or on *entradas* to establish missions among the Indians of El Seno Mexicano (as southern Texas was then known), Río Grande crossings were points of entry and the places to which expeditions returned when their missions were accomplished—or when they failed to reach their objective.

SPANISH CENTERS ALONG THE RIO GRANDE

In time three principal Spanish cultural centers near or on the river became established between New Mexico and the Gulf of Mexico. From these centers Spanish civilization radiated north, east, and west. The first and the oldest of these important centers was Santa Fe: next was El Paso, and the third was San Antonio. The country along the Río Grande looked to these towns for supplies, for military protection, and for religious support. They got their reinforcements, personnel, and supplies from Mexico, the ultimate supply reservoir and administrative center.

EARLY ENTRIES INTO WEST TEXAS

The Spaniards had not given up completely the hope of finding the Gran Quivira, or similar rewards, despite the failures of Coronado and Oñate to find the legendary place. Not long after the settling of Santa Fe stories began to circulate about aboriginal "kingdoms" east of New Mexico, where the Indians lived lavishly and enjoyed great wealth.

In 1629 interest in this land was intensified by the arrival of a group of Jumano Indians at a mission near the present city of Albuquerque. They told of a "lady in blue" who had visited their *ranchería* several times and had related the story of Christianity to them. She had also requested them to go to the nearest mission and ask a priest to baptize them. Father Juan de Salas, who heard this strange story, was so impressed by the Indians' account that he requested and obtained permission to accompany the Jumanos back to their country. Salas and another Franciscan, Diego León, spent six months in the land of the Jumanos, somewhere in the trans-Pecos region, about three hundred miles east of New Mexico.

Several months later the scholarly Father Alonso de Benavides, custodian of the New Mexico missions, returned to Spain, where he met Sister María Jesús de Agreda, the nun who, in one of her many transportation trances, claimed to have visited a distant land very similar to west Texas, inhabited by painted beings very much like the Jumanos who called at the New Mexico mission. The nun also claimed that on these transportation experiences she wore a blue cloak such as the Indians described. Father Benavides became convinced that this was the "lady in blue" that the Indians had described.

With this confirmation Father Salas made a second expedition in 1632, which took him six hundred miles southeast of Santa Fe into the land of the Jumanos. He reached a branch of the upper Colorado, near present-day San Angelo, and after a long stay returned to New Mexico. These early contacts with west Texas, while they did not result in the founding of any missions, served to establish trade between the Indians and the New Mexican settlers and also opened another buffalo-hunting region. The friendly and informal relations of many decades introduced the Indians to a civilization that they were to adopt gradually during the following century.

Thus far there had been no official *entrada* into Texas, but in 1650 the governor of New Mexico sent a military and trading expedition under the command of Captains Hernando Martín and Diego del Castillo. The party reached the Pecos, followed the valley to the south, and turned east to the Concho River, where they discovered groves of pecan trees for whose fruit they had no Spanish equivalent. They reported this discovery by the generic name *nueces*, "nuts"; a few years later the river became known as the Nueces River. On the Concho they also found opened mussels with freshwater pearls. This discovery led the viceroy to dispatch another expedition in 1654, under the command of Captain Diego de Guadalajara. In addition to searching for pearls, he was to make contact with a tribe of Indians farther east, near the Gulf Coast, about whom they had heard very encouraging reports. The Tejas Indians were members of the Caddoan family, an agrarian tribe who lived in settlements and were reputed to be the most civilized of the many tribes along the Louisiana border. The Spaniards did not reach the Tejas nation, but they came across one of their hunting parties and had a brief parley.

Peaceful relations with the Jumanos continued uninterrupted for several years; they were suddenly discontinued when the New Mexico Indians staged the successful Revolt of 1680. After eighty-two years of indoctrination by the padres and a good deal of assimilation in some of the New Mexican pueblos, all seemed to be lost in the bloody rebellion which was led by Popé. The Spaniards who survived the revolt were pushed south to El Paso, and all contact with the Jumanos seemed lost. But the missionaries still hoped to extend their work into west Texas, and the crown also planned to win allies among the more civilized tribes to help hold the frontier against foreign incursions.

CHIEF SABEATA

Relations with the Jumanos were reestablished sooner than the Spaniards had hoped, through the initiative of the Indians themselves. In 1683 several delegations of Indians visited Governor Antonio de Otermín in his new headquarters in El Paso. They asked for missionaries and for military aid against the Lipan Apaches. Nothing came of the request until the succeeding governor, Domingo Gironza Petrís de Cruzate, received a delegation of Jumanos led by Chief Juan Sabeata. He asked for missionaries as a pretext to enlist the help of the Spanish army against the Apaches. The chief declared that he represented a "kingdom" of thirty tribes, including the Tejas, and he spoke at length about this kingdom, which was ruled by a powerful king. Sabeata understood the Spaniards' desire to enlist the cooperation of a strong tribe such as the Tejas. The alluring picture drawn by him aroused great interest in Governor Cruzate, who envisioned another new world by adding the extensive territory of Tejas. He forwarded to the viceroy the information given him by Sabeata and, on receiving a favorable reply, sent Juan Domínguez de Mendoza, accompanied by Fray Nicolás López, custodian of the New Mexico missions. Principally a commercial venture in search of pearls and Indian trade, the expedition followed the well-known river trails, visited many tribes, founded a mission at San Clemente, and, after baptizing thousands of Indians, returned to El Paso without having made contact with the Tejas Indians.

THE FOUNDING OF EL PASO

The settlement of El Paso, today's Ciudad Juárez across the river, was a gradual process that took several decades to accomplish after Don Juan de Oñate, conqueror and settler of New Mexico, crossed the ford on the Río Grande in 1598. The strategic location of the pass was realized very early by priests, always alert to locations with large concentrations of Indians to civilize and bring into the fold. Father Alonso de Benavides crossed the pass in 1620 on his way to become custodian of the New Mexico missions, and he took notice of the need for a mission at that important river crossing. The man who was to establish the original mission at El Paso was a young lay brother, García de San Francisco de Zúñiga, who came over the Camino Real from Mexico with Father Perea in 1628. His first assignment was the New Mexican mission Senecú at the Church of San Antonio de Padua, on the Río Grande about six miles southeast of El Paso.

From Senecú as a base Fray García moved to Socorro, where he initiated not only the conversion of the Indians but also the raising of fruits and cereals needed at the mission. The practical-minded brother knew that a well-fed congregation was more likely to settle and accept the new civilization. Agriculture became an important basis for the progress of acculturation; once the new converts became accustomed to such products of Spanish pioneer society as cereals, fruits, wines,

The Mission of Nuestra Señora de Guadalupe, founded in 1659 in Ciudad Juárez, by Fray García de San Francisco de Zuñiga. It has gone through a number of alterations and face liftings and survives today.

and vegetables, they became more tractable. El Paso Valley eventually became an oasis in the desert where travelers and residents supplied themselves as they journeyed over the Camino Real.

Other Indians, such as the Jumanos, Mansos, Piros, Tompiros, and Zumas, occupied a complex of villages that the Spaniards assimilated into a *mestizo* culture. Today their descendants in the valley represent this cultural and physical fusion. The Hispanos, and also the Mexicans living in El Paso Valley, began with this fusion of Spanish and Indian strains, guided by a Hispanic culture that the church, the crown, and later the Republic of Mexico perpetuated over four centuries.

El Paso began with a temporary mission built in 1656 by Fray Francisco Pérez and Fray Juan Cabal, but it did not prosper. In the uprising staged three years later the Mansos and the Zumas threatened to murder the missionaries. The padres

returned to New Mexico with the Spanish commander who had been sent to pacify the Indians. Shortly thereafter, the Indians had a change of heart and made contact with Fray García in Senecú, requesting establishment of a mission in El Paso. On December 8, 1659, Fray García founded the original church. The cornerstone was laid in 1662, and the church building was completed ten years later. El Paso became the central settlement that ministered to the surrounding villages in El Paso Valley. At this center the Spaniards and their Indian allies from New Mexico found shelter during the Revolt of 1680.

FOUNDING OF YSLETA

When the Spaniards fled from New Mexico in 1680, they were accompanied by friendly Indians from various tribes, particularly the Tiguas of

The Mission of Corpus Christi de la Ysleta del Sur, built in 1682 by Fray Francisco Ayeta and Governor Antonio Otermín after the capital of the New Mexico province was moved to the El Paso Valley because of the Indian Revolt of 1680 in New Mexico. The mission is known today as Nuestra Señora del Carmen.

Isleta, twelve miles south of present-day Albuquerque. On their arrival at El Paso, it was thought best to settle the Tiguas separately at a location below the settlement on the Río Grande. They named the village Ysleta, after the original pueblo in New Mexico. Governor Antonio Otermín went to New Mexico in 1682 with an armed force and on his return took back another three hundred Indians from the Piro, Tano, Jémez, and Isleta pueblos. The Tiguas joined their own people at the newly founded Ysleta, and the others were taken farther down the river to the original pueblo of Socorro, which was later moved to its present location farther west.

In 1682, Fray Francisco Ayeta and Governor Otermín founded the church at Ysleta, Texas, and christened it Misión de Corpus Christi de la Ysleta del Sur.[1] The mission farther south established for the Piros and the Jémez Indian refugees was named Nuestra Señora del Socorro. Before long the cluster of villages down the valley included San Elizario, San Marcial, and Senecú. As part of the conversion and assimilation process the priests introduced in all the villages a Spanish way of life. Vineyards were started with vines brought from Mexico, along with fruit trees such as pears, peaches, apples, and a species of apricot known as *chabacán* (rather than the usual *albericoque*).

159

This variety of apricot is still found in Mexican gardens in El Paso. The pear introduced by the missionaries was known popularly in the valley as *pera chinche* because of its small size. It was about one-third as large as the ordinary Bartlett pear and grew on an unusually large tree whose branches rose almost vertically to a height of thirty feet. Two of these pear trees survived into the early 1930's at a ranchito in Ysleta; they stood about two hundred yards behind the mission church. The last surviving tree had a hollow trunk with a circumference of more than four feet. The Hispanos in Ysleta referred to this venerable old pear tree as *cuerpo sin alma*, "soulless body," because it was hollow and yet alive.

SPANISH PUEBLOS THREATENED

The orchards, vineyards, and wheat fields planted in the valley thrived in the fertile soil, which was irrigated by a system of *acequias* built by the Indians of Ysleta under the supervision of the padres. Supplies were plentiful, but life was far from peaceful. The uprisings of discontented Indians and the depredations by Apaches and other unsettled tribes, who raided the settlements constantly, slowed progress for two centuries. The tenuous hold of the Spaniards over a land with insufficient defenses and no regular communication over hundreds of miles of arid land, meant that they had to survive in a struggle against natural and human enemies. After centuries of struggle for survival the word Indio was an invective. When they were attacked by Apaches or Comanches, the men would shout, "¡Mal rayo te parta, Indio salvaje!" "May a thunderbolt split you, you savage Indian!" It took almost a century to reconcile the attitudes of the Hispanos to the Indians. They made the distinction between *indios mansos*, "peaceful Indians," and *indios salvajes*, "savage Indians." The return to Aztec culture is a modern attitude of Mexicans who, unlike the pioneers of El Paso Valley, never faced fierce Apaches while trying to wrest a living from the soil, or ever came home from the fields to find their houses burned to the ground and their wives and children murdered.

In spite of these hazards, the population of the valley survived and maintained a cultural continuity that in the end blended Indian and Spaniard into a *mestizo* civilization. It was a complete assimilation and was also a process of guided acculturation, because it was the original design of the conquerors for Indians and Europeans to coexist under one culture, the Spanish culture that they introduced. Today the chain of villages from Ysleta south are no longer Indian villages but are southwestern Mexican towns.

THE NEW TIGUA VILLAGE

Lately, mainly as a tourist attraction, the Tigua village Ysleta has been revived. In 1931 a letter was sent by Governor Pablo Abeyta of the Isleta, New Mexico, pueblo to the surviving governor of the Tiguas in Ysleta, Texas. The bearer of the letter inquired for members of the tribe and was directed to Dámaso Colmenero, who was believed to be the lone survivor of the tribe. When the letter was delivered to Colmenero, he read it and inquired in Spanish, "How is my brother Pablo in New Mexico?" In the ensuing interview Colmenero declared that he and his family were the last survivors of the original tribe in Ysleta and that he was the only one who could speak Tigua. He regretted that his children refused to be known as Indians and considered themselves Mexicans, spoke Spanish and English, but could not speak the Tigua dialect.[2] The same situation developed in New Mexico over the years in former Indian villages that lost their Indian identity and are now known as Spanish-American villages. The original Spanish settlers and the missionaries of Ysleta would be very pleased to learn that their efforts to Hispanicize the aborigines had proved a success. And they would also take great satisfaction in knowing that the mission they built in Ysleta in 1682 is thriving today as Nuestra Señora del Carmen, with a slightly altered façade, and is reputed to be the oldest continuously occupied church in the United States.

EL PASO OF THE LEFT BANK

Present-day El Paso is far from being as old as Ysleta or Ciudad Juárez, across the river. Nevertheless, claim to antiquity may be established by the newer city because Juan María Ponce de Leon decided to extend his rancho to include land across the river. This wealthy *hacendado* applied for a land grant to legalize the ownership to farmland that he had been cultivating for a number of years. In 1827 he paid the equivalent of eighty-two dollars for 2 *caballerías* of land, and with the purchase of these 250 acres he in a sense extended the city limits of El Paso del Norte beyond the left bank of the river. Ponce de León built the first structures in such well-known locations as today's White House Department Store, and so the growth of the city into the name El Paso was natural and legitimate. The old city El Paso del Norte across the river was extended into a suburb known as El Rancho de Ponce, a very distinguished beginning for the southwestern metropolis.

After the American occupation frontiersmen and other American travelers christened the new settlement various names, including, Franklin City, which the Spanish-speaking rancheros down the valley pronounced Franquilín (as a normal consequence of Spanish pronunciation, splitting the consonantal cluster *kl*). The adjacent Ciudad Juárez and El Paso, separated by the Río Grande, are the setting of a long, action-filled story that is dramatically told by eminent folklorist-historian C. L. Sonnichsen in his book *Pass of the North*.[3]

Hispanic culture would have taken deeper roots and thrived if there had been better harmony between church and state and more good will between representatives of both institutions. The constant vying for privileges and power between churchmen and state officials created intrigues and animosities that led at times to violent death. This undermined the well-laid plans for many projects and consumed time that could have been better employed carrying out the wishes of the crown. In addition to politics was the system of *privilegios*, which granted immunities to both churchmen and army personnel. They were responsible to different codes of law and to different tribunals for comparable offenses. When they were tried for crimes and offenses against each other, judgments were far from objective. These circumstances, added to the problems of frontier defense against incursions by French, English, and American expansionists and against a constant onslaught of Indians, make clear why there was a cultural lag and a depressed economy.

El Paso was well named by the conquistadors. It was the "Pass City," El Paso del Norte, which Indians, missionaries, traders, emissaries of the Spanish crown, settlers, travelers, soldiers, and others crossed and recrossed in search of wealth and adventure, seeking homesites—and often sanctuary from the law. The cultural influence of this important center spread north to Las Cruces and southeast to all the settlements of El Paso Valley.

Shortly after it was settled, the valley became an agricultural oasis because of the accessibility of water for irrigation, and the fertile river-bottom lands of a stream that over the years changed its course south from the nearby hills of Loma Tigua. It was culturally an intermediary for the northern province of New Mexico because of its closer contact with New Spain and because of its continuous traffic with the northern villages.

After the opening of the Santa Fe Trail eastern merchants went through El Paso on the way to San Antonio and to other trading centers in Mexico. In the days of the Chihuahua trade El Paso became the hub from which traders dispersed in various directions to trade with other settlements. The region's milder climate and longer growing season with no early frosts provided travelers and trading caravans with replenishments of supplies.

Throughout the Spanish and Mexican periods history takes note of the high quality of El Paso Valley's fruits, wines, and other products. American travelers and leaders of Civil War military expeditions spoke highly of the industrious inhabitants and their cordiality to strangers. In 1807, Lieutenant Zebulon Pike, one of the first Americans to pass through El Paso, wrote of the fine cereals raised in the valley and the excellent quality of the wines. Josiah Gregg, the trader-historian, gave more detailed impressions, telling how the fruits were transported from the old El Paso south of the river to distant markets on *carretas* and mules. He added:

The grapes, carefully dried in the shade make excellent *pasas* or raisins, of which large quantities are annually prepared for market by the people of that delightful town of vineyards and orchards, who taken altogether, are more sober and industrious than those of any part of Mexico I have visited, and happily less infested by the extremes of wealth and poverty.[4]

EL PASO AND NEW MEXICO

In addition to the uniqueness of its agricultural products, cultural differences developed because of El Paso's location at the crossroads of colonial travel. The economic stability resulting from a more productive agriculture, together with continuous trading, despite the Indian depredations and civil and international wars of the nineteenth century, gave El Paso a greater continuity of Spanish traditions. The language of the valley was not as archaic as that of the more isolated regions of northern New Mexico, and contact with a larger variety of people enriched the speech of the southern settlers with a more varied linguistic expression.

Although El Paso was still far removed from the viceroyalty of New Spain, it was considerably closer to the seats of church and state government in Durango and Sonora. After the settlement of Chihuahua and the discovery of the mines at Santa Eulalia and Parral, these new centers served to strengthen the cultural ties with the capital through increased trade and travel. Many of the leading families in El Paso originated in the adjoining Mexican states and were therefore not as ingrown culturally as were isolated settlements where the inhabitants intermarried and continued to live in the same villages for generations. The latter preserved an isolated cultural continuity within the group, while El Paso maintained a continuity with greater diversity through movement. This cultural diversity was reflected in the growth of the language. In the north many archaic expressions were preserved because there were no current ones with which to replace them.

ARRIVAL OF THE ANGLO-AMERICANS

At the beginning of the nineteenth century another cultural element arrived whose influence was to be increasingly felt until in time it superseded Hispanic colonial culture. The first arrivals were well received, as they were in California, and their trading enterprises were so successful that many chose to remain and blend into the population. After the Southwest was officially occupied by American army troops and settlers in search of land, an inevitable change took place that caused Hispanic culture to take a secondary role. The relatively peaceful region took on the nature of a frontier borderland with excesses of saloons and dance halls and the roar of the .45. But despite the uproarious interlude and the usual problems that arise when two cultures meet, the life of El Paso recovered, with a different dominant culture and the addition of another language.

The prejudices and animosities of other parts of Texas were present but not in the same intensity as they existed within the shadow of the Alamo. Eating places such as the Plaza Dining Rooms did not erect signs prohibiting Mexicans from entering but intimated their racial bias by advertising that they were "strictly American." The city's proximity to Mexico and the large proportion of middle-class property owners brought the two cultural groups into contact with each other. The *El Paso Times*, known from 1879 to 1896 as the *El Paso International Daily Times*, was owned by

Juan Siqueiros Hart, who was representative of the city's bicultural nature. By 1896, Protestant churches were flourishing. Baptists, Presbyterians, Methodists, and Pentecostals worshiped in Spanish. Some of the organizations that appeared at the end of the nineteenth century, such as La Constructora, were indications of the Hispanic population's initiative in organizing benevolent societies to protect their people.[5] Scores of families live in El Paso today in homes purchased with death benefits from this society.

El Paso's musical tradition was fashioned after the Lerdo de Tejada pattern of Mexico City, with the establishment of a *típica* orchestra, a string ensemble, marimbas, and a biblical harp called a *salterio*, somewhat like a zither. The first El Paso Symphony Orchestra was made up of members of the McGinty Club Concert Band and the Mexican Típica Orchestra. The McGinty Band disappeared at the turn of the century, but the Típica continued until the years of World War II. It was sponsored by the Chamber of Commerce and played in the lobby of the principal hotels around the plaza. As a further attraction, the orchestra added a young Spanish dancer known as La Charrita.

CULTURAL INTEGRATION

A good indication of the cultural integration that was taking place in the border city was the enchilada dinner given at the home of Mrs. John Dean, of the Matcher's Club, for the city's leading families in 1907. Mexican dinners were not generally social occasions at this early date, even in New Mexico. The social stratification of Mexico in the post-independence era was reflected among the Hispano Mexicans in El Paso, where the distinction between merchant-landowner and peon was marked. This distinction was strengthened by Anglo-Americans from the southern states who were accustomed to a caste society. When incoming Anglos married daughters of the leading Hispano families, they, like their Spanish-speaking in-laws, used the familiar and respectful *don* before their Hispanicized names. An example was Don Hugo (Hugh) Stephenson, who married Juana Ascárate, who would inherit her father's considerable fortune. James W. Magoffin, the well-known merchant of the Santa Fe Trail, joined the social elite when he married into the distinguished Valdez family and became Don Santiago to all. According to Sonnichsen, Ben (Don Benito) Dowell was "almost completely uneducated," but his

La Charrita, of the El Paso Symphony Orchestra, performing a spirited Andalusian folk dance.

clubs for their upper class. Athletic clubs and baseball clubs had to wait until the Hispanos became more sports- and action-minded. The separate social clubs were organized not to compete with each other but because that arrangement seemed more natural and enjoyable. Many of the Hispanic clubs regularly held their dinner-dances at leading hotels. Membership in social clubs was based on social distinctions and affluence. The elite in Hispanic society usually belonged to the Casino, and attendance at their fiestas and balls was only by invitation or membership. A glance at the society pages of El Paso newspapers today reveals the social life of the Hispano Mexicans. They participate in civic fund-raising campaigns, in club entertainments, and similar functions of Anglo-American society.

El Paso and its suburbs are today an international cultural crossroads, with two civilizations separated only by the Río Grande. The residents of both cities are so closely associated that many leading businessmen in Ciudad Juárez live in El Paso and many residents of Ciudad Juárez work *al otro lado*, "on the other side" (in ordinary conversation people from each city refer to the other as *el otro lado*, implying that they lead a "bilateral" existence). American traveling salesmen doing business in El Paso often register at hotels in Ciudad Juárez to be closer to that city's more active social life after working hours. This economic and cultural interaction is reflected in the coincidence of a Mexican consul in El Paso with an English name and an American consul on the Mexican side with a Spanish name. It is also reflected in El Paso's name, which it inherited from the Mexican city across the river when the latter changed its name during the Mexican Civil War.

El Paso has elected Spanish-speaking sheriffs, mayors, county clerks, and other public officials with no more than the usual political fanfare. Streets, boulevards, drives, and parks bear Spanish names, not as cultural concessions but simply because they are historically appropriate. Because both languages are as interchangeable as the peso and the dollar, no one gives the names much thought.

The interesting result is that, although El Paso is in Texas, many Texans insist that it is not part of Texas. The New Mexicans on the north do not consider it a New Mexican culture, forgetting that El Paso was the capital of the province in the seventeenth century. Mexico does not consider El Paso a Mexican city.

shrewd, enterprising nature won not only wealth but a place in society for himself and his wife, Juana Márquez.

Hispanic culture in El Paso and the valley was never totally displaced by American culture, first, because over the centuries the settlers had acquired a strong sense of identity and were loathe to relinquish it in the face of a dominant culture. Rather than a melting pot, El Paso developed a biculturalism with identical social institutions and dual communication—Anglos also spoke Spanish, and Hispanos also spoke English. Hispanos had social

To judge by its tricultural formation, this old valley with its thriving city is not any one of its components but in reality all three—a region that for centuries has been crossed by the cultures that settled the Southwest and today coexist under a relatively new nationality—a gestalt in reverse because it is the sum of its parts. Most families of South El Paso are Mexican, residents for a long or short time, depending on when they arrived from Mexico. In the heights section of the city live mostly English speakers and Anglicized Americans of Hispanic descent whose mode of living is like that of their Anglo-American neighbors. El Paso and its valley and its people are a contrast indeed to the character of the lower Río Grande as a whole.

The establishment of the first two Spanish cultural and military centers along the Río Grande was made possible by the presence of the three conditions essential for a permanent settlement. First, the missionaries needed a concentration of Indians in pueblos or nearby *rancherías* to begin their religious activities as a first step to Hispanicization. Second, a presidio with accessible supply lines was indispensable for the protection of the mission. Third, a settlement of Spanish families had to be assured. Thus was the continuity of the three-phased symbiotic enterprise ensured as part of Spain's plan for occupation of the Southwest. Both Santa Fe and El Paso del Norte prospered because the three essential conditions were met (El Paso's permanence being further assured because of its agricultural development).

CONDITIONS ON THE LOWER RIO GRANDE

In the lower Río Grande circumstances were far less favorable to permanent settlement. First, the territory extended from the semiarid expanses east of the Pecos River to the swamplands of the Gulf Coast. Second, it was inhabited by heterogeneous Indian tribes, from the nomadic Apaches and the cannibalistic Karankawas of the coast to the agrarian Tejas near the Louisiana frontier.

The Spanish crown was interested not only in converting the Indians but also in Hispanicizing them to increase the manpower needed to establish a defense against French encroachment on the eastern frontier. Spanish attempts to establish missions far from the Río Grande were seldom successful. In a few years most of the early missions had to be relocated farther west or abandoned. Most tribes were willing to be baptized in return for gifts and food. After experiencing the liberality of the more affluent whites, the Indians came to expect gifts and demanded them when they were not offered. The itinerary of the Mendoza-López Expedition of 1683 mentions that at the founding of San Clemente mission there were 56 tribes for whom the soldiers killed 4,030

buffaloes. Some historians claim that the number killed to feed the Indians during the expedition was actually about 10,000.

THE FIRST MISSION

The first mission in the Texas province was founded in 1690 west of the Neches River in what is now Houston County by Father Damián Massanet and explorer Alonso de León. They named it San Francisco de los Tejas because it was situated in the land of these friendly Indians. Encouraged by the helpfulness of the Tejas in building the mission church and impressed by their willingness to be baptized, Father Massanet returned to Mexico to request additional support to expand the work. Three years later, however, the Indians lost interest in the evangelizing efforts of the padres, refused to work for them, and in the end became dangerously hostile. The first attempt to set up a mission was abandoned.

PROBING EXPEDITIONS

One of the means used by the Spaniards to restore peace among Indians warring against each other was to send priests to try to establish missions (the Indians fought among themselves more often than they fought the Spaniards). That was the reason so many of the commanders bore the title "Pacifier of the Indians" on their expeditions. Keeping the peace also meant keeping the natives from attacking the Spaniards, of course. One of the first of the pacification expeditions to cross the lower Río Grande to quell Indian hostilities was led by Fernández de Azcue in 1655. He traveled north from Monterrey with over one hundred soldiers and three hundred Indian allies, into the land of the Cacaxtles, where one hundred Indians perished and seventy were taken prisoner. Twenty years later another reconnaissance expedition crossed the river from Coahuila under Fernando del Bosque, who was accompanied by a capable priest named Juan Larios. They penetrated north-

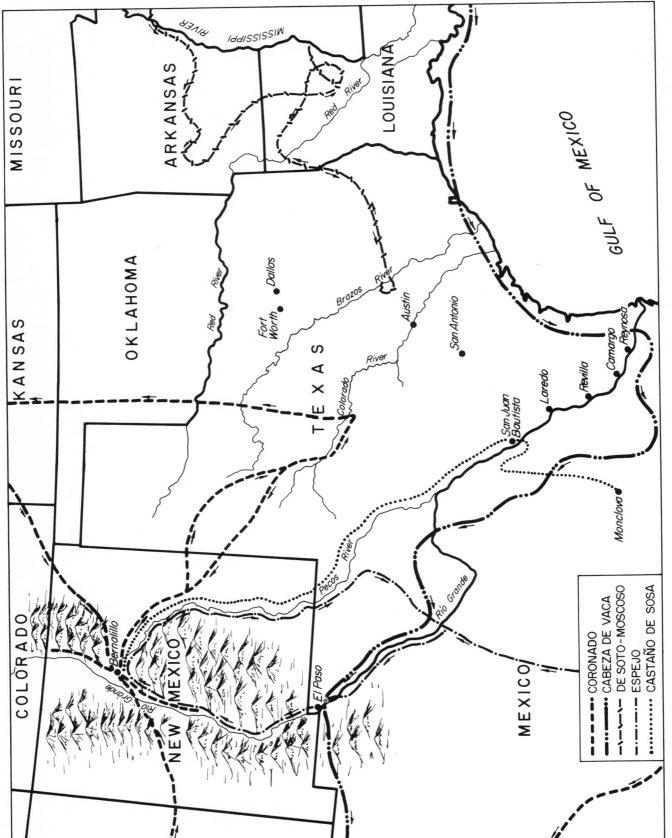

Hispanic Texas

east of present-day Eagle Pass, gathered valuable information, and gave a good description of the country.

ALARCON FOUNDS SAN ANTONIO

The establishment of the third important center on or near the Río Grande in southwestern Texas resulted from a combination of events and at least two favorable conditions. The reports received by the new viceroy, the Marqués de Valero, regarding conditions in the Texas province in 1716, revealed that the French were planning to establish a large trading colony on the Mississippi. Father Sanbuenaventura y Olivares, who had been in the region of present-day San Antonio, reported favorable natural resources on the land and large numbers of Indians along the San Antonio River. The need for the establishment of a mission with its corresponding presidio and pueblo was obvious. The added need to repel French encroachment of a land abounding in natural resources, as well as in trade possibilities, made it imperative to send some of the empire's best-qualified commanders to establish the trilogy of institutions.

The leader chosen for this important *entrada* was Don Martín de Alarcón, an experienced commander who had served the king in Spain and in Africa before coming to the New World. He had also acquired considerable administrative experience in Guadalajara and Michoacán and as governor of the province of Coahuila from 1705 to 1716. In 1718, after almost a year of preparation, Alarcón crossed the Río Grande with a force of seventy-two persons, including several artisans and a large number of livestock, more than five hundred horses and many droves of mules, cattle, sheep, goats and poultry. This was the first arrival of livestock, for which Texas would become well known by the end of the eighteenth century. On April 1, 1718, Alarcón founded the mission of San Antonio de Valero, known today as the Alamo, and named it after the viceroy, whose full name was Baltazar de Zúñiga Guzmán Sotomayor y Mendoza, Marqués de Valero. Four days later, Alarcón founded the Villa de San Antonio de Béxar, the town that would develop into today's San Antonio. The settlement was not on the Río Grande, but it was part of the expansion that began from the region crossed by this historic river.

Alarcón was one of the three most successful commanders sent into Texas to establish missions and presidios. History has recognized the importance of this Spanish nobleman's accomplishments, which have been summed up by a modern historian:[1]

Alarcón's services to the Spanish Crown can hardly be overestimated today. His founding of San Antonio ranks with the Marqués de Aguayo's later refounding of the east Texas settlements in the history of Spain's desperate attempt to control and maintain the province of Texas against French aggression.

IMPORTANCE OF THE MISSIONS

The importance of the missions extended beyond conversion and religious instruction of the Indians. They were Spain's instrument for "civilizing" the natives throughout the Southwest. In Texas the missions acquired a specific significance, because, as the northernmost frontier, the eastern part of the province was vulnerable to French encroachment. The first step in the establishment of a foothold was the conversion of the Indians. By this religious technicality the Indians could be held responsible for their conduct and for the duties assigned to them. As converts they could be, and were, compelled to obey the priests and were severely punished for any infraction of the rules. Many Indians were reluctant to trade personal liberty for the security offered by the mission. Often they ran away from the mission for fear of being whipped by the padres for breaking rules.

One of the most effective ways of incorporating the Indians into Spanish society was to put them to work under the supervision of overseers in agricultural and industrial schools provided at the missions. Teaching the practical aspects of civilization took considerably more effort, but in the end it produced more lasting and satisfactory results. The missions were thus also schools where the Indians learned the necessary skills to live in the society into which, it was hoped, they would become integrated. To become worthy Christians and desirable subjects, they were disciplined in the basics of the Spaniards' idea of civilized life. As they progressed up the ladder of civilization, they were to be introduced to other tenets of colonial society. This desideratum was achieved by very few of the converts. Most of them simply became workers in the fields and in the Spanish households. In those sections of the New World where the Indians were more highly civilized, progress was rapid. In the region of the lower

San Antonio de Valero Mission, built in 1718 by Don Martín de Alarcón and better known today as the Alamo. Courtesy of the Texas State Department of Highways and Public Transportation.

Río Grande, however, the Indians, except for the Caddoan Tejas, were less inclined to profit by the teaching of the missions. To accelerate the training process, civilized Indians from Mexico City were sent to Texas as incentives to the converts.

Missions were indispensable as sources of supplies for the survival of the Indians and Spaniards alike. They were usually established on the banks of rivers to assure water for irrigation was available. Those missions that were established too far inland did not prosper, because in their isolation they were vulnerable to attacks by the Comanches. Such missions as San Sabá and San Xavier did not last more than six lean years and had to be abandoned. They served part of their purpose by supplying information regarding Indian life, which otherwise might never have been recorded. These records have proved invaluable to historians and anthropologists who study Indian life in different regions of the Southwest. Bolton acknowledged the contribution made by the Texas missionaries in 1915, by saying: "The painstaking reports and correspondence of the missionaries as a whole will always stand as a monument to their training and intelligence, and, though yet little known, will constitute a priceless treasury of history and ethnology."[2]

THE MARQUES OF AGUAYO

The abandonment of a number of missions in southern Texas and the weakening of presidios became the chief concern of the viceroy in the early eighteenth century. To strengthen Spain's control of the Texas frontier, a second expedition was sent north to reoccupy the vacated missions and presidios. The leader of this *entrada* was a prestigious and wealthy nobleman who also had an impressive amount of administrative and military experience. In 1721 the Marqués de San Miguel de Aguayo marched north with an army of five hundred well-equipped soldiers, a large force of Indian allies, and thousands of cattle and horses. He spent a year visiting outposts as far east as the Neches River and along the Gulf Coast. He relocated missions where they could be better supplied, fortified decrepit presidios with stone structures, equipped them with brass cannon, and manned them with additional troops. In all, the marqués built and reconstructed four presidios in strategic locations, relocated and reoccupied nine missions, and left them all well supplied.

Aguayo was also responsible for a mission hastily built in San Antonio and named for him. San José de San Miguel de Aguayo eventually came to be known simply as San José. Under the patronage of the wealthy nobleman the mission's future was assured. Within a few years it housed Indians and missionaries, and it became the most prosperous agricultural center in Texas, harvesting thousands of bushels of wheat annually. The vocational centers where all trades were taught by the padres and by imported artisans were particularly useful in the program of integrating the Indians. The chapel of San José still stands as a monument to the work of the unselfish marqués, who worked diligently for years and underwrote the entire cost of his extensive expedition to Texas.

THE CANARY ISLANDERS

When Aguayo completed his tour of the missions and military outposts throughout the province, he realized that more European settlers were needed to hasten the permanence of the province, if it was to serve as a buffer to French infiltration.

It would take too long to civilize and train enough Indians to serve effectively as settlers to hold the province against foreign incursions. In his report to the viceroy the marqués recommended that Spaniards be brought in from Galicia in northern Spain, from Cuba, and from the Canary Islands. Of the one hundred families sent from the islands seven years later, only fifteen reached San Antonio. They were settled in a town lot near the San Antonio de Valero Mission. The islanders were given all the necessary supplies, seeds, and farming tools with which to begin cultivating the land allotted to them. They organized the first villa in Texas with a relatively independent government, built their homes with the quality of permanence expected by Aguayo, founded a parish church instead of a mission, and started the first school in Texas. Being more urbanized than their neighbors, they saw the need for formal education even on the frontier. The Villa de San Fernando de Béxar survives today as La Villita in modern San Antonio, and the original parish church developed into San Fernando Cathedral.

La Villita is an interesting museum where tourists can view the relics of San Antonio's Spanish period. Those who are not familiar with the history of Texas wonder at the legends on displayed items that label them as "Spanish" instead of "Mexican," as one would expect of a state that was part of Mexico when it gained independence. The labels are historically correct, because the Canary Islanders came directly to San Antonio without going through the transition of Mexican acculturation. Moreover, the islanders, all of whom were hidalgos, according to history, did not intermarry with the Mexican *mestizos* but married within their own group and later with Anglo-Americans who settled Texas before Mexican independence. In a sense these imported settlers with their own degree of self-government, their parish church, and their school, can lay claim to being the first urban, independent Texans.

JOSE DE ESCANDON'S EXPEDITION

The third of the important Spanish military leaders to undertake the settlement of the lower Río Grande was José de Escandón, whose procedures represented the best and most successful colonization efforts of the Spanish Empire in the Southwest. Some writers have been so deeply impressed by Escandón's accomplishments that they refer to his enterprise as the "odyssey of the Río Grande."

San José Mission in San Antonio, Texas, built in honor of the Marqués de Aguayo in 1720 and known in Texas as "the queen of missions" because of its size and beautiful construction. Courtesy of the Texas State Department of Highways and Public Transportation.

La Villita, a village established in San Antonio, Texas, in 1728 by a group of Canary Islanders brought to Texas by the Marqués de Aguayo. It was the first villa in Texas with a relatively independent government and was known as the Villa of San Fernando de Béxar. Courtesy of the Texas State Department of Highways and Public Transportation.

The San Antonio River, as it looked before 1963, meandering through San Antonio. In its colorful history it has been crossed by Indians, Spaniards, Mexicans, Germans, and Anglo-Americans. Courtesy of the Texas State Department of Highways and Public Transportation.

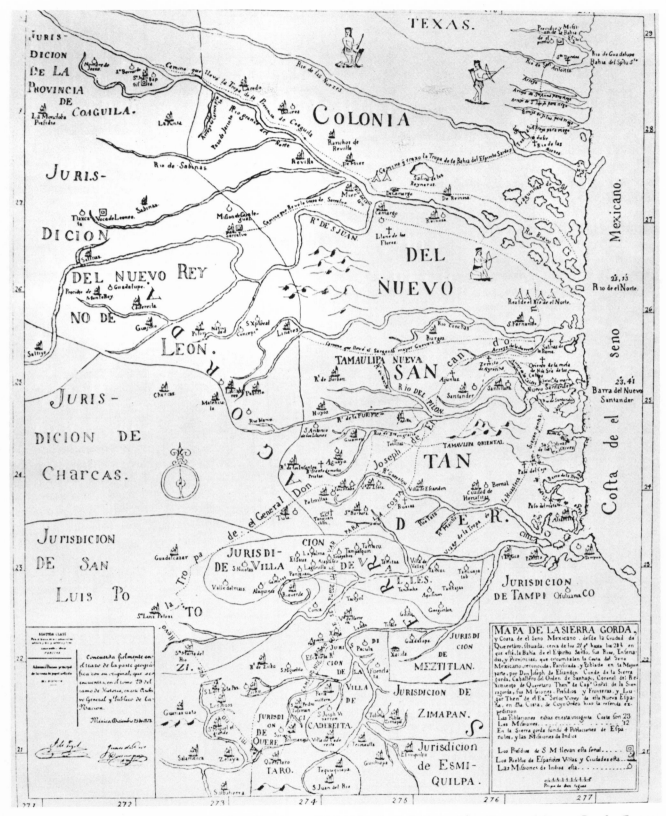

A map of southwest Texas showing the villages established by José de Escandón, Count of Sierra Gorda. Reproduced from Alejandro Prieto's *Historia geográfica y estadística del estado de Tamaulipas*, published in 1873.

The success of this project eventually influenced all of southwest Texas. San Antonio also profited by connection with the Río Grande through the establishment of Laredo directly south of what became, after Escandón's *entrada*, the San Antonio Road.

The land southeast of Laredo had been explored and crossed by several Spanish conquistadors whose explorations were not followed up with settlements. When Escandón was commissioned to undertake this important enterprise, he laid out a blueprint that was followed faithfully, with a time schedule carried out with uncanny precision. His settlement plan sounds like a modern land development of mammoth proportions, except that it was carried out under a number of adverse circumstances which the persistent commander overcame. His first step was a thorough survey of each locality: its resources, the availability of water for irrigation, the nature of the soil, and the responsiveness of the Indians. Every detail of his plan was carefully laid out before he set out with his seven captains in as many divisions to reconnoiter the territory and to prepare the recommendations they would make at the conclusion of their explorations. Following the established time schedule, all seven captains and their parties met at the end of their inspection tour at the mouth of the Río Grande to discuss the townsites with Escandón.

Two years after the survey was finished and agreed upon, Escandón petitioned for five hundred families with whom to settle fourteen designated townsites. Rules for settlement of towns, kinds of settlers, royal subsidies, supplies, livestock, and all other important matters were arranged for before the expedition departed. On March 5, 1749, he reached the Río Grande and founded Nuestra Señora de Santa Ana de Camargo, known today simply as Camargo. For several years he continued downriver, founding a total of twenty-three villages with missions on the lower Río Grande. The success of this enterprise can be gauged by the census of 1750, which credited Camargo and Reynosa with a total of 108 families and 36,000 head of stock. Escandón's expedition, like those of Alarcón and Aguayo, continued to introduce cattle to the region.

Many of the towns that Escandón founded, such as Reynosa, Camargo, and Mier, are on the Mexican side of the river, but Laredo on the United States side is now an important port of entry in southwest Texas. Escandón supervised

his project and saw it through the Acts of Possession until 1767. He did not retire until the settlement of the lower Río Grande had become a reality. His accomplishment is best summed up by Florence Scott:

North American history does not include another story or even a legend comparable to the successful colonization procedures used by this forty-seven-year-old Spaniard, who not only founded the five permanent settlements of the lower Río Grande—Laredo, Revilla (Guerrero), Mier, Camargo, and Reynosa—but many others as well, and fortunately lived to see them prosper far beyond his fondest dream.[3]

LOUISIANA TERRITORY ACQUIRED BY SPAIN

The transfer of the Louisiana Territory from France to Spain under the Treaty of Paris in 1763 put an end to the conflict that for years had been the concern of Spain in Texas. The year after the tranfer the Marqués de Rubí made a rapid tour of the northern frontier, and in his report to the viceroy he recommended a number of sorely needed reforms in army administration. With the removal of the French threat, the need for eastern frontier missions was minimal. It was therefore recommended that they be moved to San Antonio or abandoned. The capital of the province was moved from Los Adaes to San Antonio, much to the displeasure of the settlers, who had built what they thought were permanent homes. The marqués' practical recommendations were later incorporated in the Regulations for Presidios of the Frontier, enacted in 1772. The plan was to consolidate the provinces into three principal centers: Bahía, moved inland from the coast; Nacogdoches, near the Louisiana border; and San Antonio, with five missions, as the cultural and military center for the province. The marqués realized that it was virtually impossible for Spanish civilization to gain a foothold in places like San Sabá, Cañon, and other distant points that were raided constantly by the Apaches and the Comanches.

DEFENSES AGAINST HOSTILE INDIANS

Some notable progress was made after the transfer of the Louisiana Territory. It was now possible to devote more effort to defense against the Apaches and the Comanches, whose increased depredations led to a more aggressive policy by the crown. The man appointed to carry out the new plan was

Today's longhorn, a descendant of the Spanish cattle introduced by colonizers such as Escandón and Aguayo. Courtesy of Coronado Cuarto Centennial.

Teodoro de Croix, an able professional of long experience. As commandant of the Provincias Internas, he declared in 1776 an immediate war of extermination against enemies of the crown. The defenses of the Apaches were undermined by turning the Mescaleros against the Lipans.

Other experienced commanders took part in the new divide-and-conquer strategy. Governor Alejandro O'Reilly of Louisiana enlisted the services of Athanase de Mézières to win the northern tribes and the Comanches against the warlike Apaches. The Frenchman's knowledge of several languages and dialects was particularly useful in this campaign. In 1780 the Lipan Apaches came to San Antonio to sue for peace rather than to attack and steal stock as had been their custom.

When El Caballero de Croix, as Don Teodoro liked to be known, made a tour of the northern provinces, he took along scholarly Father Agustín de Morfi as his chronicler. During the comman-

175

dant's extended journey the observant padre took copious notes, from which he later wrote the first history of Texas. Another important contribution to the cultural history of the province was embodied in the reconstruction of the chapel of San José Mission in San Antonio in 1768 (this was the mission that had been erected in honor of the Marqués de Aguayo when he passed through the city in 1721 on his successful reoccupation expedition). Today San José is a national historical monument, considered by historians as one of the best examples of Spanish mission architecture.

DISSENSION ON THE FRONTIER

Of the three institutions created on the frontier for the establishment of Spanish civilization and conversion of the Indians, the most effective was undoubtedly the mission. It was planned originally as a transition for the Indians from their primitive condition to a Christian civilized state. The church envisioned a period of ten years as sufficient to transform the Indian into an urbanized individual able to live in colonial society on his own. When this was accomplished, the missions would be secularized and become parish churches.

The missions, together with the presidios and the pueblos, were supposed to work harmoniously in the conquest of the land, in the pacification and conversion of the Indians, and in the founding of permanent settlements. The history of these institutions reveals, however, that seldom if ever did they work in concert for any length of time.

Most of the dissension centered around the use of the land and the services demanded from the Indians at the missions. Constant jurisdictional controversies could not be resolved in the field and had to be referred to the viceroy and even to the king in Spain. The missionaries felt that the cruel and harsh treatment of the Indians by the presidial soldiers alienated the former from the church and interfered with their conversion efforts. The church needed additional converts with whom to justify higher subsidies and land increases for agriculture. The missions collided with the settlers, who also needed cultivable land, which they found preempted by the mission requests.

It was expected that, because they lived there, Indians would work primarily on the mission farms. The presidial soldiers and the settlers also needed the services of the mission Indians in their households and cattle lands. There was constant competition among the three institutions for services to which they felt they were entitled. The only solution was secularization of the missions so that no one could claim priority on the Indians, and they could become subjects of the crown. By 1800 all but two of the missions had been secularized in Texas, but the occupation of the land was far short of what had been envisioned.

REDUCING THE INDIANS

The Spanish crown tried to maintain jurisdiction over the province, transform the Indians from their primitive existence into *indios reducidos* who could carry on the progress of Spanish civilization and develop the land resources. The first objective was accomplished by keeping out all foreigners and by preserving the frontiers of the empire in the Southwest. Many Indians were converted, but compared with the vast majority of those still living outside the missions, the number was very small. The security offered by the mission did not compensate for the loss of freedom. The Apaches and the Comanches were seldom willing to settle down to the routine of mission and pueblo life. They preferred freedom to roam and live from pillage and hunting. Indians in agrarian settlements, such as the Caddoans, were more easily Hispanicized. Eventually these created the *mestizos*, who constituted the bulk of the Mexican population.

SPANISH CIVILIZATION BY 1800

By the end of the eighteenth century the total population of the lower Río Grande was not much over five thousand. The industry of the province consisted of cattle raising and farming, with smuggling running a close second. The latter occupation was the result of Spain's trade restrictions in the colonies. It was logical for the Texas settlers to look for outlets in neighboring Louisiana, where there was a good market for cattle. Cattle drives were made to the adjacent territory in Spanish days, despite the government's restrictions on trade. In return, the traders bought merchandise that was more expensive when imported from Mexico.

Unrestricted trade would have improved relations with the Indians in east Texas. They preferred to trade with the Louisiana French, because their policy was more liberal and open. The only export encouraged by the crown was religious conversion, offered by the missions to aborigines who did not feel a great need for Christian salvation. Moreover, the Indians realized before long that this was simply the first step toward reduction and the loss of freedom that accompanied it. Viewed in this light, the religious efforts of the missionaries were a failure. But the civilizing accomplished by teaching the Indians how to farm and to other practical skills was in the long run a greater service to both Indian and Spaniard.

Hispanic civilization in Texas around 1800 was principally agrarian-pastoral, with enough craftsmen and artisans to supply the goods and services of a pioneer culture. The expeditions sent by the government had been careful to bring along tailors, blacksmiths, weavers, carpenters, shoemakers, barbers, and other skilled persons whose services might be of use in the province. There were no lawyers, but there were notarios públicos whose duties extended beyond witnessing signatures. There were no medical doctors, but there were plenty of folk herbalists, curanderos, and midwives to serve the people's needs.

Spanish society in the nineteenth century was governed by caste, even in the provinces, but social stratification was not as strongly felt in places like Texas, where the population consisted mostly of farm hands, laborers, servants, and Indians. There was a slightly higher class, the artisans and craftsmen such as masons and silversmiths, who belonged to gremios, or guilds. Successful stock raisers and large landowners were the principal men of wealth. They enjoyed privileges not accorded to ordinary workers. Officers of the presidios and appointees of the crown, together with the landowners, constituted the upper class in urban centers such as San Antonio. Noblemen occasionally visited the province on official business or as the heads of expeditions. These representatives of the titled class kept the populace aware of a higher order of society in the viceroyalty and in the court of Madrid. Finally there were the mission churchmen, whose cultural contributions included reports and chronicles describing the country and the Indians and recording historical events. Most of what we know today about the Indians and the people of colonial days came from the pens of the padres in the provinces. Spain's class system created a social structure that continued throughout its presence in the Southwest—and to a large extent through the Mexican period until the Revolution of 1910,

for after 1822 the criollos took up where the peninsulars left off.

At the end of the eighteenth century and through the first half of the nineteenth the population in Texas consisted of a small number of Spaniards and criollos and a majority of mestizos—products of the assimilative process that took place at the missions and at the pueblos or descendants of mestizos brought from Mexico to accelerate the work of the missionaries in their craft schools. There were also a few Negroes, mulattoes, cuarterones, and other mixtures of Indians and blacks known as zambos. Other designations, such as coyotes and lobos, were used by the Spaniards for the many admixtures in the New World. The proximity of French Louisiana, Spanish territory until 1800, added a few French names to the Texas province. After Mexican independence the population became even more cosmopolitan.

AFTERMATH OF THE LOUISIANA PURCHASE

In the first quarter of the nineteenth century a number of events altered the course of Spanish life and culture in Texas and by the middle of the century spread over the entire Southwest. The first of these events was the sale of the Louisiana Territory to the United States. In 1800, by the secret Treaty of San Ildefonso, Spain retroceded the territory to France with the understanding that it was not to be alienated. When the United States discovered that it was to have a powerful, ambitious country for a neighbor, Robert R. Livingston, the American minister in Paris, made several attempts to prevent the transfer. He was instructed that, if those failed, he was to try to negotiate the purchase of New Orleans and West Florida. James Monroe joined Livingston in these deliberations with Minister Talleyrand in Paris.

The imminent war with Britain, along with the uprising in Haiti, caused Napoleon to offer unexpectedly through his minister the entire Louisiana Territory for sale. The American ministers, without instructions from Washington, boldly accepted for the United States a territory that increased the national domain by 140 percent at a cost of only four cents an acre. President Jefferson believed that the Constitution did not grant him power to acquire foreign territory, and so he proposed a permissive amendment. When it was rumored that Napoleon might change his mind, the treaty was promptly ratified on October

21, 1803. Congress was not about to dispute such a good bargain at a time when the destiny of the new republic pointed westward.

The Louisiana purchase can be considered the regressive turning point of Hispanic cultural growth in the Southwest. It is ironic that the same territory from which Spain helped the American revolutionary cause by driving the British from the Mississippi River, and from the city of St. Louis, should be lost to the same country that she once helped to free.

CONFUSING FILIBUSTERING

Once the Americans became Spain's neighbors on a long-disputed frontier, it was their turn to pose a threat to the land that Spain had tried to colonize and on which it had but a tenuous hold. The new neighbors lost no time infiltrating Spanish territory on Indian trading sorties or acquiring farmland. Some of the filibustering expeditions proposed to acquire the Mississippi Valley for Spain, others to win Texas for the United States. After the struggle for independence began in Mexico, many American soldiers of fortune joined various groups led by Mexican "patriots," whose attempts came to a tragic end. First among these filibusters was General James Wilkinson, commander of the American forces in the Southwest. He, together with a number of accomplices, began a series of filibustering expeditions undertaken under the pretext of helping Mexican patriots. These incursions ended disastrously for some of his associates and eventually involved him in treasonable acts that led to his banishment from the United States.

The filibustering period involved Mexicans, Spaniards, Americans, and Frenchmen in a series of double-dealing enterprises in which Wilkinson acted as a double agent. Despite the confusing state of affairs, Spain was able to repulse the intruders and imprison a number of them. Part of the problem was that there were no well-defined boundaries. Some considered the Mississippi the western boundary, and others believed that the Louisiana Territory extended to the Río Grande in New Mexico or to the foot of the Rockies. A confrontation about these indeterminate boundaries took place in 1806 at the Sabine River between General Wilkinson and a Spanish commander, Simón de Herrera. The American insisted on protecting his nation's interests as far west as the Sabine, and the Spanish commander declared that

he would patrol beyond it. Some historians surmise that Wilkinson was in the employ of Spain, for he promptly declared a truce.

MEXICAN INDEPENDENCE

Seven years after the rug was pulled from under the Spaniards by the sale of the Louisiana Territory to the United States, Spain had to face another crisis that lasted eleven years more. During those years the provinces suffered economically and socially, neglected because of the exigencies of rebellion.

The independence movement in Mexico in 1810 gave rise to all sorts of schemes to make Texas an independent nation, to annex it to the United States, and even to set it up as part of Joseph Bonaparte's new realm in Mexico after he lost the Spanish throne. The heart of the independence movement was in Mexico itself, below the Río Grande—the participation of the Internal Provinces was almost wholly detached from the physical struggle, although Texas was reached by the spirit of Hidalgo. Many attempts to capture and hold Texas for the Mexican liberals were abortive and lasted only until the loyalist armies arrived.

The first independence sortie, led by Juan Bautista de las Casas, came as a surprise to the Spanish garrison in San Antonio on January 22, 1811, four months after the start of the revolution at Dolores. Las Casas notified the other two centers in Texas, Bahía and Nacogdoches, that he was now the chief executive. Strangely enough, the counterrevolution was led by prominent native Texans—Erasmo Seguín, Juan Zambrano, and many others—who restored the loyalist government ten days after Las Casas had taken over. A second uprising was led by Bernardo Gutiérrez de Lara, a more imaginative leader, who saw an opportunity to enlist the cooperation of the American government, or at least its moral support, for the large number of Americans who answered Gutiérrez' call to arms. This movement was more a filibustering expedition; it began in Louisiana and so entered Texas from a foreign country and was commanded by an American, Agustus W. Magee, who resigned his lieutenant's commission in the American army to join the insurgents. They took possession of all the strongholds, beginning with the post at the Trinity River and culminating their success with the fall of San Antonio. After executing the royalist officers, Gutiérrez declared the independence of Texas. Five months later, the

Spanish royalists reversed the story and retook the city after routing the patriots and executing a number of them.

LOUISIANA BOUNDARY SETTLED

Toward the end of the Spanish regime in America, John Quincy Adams and Luis de Onís, the Spanish ambassador to the United States, spent many months trying to determine the boundaries of the Spanish Empire in North America. It was very important to define the boundaries in view of the American interest in western expansion. There were a number of provisions in the treaty, but the one that directly affected Texas was the western boundary of the Louisiana Territory. Many Americans, particularly those working on the frontier, were not happy with the provisions of the Adams-Onís Treaty; they felt that the United States had ceded too much land to Spain on the Louisiana-Texas border. Politically and diplomatically the matter was settled, but until the boundary was actually surveyed, it would continue to plague land seekers wishing to settle on American soil.

MILLER COUNTY ON MEXICAN SOIL

Miller County, on the Neches, was born of nationalism and boundary disputes. In 1820 the Arkansas Territorial Legislature created the county, and settlers moved in. Fifteen years later the Mexican government sent Colonel Nepomuceno Almonte, an educated, English-speaking officer, to survey and report on conditions in Texas. His estimates of the population, economic progress, and the attitude of the settlers toward the central government were very optimistic. When he visited Miller County, he notified the settlers that they were on Mexican soil. There was no inconvenience, Colonel Almonte informed them; they would receive land titles from Mexico. This assurance pleased the Americans, whose main objective was to get land under the best terms. At that time Mexican land laws were more liberal than those of the United States. Adams and Onís had settled the boundary problem over the conference table, but settlers would not know the physical lines of demarcation until a survey was made.

LAND GRANTS TO AMERICANS

The purchase of the Louisiana Territory was, as mentioned, the first step in the de-Hispanicization of Texas. The next step was the arrival of the American colony brought by Stephen Austin. The colony had been approved by Colonel Joaquín Arredondo, commandant of the Eastern Division of the Internal Provinces. Moses Austin, the originator of the plan, did not live to see it materialize. It fell to his son, Stephen, to bring the first three hundred American families.

Stephen Austin planned to establish his colony between the Colorado and the Brazos rivers, but his timetable was upset by the overthrow of the Spanish government from which his father had secured the grant. Austin went to Mexico City to plead his cause. There he learned that a Spanish land grant would not be honored by the Mexican government. After lengthy negotiations, however, the grant was reinstated by the government of Iturbide. His government was overthrown soon afterward, but Mexico's interest in colonizing Texas and the many friendships that Austin made in the capital won him a special and more liberal contract.

The contract allotted to every family head one *labor*, 177 acres, and Austin was given 100,000 acres as impresario of the undertaking. Taxes were waived for a six-year period to give the settlers a good start. The provision that all colonists were to become Mexican citizens was reasonable, but the requirement that they must all become Roman Catholics was unrealistic for people who came from a strong Protestant tradition with a prejudice against Catholicism dating back to Elizabethan days. The first seed of contention was planted. Historians have pointed out that the American colonists in Texas were not willing to abide by these conditions, even though they accepted land offered by Mexico. W. Eugene Hollon bluntly states: "The Anglo-American settlers who flocked into Texas after 1820 were not content with existence under a foreign government. Mexican residents quickly discovered that many of the new arrivals were aggressive, opinionated, domineering, and intolerant."[4]

The American colonists were brought in to develop the land and also to forestall further filibustering expeditions by adventurers. They were grateful for the generous land bounties offered by Mexico at a time when American land laws were considered confiscatory. The first colonists of the Austin grant entered Texas on August 18, 1824. Seven months later the authority to grant land was passed to the states under the State

Colonization Law, a more convenient arrangement for prospective colonists to acquire land. This opened the gates to impresarios who rushed to secure contracts to bring in American colonists. Unlike Austin, the impresarios of 1825 were not selective about the Americans they brought into the promised land.

The colonization law did not restrict the nationality of the colonists. Settlement was open to Mexicans, Europeans, and Americans. Mexicans had more latitude in selecting their land because, being nationals, they were exempt from the provision that foreign nationals had to settle at least ten miles from the coast. The only ones allowed to settle on land along the coast, besides Mexican citizens, were the colonists of De Witt and Austin, but, considering the record of these leaders, their special privileges are understandable. Nevertheless, Americans resented the preferential treatment given to De Witt and Austin and to Mexican nationals.

A cattleman from Tamaulipas, Martín de León, brought not only Mexican families but also Irish and American. He founded the present city of Victoria, named for President Guadalupe Victoria. Other prominent Mexicans, such as Lorenzo de Zavala and Vicente Filisola, contracted to bring in a total of eleven hundred families, most of them foreigners. Needless to say, a large number of the families contracted for never arrived. The most successful of the impresarios was Stephen Austin. Had all the settlers abided by his counsel, many of the problems that arose later might have been resolved before they reached international proportions. Unfortunately there was only one Austin.

AMERICAN INFLUENCE IN TEXAS

The impact of this enterprising, energetic army of American farmers and future cattlemen on the Hispanic population was inevitable. It was especially stressful to the upper-class Hispanos and Mexicans. The working people did not have much direct contact with the newcomers, who were largely self-sufficient and had slaves to do their menial work. One Mexican inspector who went to Texas reported that Mexicans who came in close contact with the American colonists were becoming Americanized but the Americans were not becoming Hispanicized. The Mexican government was apprehensive about the speed and efficiency with which the new Anglo-Mexicans were

setting up grist mills, opening schools, and producing crops that outdistanced by a considerable margin the yield of Mexican farmlands. Despite all this advancement, there were no visible signs of cultural adjustment to their adopted land. On the other hand, the Mexican government made a number of adjustments to accommodate the American colonists. The Coahuila legislature, which included Texas, passed reforms as a compromise to American juridical traditions, such as trial by jury, liberalization of trade laws, and exemption from slaveholding laws when President Vicente Guerrero abolished slavery in 1829. The rugged American individualists were contemptuous of any authority but their own. Although the *municipio* system of local government gave them a good deal of autonomy and self-government, the Anglo-Texans were not satisfied.

As a result of these conditions, the government sent Manuel Mier y Terán to investigate the state of affairs in Texas and to give particular attention to the colonists. He reported a very successful production of cotton and other products, great advancements in the cattle industry, and a feeling of optimistic contentment among the colonists. He reported, however, that the Mexicans living near the Americans were becoming Americanized. As far as progress was concerned, he was sorry that he could not report similar advancements among the Mexican settlers, about whom he gave an adverse report. The contrast in accomplishment was no doubt attributable to differences in motivation and personal characteristics of the settlers.

The Anglo-Texans had come in search of land to cultivate profitably as part of their thrift-economy tradition. They were products of a society for whom the cultivation of the soil was a source of pride. *Mestizos* and Hispanicized Indians, who constituted the bulk of the Mexican population in Texas, were content to raise enough to supply the needs of the moment. Many of them had never fully assimilated the culture of their Spanish-Mexican overlords in colonial days, nor had they had the opportunity to improve their retarded condition in the short, restless Mexican period. They had not developed the acquisitiveness of the Anglo and were too far removed from their own centers of culture to profit by contact with more progressive members of their own nationality. The peons of Mexican days had become inured to their lot and did not have the spirit of competitiveness of the newly arrived colonists. Mier y Terán was highly critical of conditions among the Mexican laborers, and he recommended that a better class of Mexican settlers should be sent to Texas to help maintain a proper balance of progress. José Vasconcelos, the Mexican philosopher, writing in 1952, reiterated the opinions of Mier y Terán.

OTHER INTERCULTURAL INFLUENCES

The arrival of Anglo-American colonists did not revolutionize the agrarian culture of the Hispanic population in Texas. It was for the most part an intensification of the agriculture already in existence. The Anglo-Americans, on the other hand, added a different form of animal husbandry that changed the character of Anglo-Texans and gave them the individuality associated with the open range. The Mexican vaqueros in the Texas ranchos had a well-developed cattle-raising industry that, if it lacked selective breeding, was extensive in quantity. The *chaparrales* of the province were full of wild cattle that had multiplied from the original Andalusian breed introduced by the expeditions of Alarcón, Aguayo, and Escandón in the eighteenth century. The new Anglo-American colonists were quick to adopt open-range stock raising, together with the Mexican nomenclature and *indumentaria*, including sombrero, chaps, boots, and saddle. The Spanish vocabulary assimilated by the Anglo-Texans was the natural result of the adoption of an ongoing industry for which they had no equivalent nomenclature. Moreover, the colonists were now Mexican citizens living on land granted to them by a country whose national language was Spanish. Whenever possible, the language was Anglicized, producing such variations as *lariat* for *la reata*, *hackamore* for *jáquima*, *dally* for *dale vuelta*, *mustang* for *mesteño* or *mostrenco*, *chaps* for *chaparreras*, and *buckaroo* for *vaquero*. Some Spanish words, such as *remuda*, *látigo*, *pronto*, *rodeo*, *sombrero*, and *tapadera*, were adopted unchanged, although they were pronounced in characteristic southern or western Anglo-American fashion.

ADDITIONS TO THE TABLE FARE

The American colonists in Texas also added a few items to their daily fare from the tables of Hispanic folk. Both had in common the usual staples of beef and potatoes, but pinto beans, known at that time as *frijoles garrapatas*, chile con carne without beans, corn tortillas, tamales, and dishes prepared with these ingredients were added to the Anglo-Texan cuisine. A meat dish that appealed to the new colonists was *barbacoa*, a special way of preparing a side of beef or a quarter, depending on the number of dinner guests. It was not only adopted but appropriated by the newcomers under the name "Texas barbecue." The *barbacoa* that the Spaniards had imported from the Caribbean appealed to the Anglo-Texans, who liked to do things in a big way. The best way to roast a whole steer was to barbecue it in a preheated pit and then skewer it on a revolving spit, where it was basted with a special sauce. The name was changed from the Spanish to *barbecue*, but the quality and the flavor remained unchanged and stable—in Texas.

Hispanic cuisine was basically Spanish, with a number of added Indian variations from the Mexican plateau. In San Antonio particularly the people continued to prepare a large variety of Mexican dishes alongside the traditional *puchero* or *cocido*, *arroz con pollo*, *pipián*, *albóndigas*, and many other dishes of Spanish provenance. They did not add any of the southern American dishes prepared from corn, because Mexicans were the product of a maize culture whose corn preparations were more sophisticated than grits and corn pone. The mutual intercultural influences in Texas were strongly apparent in concrete, material things. Food habits, dress, language, arts, and crafts reflected the assimilation that took place within a few years. According to Hollon, in his *The Southwest, Old and New*, the Mexican decorative blanket was considered the height of rural fashion in the early days of the republic in Texas. The lack of acceptance was in nonmaterial things, such as value systems, religions, familial folkways, and a number of legal concepts.

MUTUAL MISUNDERSTANDING

In a period of fifteen years Anglo-Texans (who politically were Anglo-Mexicans) discovered a number of traits and social concepts of their adopted country that they found especially difficult to accept. Likewise, Hispanic residents in Texas noticed a number of customs and attitudes that made them suspicious and cautious in dealing with the Anglo colonists. Mexican officials interested in the progress being made by the new colonists applauded the successful results gained by them and deplored the deficiencies of their

Mexican compatriots. The more liberal members of each group, such as Austin and other members of his colony, were willing to compromise on some of the political and cultural differences. But these men were too few to stem the tide of intolerance and misunderstanding.

TEXAS WAR OF INDEPENDENCE

The catalyst that fused ulterior motives, dormant hatreds, and political differences over the Centralist-Federalist issue was President Santa Anna's betrayal of the Federalist cause, which he had openly sponsored in Mexico. Both Anglo and Mexican liberals had sought the creation of a separate state of Texas within the republic, a practical possibility that they expected to realize under the federalist system of government. When the opportunist Santa Anna turned Centralist overnight, the citizens of Texas felt that they had lost their autonomy and a good share of their personal freedom. The Anglo colonists, together with some of the leading Hispanic ranchers, may have taken an exaggerated view of the political order and escalated issues that might have been resolved in time. As the issues became heated, hatreds and prejudices that had been held in abeyance suddenly came to the surface and grew to the point that what had begun as a political problem flamed into armed resistance against the Mexican nation. Once blood was shed, the latent feelings of rebellion, a desire for full independence (with more than spiritual backing from the United States), and racial prejudices coalesced, dividing the people of Texas into two belligerent groups. The defeat at the Alamo, with all its unmilitary consequences, was the point of no return. The conduct of what began as a punitive war against rebellious Texans grew into an armed struggle for independence. Mexico had enough manpower and military resources to have quelled the Texas uprising handily, but Santa Anna's leadership left much to be desired.

In retrospect, historians and social scientists have tried to appraise the causes of the war. It is a long story in which no single cause for the war is attributable. It is safe to say that war could have been averted had there been at the helm of the Mexican government a statesman rather than an ambitious military dictator. José Vasconcelos gave his estimate of Santa Anna: "This contemptible man represented all the vices of the military caste dedicated to controlling and not to defending

General Antonio López de Santa Anna, president of Mexico during the war with the United States. Courtesy of the Arizona Historical Society Museum.

the country."[5] Some scholars believe that the inability of Anglos to bridge the cultural gap, accentuated by religious differences, was the principal cause of the Texas rebellion. But it does not explain why Zavala, Seguín, Navarro, and many other rebels of Hispanic ancestry joined the war against Mexico. The Federalist-Centralist political tug of war applies to the many Mexican citizens who died in the struggle. Mexicans fought and died in political struggles in Mexico by the thousands before and after the Texas rebellion.

Culturally the outcome of the Texas war was tragic for Hispanic residents; thereafter, Texans equated every Mexican with the fall of the Alamo. Spanish-speaking settlers became less than second-class citizens of the new republic. The vindictiveness that rankled the hearts of Texans whose relatives died in the struggle was visited on Mexican folk who had hardly participated in it. In a few more years their lot would be worsened, as Mexico and the United States became involved in a war for which the Texas episode was a stepping-stone to the fulfillment of manifest destiny.

THE MEXICAN WAR

The mutual hatreds and animosities that built up between Mexicans and Americans during the Texas rebellion became intensified in Mexico when the United States recognized the independence of Texas. A diplomatic crisis developed when Texas was admitted to the Union. Mexico interpreted these events as direct insults by the United States and a belligerent manifestation of American expansionism. As tensions mounted, both countries began mobilizing their armies to the frontier long before hostilities broke out. The presence of troops poised on either side of the Río Grande needed only a spark to ignite the powder keg. North of the river there was a feeling of superiority and contempt for a nation that had lost a rebellious state. On the south there was a feeling of confidence in a European-trained army, in internal defenses, in a cavalry that was second to none, and in the advantage of well-known terrain. Added to this was the strong belief that intervention would be forthcoming from Europe in the event of war.

The main weakness in Mexico was the political instability of the central government after the Texas rebellion. Presidents succeeded each other overnight, and diplomats were unable to cope with the problems that arose between the two nations. The outbreak of hostilities resulted from an incident on the Texas border that the United States interpreted as invasion of its territory. Mexico, which had not recognized the independence of Texas, felt that it was within its rights to cross the Río Grande into territory still considered Mexican soil. At the end of the war Mexico ceded territory that extended the American domain to the Pacific coast.

CULTURAL SETBACK

Before the war with Mexico all social, economic, and legal institutions were those established by Spain and Mexico. The language too was Spanish, but after 1848 it was replaced by English, thenceforth the language in which all business trans-

actions and official affairs were to be transacted. As was to be expected, this was a shock for a region that for several centuries had lived under the Spanish-Mexican system, and to whom communication in Spanish meant *hablar en cristiano*, "to speak like a Christian." It was a cultural shock from which many never recovered, and echoes of that shock persist to the present day. The Mexican people had lost half of their territory. Those who remained in the Southwest were members of a defeated culture, under the direction of a victorious nation whose people spoke a different language. In Texas, where Mexicans had suffered two setbacks, the incentive to cultivate a culture that was viewed as inferior because it was defeated, languished for a long time. The new government under which the Mexicans were now living offered no encouragement. The traumatic experience of the postwar period was a psychological setback to the Spanish speakers of the lower Río Grande. The memory of the Alamo and Goliad was alive in most Texans, who had fought twice against Mexico, not so much because they had lost the battles as because they had been defeated by people for whom they had a deep-seated contempt.

During the Mexican War the behavior of the Americans after taking Monterrey was part of the pillage that marked the route of the victorious army all the way to Mexico City. An observer was quoted as saying, "Nine tenths of the Americans here think it a meritorious act to kill or rob a Mexican."[6] The behavior of the Texans in particular was so reckless that General Zachary Taylor finally had to muster the Texans out of the service and send them home. General Winfield Scott was faced with the same problem in Mexico City and was forced to move the Texans out of the city as a step toward the restoration of order. The behavior of the American troops during the Mexican War had the same effect on the Mexicans that the Alamo had on the Texans. The only difference was that the Mexicans remained in Texas and suffered the reprisals of the postwar period.

General Scott felt so remorseful about the treatment accorded the Mexicans by the American soldiers that in his memoirs he wrote: "The soldiers committed atrocities to make Heaven weep and every American of Christian morals blush for his country . . . Murder, robbery and rape of mothers and daughters in the presence of tied-up males of the families have been common all along the Río Grande."[7]

AFTERMATH OF THE WAR

Under the unfavorable circumstances that followed the war Hispanic culture receded. The colonial life enjoyed by families in Spanish-Mexican days became a nostalgic memory. At the end of the war they were given a choice to stay in conquered territory or move to Mexico, a difficult choice for people who had lived for generations in a land that now in the space of two years had become foreign soil. It was tantamount to saying to them, "If you don't like this country, get out." Most of them chose to stay rather than risk starting a new life in a country that was war-torn, bankrupt, and politically unstable. It was difficult for them to accept the new roles as members of a culture ignored or looked down on by people who ironically had once been invited by the Spanish and Mexican governments to settle on liberal land grants.

THE PERVASIVE "WHITE" CONCEPT

Cultural, political, and religious differences tended to polarize Mexicans and Anglo-Americans, but the most persistent reason for the prejudice felt by Americans was that Mexicans were dark-skinned people. Despite the rhetoric used to rationalize prejudice in the Southwest, the lack of acceptance of darker skins by most Europeans is by and large the most obvious. In the United States there is a tendency to speak of "white bread," to market white-shelled eggs exclusively, to use tons of bleach to make things white, to refer to the "first white man" to set foot on southwestern parts of the continent where Spanish Caucasians had preceded Anglo-Americans by several centuries. The same magic color is by extension the mark of distinction of men who, according to *Webster's Dictionary* are "honorable, honest, and square dealing." The symbolism attains national significance when the residence of the chief executive is called the White House.

Mexican *mestizos*, who made up most of the Spanish-speaking population in Texas, did not fit this white concept and so were socially unacceptable except as underpaid laborers. The natural sequence was prejudice and discrimination, followed by segregation, and, more significantly, by what Kidder calls "cultural decapitation." This is what happened when schoolchildren in Texas were forbidden to speak Spanish on the school grounds—denied the only language most of them knew on entering school.

The mellowing of this attitude became apparent by the acceptance of Hispanic culture, somewhat whitewashed by being called Spanish. The acceptance of a cultural heritage, however, does not guarantee the acceptance of the people who represent it. A school superintendent on the New Mexico–Texas border once asked a visiting team of a state university to recommend a Spanish teacher for his school. He felt that high school students could enrich their cultural background by studying Spanish. The superintendent added as the visitors were leaving: "I want a good teacher who can speak the language good, but please don't send me a Mexican. I want a white man."

MEXICAN LABOR CONTRIBUTION TO TEXAN AFFLUENCE

After they began adjusting to the new order, the Hispanic peoples in the lower Río Grande found themselves detached from the general life of the country. Part of this isolation was self-imposed; the people wanted to recoup some of their own way of life, their own customs, traditions, folk songs, folk drama—in short, those things that would help restore to them a sense of identity apart from the Anglo-American world. There were two classes of Hispano Mexicans: the Spanish settlers from the Canary Islands and the landed estate owners from the days of Escandón in the lower valley and the *mestizos*. The latter became the labor force who cleared the chaparrals of southern Texas for the agricultural development that took place at the end of the century. The work in the cotton fields and the pecan and citrus-fruit orchards, along with truck farming, was done by these Mexican *peones* who did all the stoop labor.

In 1926, *Century Magazine* acknowledged that the basis for the pyramid of economic prosperity of the Southwest, and particularly Texas, was the labor of the Mexicans who picked the cotton and tilled the land. *Literary Digest* commented in 1930 that the Mexicans put Texas on the map agriculturally. It is an accepted fact, reiterated by Texans, that, "man for man, a Mexican can outplant, outweed, and outpick anyone on the face of the earth." Others are frequently heard to comment, "if it weren't for those hard-working Mexicans, this place [Texas] wouldn't be on the map." The same Mexican *mestizos*, whose lack of initiative had been deplored by Mexican government inspector Mier y Terán in the 1820's, made possible, by the end of the same century, the great development that took place in the lower Río Grande in the days when there was little mechanized agriculture.

The Hispanic population of Texas has increased and decreased over the years, depending on political and economic conditions in Mexico and available jobs in the United States. Despite these fluctuations, a large permanent nucleus of Mexican residents has maintained a continuity of Hispano-Mexican culture along the Río Grande and also in larger urban centers, such as San Antonio, Laredo, and others downriver to the Gulf of Mexico.

HISPANIC CULTURE SURVIVAL

Hispanic culture has survived in a climate that for years was not particularly encouraging to the Spanish speakers. In San Antonio the Alamo casts its ominous shadow over Mexican culture, though eight Spanish names are listed on its walls alongside those of Bowie and Crockett—whose wives, incidentally, were Mexican women from Monterrey. The Alamo, originally the Spanish Mission of San Antonio de Valero, has become a monument to man's inhumanity to man and stands as a reminder of hatreds and reprisals. Mexicans who pass by the old mission overlook the battle they once won there and simply remember it as a symbol of the days when their ancestors named this region Tejas and everyone spoke Spanish. Louis Ruybalid, former director of the Community Welfare Council of San Antonio, has written: "The maintenance of the Alamo with all it symbolizes, with every parade ending at the foot of the monument, is a constant reminder of the cleavage that is sustained by a parade of tourists."

Attitudes have been modified over the years, and enlightened Anglo-Texans are no longer so inimical to Hispano-Mexican culture. The postwar period has given a renewed vigor to the legacies of the original Texans, helped by the large numbers of Mexicans who have settled in the state over the past fifty or sixty years. One author who feels that there has been a change in Texan attitudes is Stanley Walker who believes that "Texans seem to be improving their manners a little."[8] He relates an interesting incident at a luncheon in Austin attended by a group of Mexican government officials. Some of the Texan speakers alluded to "certain Mexican misdeeds of other days," and when W. John Garwood, justice of the Texas

Supreme Court, rose to speak, he delivered his remarks in Spanish.

THE RISE OF HISPANIC AND MEXICAN-AMERICAN ASSOCIATIONS

It is interesting to note that it is in that part of the Southwest where antagonism and prejudice have been more intense that many Hispano-Mexican organizations originated. The Sons of America was one of the first groups to organize. It was founded in 1921 to help Mexican Americans realize their legal rights. Six years later, in Corpus Christi the League of United Latin American Citizens (LULAC) followed suit and included some of the members of Sons of America. LULAC addresses itself to twenty-four areas, including education, citizenship, civicmindedness, patriotism, and pride in Hispanic origin. After World War II, Hector García, of Corpus Christi, founded the G.I. Forum, a national service organization of Mexican-American veterans of recent wars. The aims of this association also include educational goals and stress raising funds to provide scholarships for Mexican-American students. The Forum's slogan, "Education is our Freedom and Freedom should be everybody's business," indicates the importance the group attaches to education as a means to be free. In the last ten years, these organizations have urged their members to take an active part in politics, to assure themselves of a greater say in policy making.

Many other organizations throughout the Southwest have similar objectives. Membership is determined by the nature of their concern. Mexican-American agricultural unions represent farm workers. Educational associations, such as United Mexican American Students (UMAS), are especially concerned with the welfare and advancement of college students, although some of the more socially sensitive chapters also become involved in community affairs. Some groups such as the Mexican American Youth Organization (MAYO) in southern Texas, are more adamant in their demands than some of the others, partly because of their youthful membership. Those associations emphasizing Indian ancestry, in preference to a Hispanic cultural heritage, tend to assume a negative self-assertiveness. The Brown Berets go to such extremes as to state that they will kill for their race—"por mi raza mato." The points in their Ten-Point Program begin, "We demand" and vow to use arms against "any threat-

The Spanish presidio, La Bahía, in Goliad, Texas. It was the site of a famous battle during the Texas Revolution of 1836 and has been fully restored as a Texas shrine. Courtesy of Texas State Department of Highways and Public Transportation.

ening elements from outside of our community such as the police."

NONACTIVIST ORGANIZATIONS

Some clubs are not separated from Anglo-American society. They try to reach their objectives, cultural or economic, by working with the establishment. The Mexican-American Chamber of Commerce and the Mexican-American Lions Club cannot be divorced from the business and indus-

trial community of San Antonio. According to some observers, although they identify themselves with Mexican Americans, members of these clubs belong to a higher economic level of Mexican society, "have very lucrative jobs and try not to speak Spanish too loudly in the exclusive sectors where they live."

There are other centers in San Antonio whose principal objective is "to help raise the consciousness of a positive image of Hispanos in the United States," as Virgilio P. Elizondo, president of the

Mexican American Cultural Center, says. They conduct workshops on cultural topics at the San Antonio Center and expand their work through television appearances throughout the Southwest. The center has an extensive library, a bookstore where books in Spanish are available, and a good film-rental collection. A very strong program of folk activities is carried on by Bishop Patrick Flores in order to maintain the cultural identity of the Hispanos and also to provide enjoyment. At Christmas the center holds a *posada* at the market place, with candle-bearing processions as in the Spanish-Mexican days of San Antonio.

For many years the late Eulalio Gallardo Luna had a very successful program at the Neighborhood House in the Mexican-American sector of San Antonio. Through the Neighborhood House, which was sponsored by the Presbyterian church, he raised funds with which to build a modern clinic where San Antonio's medical doctors and dentists took turns donating a day's service on scheduled days. Luna's success arose in large part from his ability to work with the community, including members of all faiths and ethnic groups. He believed that an effective way to raise the cultural and living standards of the poor was to provide them with social and medical services simultaneously. He also insisted that a library at a social center should contain current, useful books instead of the usual discards sent by donors as a charitable gesture. He accepted only current and well-preserved editions.

A practical observation made by Luna indicated the progressive levels of culture among Mexican Americans in San Antonio. He would drive visitors through the various sectors of the city to show the vertical movement of Mexican Americans and thereby help dissipate the general notion that they were all socially static. He began with the poorest sections, inhabited by migrant workers and wetbacks. Next he drove to a section with housing projects and a more settled population who owned modest homes. The next section comprised well-kept front lawns, and house and garage combinations in well-groomed surroundings. These homes reflected a higher and steadier income among residents with a noticeable pride of ownership. The last section consisted of upper-middle-class residents, businessmen and professionals who had "made it," according to Luna. As was to be expected, the last group of families had become integrated into the economic and social life of the city, spoke English more often

Eduardo Gallardo Luna, active social worker and director of the Neighborhood House in San Antonio, Texas.

than Spanish, and had developed life-styles like their Anglo-American neighbors'. They were bilingual and bicultural, the desideratum of many Hispanic residents in the United States.

The indigenist Chicanos claim a closer spiritual kinship with Emiliano Zapata and Pancho Villa, and even with the heroic Cuauhtemoc, "roasted feet and all," as Américo Paredes says. The issues conjured up by those names were of concern to Mexico many years ago, but today the country is more interested in becoming industrialized, developing its agricultural industry, and keeping up with world developments in business, commerce, and technology. The descendants of Mexicans living in the United States wishing to cultivate their Mexican heritage will have to consider the goals and aspirations of modern Mexico, which in many respects are comparable with those of the United States. Among other things, Mexico continues to cultivate its Spanish cultural heritage, enriched by its own contributions, and complemented by elements of indigenous culture, all of which in the end produce the Mexican nationality sought by the revolution.

Another Hispanic cultural organization in San Antonio is one known to some as the Hispanic Society and to others as the Hispanic Foundation. It is composed principally of descendants of the Spanish Canary Islanders sent there by the Spanish crown in 1731. According to José San Martín, a society member, the organization has long been interested in preserving the cultural heritage of San Antonio. Thirty years ago Rómulo Mungía went to Mexico City to petition the National University for an extension, or *sucursal*, in San Antonio. Official arrangements were made whereby the city would provide the buildings and the university would provide a staff to teach a full curriculum leading to a degree. The project has been very successful; hundreds of students have taken courses in language, literature, and other subjects related to Hispanic culture. Half of the students are Anglo-Americans specializing in Spanish. The society also petitioned the Texas legislature for a bilingual educational program and was successful in establishing it in San Antonio, where more than half of the population is Spanish speaking. A number of the society's members are concerned with promoting Hispanic cultural events. Dr. Daniel Saenz, a medical doctor, is also an authority on Spanish philosophy. He was instrumental in helping to bring Spanish philosopher Ortega y Gasset to the United States many years ago. Dr. Saenz also gives lectures regularly on both Ortega y Gasset and Miguel de Unamuno, another Spanish philosopher.

The society holds annual social affairs, to which San Antonio's leading citizens are invited. In 1972 a dignitary of the Spanish government was invited to their annual ball and was named honorary *alcalde* of San Antonio at an elaborate ceremony. According to San Martín, the center also includes in its program cultural leaders from Mexico, an acknowledgment of the two peoples' common Hispanic heritage.

Most of these organizations address themselves to problems that they believe confront Mexican Americans and Hispanos alike. The Mexican-American Political Association (MAPA) seeks to develop self-determination and self-sufficiency to help the Spanish speakers be more independent, able to rely on their own resources and initiative. In addition to whatever specific mission the organizations have, they all express deep concern for the preservation of their Hispano-Mexican heritage, with varying degrees of emphasis on what they consider Spanish or Mexican. Hispanos and Mexican Americans interested in the cultivation of their cultural heritage need turn only to the traditional customs and practices in their own families, who are for the most part products of a folk culture, despite being domiciled in urban centers. With these elements as a basis the more advanced forms of Hispanic culture can be more easily cultivated. Many individuals are well acquainted with the roots of their Hispanic culture. President Echevarría of Mexico, visiting San Antonio, greeted the Mexican children, who as they approached him placed their hands on their heads, to forestall *mal ojo*, or evil eye.

Educational institutions in the lower Río Grande, such as the Extension Service of the University of Texas, Trinity University, and Lady of the Lake College, also make a significant contribution to the culture of Spanish speakers by offerings in Hispanic fields. The University of Texas has one of the leading centers of Latin American studies in the nation, with a publication program by the Texas University Press that includes not only original documents but also current studies and translations of some of Spain and Mexico's leading scholars. In fact, many students learn about the accomplishments of Spain and Mexico's leading men for the first time in English versions provided by the University of Texas and by other university presses in the Southwest, such as Oklahoma, Arizona, and New Mexico. Members of the faculties of these institutions have published books in the fields of anthropology, folklore, education, and sociology on specific subjects of Hispanic culture.

In the early Southwest life was lived on two levels: the official world, consisting of church and state authorities whose responsibility was to administer the laws and regulations entrusted to them by the viceroyalty in Mexico City, and the folk world. The few emissaries who made up officialdom in the provinces did not share in the cultural life of the community, because they were regularly transferred or replaced. The settlers, who were mostly "folk," provided the unbroken cultural chain that bound them as a people whether in New Mexico, California, Texas, or Arizona. There was greater continuity among the folk, first, because they were permanently located, and, second, because they guided themselves by traditional ways and customs enriched by improvisations determined by necessity. Local improvisations became in time part of the body of regional customs. These additions eventually gave each region the characteristic stamp that produced New Mexicans, Californios, Texans, and Arizonians and determined each succeeding change in the folk culture of the internal provinces. Although each region had its own personality, the people shared a common bond of Spanish heritage, a traditional heritage that is still evident throughout the Southwest.

Many of the practices that became traditional over the years were adaptations of comparable customs from Mexico and Spain. There were accepted ways of farming in arid lands, in those with abundant rainfall, and in those where streams could be diverted into canal systems called *acequias*. Crops raised with rainfall were referred to as *de temporal*; those under irrigation were called *de regadío*. Some writers claim that the early colonists learned the art of irrigation from the Indians, simply because both cultures were familiar with dry farming. No doubt the colonists picked up a few pointers from their pueblo neighbors,but irrigation was so commonly used in Spain that the early peoples of the Southwest simply transferred to the New World the practices they already knew together with administrative regulations that most

southwestern states incorporated years later into their own laws.

ACEQUIA ADMINISTRATION

One of the provisions of land apportionment by the crown was that the grantees assume communal responsibility for the upkeep of their waterways. That led to the adoption of overseers called *alcaldes*, *mayordomos*, or *zanjeros* from Texas to California. In addition to the upkeep of *acequias* and *contra-acequias*, there were additional responsibilities for landholders in El Paso Valley, whenever the main canal, or *acequia madre*, intake at the junction of the Río Grande became filled with sediment and debris and stopped the flow of water. All the rancheros using water from a given main ditch contributed a proportionate number of men, horses, scrapers, and wagons to help clear the ditch head every spring. This annual project was appropriately called *la fatiga*—it was fatiguing indeed to clear out tree branches, trunks, and boulders washed in by the river during the spring thaw. This traditional arrangement was a communal practice rather than a legally established irrigation service. Its functioning and the settlers' respect for custom bore a close resemblance to the Tribunal de las Aguas, which has been meeting regularly on the steps of the Cathedral of Valencia since the Middle Ages. The Hispano Mexicans of the Southwest modestly referred to their ditch meetings as La Junta del Agua, a group that assembled whenever there were problems. This practice continued in the lower Río Grande until the early 1930's.

In the days when there were no government-aid programs and very little currency was in circulation, cooperative arrangements were made informally by the colonials and their descendants for enterprises of common interest. Manpower shortage was often a problem in the days before mechanical farming, but when Indian labor was available, the problem was solved by the "contributed" services that the neophytes rendered as part of their responsibility to church and state. In California the missions were paid for the services rendered to the rancheros by the Indians. Other farmers in the Southwest who could not draw upon Indian labor resorted to a system of *peonada*, an informal but effective mutual-assistance program among neighboring ranchos. When a farmer's wheat was ready for cutting, he would ask his neighbors for a given number of *peones* to bring in the harvest, and he would contribute an equal amount of help to his friends when their turns came.

THE *CIGARRO* BREAK AND OTHER CUSTOMS

When wage earners replaced the *peonada* system, after the Anglo-American occupation, the *peones* in the field devised an interesting custom that may be considered a forerunner of the present coffee break. Most ranch hands made their cigarettes, and they had to stop whatever they were doing to roll a *punche* cigarette or, later, a Bull Durham. It was tacitly understood that a field hand became entitled to this privilege simply by announcing, "Voy a torcer un cigarro," "I'm going to roll a smoke." The rest of the men slowed down while their companion leaned on his shovel and leisurely rolled a cigarette. The ritual was never hurried; it was prolonged as much as possible so that the workers could enjoy a rest on the employer's time. Nonsmoking employers frowned on the custom, but unless they hired nonsmokers, they had to put up with the cigarette break.

In a land where colonists were also pioneers, they relied almost entirely on custom to guide them and in the process preserved many a tradition for which no explanation was given other than that it was the way it had always been done. The folk enjoyed doing things according to this folk heritage, and any deviation from it was discouraged. Folkways were explained and justified simply by saying, "Es la costumbre de nuestra gente," "It is the custom of our people."

One of these interesting *costumbres* was the unusual names given to Hispano-Mexican children. Some were taken from pastoral novels of sixteenth-century Spain, and some even harked back to Roman times. Names such as Filadelfio, Predicando, Policarpio, Secundino, Sixto, Tircio, Octaviano, Zoraida, and Zoila recalled the Romans, the Moors, and the Spaniards of centuries past. Much of this picturesqueness has been lost by the adoption of less historical (but more practical) names like Sandra, Karen, and Yvonne, with a sprinkling of Joes and Bills.

For two and a half centuries the people of the Southwest guided themselves by customs handed down by word of mouth from one generation to another, until the arrival of another culture disrupted age-old habits. There was a customary way of conducting a *casorio*, a wedding, a *prendorio*, an engagement, or a funeral. There was also a way of planting and harvesting. There were things a girl could not do when she was single, and things she could do after she was married. From the time a child was conceived, the expectant mother relied strongly on tradition to guide the course of her future child, and she obeyed taboos and practices recommended by the *curanderas* and other folk healers to ensure her welfare and that of her potential offspring. For instance, to prevent the child from being born with a harelip, she carried a key in her pocket, and under no circumstances would she be exposed to either *susto* or *espanto*, lest the child be born deformed. *Susto* was self-induced fear resulting from some organic imbalance; *espanto* was a fright caused by an outward agent, usually something supernatural—a ghost or an apparition. It was also understood that an expectant mother would have cravings that should not be denied. She could develop an *antojo*, a strong craving for some special dish that she did not ordinarily have at home, and it was the husband's responsibility to provide it (this custom is also found in the folk culture of other nations).

No doctors attended the birth of a child, but there were *parteras*, midwives, on hand in every village. They had practical knowledge of such matters and, except for complications that might set in, they managed to care for the mother and child. They may not have observed all the sanitary precautions of the modern clinic, but their patients balanced this deficiency by the immunities they had developed in their hardy lives. Unlike the Indians, who hardly interrupted their daily routine with the birth of a child, the Spanish mothers spent twenty to thirty days in bed, during which they were customarily nourished with chicken and chicken broth, recommended by accepted practice as the best fare for a convalescent mother.

Children matured into young adults, unburdened with problems of choice of behavior. Because they were products of a folk culture, they, like their parents and their ancestors before them, followed the dictates of custom and tradition. They wore religious amulets around their necks to protect them against evil, a piece of silk inside their hats to ward off lightning, trousers above the ankles for good luck. They left their shoes at the foot of their beds at night for protection and avoided stumbling on their left feet. The Anglo-American beliefs in throwing spilled salt over the left shoulder and avoiding black cats crossing one's path never found their way into Hispanic superstition.

THE EXTENDED FAMILY

Another practice that tied communities together was what is now called "the extended family," provided through *compadrazgo*, particularly in the small villages. The christening of a child called for *padrinos*, godparents, from the same community who were bound by friendship or by the relationship of worker and *patrón*. The latter relationship was particularly desirable, because it provided more security in the event of loss of a parent. The entire community participated in the christening ceremony, providing a *canastilla*, or layette, for the newborn (with the understanding that the value of this contribution was not to exceed fourteen dollars).

The formality of established custom was observed when a child was returned to the parents after the christening ceremony by recital of the following quatrain:

> Aquí les traigo esta prenda
> Que de la iglesia salió,
> Con los santos sacramentos
> Y el agua que recibió.

> I bring you this precious jewel
> Just returned from the church,
> After the holy sacraments
> And the water it received.

The parents accepted their child and answered:

> Recíbote, prenda hermosa,
> Que de la iglesia saliste
> Con los santos sacramentos
> Y el agua que recibiste.

> I accept you, precious jewel
> Having returned from the church
> After the holy sacraments
> And water that you received.

On the way to the house or from the church, the party was assailed by all the village children, who shouted, "¡Pastilla!" This meant that the godfather, who usually came prepared, was to distribute candy and small coins to the young celebrants. In southern New Mexico and Texas the children shouted "¡Bolo!" a contraction of the Greek *óbolo*, which meant a sixth part of a drachma in ancient Greece, and equivalent in colonial days to twenty *céntimos*. The nonfamilial relationship resulting from the christening ceremony eventually involved entire communities, and everyone became a *compadre* or *comadre*. The intrafamily relationship was patriarchal, with consistent roles for male and female children.

In addition to baptismal *compadres*, the *padrinos* were also present at a wedding and the *primos* from both families attended a *prendorio*, or announcement party. In *compadrazgo* relations, the women usually maintained the closeness of both families. *Compadres* could be cordial and helpful, but *comadres* were sometimes inseparable and were closer than nuclear relations. Another family relationship was that of *concuños*. Men who married sisters became *concuños*; sometimes those who simply married into the same family were given the same appellation.

COURTESY AND PROPRIETY AMONG THE FOLK

There were no *reglas de urbanidad*, or rules of etiquette, to follow as there were in the large cities, but custom governed the behavior of children within the family and before their elders. Should a caller arrive while the family was seated at the dinner table, the former would invariably be asked to join the others at the table. The visitor would decline, saying that he had already eaten and would add, "Buen provecho." This custom was practiced by urban dwellers as well. A child taking a drink of water before a guest always proffered the glass and invited him to drink first, asking, "¿Gusta usted?" It was understood that a young person never addressed his elders with his hat on, and sometimes young people crossed their arms as a gesture of respect while speaking.

The roles of men and women young and old were so prescribed by custom that, despite the folk's candid speech and frank discussion, certain topics were not mentioned in the presence of the opposite sex or before children, especially girls. Should it become necessary to mention sex or any intimate matter, the speaker would take note of his hearers and preface his remarks by saying, "Con permiso de la gente." Once a girl was married, she would be included in the conversation.

In 1929, while I was traveling over the Southwest collecting traditional lore, I came across several centenarians, including one who was reputedly 135 years old. These oldsters provided me with an opportunity to inquire far back into their parents' and grandparents' experiences to ascertain the history of some of these social practices. After relating how things were "in the old days," I would ask them if that was the case also in the days of their parents, to which they would answer, "Oh, it was much stricter then!" This oral history, going back to the middle of the eighteenth century, showed an unchanged continuity over more than a century and a half.

One of the customs that, until recently, changed very little from colonial days is the manner in which women smoked. The older peasants wore long black skirts made from homespun materials of their own manufacture and had pockets on the side like men's trousers. In these pockets, buried in the folds of the full, simple skirts, the older ladies carried their *cajitas de fumar*, boxes with all the makings for rolled cigarettes. When they sat talking, each one would take out her wooden box, select a thin corn husk, put on it several pinches of *punche*, roll it carefully, and hold it inside her hand while lighting it with a *mecha*, a live coal, or, later, with a match. It was not considered ladylike to hold a cigarette between the fingers like a man, but between thumb and index finger, with the rest of the hand over it as a shield.

When a young man was old enough to smoke, he was allowed to do so, providing he did not smoke before his elders. Under no circumstances could he ask for *lumbre*, a light, from an older person. The old-timer in the Southwest hung on to this taboo until around World War I and would bring down a cane over a young fellow who dared ask him for a light.

One of the significant characteristics of Hispanic life is that it is not highly institutionalized, although it is closely knit by the strength of ethnic customs and traditions. The people act not in concert but as individuals, even though they may all do the same thing. Personal relations, neighborliness, community activities, wakes, burials, charity, and the myriad activities that make up communal life are initiated by individuals behaving so consistently that, when viewed collectively, the behavior seems to be institutionalized. This is in direct contrast to the Anglo-American tradition of the town hall, where everyone congregated and decided on a common course of action. In Hispanic communities concerted effort and collective action result from individual accumulation.

In colonial days, and far into modern times, there was a custom of sharing each other's best culinary successes, which was comparable with today's pot-luck dinners. But it was not organized as a collective effort. Whenever a dish turned out particularly well, the lady of a Hispano home would take a *cazuelita*, or clay bowl, fill it with the particular *guiso*, or dish, cover it with fresh-baked bread or *tortillas*, and send it to a *vecina*, or neighbor, by one of her children, saying that she had been unusually lucky in the kitchen that day and wanted her friend to taste this *bocadito*. The receptacle was never returned empty; it would be a rejection to do so. The receiver waited until she too had had a good day in her kitchen and returned the *cazuelita* with another *bocadito*. The highest praise for the cook was to hear that the neighbor's husband had liked the dish, and it was also a way of saying thank you.

GROWING UP TO BE AN HOMBRE

In the rugged life of the West, where men had to survive by ingenuity and hard work, it was essential that young boys become men as early as possible. Being *muy hombre* was a virtue aspired to by both young and old, for it meant that a man was able to give a good account of himself in a crisis. The same was said of the girls who stayed home and learned to be able housekeepers and eventually wives. Of them it was said that they were *muy mujerotas*, or *señoras de sus casas* when they set up housekeeping. The mothers attended to this training at home, but the boys who grew up in the open learned from other men the skills by which the colonists survived: planting, hunting, house building, stock raising, and all the details attendant on each occupation. Necessity dictated, above all, that men become horsemen. That meant learning all they could about these useful animals. Horses had to be loved, raised, cared for, broken to the saddle and the plow, and trained for the hunt. It was here that the *caballerango*, the "horse wrangler" of many decades later, developed in the West from the Spanish *caballerizo*, who had groomed the king's horses.

One of the necessary roles for a family man in

New Mexico and Texas was that of buffalo hunter, supplying his household with meat for the winter months and hides for trade. He had to become a *cibolero* who, lacking firearms (which were owned only by the soldiers of the presidio), used the Indian lance and bow and arrow. These *ciboleros* were known in colonial days and late into the nineteenth century as the best mounted hunters in the Southwest. Hunting buffalo on horseback meant riding into a fast-running herd, driving the lance on the run, and cutting out quickly to avoid being trampled. It took skill, speed, and courage to bring down a one-ton bull with nothing but a wooden lance, a skill more to be admired than the wanton shooting of grazing beasts with a rifle by later "hunters" of the plains.

After the kill came the long and tiresome work of cutting *perchas* from the buffalo's hide, upon which to string up the *cecinas* of *charqui*, which, when partly dry and partly frozen, were baled and loaded on pack horses for the return to the villages. The whole operation matured the young men who went along; it taught them how to help provide meat for the larder and converted them into thoroughgoing *hombres*.

It was not all work and toil for young men in the Southwest, however. There were more pleasant ways to prove their manhood, such as a few runs in a *corrida del gallo*. This was a game played on horseback by two teams sometimes from the same village but generally from two different towns. The trick was to ride past a rooster buried the ground up to its neck, seize it at full gallop, and cross the goal line with the opposing team in hot pursuit. Many Anglo-American travelers who came into the Southwest at the beginning of the nineteenth century commented disapprovingly on this sport. Later, the ASPCA entered the arena, and rooster pulls are no longer held in public view, except in remote mountain areas. Not very long ago, a father spoke to me proudly of his young son's success at "riding the rooster," as they called it. The young man was *muy hombre* who could outride a whole group of seasoned horsemen and bring home the rooster, so to speak. The sport was popular in the fiestas of California, New Mexico, and Colorado, but has survived longer in New Mexico.

MUY HOMBRE, MUY MACHO, MACHISMO

The preoccupation with being *muy hombre* in colonial days cannot be equated with present-day *machismo*, although they have in common certain manifestations of maleness. *Hombre* meant courage to work hard, to endure hardships, to face the enemy no matter what the odds, to wrest a living from nature, and to survive. In Spain this is known as *hombría*.

Machismo is a display of daring with no useful purpose, a show of maleness in the animal sense, a provocative show of courage that encroaches on the rights of others, with no more end in view than selfish satisfaction and dramatic display. Many writers confuse *machismo* with what Mexicans refer to as *muy macho*. The latter is used to describe men who exude maleness, sometimes without knowing it. When they are aware of it, they may capitalize upon it and become Don Juans. Being *muy macho* does not preclude being *muy hombre*, and when the two qualities are combined in a man, they constitute a threat to the romantic aspirations of other male members of society. *Machismo* has been loosely interpreted and overplayed; some try to account for all sorts of behavior by attributing them to *machismo*. More often than not, it is a compensation for an inferiority complex, a defense mechanism for men who are frustrated because nature has not endowed them with admirable qualities, either physical or moral. They find an easy way out by showing sexual potency in order to prove to themselves and others what powerful males they are. A man who is *muy macho* by nature or *muy hombre* by principle has no need for *machismo*.[1]

Being *muy hombre* also had a moral significance, a meaning embodied in the expression *palabra de hombre*, "word of a man," a phrase assuring veracity and honesty. Eventually the expression was shortened to simply *palabra, hombre* being implied. The word of a man was his bond. With *palabra de hombre* and a handshake, contracts were made without written documents, and statements were attested to without witnesses. Years ago this was the way of Hispanic people of the Southwest who, lacking writing skills, had to rely on verbal assurances. There have been countless instances of this culture trait of colonial days, which survived until recently.

The well-known Sheriff Lucero, who was active in territorial days in Doña Ana County, in southern New Mexico, did not carry a gun and had no jail for his prisoners. At a *baile*, when things got out of hand, he would arrest the culprits and have them sit under a large cottonwood tree. He would order them to stay put because they were in jail

Sheriff Felipe Lucero, of Las Cruces, New Mexico, who always got his man without a gun.

and then ask each one, "Will you give your *palabra de hombre* to stay here until I return?" The whole group, who had imbibed too much, fought too much, and talked too much, would answer, a bit thick of tongue, "Yo soy hombre," "I'm a man," and proudly sit down under the cottonwood tree. The next morning all the *hombres* would be lying asleep "in jail," thoroughly imprisoned by their word. Sheriff Lucero was not a highly trained man, but he understood the cultural climate in which he had to work and used it to his advantage.

Under constant threat of Indian attacks, particularly after the crops had been gathered, boys became men overnight. These encounters meant defending their homes and property with weapons that were no different from their enemy—no Winchesters and Sharps against bows and arrows as seen so often on television shows today, but man-to-man combat, the kind of resistance that held

the Southwest for centuries. This too was the sort of experience where an able-bodied young man became *muy hombre* in order to survive.

COURTSHIP AND WEDDING CUSTOMS

When he had grown into manhood, there remained the last hurdle for the young man who aspired to full participation in the life of the community, and that was matrimony. The girl's father wanted proof that his prospective son-in-law was worthy of his daughter. He took him along on one of his trading expeditions to Chihuahua. On this long trek the young man learned the skills of the *atajo* and the caravan. By loading pack mules at daybreak, driving on the trail, finding water holes, setting up camp, guarding the stock, and living exposed to the arrows of the hostile Apaches, the young man had to prove his worthiness—again *muy hombre*—if he aspired to the girl's hand.

Sometimes, on reaching Chihuahua, the young man would find another girl more attractive than the one he had left behind. But should the young man decide to take a bride at home, there were certain customs to be observed, those his father and his grandfather before him had followed. At the village fiestas, at folk dances, and at church he would meet the eligible girls from whom he would choose the one he wanted for a wife. First he would be a simple *pretendiente* who could call on the family and become better acquainted. He would not have an opportunity to be alone with the girl, but he would manage to send messages, if he could write, or oral messages conveyed by young *primos*, or mutual friends—never by brothers of the girl; they were supposed to stand guard against such invasions. If his bid progressed, and he made up his mind about the young lady, he would ask his parents or his uncles to prepare a *carta de pedimiento* or simply speak on his behalf. The intermediaries would press the young man's interest, but the parents and the lady in question would never answer outright lest they seem too anxious. They would set a *plazo*, when the aspiring swain would receive *el sí*, if approved, or *calabazas*, if refused.

Once he became the formal *novio*, he could call and talk with the girl in the parlor within earshot or in the presence of a chaperon, who could choose to be strict or understanding. The next ceremony was the *prendorio*, the folk equivalent of the announcement party, when both families met at the girl's home. The prospective bride and groom went around the room greeting everyone, whom they already knew anyway, with a courteous and blushing, "*Servidor[a] de usted.*" Through this simple ceremony the family became extended, and thereafter all members were *primos* and *primas*. It was a nicety that brought families closer together.

Next came the *casorio*, and if there was a church with a priest who could insist on making them *rodar* (the equivalent of publishing the bans), they would wait the time prescribed, after which the marriage ceremony was arranged with *padrinos* and *madrinas* in readiness for the final event. If the village had only a visiting padre, and the time for his next visit was far away, a judge would perform the ceremony, which could be repeated later when the priest arrived. In the larger villages and towns the groom would be expected to give his prospective bride the *diario*, or daily allowance, either in coin or in kind during the interim between *prendorio* and *casorio*. The best products of his garden, the fattest lamb, and the best chickens were left at the doorstep of her home until the day of the wedding (this meant short engagements).

Until recently it was customary for the groom to observe a very old Spanish custom of presenting *las arras* to the bride at the wedding ceremony, a practice that is still observed in northern Spain. In the Middle Ages the groom gave his bride thirteen gold coins in exchange for the dowry that she brought to the home or as a gesture in appreciation of the bride's personal virtues. The Spanish Goths of the seventh century had a custom very similar to this, from which the Spanish practice may be derived. In the Southwest the sum given by the groom at the altar was fourteen *reales*. It was always given in silver (when American currency came into use it was never referred to as "one dollar and seventy-five cents"). The best man carried the satchel with the coins and delivered it to the groom at the proper moment, for the latter to place in the bride's hand.

The bride's wedding dress often came by trading caravan all the way from Mexico City, or in later years the traveling *varillero* was given the order in advance. The bride's ensemble, according to custom, was paid for by the groom, but the best man paid for the *baile* and the banquet after the wedding. The procession following the wedding at the church led to the home of the bride and was almost identical to the one at the wedding of El Cid to Doña Jimena in the eleventh century. Until

recently, Taos has seen wedding processions in which even the order of the wedding party was the same as that described in the old Spanish ballad. *Músicos* playing guitars and violins preceded the bride and groom, who were followed by the *padrinos* and the guests. Children shouted requests for *pastillas*, to which the *padrino* promptly responded by scattering a few coins on the ground.

Finally, when the celebration was over, far into the night or early morning, the wedding couple retired to the privacy of their new quarters, where the bride most likely spent the rest of the night nursing a very new husband a bit the worse for wear, as a result of the *brindises* that his friends managed to contrive during the fiesta. The last of the chain of customs accompanying the wedding was performed by the village troubadour, who sang admonitions and advice for a happy wedded life in a long ballad entitled "Entriega de Novios."

For the first week or so the newlyweds were not to be disturbed. Sometimes they remained in the home of the bride until the proud husband took his lady around to all the village and introduced her as his *señora*. On that day they left the parents' home and took the mattress, unless the families had arranged beforehand for the newlyweds to take the *cama matrimonial*, or even a complete bedroom suite if they could afford it. And so was the quest for a wife happily concluded by the young man who chose to woo his bride by following the traditional practices which colonial folk evolved from their Spanish heritage—and have continued to modify over the years. These customs, with few variations, were followed in all the southwestern states. In California the affluent rancheros held week-long wedding fiestas.

The final rites among Hispano and Mexican folk in the Southwest were also carried out according to custom and tradition, with the usual few regional variations from southern Texas to California. When a person passed away, the *dolientes*, or bereaved, engaged the services of the village coffin maker, the *cajonero*, "box-maker." The coffin was not usually referred to, particularly in New Mexico, by the Spanish *ataúd* but was given the down-to-earth name *cajón*, "big box." If an *inocente*, a baby, had died, the coffin was trimmed in blue for a boy and in white for a girl. In some homes a bow was placed on the door so that people would know that they were *de luto*, in mourning, and observe the usual courtesies. This custom varied according to the deceased's relation to the family. The death of a father or mother called for a longer period of mourning, as in most places. Some families covered all mirrors in the house with black cloth called *crespón*, but this again was an individual variation. The practice was comparable with the one in Ireland, where all mirrors are covered so that the soul may not see itself before departing.

WAKES AND FUNERALS

Wake observances have at times led outsiders to remark that the Spanish folk in the Southwest had a gay fiesta during a funeral. The fact is that a wake was, and still is, a solemn affair where people came quietly to pay their respects and to offer their *pésame*, condolences, with the assurances of help and cooperation characteristic of a highly cohesive folk society. The extended family relationship, through *compadrazgo*, played an important role, particularly if the head of the house had passed away. The wake ceremony began early in the evening and was consistently observed until the era of the funeral parlor. It was a combination of Catholic ritual and folk tradition comparable with Spanish practices centuries ago. The vivid account of a young girl's funeral given by Spanish poet Gustavo Adolfo Bécquer was duplicated in many homes in the Southwest two centuries ago, and in remote villages it continues today.

Usually the furniture was removed from the largest room in the house, and chairs were lined against the walls. The deceased was laid out on a table in the center of the room, surrounded by lighted candles. Those who came to offer their condolences sat on the first chairs by the front door and progressed clockwise to the room where the immediate members of the family were gathered. In this room the phrase "Le acompaño en sus sentimientos," "I sympathize with your sorrow" was repeatedly heard, followed by an *abrazo* and a few tears. From this mourners' room, the visitors proceeded to the kitchen, where black coffee and *empanaditas*, meat or fruit turnovers, were served by neighbor women. The grieving family was usually relieved of this responsibility.

In the back room or kitchen, where friends gathered and remained until daybreak, anecdotes and stories related to the deceased were shared. As they sat around the room with cups of black coffee, some old friend of the family would begin in low and measured tones: "I remember the time when the late *el finado*, Don Telésforo, and I were coming back from a buffalo hunt . . . ." The story invariably took many detours in order to pinpoint the place or the time: "It was in the winter of 1880; I knew it was then, because the last spur of the railroad still had about a mile to go before coming through town."

Sometimes the village troubadour came and sang the age-old religious chants called *alabados*. They gave the gathering an eerie feeling, because these songs were anything but gay. In New Mexico many people refer to them as "Penitente songs," because they have been preserved by this religious sect in their Easter ritual. Just as the first light of dawn began to appear, the *rezadoras*, women who recited prayers from church ritual, knelt and prayed aloud in monotone with the usual antiphonal responses from the gathering. This usually terminated the wake, after which all departed sleepy and worn from the all-night vigil.

Later in the day, at the agreed hour, some came back to carry the coffin to the *camposanto*, or cemetery, where the body was interred to the accompaniment of more *alabados*. Some families thought these songs were too sad and funereal, and asked that they not be sung at wakes or funerals. Thus ended the traditional cycle of life that began at the cradle and ended at the grave.

Although some of the beliefs and practices observed by the Spanish colonials and their descendants can be traced back to Europe, many superstitious practices are lost in hoary antiquity. Superstition was one of man's early attempts to understand the inexplicable phenomena of nature. Impelled by the will to survive, he evolved animistic beliefs sometimes based on sympathetic and mimetic magic; then, through emulation or by word of mouth, they were transmitted to future generations. Superstition may mean an unfounded belief implying a casual relationship or the lack of relationship verified by mere coincidence. Some of these practices seem today anomalous, because in a sense they are outmoded in a more enlightened society. However, there is nothing degrading in certain adherences to superstitious practices among the folk; sometimes these beliefs are simply a manifestation of a fundamental thought. When speaking of superstition, Thomas de Quincey once said:

Superstition, indeed, or the sympathy with the invisible, is the great test of a man's nature as an earthly combining with a celestial. In superstition lies the possibility of religion, and though superstition is often injurious, degrading, demoralizing, it is so, not as a form of corruption or degradation, but as a form of nondevelopment.[1]

Superstition may suggest degrees of folly, and belief in it may manifest a lack of good judgment. In many instances the difference between superstition and good sense is about the same as that which Bishop Washburton indicated when he defined orthodoxy and heterodoxy. "Orthodoxy," said the bishop, "is my doxy; heterodoxy is another man's doxy."[2]

Superstition, whether a transmission from antiquity or a casual relationship unverified by scientific process, is one of the universal forces that humanity, and particularly the folk, has utilized knowingly or unconsciously in attempting to keep his culture from crumbling or his personality from deteriorating. The Spanish people of the Southwest, the folk who compose the bulk of the population even today, were no different in this respect and sometimes relied on superstition and practices endorsed by tradition for more profitable and happy living.

It is interesting to observe the manner in which Hispanic folk achieved security. The individual would usually do something negative in order to achieve something positive: avoid marrying on Tuesday, avoid cutting a child's fingernails before the baby was a year old, or refrain from eating fruit on an empty stomach in order to forestall evil consequences. These negative taboos were actually turned into positive factors that often helped preserve the well-being of the individual. Moreover, no one could tell what might have happened had the taboo not been observed, so there were no data to disprove the efficacy of the practice.

SUPERSTITION MEANINGS LOST

In time many superstitious practices lost their meaning; that is, people no longer believed their original intent, but preserved the outward form as a way of doing, with no thought of evil consequences, simply for sentimental reasons. In like manner Anglo-American brides continue to wear on their wedding day something old, something new, something borrowed, and something blue. Male babies are dressed in blue and female ones in pink. Why? It is simply a way of doing, which people observe without question. The Spanish folk explain and justify their actions by saying, "Es la costumbre de la gente," their way of doing.

Some popular writers in the Southwest see symbolism lurking in every corner and attach meanings to practices that, when explained, prove to be nothing but traditional expediency. Some claim that the Hispanic population in the Southwest, and particularly in New Mexico, paint their doors blue to ward off evil spirits. Others insist that the people in the Río Grande Valley hang their strings of red chile over their housetops because of a superstition regarding the preservation of the palatable *Capsicum annuum*. The practical-minded Hispano Mexican knows that hanging *ristras* of chile over the housetops ensures they will dry properly and will also be out of reach of the chickens roaming over the patio.

Many superstitions are no longer observed or believed but are still remembered by the folk. A young woman may remark, as she sweeps her kitchen at night, that it is very bad luck to do so but continues this household chore with no apparent misapprehension. Again, she may sweep the feet of an unmarried male guest who is in the path of her broom, to which he will remonstrate playfully by assuring her that this means he will marry a hag or an old widow. Some of the folk today do observe and believe these superstitions, but even those who do not observe them derive some satisfaction from knowing what they should or should not do. This behavioral pattern occurs in any society that knows the consequence of breaking natural law. But this knowledge does not keep them from overeating, drinking too much, chain smoking, and doing a number of other things known to be detrimental to health.

NO INDIAN SUPERSTITIONS

It has been often said that the Spanish colonials adopted a number of the superstitions of the Indian servants who worked in their homes and eventually became absorbed into the household. Warren Beck states that "contacts with their Indian servants accrued many superstitions and practices." It would be interesting to know what particular Indian superstitions have been adopted by the Hispanos of the Southwest. The fact is that the Spanish in Spain, and also in the New World, were reluctant to adopt any belief and religious rite that was un-Christian because of their long struggle against the "infidel Moor." They adopted Indian plants, foods, and processes that they found practical, as well as words for which they had no Spanish equivalent. But in religious and supernatural matters they went so far as to eliminate such intermediaries as fairies from their own folk tales and substitute the Virgin Mary or some saint to strengthen their religious faith. When they found a similarity to Christianity in Indian worship, they took advantage of it by substituting the name of a saint or a part of the Trinity so that the Indian might be better inclined to accept concepts of the religion that they were

trying so hard to implant. But the last thing they would do would be to adopt a "pagan" ritual or a practice that they considered heretical, the work of the devil himself. This attitude would preclude the adoption of Indian sorcery and superstition in Hispanic homes, either in colonial days or later.

Moreover, the Spaniards did not need to resort to Indian superstitions; they had enough of their own for whatever occasion should arise. It must also be borne in mind that the word *indio* did not conjure any superior qualities in the mind of the Spanish population. In fact, the word was used as a pejorative and is still hardly complimentary today, except among indigenists who consider themselves Indians to begin with. In bringing Indians into the fold of Christianity, the missionaries tried to cleanse them of their superstitious practices, and when they were absorbed into the family, their acceptance depended on the degree to which they had been Hispanicized.

WITCHCRAFT

The *brujas*, or witches, who are so much a part of Hispanic tradition, were not necessarily bad; in fact, they were considered useful to jealous husbands and wives, even in the Spanish colonial world of the sixteenth century. In his *El Carnero*, Juan Rodríguez Freile tells the interesting story of the witch Juana García and how she helped a jealous wife trap an unfaithful husband.[3] In the Southwest, Indians, Spaniards, and later Anglos also had some deep-seated beliefs in the supernatural. The Navajos believed in human wolves, men and women disguised in animal skins whose maleficent practices brought grief to their victims unless the latter chose to remain friendly with them. In west Texas "water witches" tied a string around the Bible and twisted it around a door key. As the Holy Book unwound, they measured a foot for every turn and drilled at the end of the last turn.

Before the broom riders fell into disrepute, the theologians of the thirteenth century had to work out their theory of human relations with Satan; and the Holy Inquisitors, as well as the good citizens of Salem, drew them into their own jurisdiction by confusing witchcraft with heresy.

Both good and mischief may be accomplished by *brujas* in the Southwest, but the devil is the gentleman who dispenses love potions and favors to those who have entered into a Faustian pact with him. These pacts are generally referred to as *pactados con el diablo.* Witchcraft is an accepted culture pattern about which clerics, when asked, will answer, "Sí, hay brujas, pero el cuento es dar con ellas"; "There are witches, but the trick is to find them." When their mischief is reported, investigators usually arrive after the witches have done their evil work. Houses are turned topsy-turvy, pictures fall from their places on walls, the coffee pot boils with no heat under it, and flowers are thrown through window panes without breaking them. These are some of the less-damaging antics of witches, but there are also instances where lives are lost. The story is told of a miller in Las Cruces, New Mexico, who died unexplainably one night while working at the mill. His replacement suffered a similar fate the next evening. Finally the third miller closed and locked every exit and, after starting the mill, stationed himself at the main door with a sharp axe. Around midnight he heard a very sweet and enticing female voice speaking through the keyhole, but the miller would not yield to her tempting entreaties. He asked her to stick her hand through the crack of the partly opened door. As she did so, he drew the sign of the cross on it with his finger. When the voice turned into a wild screech, he trapped the arm and chopped it with his ax.

Frogs have entered rooms in the dead of winter and tried to attack sick people in bed; they disappeared when impaled by a hot poker or when thrown into the fireplace. Women who harbored in their homes a hole filled with snakes have been brought to trial, and even today *brujas* are fined for practicing witchcraft in the Southwest. In localities where the belief in witches is strong, stories about them are set in other villages and the characters are impersonal. In the more credulous towns witches and their work are known by name and are consulted regularly, though not openly, by those who seek the witches' intercession in matters of love, vengeance, and spells.

One interesting story concerns a man whose curiosity led him to investigate the secret rites of witches in a remote area between Taos and Mora, New Mexico. When he saw a lighted house, he left his car by the road and walked over to investigate. Looking through the window, he was surprised to recognize women from his own village, who were dressed in black and were dancing with a gentleman whose tail protruded under his coat and who wore hooves instead of shoes. A big billy goat entered the room, followed by a serpent, who kissed the women with his forked tongue. Finally a group of skeletons entered carrying a coffin. When the women fell to eating the corpse, the man at the window felt such revulsion that he exclaimed, "¡Ave María Purísima!" and was catapulted to the road as the house disappeared in a puff of sulfurous smoke.

Should anyone want to see the devil in person, all he needs to do is grab a black chicken on the dark of the moon and take it to a place where five roads meet, wring its neck, suck the blood, and start turning clockwise until he falls. As he gets up, an unknown hooded being will take him where he can see the devil face to face. Aurelio Espinosa speaks of a school for witches, which is supposed to have existed in the mountain town Peña Blanca, New Mexico. There the devil presided in a cave, teaching witch aspirants how to turn into doves, owls, and finally dogs.

ARBOLARIOS VERSUS *BRUJAS*

Man has always been curious, credulous, or intrigued by the supernatural. Whereas some people are content simply to believe in beings from the unknown, others fancy that they can contact them and acquire the powers of the occult. Such beliefs cut across social caste, and society's acceptance of their ability to communicate with the supernatural changes from one generation to another. Today, when world society is so splintered, witches are not only about, but even appear on television. There is also a noticeable increase in the activities of these beings among southwestern Hispanic folk.

One character who has not entirely disappeared from the scene is the *arbolario (herbolario)*, the individual who began by dispensing herbs and household remedies centuries ago and then undertook to undo the evil work of sorcerers and *brujas*. In the days before scientific medicine the folk relied on empiric knowledge for the alleviation of their ills. There was always someone well informed on the curative virtues of plants, wild and domesticated, who could prescribe a potion, a tea, a rubefacient, or a purge for a given ailment. Eventually these village medics entered the field of the supernatural to counteract the effects brought about by village witches. It was a handy way to diagnose a malady that the village *curandero* could not cure. The *arbolario* simply declared that the patient was bewitched or that someone had cast the evil eye on him; to bring him out of it, a complicated ritual was called for.

The diagnosis was based on the patient's recollection of events over the past year. Had an owl followed him home, flying from treetop to treetop? Was there a woman who had been in love with him at one time? Was there an enemy who could profit by his sickness or death? Was someone trying to harm a member of his family indirectly? (One of these possibilities usually applied.) The *arbolario* went to work for a fee.

A ring of salt was laid around the suspected witch's house, crossed needles were placed on the window sills. If an owl emerged through the chimney, the witch doctor threw salt into the air in the form of a cross and then shot the owl down. The next morning a very sick witch called for him. When confronted, she confessed her evil doings and begged him not to harm her further. From under her pillow she pulled the effigy of the sick man and removed the needles that she had put through his liver, whereupon the village patient immediately recovered. The *arbolarios'* work was always positive and consisted of curing ailments and breaking spells. These village healers have continued to be active; unlike the *brujas*, they need not do their work covertly, because they are not censured by the community.

BASILISCO AND ESPANTOS

Despite the efforts of the church to dispel the belief in the supernatural, *monos* and *muñecos*, rag dolls and wax figures, are still being made according to directions given in the *Libro de la Magia Negra, The Black Magic Book.* Some of the *monos* are realistically covered with mouse fur. A secondhand car dealer in Albuquerque once found a bundle in the trunk of a trade-in containing, among other things, a good specimen of a fur-covered *mono.* There was also a *piedra imán*, a lodestone, or magnet, which according to directions was fed steel or iron filings every Friday in order to maintain its strength. The lodestone goes back to Roman times and is an age-old, universal adjunct to the practice of magic.

Another denizen of the supernatural world, which is referred to in the shepherds plays of the Hispanic Southwest, is the *basilisco*, that ugly bird born from the last egg laid by an old hen. Anyone looked upon by this creature dies instantly, according to tradition. Near El Paso was a spot on the old road down by the river where people dropped dead for no apparent reason. Finally someone discovered a *basilisco* in a crow's nest. A mirror on a pole was raised to the nest,

and the old bird died from the shock of seeing his own image, as prescribed by tradition.

In a land that abounds with legends of buried treasure trove—"Spanish chests" filled with gold—there has been a very strong belief in supernatural forces that guard such troves. There are *espantos* and apparitions that plague those who go looking for instant wealth. At the crucial moment bones rattle, skulls fall, and fumes emanate from the earth, overcoming the searchers. Graveyards abound with *ánimas en pena*, who in the middle of the night ask passers-by to pray them out of purgatory. Spanish ghosts have been known to be not only polite but amorous. A harassed husband in southwestern Texas complained about the *espanto*, or ghost, who got into bed with his wife every night and refused to allow the husband to retire until he said, "Con su permiso," "With your leave." The intruder was the ghost of his wife's first suitor, who had died before she married.

These ghostly apparitions can cause *susto*, a mental ailment that can be cured by an *arbolario* and sometimes by a witch. The victims foam at the mouth, turn blue, and roll their eyes in desperation. The cure is simple. A pinch of dust from the four corners of a graveyard is placed in a piece of red flannel and boiled with the mother's wedding ring. The brew is placed in a cup over which the *médico*, the village *curandero*, or an *arbolario* makes the sign of the cross with a cupped hand and gives it to the patient, who takes three swallows, repeating between each draught: "Alabado sea el Santísimo Sacramento del Altar." This combination of church symbolism and witchery is common in antidotes for spells cast by *brujas* and sorcerers of all sorts.

LA LLORONA

One of the most frightening *espantos*, which could cause a person to suffer a sudden attack of *susto* in the colonial countryside, particularly in Mexico and the Southwest, was the wail of *La Llorona*, that nocturnal mourner who roamed at night looking for her lost children. Some say she was a widow and drowned them in a pond or a well to be free to marry another man. Should she find other children like her own, it was said, she would probably kill them too, or she would cast an evil spell on whoever saw her. Naturally no one has ever seen her, but in the middle of the night her crying would be heard as she passed by. Her constant crying was like the wailing of a siren approaching and dying faintly in the distance. When *La Llorona*, The Weeper, stopped to wail at someone's doorstep, there was sure to be a death in that household. This unfortunate, unseen woman began wandering over the Southwest two centuries ago. Some say that her history goes back to the days of the Conquest. After all these years, she still roams at night over the country in search of her lost children.

THE EVIL EYE AND THE WHIPSNAKE

An evil once feared by folk in the Southwest was *mal ojo*, the evil eye. The spell could be cast by anyone in spite of himself, even when he meant no harm. Mothers objected to someone looking too intently, though admiringly, at a baby for fear of *el ojo*. High fever, vomiting, and even blindness could result from such a spell, unless the person who caused it could be found. The yolk of an egg was placed on a plate, and the person's face who caused the evil eye was reflected in it. The culprit was summoned immediately and was asked to spit in the child's face in order to remove the spell. Until a few years ago children all over the Southwest used to wear strings of coral beads around their neck to prevent the evil eye. Social workers throughout the Southwest still find this belief very much alive among Americans of Mexican descent today.

Many beliefs are a mixture of superstition and a folk interpretation of the behavior of the fauna of the region. A horned toad, so they believe, rolls into a ball at the approach of a snake and, once being swallowed, expands within the reptile and splits it open with its horns. Some snakes, such as the *chirrionera*, or whipsnake, can perform incredible feats. When this red-bellied snake is being chased and is about to be caught, it rolls itself into a hoop, turns cartwheels, and rolls away from danger. It also lies in the grass in wait for a good milk cow, around whose legs it wraps itself tightly and enjoys a good drink of milk (the cow goes dry as the result of this unexpected reptilian milking).

At night a whipsnake wraps itself around the neck of a nursing woman and sucks her breasts, meanwhile keeping the infant contented by putting its tail in the baby's mouth. It also is known to stand up on its head and administer a whipping to men in the fields, who claim it is like a cat-o'-nine-tails.

More feared than the *chirrionera* is the *ajolote*, or waterdog, referred to in northern New Mexico as *guajolote*, the Mexican word for turkey. This amphibian was particularly dangerous to young girls who bathed in the ditches of the Río Grande. Many a mischievous boy emptied a ditch of its feminine bathers by shouting, "Ajolote!"

WEATHER FORECASTING

Those who listen to weather forecasts on television every evening will appreciate the simplicity with which the colonials in the West could forecast not only the morrow but a whole year in advance. The system for computing the weather was called *las cabañuelas*, but it took someone who knew *números*, that is, arithmetic, to make the computations. According to tradition, the weather of the first twelve days of January corresponded to the twelve months of the year. Beginning with the thirteenth day, each day represented the months of the year in reverse. From the twenty-fifth to the thirty-first, each half-day represented the weather for each month in succession, and the weather of the first twelve daylight hours of the last day of January also corresponded to the twelve months in regular order. The average of these observations was the weather forecast for the entire year. Only very special observers could *echar las cabañuelas* accurately.

The Spanish colonials had other ways to help them tell what weather to expect, such as omens and observations of all sorts of natural phenomena. If the roosters crowed early in the evening, the weather was sure to change the next day; if the cattle were frisky, if the snails were climbing, if snakes appeared in large numbers or a donkey's bray was answered, rain was sure to follow. A ring around the moon announced a coming storm.

HEALERS AND THEIR ART

There may have been no medics in colonial days, but, as mentioned before, *curanderos*, *médicos*, *parteras*, *arbolarios*, and *sobadores* could prescribe a brew, recommend an herb, perform a ritual bordering on the supernatural, attend a birth, and rub a dislocated joint into place. There was hardly a root in the Southwest whose virtues were unknown to these folk healers. A newborn pig was rubbed on the patient with epilepsy; ground baked badger mixed with magpie soup was good for asthma and cat's flesh for tuberculosis; a wife's or husband's drawers around the neck would relieve a crimp in the neck; and bleeding from an open wound could be stopped with a compress of cobwebs. Many a man went to work years ago with the labels from a sack of Bull Durham or Tuxedo tobacco on the sides of the forehead to relieve a headache. There were also oils from snakes, skunks, coyotes, and virtually any denizen of the forest, for rheumatism, arthritis, or whatever ailed the patient. And for those who wished to win the heart of a young lady, a pinch of dried jackrabbit bone was placed in the lady's soup or coffee.

The *curanderos* of the Southwest were a group of specialists whose services depended on the nature of the ailment to be treated. In some instances, a sort of family history and mental diagnosis became necessary, particularly when an *arbolario* was trying to ascertain the cause of a certain hex, or *embrujo*. Inadvertently this practitioner was acting as a sort of folk psychiatrist, and in many cases he helped relieve anxieties of his patients. The *arbolario* (properly spelled *herbolario*) was originally an herb dispenser, but in time he extended his activities to casting out evil spirits and undoing mischief done by witches; because that practice was more lucrative, he became a specialist.

The acceptance of folk practitioners is usually referred to as *curanderismo*, and at times there is a tendency to ascribe to this healing art much more than it embraces. It has become as pervasive as *machismo*. All the different classes of folk healers have in common a good knowledge of herbs and their curative powers. Some of them have become proverbial and are known to every housewife, as it happens in Anglo-American folklore. Herb peddlers are responsible for much of the widespread knowledge of both wild and domestic herbs. At one time they traveled throughout the Southwest and did a good business replenishing the *alacenas*, or medicine chests, of the folk who tried to keep a good supply of basic remedies, in the days when medical doctors were not available. The Aztecs prepared one of the first herbals in the new world and set the pace for the ones that followed through colonial days. When the Old World plants were added to those of the New, the list became interminably long. Some of the vendors would come to a village and recite their wares loudly so that housewives could check to see that they were well supplied.

A collection of medicinal plants used in colo-nial days in California was recorded by several priests from San Antonio de Padua in 1814. Eventually Father Zephyrin Engelhart had it published in *The Mission of the Sierras* in 1929. Archer Taylor asked me to annotate and identify the herbal list, which was later published in *Western Folklore*.[4] Many of the herbs used today are found in this list of plants, and the uses to which they were put in the early days of California are very little different from those of today.

The healing arts among the folk were more specialized in years past than they are today. At one time the *partera*, or midwife, had only one function to perform, and if she prescribed household remedies to her patients they were usually those connected with her trade. Because midwives are not in such great demand today, it is natural that these women should expand their practice to the prescription of herbs. The services of *curanderas* were requested by mothers with ailing babies and young children. They knew what was good for *empacho*, a very common ailment among babies resulting from indigestion. They advised young wives concerning the care of their offspring and recommended all sorts of rubefacients and brewings for growing children. They also attended adults, but men usually preferred the male *curandero*.

The *médico*, another variant of the *curandero*, has a status beyond that of a mere folk healer. Many of these healers, particularly the women, combined religious practices by calling on the deity or a particular saint when dispensing a brew. Usually they would make the sign of the cross over the receptacle before offering it to the patient and in some cases utter a benediction that gave the patient greater faith in the medicinal brew. (Religious utterances were also used as a sort of incantation on putting out a light or when beginning a journey. As the light went out, the grandmother would say, "Alabado sea el Santísimo Sacramento del Altar." When starting on a journey, the driver would take the reins, urge the horses forward, and say, "Nombre sea de Dios," "In God's name." Protestant Hispanic folk continued this practice because they saw nothing different in invoking the blessing of the Almighty when applying an ointment or taking a prescription. The Pentecostals were more lengthy and profuse in their acclamations and prayers that accompanied these proceedings.)

Another name used for these folk healers was *sanador*, which literally means "healer." A few of these traveled over the Southwest, and at one time there was a healing salve by the name of Sanadora, which was marketed until the sales were stopped by the United States Post Office on a legal technicality. The product was advertised widely in local Spanish newspapers. The *Las Vegas Optic* carried a story on July 29, 1905, in which one Vicente Leal, from Union County, spoke highly of the medicine, saying that he had applied it to his hand after a severe rattlesnake bite and in twelve hours had recovered completely. Benigno Romero in Albuquerque did a brisk business with this bottled medicine until 1919.

Whether as *sanadores* or *curanderos*, Hispanic folk were not as spectacular as were their Anglo-American counterparts, who combined showmanship with their wares. The renowned healers in the Hispanic community were more on the order of miracle performers, who used a combination of healing with Catholic religion. Usually there were *niños* who were vested with religious healing powers. Newspapers acclaimed their performances in vivid accounts as they traveled from place to place. It was thought that young boys were more *inocentes*, devoid of guile and less susceptible to worldly temptations.

The usual village practitioners, from *curanderos* to *arbolarios*, had a broad knowledge of folk pharmacopoeia and usually had on hand many of the herbs that they prescribed in case the people did not already have them in their own *alacena*, or cupboard. Most of their prescriptions called for teas, brewings, and compresses. High on the list of remedies were animal oils and fats such as skunk oil, coyote salve, and snake oil, some of which are still available today. Almanacs printed in the Spanish language carried long advertisements of folk medicines and herbs.

One of the most popular in the Southwest was Té de la Abuela, or Grandma's Tea, which some families used at regular intervals. Medical doctors who had a large Hispanic clientele would give a prescription to the patient and just before leaving would recommend to the lady of the house that she continue giving the patient *sus yerbitas*, "your herb brewings," to establish the necessary rapport. The medics knew that it was good psychology to place the patient in a receptive frame of mind. The folk reliance in the use of herbs was a boon to Chinese doctors, who used to advantage the rich herbarium they had at their disposal. And in such Hispanic population centers as El Paso, San Antonio, and Los Angeles the *doctores chinos* usually had a sizable Hispanic clientele.

THE FOLK CHIROPRACTOR

One kind of specialized folk healer relied more on his knowledge of anatomy than on herbs and potions in ministering to his clients. He is not so much in evidence today as he was in the days of the Santa Fe Trail, when men had to sit on a freight-hauling wagon behind a string of mules or yokes of oxen for days and months. At the end of the day or when they had a rest stop for meals, the drivers would usually ask someone to give them an *apretón de arriero*, a "driver's hug." This is a form of folk chiropractic learned from a healer known as a *sobador*. This man was a combination of osteopath and chiropractor, who did not prescribe a series of expensive treatments but would relieve the patient on the spot.

The driver's hug was just one of his effective practices for a man who was ailing with aching back and shoulders, resulting from long periods of sitting, driving over trails that were anything but smooth. The procedure was simple. The patient would stand in front of a strong man, preferably one who was taller than he and lace his hands behind his neck with elbows bent down close to his chest. The man behind him would encircle his arms around the driver's arms, raise him by leaning slightly back and simultaneously giving him a strong, sudden hug. The driver's spine would crack like popcorn, and when he was dropped back on his feet, he would stretch out his arms, turn his neck around a few times, and smile with apparent relief. Women were given a less enthusiastic hug because their shoulders were not as strong as a driver's back.

The *sobador* was also very efficient in setting a dislocated shoulder, knee, or ankle. When a man slipped, fell, or wrenched a limb, the call went around for the *sobador*. With his knowledge of the human body he could set a joint back in place with a slight turn and a single jerk. A compress of cold water would finish the job and keep down the swelling for the afflicted patient. If the person's ailment called for simple massaging and manipulation, the *sobador* simply gave his patient a good rubdown. The word *sobador* simply means masseur, and he had none of the paraphernalia and prolonged series of treatments. The folk of colonial days were usually accustomed to withstand pain and recovered much easier than their frail brethren of today who do not usually have to exert themselves so much.

The superstitious and healing practices of southwestern Hispanic folk were part of a life pattern that provided them with a degree of comfort, security, and peace of mind in a land that until recently lacked effective medical treatment or opportunities to rise to a higher socioeconomic level. Their attempts to explain and control the vagaries of fortune, influence the course of fate, and direct the results of natural law took the form of proverbs, maxims, beliefs, omens, and other expressions of folk wisdom, not least of which were religious propitiations, amulets, and exorcisms in the name of the deity. Their interpretation of religion was based not on profound concepts of theology but on a set of practices that reduced religious worship to a simple formula of mimetic and sympathetic magic.

Nowhere did the mimesis of religious fervor reach so marked a climax as it did in the Easter observances practiced by that strange order of flagellants known in northern New Mexico and southern Colorado as Los Hermanos Penitentes. (A Penitente church, or *morada*, has been set up in Denver, but no instances of flagellation have been observed.) There is still a good deal of conjecture concerning whether this penitent order is part of the Third Order of Saint Francis or whether it is simply a survival of some medieval organization stemming from the Cofradías of Spain. Flagellation was practiced in Spain long before the Conquest and later, during the Golden Age, when the great Lope de Vega scourged himself until blood splattered the walls of his room. Those who have read Villagrá's poetic account of the Oñate Expedition into New Mexico in 1598 know members of the expedition celebrated Good Friday by flagellating themselves in public and that Oñate scourged himself privately in expiation of his sins. The Indians who witnessed these acts of contrition thought that the Spaniards had gone crazy.

The Penitentes have been studied by anthropologists, historians, sociologists, and literary men and women. They have been written about by Protestant clergymen, by Catholic priests, and by professional writers whose primary object was to sell feature articles to the newspapers. This array of authors presents a kaleidoscope of information, misinformation, bias, and romanticism, but there has been no consensus among them regarding the origin of the Penitentes.

Some writers draw a parallel between these religious fanatics and the bloodletting of Aztec worship. The secretiveness of the *morada* is also thought to have originated with the Indian kivas of the pueblos, whose ceremonial meetings are not open to outsiders. This is hardly the case, because Indian religion was influenced, sometimes superficially, by Christian worship, but there is no evidence to support the claim that Catholicism as practiced by Hispanic people of the Southwest was affected by Indian rites. A few persons

in Hispanic communities may have residual evidences of aboriginal worship, but that is because of the Hispanicization of Indians living in the Hispano community, who may still cling to vestigial forms of their original religion.

Flagellation as a form of exalted devotion occurs in most religions. The Egyptians beat themselves at the annual festivals in honor of the goddess Isis. The Romans too practiced flagellation, though not often self-inflicted, and the Christian Church adopted it originally as a form of punishment and later as a form of penance. The purifying agents blood, water, and fire were used by religions of antiquity. The Christian Church adopted all three symbolically in the "blood of the Lamb, the water of baptism, and the fire of the Holy Spirit."

One of the reasons that the origin of the Penitentes is difficult to establish is that the Catholic church itself has been ambivalent in its permissiveness. Saint Anthony of Padua not only practiced flagellation but extolled its virtues and recommended it. Organized flagellant groups appeared

A Penitente procession on the way to the *morada*, or church, in Truchas, New Mexico, spring, 1933.

in northern Italy in the middle of the thirteenth century, and the practice spread into Germany and Holland. Strictly speaking, the Catholic church has never sanctioned this extreme manner of expiation, although for practical reasons it has been acquiescent at times in the Southwest. Pope Clement VI was so opposed to it that he issued papal bulls prohibiting it, and many zealous Catholics were burned at the stake for proved violations of those edicts. After the arrival of the French Bishop Lamy in New Mexico in the early nineteenth century, and of Protestant missionaries, whose religious ethic did not approve of flagellation, the Penitentes had a turbulent history, and the road has not been smooth until the last few years. Intolerance lessened, with the waning of nineteenth-century religious fervor, and today the Penitentes are not looked on with distaste, nor are they made to feel that their religious observances have no place in present society.

THE PENITENTES BEFORE 1848

Before the arrival of the Americans in the Southwest, the Penitentes practiced their rites more or less openly, not because every Hispano was a member of the fraternity, as some writers allege, but because of the innate individualism in Hispanic society, where a person feels free to be whatever he wishes without conforming to the dictates of the majority. Newcomers to the Southwest manifested great interest in a religious practice that was so foreign to their concept of religion. The insistence of strangers on watching what they considered a spectacle, rather than a religious ceremony, caused the Penitentes to go into virtual seclusion and also to prohibit attendance at their rites by sightseers. But when a person approached the *hermano mayor,* or head man, in advance, requesting permission to attend the ceremonies, it was usually granted with the explanation that it was a religious meeting and that the visitors were asked to be respectful and quiet during the ceremony. The more intimate rituals were never open to visitors, but only to participants or initiates.

BECOMING A PENITENTE

Early in the spring novices who had applied for membership were advised of the first obligation, which was that no information about what went on inside the *morada* was to be divulged, "neither

to thy wife, nor to thy neighbor, under penalty of flogging." If the novice was not ready to accept all the obligations of the order, he was denied admission, but he could reapply when his wife or his parents gave their consent. At that time he went to the *morada's* door carrying two lighted candles and accompanied by a *padrino*. When admitted, he lay prostrate, kissed the earth and said: "My Lord Jesus Christ, I am a poor Penitent who comes to perform my exercise and fulfill my devotion."

The Brothers answered together, "God carry thee forward and increase thy devotion."

When the *novicio* had subscribed to all the regulations and accepted the obligations imposed by the order, he was inducted into the rituals and ceremonies that took place within closed walls, as well as those performed in public. The initiation rites included three gashes cut on his back by the *sangrador* or *picador* with a flint knife called a *pedernal*. (This distinguishing "brand" was sometimes seen at the state penitentiary on the backs of those committed, and it was often rumored that aspiring politicians wishing to gain favorable endorsements from regions of northern New Mexico that were Penitente strongholds also underwent this initiation.)

Subsequent entries to the *morada* followed a ritual. The Penitente knocked at the door and said: "God knocks at this mission's door for his clemency."

From within the Penitentes would answer: "Penance, penance to seek salvation."

The caller would continue: "St. Peter will open to me the gates, bathing me with light in the name of Mary with the seal of Jesus. I ask the Confraternity, Who gives light?"

Then from within: "Jesus!"

Caller: "Who fills it with joy?"

They: "Mary!"

He: "Who preserved the faith?"

They: "Joseph!"

On entering, the newly initiated brother genuflected before all the images on the walls and then addressed those present: "Pardon me Brothers if I have offended anyone, or have been guilty of scandal."

They answered him: "May God pardon him who has been pardoned by us."

The brother passed around on his knees, asking the blessing from all the brothers present, and then rose, saying: "Holy and good night may God give us. How do you do?"

Flagellants on the way to Calvary in the countryside near Abiquiu, New Mexico, in 1893. Courtesy of Fred and Jo Mazzulla.

FLAGELLANTS

Certain ceremonies were carried out on given days during Holy Week, but any member who felt compelled to do so applied the flagellum either in the *morada* or on some secluded pathway in the mountains surrounding the village. The Swedish painter Carl Redin, of the artist colony in Albuquerque, was sketching in the mountains early one morning when his attention was drawn to a swishing sound, accompanied by a low-pitched mumble that he could not understand. In a minute or so he noticed a man coming along a mountain pathway, bringing a whip over his back at every third step and repeating a prayer as he walked. The artist concealed himself in the undergrowth and watched fascinated as the penitent man, stripped to the waist, applied vigorously the *disciplina*, a flagellum made from strips of yucca. The man continued up the mountain slope castigating himself in an ecstasy of religious fervor.

This is the kind of scene that "Penitente hunt-ers" used to seek out surreptitiously wherever the flagellants tried to find not necessarily secrecy but privacy for their religious practices. During the Lenten season, groups of young men and women, most of them university students, went out to the mountain villages of northern New Mexico to watch the Penitentes, and, now and then, they were intercepted by armed guards. Most of the stories told by imaginative people who claimed to have "shot it out with the Penitentes," were romantic exaggerations of adventure seekers. But there were isolated instances in which the fanatics' insistence on privacy clashed with the determination of interlopers who went armed, in the days when the carrying of firearms was unrestricted.

PENITENTE RITUALS

Most of the writers who witnessed the Penitente ritual, after the Anglo-American occupation of the Southwest, agreed in their descriptions of the basic rites and, except for the condemnation by

207

A Penitente procession bearing the Cristo statue preliminary to the Procesión de Sangre in Truchas, New Mexico.

those who considered extreme penance savage and abhorrent, they all described the same processions and the same scenes that may be observed today in the few places where the order still practices the rites.

The climax of the Easter ceremonies was reached on Thursday and Friday of Holy Week, following the events in the life of Christ. The main event on Thursday, called La Procesión de Sangre, left the *morada* at noon, led by the crack of the flagellum on the already bleeding backs of the twelve members of the order. The Cristo was bent low under the weight of the heavy timbercross, but he labored on, stopping for rest and prayer at the stations of the cross. A few *alabados* and prayers were intoned at each station, and then the file of worshipers wended its way over the hillsides to Calvary, a place selected in advance for the cross to be erected. On this spot the crucifixion took place —an event that no outsider ever witnessed, including Charles F. Lummis, who first reported the Penitente rites in *The Land of the Poco Tiempo.*

It has been surmised by students of this subject that two hundred years ago actual crucifixions took place, and the belief persists today because of a subsequent story that the Cristo's shoes were placed at the doorstep of his home when he did not survive the ordeal. The crucifixion was simulated in later years by tying the man to the cross and keeping him on it until he began to turn pur-

ple. Then they would bring him down, and the coadjutor would bathe his wounds with rosemary water and revive him. Being selected as the Cristo was considered a great honor, which usually required the permission of the wife or mother of the candidate before he could be accepted.

On Friday night another important event, called *tinieblas*, took place in the chapel. Many residents in the areas where the Penitentes lived claim that the actual crucifixion took place during this evening and that people were brought together in the *morada* to draw attention away from the culminating event. Although the Friday evening meeting was open to outsiders, who had arranged for admission in advance, the *morada* was not open to the public. Today a certain amount of notoriety is involved in Penitente rites, and the shroud of secrecy is maintained to give greater publicity to a ceremony that is not supposed to be public.

Another factor that gives the institution of the flagellants a flavor of exoticism is the use of Spanish terms for the parts of the rite. Actually these words have a very ordinary meaning for anyone who is familiar with the Spanish language.

TINIEBLAS

In years past, *tinieblas*, an exotic form of Tenebrae, was an interesting experience to witness because of the uniqueness of the ceremony. The interior of the *morada* was simple and unadorned, mostly because the members of the order were very poor people. Their holy images and *retablos* were also products of folk art, not so much traditional folk art as attempts at reproduction of models by simple people who knew little about carving and less about art.

When the ceremony was about to begin, the *celador*, or sergeant-at-arms, took his place by the door and allowed the villagers to enter whether or not they were Penitentes, but he kept out visitors who had not been given permission by the *hermano mayor* to attend. The altar at the back of the *morada* was simple: a table on which was set a triangular candleholder, or sometimes two, with twelve candles representing the twelve Apostles and a larger candle for Christ. These candles were the only light in the chapel. On the earthen floor of the altar was a bed of broken glass and a stout, round cactus with sharp spines. From the side door by the altar, a man in white trousers and nude to the waist entered, carrying a heavy cross about ten feet long, followed by two men who were lashing themselves with a yucca whip that drew blood at every blow. Another, who had just received the "five wounds of Christ" on his back, entered, the blood streaming down his back and gathering in clots along the waist of his trousers.

Each participant tried to devise the most ingenious form of penance commensurate with the magnitude of the sins that he was expiating and with his ability to withstand the ordeal. One man crawled on his bare knees across the bed of glass, cutting deep gashes in his flesh. In an effort to emulate the suffering of Christ, a member of the order walked with a crown of thorns, which he pulled down over his temples to increase the flow of blood down his cheeks.

One of the last to enter, also stripped to the waist, walked deliberately to the thick cactus and, kneeling before it, engulfed the prickly plant in a tight embrace as he turned his eyes to heaven and uttered a quavering prayer. He remained on his knees for a long while, pressing the cactus closer and closer to his body. As he drew away, the spines clung to his flesh, where they would remain until they festered and fell out. Despite their fortitude some of the men collapsed from sheer exhaustion and loss of blood. They were carried to the adjoining room, where the coadjutor and *enfermero* bathed their wounds with rosemary water.

When enough of these acts of penance had been performed, the *hermano mayor* and *pitero*, or flute player, took their places by the altar with open notebooks in hand. Twelve Psalms were recited or *alabados* were sung, and a candle was extinguished after each hymn, until only one was left lighted in the dim interior. The *hermano mayor* stepped forward to warn those who were nervous and women and children to withdraw. The front doors were shut once more, and, as the leader snuffed out the last candle between his fingers, he intoned, "And now the veil is rent asunder! The firmament trembles, the gates of Hell are opened, and the spirits will rise from the dead!"

Hardly was the last word uttered when pandemonium broke loose with the rattling of chains, the beating of pots and pans, the crackle of *matracas*, or rattles, and the wailing of women. This deafening noise went on for several minutes and then stopped as suddenly as it started. The shrill notes of the *pito* alone could be heard as the leader announced a *sudario* or a Pater Noster for the departed soul of one of the brothers. Twelve prayers relighted the candles in reverse order.

Flagellants at the Calvary site with other *hermanos* of the fraternity in Abiquiu, New Mexico, in 1893. Courtesy of Fred and Jo Mazzulla.

When all twelve were once more burning, an *alabado*, sung by the leading brothers at the altar, ended the service. Whether or not the Cristo was crucified during the noisy rites was left for outsiders to conjecture.

PENITENTE POLITICAL INFLUENCE

The claim that the Penitentes hold political sway in the mountain counties of northern New Mexico is probably true, not because they are members of the secret order but because in many of the villages they are a majority. This religious sect has also been accused of taking human lives whenever they have been opposed or openly censured, but again public opinion equates self-inflicted bodily punishment with a tendency to do bodily harm to others. In 1936, Carl Taylor, a writer who lived in the mountain village of San Antonio east of Albuquerque, was found murdered at his desk in his cabin. The killing was immediately attributed to the Penitentes who lived in the village, because Taylor had just published a magazine article about the Penitentes. As it turned out, he was killed by his houseboy, who thought the author had a large sum of money in the house.

As the New Mexican folk move to larger population centers and through education and acculturation abandon extreme forms of religious worship, the Penitentes dwindle in numbers. But the canyons of northern New Mexico will continue to echo for many years with the resounding crack of the flagellum. Late at night during Lent the mournful *pito* will beckon the flagellants to cleanse their souls with the sharp strands of the Spanish bayonet soaked in vinegar, and ghostlike forms wrapped in sheets will slip away from the village on secluded paths to the mountains, where, unmolested by curiosity seekers, they can administer punishing lashes in expiation of their sins. They will return to the *morada* at dawn to have their wounds bathed in *agua de romero*, as they have done for centuries.

The reenactment of the passion of Christ by the Penitentes is referred to loosely as a "drama," but it is not drama, in the strict sense of the word. Alfred Bates makes the distinction clear when he says:

When is a play not a play? The answer is, when it becomes the real thing: when torture is inflicted in order to cause suffering, rather than to strengthen and prove. Then it is no longer dramatic in character, and is, rather than presents.[1]

A century and a half of association has inevitably resulted in some degree of acculturation of both Hispanos and Anglo-Americans in the Southwest, but there persist today certain culture traits that neither group has relinquished altogether. Nothing is more disquieting to Anglo-Americans who feel that time is money than the time perspective of Hispanos. They refer to the manner in which Hispanos deal with time as the "*mañana* psychology" and add that they leave everything for the morrow. Actually, upon analysis it is more of a "today psychology."

Hispanos, with a deeply ingrained sense of realism, cultivate the present to the exclusion of the future, because the latter has not yet arrived and hence is not a reality. In the trinity of past, present, and future, the only reality, timewise, is the present. The past is the recollection of a spent reality, and the future is an unrealized hope. Hispanos are so reluctant to relinquish the present that they hold onto it until it becomes the past, which in terms of clock timing means that an eight o'clock appointment can take place any time until nine, because the hour of eight stretches out until nine. This may be the reason that the clock is slowed down to a walk (*andar*) in Spanish, while in English it "runs."

In the future-oriented Anglo-American civilization, many things are planned so far in advance that the present loses its meaning. January magazines come out in December, and next year's automobiles are on sale long before this year is out. Even cemetery plots and funeral arrangements are bought and paid for in advance or on the installment plan. To a Hispano who lives *today*, the very idea of planning his funeral sounds like the tolling of the bells. In industry the designers go one step further; they plan a built-in obsolescence that determines the length of time that an article can last.

It naturally follows that a present-oriented person should be compensated by the ability to improvise, something that most Anglo-Americans are reluctant to do. Faithful to their slogan, they prefer to "be prepared" and are usually told to have an impromptu speech ready before attending a meeting where they will be called upon to say a few words. A Hispano, on the other hand, can usually improvise what he wishes to say because, as the Spanish humorist Julio Camba says, "Nosotros lo improvisamos todo."

But what about *mañana*? Like the shrug of the shoulders, it implies an indefiniteness that can be made definite only when the future arrives and becomes the present. Meanwhile, all else is postponed, except that which can be done only today. If one is having a good time, he never allows the future to intrude by worrying about it. The future-minded individual who looks at his watch when the party is in full swing and breaks in with: "Sorry, folks, but we must be running along. Tomorrow is another day," is either a practical-minded Anglo-American or a "reconstructed Hispano." In Spanish, *actualidad* is a combination of an extended present at a party, at an interview, or even in speechmaking, because, to a Hispano, *mañana* is today.

THE LAND OF *MANANA*

The Southwest is often referred to as "the land of *mañana*," implying that there everything is left until the morrow. It is simply a matter of priority, where the unreality of the future is procrastinated, even though such a time priority often leads to improvidence. The choice that Hispanic people make of past, present, and future is logical in that it is consistent with other values with which it is combined. This time perspective differs somewhat from that of Anglo-Americans, who also combine their time orientation with the values that they profess.

Both cultures try to achieve fulfillment and satisfaction. But Hispanos, being realists, seek the fulfillment of their desires *now*, and are not easily satisfied by waiting for the future. This trait has led some sociologists to say the Hispanic people follow an undeferred gratification pattern. The analysis would be correct if they did not add that it is a pattern of the lower classes. The tendency of Hispanos to gratify themselves today at the expense of the morrow has nothing to do with economic or social condition. It is an awareness that the present is a reality, a basic essential in their realistic culture; hence happiness must be the fulfillment of a desire that can make them happy today.

As we shall see, the attainment of something that provides an enjoyable satisfaction to the individual means that he must give up something. Hispanos and Mexicans prefer to give up the future when choosing reality, whereas Anglo-Americans give up present enjoyment to reach for a goal that they have set for themselves in the future. In the process of acculturation many Hispanos have become ambivalent about these two attitudes and compromise by being provident on the one hand, which is a future orientation, and still insist on the cultivation of the present as the fulfillment of reality, particularly if the fulfillment is concerned with humanistic values.

THE REALITY OF THE PRESENT

The present is a reality that we can all sense because it is with us; the past is a recollection of what once was a reality; and the future is conjecture, a hope of what may come to pass. If we consider romanticism an attitude, or a state of mind created by the imagination, as opposed to realism, we may safely assume that both Hispanos and Anglos are romanticists, except that Hispanic romanticism is based on the past, and Anglo-American romanticism is future-oriented.

In this trinity of time the present is greatly modified by the choice that each culture makes of what has gone before or what will eventually come to pass. In America, children are prone to forget the past and to consider the present a preparation for a future that will bring the fulfillment of their goals. In the schoolroom they constantly hear about "objectives and aims," and the present becomes a constant struggle to reach these objectives. Not having had the same orientation, Hispanos have to put forth greater effort to perform on a par with their Anglo classmates.

Even the slogans used in American life emphasize the future and not the past: "Don't cry over spilt milk," "It's water under the bridge," "Hitch your wagon to a star," "Save for a rainy day," "Be prepared." The past is so little regarded that special efforts have to be made to preserve it. Traditions are looked on by the younger generation as the mistakes of their ancestors. The present, on the other hand, is projected into the future to such an extent that children look forward to the day when they can become managers or presidents of firms. When they apply for their first job, they inquire about the opportunity for advancement. Such an orientation produces people of vision, of imagination, who live constantly in the hope that some day "their ship will come in" or that prosperity is around the corner. Such romanticism is effective in the formative period of youth. The young are willing to do all sorts of menial work, deny themselves untold enjoyment in the present, to achieve the fulfillment of their desires.

When people have grandiose visions of the future, they are often said to be "building castles in Spain." Spanish castles to a Spaniard are a reminder of a past greatness that was once a reality. Castles built on the future are American paid-up homes. American life is so inexorably geared to the future that the Hispanos, who enjoy the reality of the present, often reject some of the advantages that orientation on the future provides. For example, they are less likely to buy insurance, because it seems like an anticipation of misfortune. Some of them even go so far as to say, "When you buy insurance, you are inviting trouble." Savings accounts too are not as automatic with Hispanic people as they are with Anglo-American families, who open an account or buy bonds in the name of a child when he or she is born.

DESPRENDIMIENTO IS TODAY

The insistence on enjoyment of the present gives rise to a number of corollaries, particularly when this concept is combined with the way money is spent. Hispanos would rather spend their money today, and most of them enjoy doing it to the point where they are said to be "muy desprendidos," "unattached to money." This desprendimiento or unattachment was what moved the rancheros of California in colonial days to offer hospitality to travelers; provide them with lodging, food, a change of horses if necessary; and also leave a few coins in each guest room for the visitors to take if they needed them. (According to Mexican tradition, this virtue does not extend to the people from Monterrey, Mexico, whom they claim are very codo duro, "hard-elbowed"; that is, their elbow must be tapped to loosen their tight fist. In Spain, the Gallegos and the Catalonians are supposed to be equally reluctant to part with their money. These regional individuals are all very thrifty businessmen in Mexico as well as in Spain.)

The general tendency among Hispanic people is to disassociate themselves from material things, or at least to keep this association to a minimum. This is why money is considered something to part with, and when this trait is combined with the sense of the present, Hispanos and Mexicanos are known to be so *desprendidos* that they live beyond their income, and "echan la casa por la ventana," "they throw the house out the window," or spend what they have with reckless abandon.

There is even a reluctance to refer to money as such; in Spanish cash is called *efectivo*, and a man with nothing in his pockets says, "No traigo suelto," "I have no change." This unattachment is so extreme at times that it is amusing. José de Espronceda, great Spanish poet of Romanticism, went to Portugal as a young man. As he crossed the Tagus River, he flung his last *peseta* into the river because he did not want to enter Lisbon with such limited means. A Hispano college student out of a job in St. Louis several years ago had only a dollar in his pocket. He could not defer his gratification when he saw the theater marquee announcing his favorite opera; so he spent his last cent on it and enjoyed a performance by the Metropolitan Opera Company. Being Hispano, he preferred to enjoy himself in the present by a bit of *desprendimiento*, or unattachment, to a dollar even if it meant skipping a meal in the future.

This unattachment is well portrayed by John Steinbeck in *Tortilla Flat*, where the poorest Mexicanos share their meager lot with visitors, as though they were part of an affluent society. The man who hoards his money is looked on with suspicion by Hispanos. They try to imagine where he hides his wealth. Many treasure stories grow out of these conjectures. In Anglo-American society, the man who saves his money is respected, and he takes pride in his bank account. Charles Dana could not understand how a Californio could be proud though he did not have a *real* on his person. If an Anglo-American is prodigal with his money —that is, if he begins to practice *desprendimiento* too obviously—the Internal Revenue Service is moved to investigate his liberal spending, because it is not considered "normal" for a person to be so free with his money.

TIME PERSPECTIVE

The difference in time orientation is further exemplified in Anglo-American society by a constant running ahead of the calendar; cars, magazines, and clothes are displayed in advance of the season. Of recent years concern has been expressed over the showing if winter clothes in summer, which sometimes makes the current fashion unavailable because the stock is put on clearance sales or stored before the season is over. Magazine subscriptions are sold for years in advance. Newspapers advertise "Tomorrow's News Today." In Latin America as many as three past issues of the important magazines are carried on the newsstands, and unless the customer specifies the date he wants, he will be given whatever the stand has in greatest quantity.

It is interesting to note that, although our magazines and professional journals are issued months in advance, the *Revista Iberoamericana* until recently used to be one year behind, a puzzling situation for American professors, who never knew whether they were paying their subscription for the current year, the year following, or the year past. The sense of actuality among Hispanic peoples consists of prolonging the present until it becomes the past. There seems to be a reluctance to release the present, as a result of which a celebration will continue as an *actualidad* until the following morning, as they did in old California, where wedding feasts continued not only until morning but for several days.

Lately the extended travels of Anglo-Americans in Spain and in Latin America are beginning to modify their time perspective, and what was considered lack of foresight, procrastination, or utter disregard for the future among Hispanos is looked on in a different light—something enjoyable that Anglo-Americans would do well to adopt as a preventive of ulcers. In the United States life is governed by time schedules that are in turn governed by strict observance of the clock, an understandable necessity for an industrial society. Hispanic countries are also becoming industrialized, but they have not yet become tyrannized by the clock.

The attitude toward time seems to be accepted by Hispanic people everywhere. It is part of the heritage of cultures that are not greatly industrialized. In Peru, far from the American Southwest, the same tendency has been observed. At the American embassy newcomers have been warned not to expect all their dinner guests to arrive at the hour indicated in the invitation. A newly arrived Anglo-American couple gave their first dinner party at eight, and were at a loss when no one arrived. The maid was not surprised. She simply said, "Señor, it is too early yet. The guests will begin coming later on." A few weeks later, when the Americans were invited out, they arrived at the hour indicated in the invitation and were surprised when the *mayordomo* escorted them in an empty living room. For a moment they thought that they had misread the date, but the young man assured them that it was indeed the right day and added, "Please come in, the lady of the house isn't here yet." When the embassy wanted guests to be prompt, they printed a note on the invitation that read, "Hora Americana." It was a practical and diplomatic way of dealing with the differences in time perspective.

MODIFIED ATTITUDES

Hispanos in the Southwest who have to work in an Anglo-American milieu naturally tend to alter their traditional Hispanic behavior patterns, but it is difficult to abandon completely ways and attitudes of time perspective that bring so much satisfaction and enjoyment to all Spanish speakers, whether Hispanos, Mexican Americans, or Chicanos.

The advantage of a future-oriented society is that, while temporarily dissatisfied, it is always hopeful and can express its faith in the future by saying in the midst of a depression that prosperity is around the corner. Under the same circumstances Hispanos simply adopt a fatalistic attitude and accept "Lo que será, será," "Whatever will be, will be," because the future is an unreality of which they can be conscious only insofar as it can be projected into the present.

Anglo-Americans see the future as a hypothesis on which to speculate safely, sell on the installment plan, or buy investment insurance. Investment in the future was expressed by Hispanic folk until recently by a semiphilosophic "¡Ojalá!" from the Arabic *Ah Ala,* "Would to God!" The tendency of the Hispanos to hold onto present reality until it merges with the past causes some observers to say that they walk with their backs to the future. There is some truth in this observation, and for this reason it can also be said that they live reality twice, once when living it in the present and again when recalling it.

Mexican songs do not speak of "the love I left

behind me," but of "un amor que no se olvida ni se deja," that is, "a love one never forgets or leaves behind." The Anglo-American does not mind "shaking the dust" off his shoes and can easily project himself into a happy day to come by singing "Silver Threads Among the Gold," with a future nostalgia, to use an anachronism. The former sings of a love that was, while the latter of a love that will be. The point may seem belabored, but it is a fact that Hispano Mexicans may seem improvident because they see nothing romantic in future old age.

ENJOYMENT TODAY

The importance of the present is expressed in a story told years ago about a young Hispano in New Mexico whose wife ran away with another man. The judge to whom he took his complaint tried to counsel the brokenhearted husband and, by way of consolation advised him to forget the unfaithful woman, adding, "Who knows, Juan? Tomorrow you may find a better girl and you can be happy." The injured husband answered characteristically, "Oh, yes, *mañana,* your Honor, but what do I do *now?*"

Juan did not have the *"mañana* habit"; on the contrary, he was unwilling to postpone for the morrow what he thought he should have today. *Mañana* is conceived in an undetermined time and is therefore expressed in an equally indefinite term. *Mañana* expresses a remoteness that the word "tomorrow" does not convey, and those who translate it literally may be disappointed, like the hunter in Mora County who tried to cross a broken bridge on a hunting trip. When he complained to the landowner about the damaged bridge, he was assured that it would be fixed *mañana,* but on his return a month later, it was still impassable. Whoever was supposed to fix the bridge had something more important to do today, and so he postponed the less important detail of the bridge into a future indefinite time, in other words, *mañana.*

In present society, Hispanos who have become acculturated to American life find themselves falling into the usual routine inescapably; that is, they plan their activities in advance and sometimes have to forego something they would rather do because they agreed to do something else. But even the most urbanized Hispano reverts to his "present" orientation, particularly when in the company of other Hispanos.

214

Call on a Hispano friend, and the evening may turn into a social gathering, a dance, a love affair, or even a fight, but none of it will have been planned beforehand. In Anglo-American society one usually has calling hours arranged in advance, and it is considered poor manners, or at least thoughtlessness, to go knocking at a friend's door without calling in advance. That is undoubtedly a carryover into domestic life of the scheduling in organized industry, where a timetable is indispensable for efficiency, but it seems dehumanized to most Hispanos. In New Mexico they hail a friend going by and say, "¡Llegue, llegue!" asking him to drop in, not someday but at that moment. It would be a bit difficult to imagine an Anglo-American asking a person passing by to drop in without planning in advance.

It is inescapable that the interaction between Hispanic and Anglo-American cultures should modify both of them by mutual influence, but it is important, and interesting, to note the ingredients that are being combined. The realism exemplified by most Spanish speakers, who do what they personally consider important to their enjoyment of the present and postpone unenjoyable necessary chores for the morrow, runs contrary to the Anglo-American practice of getting the onerous things out of the way first.

TIME TO WORK AND TIME TO ENJOY

A school superintendent from Minnesota was being shown through the rural mountain villages of New Mexico late one fall, during a state teachers convention. As he was being driven around, he inquired from his guide what sort of fuel was used by the New Mexican mountaineers in the winter. He was told that they used firewood. "But," he asked, "where do they store it?" He was told that the firewood came from the neighboring woods and was never stored by the mountaineers. The superintendent—who believed in using the present to provide for the future—was concerned that these people made no advance provisions for the coming winter. He asked, "What do these people do when they need wood?" The answer came: The New Mexicans got their wood when they needed it, and not before.

To many Anglo-American observers such an attitude toward life means indifference or laziness; to others it seems a contradiction that does not make sense. It is contradictory if we call it laziness and sheer indifference, not that there may not be,

as in all societies, those who are in reality indolent. But laziness is an indisposition to exertion, and not a sequence of activity and inactivity.

Until recently, Anglo-Americans, like most other people, were wont to generalize, saying that Mexicans were naturally lazy and would rather sit in the sun under a big sombrero than work. The same observer would go to the Mexican markets, where he found thousands of handmade products of excellent craftsmanship from which to choose. The peasant who could enjoy the sun when the sun was out (since he had no guarantee that it might shine mañana) also turned out sarapes, crockery, and carved-leather goods for the tourist—a simple difference of time value in a culture where time is not money but a philosophical concept.

Mexicans, Hispanos, and Mexican Americans have been enjoying life today for many generations. Their Anglo-American friends have had their sights set on the future with bank accounts for their children. The Hispanos work when it is necessary, and they pay for the brides' ensembles when they marry. When they wish to relive this reality, they will talk about "allá en mis tiempos," "back in my day"; and when they sing, they will recall the life back on the old rancho where they once lived: "Allá en el rancho grande, allá donde vivía."

Even in the Spanish language the future is of little importance. During the past decades the future subjunctive has disappeared, and the simple future is formed with the *present* of the auxiliary verb *to be*. The present tense can also be employed to express futurity by saying, "Mañana vengo a verle," "Tomorrow I come to see you."

One of the important characteristics of the fickle Don Juan of Spanish literature was the way he enjoyed a succession of present realities. When he was threatened with future punishment for his misdeeds, the young scoundrel answered, unimpressed by his future fate, "¡Tan largo me lo fiáis!" "It's a long time hence!" A story is told about a Mexican *abonado*, or a boarder, who failed to pay his board at the *fonda* where he ate. The *madre*, as the owner-cook was called, said to him as she served him: "You haven't paid me for the last two weeks," and reprimanded him by saying, "¡Allá la verá con Dios!" meaning that he would pay in the afterlife. The unmoved boarder looked her in the eye and answered mischievously, "Si para entonces me las guarda, sírvame otro plato": If she was willing to wait that long, she could serve him a second helping.

Emphasis on the present and unconcern for the future were utilized by a student at the University of Denver who was working part time as a door-to-door salesman. He was having difficulty collecting monthly installment payments in the Mexican-American part of the city, though his clients were all wage earners. When asked how he went about collecting, he said that he usually gave them up to ten days after the first of the month. He was then advised to call on payday. He did so and was greatly surprised to discover how promptly his clients paid. The time to collect was now, when they had the money to pay with, before they spent it on something they thought was more important. In fact, he took other items along in case someone was interested, and discovered that his "bad debtors" bought items he had never imagined they could afford.

In Mexico they tell of an altruistic employer who decided that his workers were not being paid enough, and so he raised their wages. The following Monday nobody showed up for work; the new wages were high enough to enable them to work one day less. A similar tale is told about a fisherman in Tampico who fished every day in the week to make a living, but during a season when the fishing was good, he worked five instead of six days because the catch of five days was enough to tide his family over the weekend. These stories may be apocryphal, but they illustrate the importance with which the present is looked on in Hispanic culture and the lack of thought of that morrow, which they like to call *mañana* because it is so indefinite and unreal.

The Spanish language in the Southwest reflects the history of the people who have spoken it since it was introduced by the Spaniards at the end of the sixteenth century. The language spoken by the colonials then was virtually the same as the one spoken in Spain and was not much different from the speech of other colonists in Latin America. Like all languages of the Western world, Spanish maintained standards of usage through its written literature and also developed a language of the hearth among speakers who relied entirely on oral transmission because of their inability to read or write. Both levels of Spanish co-existed and fulfilled the varied needs of all sectors of society.

As time wore on, folk Spanish and the language spoken by the educated classes developed differences in pronunciation along phonetic lines common to the language. In 1915, Aurelio M. Espinosa made a complete study of the morphological and phonetic changes in New Mexican Spanish, which apply equally today.[1] The changes that occurred in the language of colonial literate society are developmental, whereas those that occurred in the oral language of the folk were a form of "deterioration" brought about by a relaxed pronunciation and by a limited familiarity with the written word. The folk's inability to read and write led them also to preserve many forms that were current in the seventeenth century but today are archaic or obsolescent. The current use of some of these archaic words among southwestern folk gives a charming historical flavor to the language, but it does not mean that the people today speak the language of Cervantes.

A small number of crown representatives, administrators, public functionaries, and churchmen in the principal cities of the Southwest, such as Santa Fe, El Paso, and San Antonio, were familiar with the language of the folk. But their duties required them to use also the more formalized language when attending to official dispatches, documents, contracts, and legal matters connected with their offices. This form of language was less subject to change because it consisted for the most part of formulae, some of which are still current in Latin America. The language spoken by the educated *criollos* and by the administrators was not static, however, and continued to develop along linguistic lines until it was replaced by English.

The folk who lived outside this small cultured circle did not keep pace with the normal language changes that occurred over the next three hundred years. They continued their form of popular speech and preserved unchanged expressions that now are considered obsolete. At the same time they developed the apocopations, elisions, and syllabic inversions that linguists call ellipses, metatheses, and epentheses. Eventually, as the Hispanos merged into one class, the spoken Spanish became uniform, and the differences between cultivated Spanish and folk speech disappeared. What is commonly heard today in the Southwest among the residents is traditional folk language, together with Anglicisms, literal translations, and accretions from artificial sources such as Pachuco, and what in Spanish is labeled *jerga callejera*, or street slang. Ironically a "truer" Spanish can be found in the isolated villages and remote mountain valleys in New Mexico than in the cities where Spanish is taught in the public schools. The older Hispanos are more likely to greet a stranger by asking, "Where does your grace come from?" when they say, "¿De 'ónde viene su mercé'?" They may drop the *d* from *dónde*, and the final one in *merced*, but those are normal changes that occur in folk speech throughout the Spanish-speaking world.

FACTORS THAT HELPED TO PRESERVE THE LANGUAGE

Many factors have been instrumental in preserving the use of the Spanish language, despite all the imperfections that characterize it today. First and foremost, the proximity of Mexico along the Texas, California, and Arizona borders and the constant traffic of people coming and going have kept the language alive. Recent arrivals from Mexico contribute additional vocabulary to the language and help keep it current. In spite of the limitations imposed on the use of Spanish by circumstance or by design, it continued to be used by Hispanos. In regions of the Southwest where the Anglo-Americans were a decided minority, the tables were turned, and the Anglos learned Spanish in order to communicate with their friends and neighbors.

Another important factor in the preservation of the Spanish language was the church, which continued to assign Mexican or Spanish priests to the missions. The close association of the village priests with the inhabitants provided them with oral Spanish of better-educated individuals. Some of the more concerned padres taught the language to the young in their spare time. One well-known priest who worked diligently in trying to provide schooling for the children of Taos was an independent priest named Martínez, who published a few issues of a newspaper in Taos called *El Crepúsculo*. Some writers claim that the printing press used by "El Padre Martínez" was brought into the Southwest by Josiah Gregg. Actually Antonio Barreiro brought the press from Mexico City and sold it to Ramón Abreu, who in turn passed it on to Padre Martínez.

Shortly after the American occupation, Bishop Lamy was assigned to Santa Fe. One of his main concerns was the strengthening of the educational system in the state. He brought with him a number of French priests to help him revamp church work under his jurisdiction, but their main interest lay in establishing educational institutions, where Spanish was part of the curriculum. The extensive schoolwork initiated and directed by Bishop Lamy was not primarily designed to teach Spanish to the New Mexicans, but it did serve as a transition from Spanish into English for many new citizens under circumstances that were more favorably accepted by a predominantly Catholic population. In California the missions were established for the conversion of the Indians, but the presence of an institution whose work was carried out in the Spanish language was influential in maintaining a linguistic continuity.

A year after the American occupation Protestant church schools opened in New Mexico, led by the Baptists, who established the first school in Santa Fe in 1849. After the Civil War the Presbyterians and the Methodists built schools in Santa Fe and in Albuquerque, and eventually in Texas and Arizona. Some of these institutions have continued as boarding schools until the present day.

The Protestant schools also emphasized an English curriculum and tried to act as a bridge between Spanish and Anglo-American culture. Spanish was an important subject in the course of study, included with a view to preparing some of the young men for the ministry. Because the congregations they would eventually serve were Spanish-speaking, it was necessary for these future ministers to improve their public-speaking proficiency in that language. Both Protestant and Catholic churches have conducted services in Spanish throughout the Southwest so that, indirectly, those who attend services during the week are exposed to a more formal version of the language than they use at home. Other activities supervised by the churches during the Christmas season and other church holidays gave the parishioners and the congregations an opportunity to use Spanish freely.

THE ROLE OF NEWSPAPERS AND JOURNALS

The publication of newspapers and *revistas* in Spanish from Colorado to California and all along the Mexican border was another means by which the Spanish language continued to live with a fluency that oral transmission alone could not have provided. Over the past 125 years more than five hundred newspapers have been published in the southwestern states, beginning with a periodical that Antonio Barreiro published in 1834, when he imported the printing press mentioned earlier. Many of these newspapers had a very short life, but another paper was always started to replace the one that closed down. *El Crepúsculo* published only a few issues in 1835, but the people in Taos always remember the name of their first newspaper. *El Nuevo Mexicano* in Santa Fe had the longest life of any newspaper published in Spanish in the Southwest. It continued with the same masthead from 1849 until 1965, and during the time that it was owned by Cyrus McCormick, it made a definite attempt to upgrade the quality of the language and the content by employing an able editor from Chihuahua. Members of the Spanish faculty of the University of New Mexico and other institutions were employed as contributors and feature writers. Many of the leading citizens of Santa Fe were also asked to contribute regularly, and for a number of years the traditional lore of the Hispanos was featured in every weekly issue.

One of the most widely distributed and influential Spanish newspapers in the Southwest was *La Prensa de San Antonio*, published by Ignacio Lozano. It was a complete newspaper with all the usual sections and supplements of large urban dailies. It was used by Spanish classes in the colleges and universities of the Southwest and helped acquaint English speakers as well as Hispanos with Mexican journalism.

The names of some of the newspapers indicate their objectives and editorial policy. Such newspapers as *El Defensor del Pueblo*, or *The People's Defender*, published in 1882 in Albuquerque alongside *Opinión Pública* and *Nuevo Mundo* clearly indicate their mission. In the early 1900's *El Independiente* appeared in Las Vegas; *La Vía Industrial* in—non-industrial—Antonito, Colorado; *La Opinión Pública* in Walsenburg, Colorado; *El Heraldo del Valle* in Las Cruces, New Mexico; and *La Revista* in Taos. Even a small village like Roy, New Mexico, had a short-lived paper called *El Hispano Americano*.

California had one of the most vocal newspapers, edited by a young Californio barely twenty years old, who gave his editorials an emphasis seldom seen in other parts of the Southwest. From 1855 to 1859 Francisco P. Ramírez was, according to Leonard Pitt, a self-styled champion of the Spanish Americans in California. He named his newspaper *El Clamor Público*, *The Public Outcry*, and when he felt that the Californios were being "sacrificed on the gibbet and launched into eternity," he expressed his sentiments on the editorial page. The Californios had not been separated from Spanish literary sources as long as the New Mexicans, and so they were more familiar with a fuller and more current use of the language. Other newspapers in California were published in Spanish for the benefit of those citizens who were more accustomed to their original language than to the newly arrived English. In San Francisco they read *El Eco del Pacífico* and *La Crónica* until 1856, when they ceased publication.

It is interesting to note the variety of readers that *El Clamor Público* had in southern California; Ramírez complained that his paper was read by more Yankees than Californios. The large number of Spanish-language newspapers published was undoubtedly a factor in keeping the language alive. Many Hispanos and Mexican Americans today may not be able to read English, as is disclosed by adult-education programs in San Antonio and other large population centers. But many of them are able to read Spanish, and they

continue reading it today in the local newspapers.

Reading, like many other skills in the Spanish Southwest, was transmitted by tradition; that is, a father who could read taught his son enough to get him started, and if he was lucky to receive instruction from an itinerant school teacher or at a church school, he would learn not only reading but writing and arithmetic. The well-written letters and official records found in the villages and towns throughout the Southwest attest to a greater literacy than is usually attributed to the inhabitants. Books were not numerous in the Southwest in colonial days and were not particularly abundant in American territorial days, but newspapers provided reading material for those who could read.

Occasionally interesting editions of books are found in the possession of Hispanic families. Eighteenth-century editions of Calderón de la Barca's plays, and several volumes dealing with agriculture, bound in vellum and published in Spain in the 1700's, have been found. The mountaineers who owned these books complained that they were filled with spelling errors, not knowing the changes that had taken place in Spanish orthography in the past three centuries. In a study made in 1942 by Eleanor Adams and France V. Scholes of books in New Mexico between 1598 and 1680, they discovered that, other than the missionaries and the Spanish governors of the province, the settlers had only eleven books among them, all but one religious publications.[2] It is likely, however, that a search of old chests owned by the Hispanos would bring to light some interesting additions.

FOLKLORE AS A FACTOR

The most important factor in the preservation of the Spanish language is the rich body of traditional lore that abounds throughout the Southwest in the form of folk songs, proverbs, riddles, games, and folk plays. Even more important are the troubadours and village poets who for centuries have composed songs and ballads in every village of the region, and who, in addition to their own compositions, have learned the traditional songs and verse of years gone by. The language of these bards of tradition is surprisingly broad and rich in content. They can express themselves much better than most of the village people. In trying to put across a message in rhyme, they study and use forms of expression that the average individual seldom uses. Many present-day urbanized Spanish speakers find it difficult to express themselves in standard Spanish and must recur to Anglicized expressions that are neither Spanish nor English but a bastardized form of communication used by those who have lost touch with the language of the people. Many today advocate that the atrocities that are currently used in the name of Spanish should be taught and cultivated, under the impression that this is the language of the people. The real Spanish-speaking folk whom they are trying to emulate have always had a respectable command of Spanish. The deteriorated forms of expression one hears today are, for the most part, arbitrary neologisms or Anglicized forms that would horrify their ancestors.

REGIONAL DIFFERENCES

The Spanish language has had a different development in each of the principal regions that comprise the Southwest: New Mexico, California, and the Texas-Mexican border. New Mexico was the first province to be settled and was the most isolated from the very beginning. The region north of Albuquerque, where most of the original colonials settled, was far from the cultural centers of New Spain, as well as from those of Mexico after independence. The only contact that the New Mexicans had with people on the south was that during the annual Chihuahua fairs and the trading caravans over El Camino Real. This isolation, covering two and a half centuries, gave the language of this northern region a distinctive character, different from that of the other two regions.

Language learning, like other skills in the country, depended to a large extent on oral transmission, with the resultant dislocations and mutations to be expected in an isolated region lacking the modernizing effects of a written literature. In addition to the obsolescent words of seventeenth-century vintage, there developed in northern New Mexico an intonation not found elsewhere and a pronunciation that is readily recognizable as a distinguishing characteristic of the northern New Mexican colonial. In current usage are a number of expressions and words that have fallen into disuse in most sectors of the urban Hispanic world. These outmoded forms provide the linguist with interesting material for study, but they also curtail the use of current Spanish. The use of such historical forms as *vide, truje, ansi, mesmo, dende, agora*, and a host of other archaic words does not mean that the New Mexicans are speaking incorrect Spanish. It was the language used in the Spanish world when the province was settled at the end of the sixteenth century. It simply means that part of the language that these people speak is outmoded elsewhere.

INFLUENCE OF ENGLISH ON SPANISH

Until recently most of the people of the Southwest were pastoral folk, *mestizos* and Hispanicized Indians who relied on orally learned speech, because they lacked, with few exceptions, the basic skills of reading and writing. As they were introduced to the English language, they Hispanicized unfamiliar words and extended that practice to everyday Spanish idiom. English words such as *park, flunk*, and *brake* were not common in Spanish days, so they simply converted them into *parquear, flunquear*, and *brequear*. Sometimes they transferred words that in Spanish were used in comparable situations, such as *arrear* for "to drive." The Spanish *arrear* is used to mean to drive cattle and horses instead of cars. The modern word in Spanish for driving a car is *dirigir*. Another form of Anglicization is the literal translation of expressions from the English, such as *aplicar* for "to apply," and the corresponding noun *aplicación* for "application." In older Spanish one "applies" a compress, but *aplicación* means "laboriousness." The standard Spanish rendition is *solicitar* meaning "to apply for a job" and *"solicitud"* for a "job application."

In the Southwest, Spanish began to deteriorate gradually as it ceased to be the language of commerce, industry, and public administration. The mandatory translations into Spanish of legislative proceedings in New Mexico, Colorado, and California helped Anglicize the Spanish language. On the surface it seemed that both languages were on a par with each other, but actually they were not, because English was the base on which the Spanish renditions were molded. As the Spanish speakers gradually improved their English, the use and quality of Spanish began to diminish proportionately, until it became a familial tongue used in interpersonal relations among friends and for household needs. The diminishing quality of the language can be observed in the translations made in the legislature. The earlier translations were made in standard Spanish with occasional Anglicisms, but these increased in geometrical progression in the ensuing years, as the translators and interpreters became more familiar with English and less so with Spanish. Those who witnessed simultaneous interpretations in the legislative chambers were greatly amused by the renditions of the interpreters who would rush to the side of an English-speaking legislator as he launched into a long and involved dissertation.

The substitution of English for Spanish in public and then at home gradually pushed the latter into the background. This process was not unique in the Southwest; the same happened to the German of Pennsylvania, the Italian of New York, and the French of Louisiana. It is very difficult for people to become bilingual when they are surrounded by a unicultural society, unless a very special effort is made by those who wish to preserve their own language at the same level of proficiency. Bilingualism means, in effect, biculturalism as well.

The introduction of the English language in the Southwest affected spoken Spanish in all regions in much the same manner, but with different degrees of intensity. In the northern villages of New Mexico no changes became apparent at first because the few Anglo-Americans who settled in this region learned Spanish and used their own language principally for official purposes. The central part of the state, where industry and trade centers were established with the coming of the railroad, had a larger influx of Anglo-Americans. The language lines were soon divided as the modern cities like Albuquerque and Las Vegas grew up near the railroad, and the original settlements remained apart about half a mile away (and were soon known as "Old Town"). This division was characteristic of many cities and towns in the Southwest and determined the fate of the two languages. English, as mentioned earlier, was used in business transactions, government administration, legal matters, and industry. The Spanish language gradually became the language of the hearth that did not influence the cultural growth of the community. Exposure to English forms of expression, however, did expand the language of the Hispanos, who found it more effective to translate literally the new concepts from English into a Spanish that was structured on English syntax. This gave rise to such forms as *hacer su mente pa' arriba* for "to make up your mind"; *tener buen tiempo*, "to have a good time"; *démelo pa' atrás*, for "give it back to me." These expressions, so widely used in northern and central New Mexico especially, were hardly conducive to bilingualism, much less to the preservation of correct Spanish diction.

The influence of English on the Spanish of the borderlands was inevitable after 1848, again because all official and business transactions were carried on in the national language. But it was a mutual influence. Taking over of the cattle industry meant adopting the language of the vaquero. Such words as *lariat, lasso, wrangler, remuda, hackamore, corral, mustang,* and *buckaroo* were not far removed from the original Spanish *la reata, laso, caballerango, remuda, jáquima, corral,* and *vaquero.* This aspect of western English has been studied for many years. An early example is Harold W. Bentley's *Spanish Terms in English with Particular Attention to the Spanish Southwest.*

BORDERLANDS INFLUENCE

The constant border traffic of Mexicans and of Americans of Mexican descent has served to keep the Spanish language, including regional Mexicanisms, current and alive in the Southwest. The full meaning of expression, available in Spanish from neighboring Mexico, has also helped maintain the fluency of language along the international border, except in isolated northern New Mexico. Full communication developed along the borderlands, with a minimum of Hispanicized English until recently. Great numbers of border residents are fluent in both languages and are truly bilingual because they are bicultural. That is a normal development among people who grow up in a natural human laboratory, where both cultures can be lived and where, as in this instance, both English and Spanish are used socially. Along the border there are Anglo-Americans who know the Spanish language better than many Mexicans do; conversely there are also Hispanos and Americans of Mexican descent who have a better command of English, both written and spoken, than a large number of Anglo-Americans have.

Among the Hispanos of the borderlands from California to southern Texas there are actually three language groups: those who have cultivated English and are more at home in that language; those who prefer Spanish and know it well, along with a working knowledge of English; and the fortunate ones who have become bilingual for practical reasons. Many professionals of both cultures have found it greatly advantageous to be bilingual.

Some of the universities in the borderlands have helped to further the cross-cultural flow by undertaking programs in depth in centers of Latin

American studies. The Mexican universities became aware of this interest half a century ago, and began offering summer courses for Anglo-American students. From these early efforts the field has grown to such proportions that Mexican universities along the bordering states, as well as the better-known ones in the interior, have developed extended programs by adding bicultural Anglo-Americans to their faculties.

Many American universities, wishing to take advantage of the cultural climate of a Spanish-speaking country, hold summer sessions of their own all over the neighboring republic. One result of this mutual program is an American university in Puebla, the University of the Americas, and an extension of the National University of Mexico in San Antonio.

CALIFORNIOS BECOME ANGLICIZED

In California many of the original settlers, particularly the more prominent rancheros, became assimilated through intermarriage with the incoming Anglo-American traders and sea captains who retired on the West Coast. Most of their descendants became English speakers. The Spanish-Mexican period in California was short compared with the settlement of New Mexico. That is why there are no linguistic archaisms in the language of the Californios and the later Californians, except those brought by settlers from regions where the language forms developed from an earlier-vintage Spanish. The close relations between the original settlers and the Anglo-Americans in the southern part of the state gave rise to language mixtures that Mexicans have always referred to as *pochismos*. In the years that followed the American occupation, the nickname *pocho* was applied to any person who used an Anglicized version of Spanish or expressions that were not strictly of Spanish provenience. Some mildly critical quatrains, tempered with Spanish wit, sang the failings of the California *pochos* and chided them for their deculturation.

The influx of Mexicans into the state over the past fifty years has created barrios where Spanish is spoken almost exclusively. But as the children enroll in the public schools, where English is taught, Anglicization begins to take place. Unlike the Texas-Mexican border, California does not have good-sized cities adjoining each other along the border where people can freely come and go. As a consequence there is not the extensive carryover that occurs in cities such as El Paso, San Antonio, and Laredo. Both San Diego and Los Angeles are many miles from the Mexican border, and the heavy seasonal traffic of migrant workers on their way northwest provides the only close contact with Mexicans. On the other hand, opportunities to work and mix socially are considerably better in California than in Texas, and the cultural climate is more conducive to acculturation. In Texas, with the exception of El Paso and to some extent Laredo, the cultural lines are more strictly drawn.

EL PASO VALLEY

The one region of the Southwest that probably developed the most nearly complete and also the most colorful Spanish was El Paso Valley, extending north to Doña Ana in southern New Mexico. At the crossroads of trade routes, the valley was never isolated, and therefore its people did not preserve exclusive linguistic forms that eventually would become archaisms. They did preserve, however, a very rich agricultural vocabulary that was not entirely current in other parts of the Southwest. Some of this vocabulary was composed of old expressions that disappeared only when modern methods of agriculture were introduced. An early study of the Spanish language of the region reflects the life that these people led in the country. The urban Hispano, having constant contact with Mexico across the border, generally spoke the language of northern Mexico. Naturally, as the Spanish speakers learned English in school and began working in industries established by Anglo-Americans, they found it easier to Hispanicize some of the concepts that did not come readily in Spanish, though not to the same extent that the Spanish speakers did in New Mexico. The diversified agricultural products of the valley required a functional language to use in such broad and varied activities.

AGRICULTURAL VOCABULARY

Because agriculture could be carried on only with irrigation, the first residents of the valley had to build a network of ditches based on the guidelines that were given by the Spanish crown when land was parceled out to settlers. Through the *acequia madre*, "mother ditch," water was diverted from the river and distributed throughout the valley farmlands by a network of smaller *contra acequias*. The man in charge of administering the water distribution was called *alcalde del agua* in El Paso Valley and *mayordomo del agua* in northern New Mexico (names later replaced by the less picturesque "ditch boss"). In Arizona this official was known as *zanjero*. In El Paso Valley, the title *alcalde* was a carryover from Spanish colonial days, as was *mayordomo* in the north. The Anglo-Americans also perpetuated this title by using the English equivalent "majordomo," which was close enough to the Spanish word from which it originated. But for *acequia* they followed the southern mountaineers' tendency to use the duonominal combination *acequia* and "ditch" or "*cequia*-ditch," much as the mountaineers would say "man-child," "rifle-gun," and "hound-dog."

The preparation of the land for planting had a varied vocabulary in El Paso Valley, where winter plowing was called *barbecho*. In the spring the land was molded into *melgas* or *tablas* for planting alfalfa and wheat, *surcos* and *camellones* for chiles and sweet potatoes. The plow opened a *besana*, "furrow," to provide *bordos* to hold the water. Plants were cultivated with the hoe, or *escarda*. To dig the soil deeper was *traspalar*. For that an *azadón*, "grub hoe," was employed rather than the lighter *cavador* used for surface hoeing.

In the fall farmers who had been working on *la labor* (which originally was 177 acres of farmland) gathered the hay and placed it in an *arcina* (stack) for the winter or in a *tejaván*, "shed," if there was one. Perishables such as fruits and vegetables that the families wanted to keep for the winter were placed in an *almárcigo* dug partly into the ground, much like a potato cellar.

UNITS OF MEASURE

This industrious valley, where so much history has been made, had occasion to use much of the Spanish language of colonial days. In trading and selling, the settlers needed to measure or weigh their products. The *almud*, an ancient measure for dry cereals and grains used in northern Spain, was regularly employed until the turn of the nineteenth century. Some of the quaint measuring boxes, varying from one-half to one gallon, were still around in some of the old ranchos of El Paso Valley during the early days of this century. For larger quantities there was the *arroba*, four of which made a *quintal*, or approximately a hundred weight; and a *fanega*, which amounted to a bushel and a half.

Length and height were indicated by a nonverbal system consisting of a number of signs made with hand and arm. It was considered an insult to refer to the height of a boy, for example, by stretching the arm palm down to indicate how tall he was. The insulted party would say, "He's not a horse or a cow!" The proper way to indicate the height of a boy was to hold up index finger and thumb outstretched with the index pointing up. An outstretched arm with hand palm down was used for an animal higher than a man's waist; the hand was held vertically to indicate the height of an animal no higher than the waist, such as a pig.

Before standards of measurement were established, the folk used the traditionally accepted system, which served well enough, since there was no need for the precision of modern technology. They could not carry measuring instruments, so they used parts of the body to indicate length. The shortest measurement was the inch, indicated by the first joint of the thumb, *pulgada*, derived from the word for thumb, *pulgar*. The next length was the *jeme*, the distance between index finger and thumb outstretched. Like the English, the Spanish colonials also used the span of the hand, called *cuarta* or *palmo*. The unopened hand and the individual fingers were also occasionally used in measuring liquids in a receptacle. The next measurement was the *codo*, the distance between the tip of the middle finger and the elbow; and the *vara* measured from the center of the chest to the tip of the fingers, an equivalent of 33.5 inches.

There were other traditional ways of measuring length, as when a mother took her son to market to buy him a pair of trousers. She would ask him to hold the trouser legs outstretched across his chest, assuming that the length across the chest and arms was equivalent to the length of his legs. The same method was used to measure the length of a saddle stirrup—by holding the stirrup under the armpit and touching the saddle with the fingertips, as any horseman knows today.

In measuring land grants, the people of the valley were not as exact. Distances were calculated by so many cigarettes or by a day's journey from sunup to sundown, *de sol a sol*. But an official grant was expressed in *sitios*, *labores*, and *haciendas*; the last consisted of 5 *sitios*, or 5 square leagues, which in acres amounted to 177.1 for a *labor*, 4,428 acres for a *sitio*, and 22,140 acres for an *hacienda*. The English rod and chain, called a *cordel*, was the equivalent of 50 *varas*.

OTHER ARCHAISMS

Other interesting archaisms known around El Paso Valley but not current in northern New Mexico or California related to everyday living. When speaking about a contemporary of the same age, a person in the valley would say: "You and I are from the same *camada*," a word that originally meant "litter." In the summertime the men wore cotton shirts, called *cotones*, which were cool, had no buttons, and were loose-fitting. The name derives from the *cota de malla*, or coat of mail used by soldiers in colonial days. When these shirts were made of homespun, they were called *cotón de jerga*. In Spain the name *jubón* was generally adopted for this shirt, but in the Southwest the older name was preserved. Many old Spanish words had their origin in colonial military dress. *Capacete* is a good example. Originally it was the Spanish helmet worn by the army, comparable to the morion. In the Southwest, and particularly in El Paso Valley, it was not a covering for the head but a shade for the front seat of a wagon or buggy. Covered wagons were called *carros encamisados*, that is, "wagons with shirts." In addition to the old words the El Paso region also adopted linguistic forms with which they came in contact over El Camino Real. This contact with current language has continued to the present day, giving the people along the Mexican border a much broader and more up-to-date Spanish vocabulary than those in the north.

PACHUCO DIALECT

It is interesting to note that this same region gave rise to the much misunderstood urban argot called *pachuco*, a sort of dialectal Spanish derived arbitrarily from a combination of old Spanish words, Anglicisms, and specially created neologisms common among young people, particularly newsboys, Western Union messengers, and delivery boys. At first it was used only in El Paso, but eventually it spread farther north and particularly to California. *Pachuco* meant simply a person from El Paso.

Many original expressions of El Paso argot have become obsolete and have been replaced by a more modern *pachuco* dialect. If someone wished to call a friend's attention to a good-looking girl going by, the girl watcher would say, "¡Echale agua, mano!" which literally meant, "Throw water on her, friend!" If attention was being called to something before it passed out of the field of vision, the call was, "¡Lícalo, lícalo!" To go out on the town, so to speak, was expressed as *dar verde* (a different color from "painting the town red"). If a baseball player pulled a grandstand play by catching a fly with one hand, he was said to be giving *changüi*. When a boy was looking for work, he wanted *jale*; if the work was heavy, it was called *camello*. A hungry El Paso boy would say that he had *jaspia*, a condition he easily remedied by going home to his *chante* and *martillar* with his father, whom he respectfully referred to as *jefe*. After dinner, consisting of *maromeros*, pinto beans, he was ready to *caldear* with his *huisa*, and if the girl he made love to objected to being called by this strange appellation, she would tell him, "¡Pinte!" which meant, "Take off!"

These and scores of other similar expressions current before World War I, were so unfamiliar to people in other parts of the Hispanic world that El Pasoans, who were members of the clan, delighted in speaking their amusing argot in the presence of outsiders to confuse and impress them. While this *jerga callejera* was originally contrived as a dialect for the street "four hundred," it eventually spread all over the Southwest from California to Colorado and to southern Texas, where it expanded with many borrowings of English slang. This argot did not gain much acceptance in New Mexico north of Albuquerque, whose culture was largely pastoral.

Cultured individuals found the slang amusing and used a few expressions now and then when speaking to close friends. A doctor showing his new car to a friend would say in jest, "Echale agua a mi nueva catalanga," "Throw water on my new chariot." The other would answer in like currency, saying, "¡Tres piedras, cuate y un ladrillo adrenical!" meaning that he highly approved, although what he actually said was: "Three rocks, my twin, and a brick to boot!" Later, *pachuco* assumed social implications, and for a while it was associated with the questionable elements of society in the Southwest. In many sectors of Texas and California it was considered for some time the language of the marijuana smokers, the *grifos* or *los del tres*, so called because they inhaled the smoke in three gulps.

Pachuco is applied both to the speakers and to the dialect because the two went hand in hand, but it should not be assumed that those who are familiar with this dialect were also members of the group designated by this term. Like any artificial form of expression, this widely publicized speech now lacks originality and has lost much of its former picturesqueness. It ascribes arbitrary meanings to words already in the Spanish lexicon; sometimes the speakers stumble on archaic words unknowingly, as in *calcos*, from the Latin *calceus*, "shoes," but when they refer to the same article as *boris*, it becomes an arbitrary invention that is made respectable by being called a neologism. There is no attempt to use figurative words or expressions that manifest a sense of aesthetics; on the contrary, *pachuco* is somewhat depreciatory and inelegant. *Pachucos* have often been likened to the Los Angeles zoot-suiters of World War II. The latter attained their designation from their manner of dress and their duck-tail haircuts. The *pachucos* originated as a linguistic group and have no distinctive dress style.

Folk speech such as is heard among the mountaineers of New Mexico and the country folk in Mexico is based on observation of nature, expressed in colorful figures of speech. For example, people who handle stock have learned that the way to hold a horse with a rope is to lean sideways on the hip, and so they say figuratively, "¡Echale cuadril!" which English-speaking folk working with wagons would render, "Put your shoulder to the wheel." The Hispanic cowhand speaks of being thrown over the head when let down by someone and expresses it by saying, "Me echó por la cabeza." The *pachuco* dialect, on the other hand, is a product of an urban environment and revives a few obsolescent words, makes up a number of Anglicisms, and ascribes arbitrary meanings to current Spanish words. Students who have researched the *pachuco* argot have assumed that all of the vocabulary is original, but a reference to the dictionary of the Spanish Academy, or to a good Spanish-English one, will reveal that such words and expressions as *chavalo*, *hacer ronda*, *garra*, *greña*, *controlar*, and *chaveta* and a number of others thought of as *pachuco* are standard or colloquial Spanish.

A CHOICE OF LANGUAGE

Attempts are being made today throughout the Southwest to reinstate the Spanish language among Americans of Mexican descent, Hispanos of New Mexico, and members of the Chicano movement.

One of the problems faced by advocates of what is termed "bilingualism" is the selection of the Spanish that should be taught. Some object to the literary Spanish that forms the standard of Mexico, Latin America, and Spain on the grounds that it is academic language and not the "language of the people." They therefore insist that the language must be taught "as people speak it." The only problem is the selection of the people to use as the models of linguistic expression. If the object is to preserve the Spanish language as an instrument of communication among the Mexicans, Hispanos, and Chicanos, the use of a dialect plagued with Anglicisms and syntactical forms derived from the English language would be counterproductive, because it is partly molded on the very language that they are trying to avoid.

Some Chicano activists advocate what they call "Chicano Spanish" and insist that it should be taught to them in the public schools because it has more relevance for their culture. This would be a practical consideration if the Chicano adherents did not have to communicate with the rest of the world in which they live—if in reality they had a culture of their own. In the Hispanic world the deteriorated dialect that they propose is not acceptable, and, because they are not self-sufficient, they must use a language that is understandable and acceptable to both the Spanish-speaking and the English-speaking world. Moreover, the number of Spanish speakers who accept the name Chicano as the label by which they should be identified is indeed small.

The current interest in the use of the Spanish language, and the conscious attempt being made to include courses on Mexican and Hispanic culture, should expand the use of the language. In looking through the published efforts of advocates of this movement, however, one finds a limited use of Spanish and a quality in what is used that does not come up to expectations. It is too early yet to expect measurable results, but another generation should see a reflection of the present interest in the language, provided what is taught and spoken is allowed to develop freely and responds to cultural conditions rather than to political and propagandistic considerations.

On April 20, 1598, Oñate and his band reached the Río Grande, where the general took formal possession of New Mexico and all the adjoining provinces, in a long and verbose act celebrated with masses and other rituals accompanying such ceremonies in the presence of the army, the officials of the crown, and the friars. "And finally, in the evening the performance of an original comedy written by Captain Farfán on a subject connected with the conquest of New Mexico—early days of the drama, indeed."[1] So wrote historian Bancroft.

The establishment of the first province of the Southwest began auspiciously with a folk play in the open air, and that custom has continued to the present day. The representational tradition was so well established by the end of the sixteenth century that the soldiers of the first settlement promptly presented one of their own invention. In addition, so history tells us, they performed *morerías*, traditional plays about the struggles between Christians and Moors. This drama has survived in the Southwest under the title *Moros y Cristianos*, or simply *Los Moros*.

The continuity of the folk theater is unbroken among Hispanic peoples throughout the New World, dating back to medieval times in Spain when the first *autos sacramentales*, as the religious dramas were then called, were performed in and outside the churches of Europe. This wealth of liturgical drama was drawn upon by the missionaries when they sought to convert the Indians in Mexico, and they produced the large number of religious plays in New Spain, which eventually came into the Southwest as the empire expanded its northern frontiers. The name *auto* was preserved in most of these plays, but instead of adding *sacramental*, most of them usually carried the name of the principals such as *Auto de Caín y Abel* or *Auto de Adán y Eva*.[2]

The mystery plays were a practical vehicle for the transmission of church doctrine and the plan of salvation to aborigines. Many tribes were accustomed to the pageantry of their own festivals and to the representation of events, either by picture writing, as among the Aztecs, or by the lively dance drama of southwestern tribes. The religious significance of the Christian plays appealed to the missionaries as a practical teaching instrument and compensated for the absence of a common tongue.

FOLK DRAMA ADOPTED

Eventually the Spanish folk, particularly in the Southwest, adopted the simple folk drama with few additional props or theme variations. Folk drama gave the settlers an opportunity for religious participation in a region that was not well supplied with churches and priests. This rich heritage also filled the need for entertainment, otherwise unavailable because of the long distances, limited funds, and the hostility of the warring tribes. Eventually the folk plays became part of the traditional repertoire of the Hispanic population even in remote mountain villages because the Franciscans took the plays with them wherever they went. It is also likely that they were written by the missionaries in various parts of Mexico and the Southwest.

Because only a few settlers could read and write, either the priest or a *mayordomo* in the church or a *director*, who usually had a manuscript, supervised the village presentations. At times no manuscripts were available, but those who had participated in similar plays at home or in other villages knew their parts by heart and continued to play the same roles year after year.

When the villagers moved to a new community, and a *director* began to put his cast together for a folk play, he used experienced participants who had played the roles elsewhere. The only problem was that, although the plays had the same title, they had been composed by different authors, and the speeches did not always coincide. The incorporation of these variations gave rise to a number of variants of the original composition. In time the most popular folk plays became so mixed that

A New Mexico Hispano ready to participate in the traditional drama of Christians and Moors. Courtesy of Coronado Cuarto Centennial.

it was virtually impossible to know which was the original script.

Authorship also became practically impossible to determine, because the missionary authors borrowed freely from each other and also took names and lines from familiar medieval *autos*. The names used for some of the shepherds in these plays indicate that the authors were well acquainted with Latin and Spanish pastoral poetry and novels. Such names as Matatías, Sarababel, Selastiel, Deidoro, Erás, Afrón, and Tetuán are definitely from literary and/or biblical tradition.

FIRST PLAY IN THE NEW WORLD

The earliest *auto* in the New World was *Adán y Eva*, presented in Mexico City by Toribio Motolinía in 1531. A firsthand account of this presentation was discovered by Carlos Castañeda in the archives of the García Collection in the University of Texas.[3] The attempt was, as Motolinía stated, to present the fall of man with the collaboration of the Indians. The presentation was so realistic that both Indians and Spaniards were deeply moved by the setting and the acting. A play of the same name came to form part of the folk-drama repertoire of the Hispanic Southwest in colonial days, although it was not the original play but one of its many variants.

It is interesting to note that, after Protestantism became established in some sectors of the Hispanic population of the Southwest, these same plays, particularly the Nativity play, were performed in Methodist and Pentecostal churches during the Christmas season. The folk did not give up their folk theater when they were converted to Protestantism because the plays did not alter the story of Christ. In these celebrations both Catholics and Protestants took part, with little concern for theology.

ECCLESIASTICAL DRAMA

Theater in France, England, and Spain began with religious drama, and folk plays are found in all three of these cultures, often with identical, or at least very similar, episodes, because they had a common subject. A very close resemblance is found in one of the Wakefield shepherds' plays of England to the one that has been so popular in the Southwest since colonial days, *Los Pastores.* In the Wakefield play *The Shepherds*, a shepherd named Mack has a wife named Gill. In *Los Pastores*, the Spanish play by the same name, the wife of a comparable character is named Gila. The general theme is identical, and both compositions abound with songs.

Historians of Spanish drama consider *El Auto de los Reyes Magos* the beginning of Spanish national drama. This play, of which only a few verses are extant, was probably written in the twelfth century, but the same title has been consistently used throughout the Southwest. When I first heard of this play in 1928, I became hopeful of finding a version, or even a copy or variant of the original medieval *auto*, but I soon discovered that the folk play in the Southwest was a comparatively modern version with the same title. Nevertheless, it showed how consistent the religious-drama tradition has been.

OLD TESTAMENT AND NEW TESTAMENT CYCLES

A number of plays based on Old Testament themes in a sense form a cycle depicting the salient events of Judeo-Christian religion. It was logical that the first enactment should be *Adam and Eve*, telling of the fall of man, useful in catechizing the neophytes of Mexico. The second was entitled *Caín y Abel*, with the subtitle *El primer Crimen.*[4] But the cycle that became most popular and enduring was the one around the life of Christ, with preference given to the drama about the Nativity. An addition to the New Testament drama sequence of New Spain, introduced during the reign of Charles V, was based on the apparition of the Virgin on Tepeyac Hill outside Mexico City, where the shrine of the Virgin of Guadalupe now stands.

An interesting and controversial episode arose regarding the historical expediency of this "miracle." A play by Mexico's leading contemporary dramatist, Rodolfo Usigli, entitled *Corona de Luz*, very strongly suggests that the apparition in early colonial days had religious and political significance. The apparition was in fact arranged, so the dramatist suggests, to involve the incredulous Indians in an event that would be theirs and would thereby create a link between the neophytes and Catholicism.

In any event, a play known as *La Aparición de Nuestra Señora de Guadalupe* was written soon after the event, a play that fit very well into the New Testament cycle. In the Southwest the folk play is known by the shortened title *La Aparición* and is played on the Day of the Virgin. It is followed by another ingenious presentation, clearly designed to continue the history of Christianity as it emerged from its Hebrew origins. The play *San José*,[5] in addition to introducing Joseph into the play sequence, dramatizes the manner in which the future husband of Mary came into the story. Briefly, the patriarchs are summoned to a meeting designed to choose a husband for the future mother, and each man is given a reed with the understanding that the reed held by the one chosen will miraculously bloom. In a number of scenes such virtues as modesty and honesty are carefully worked into the theme. The reed held by José suddenly bursts into bloom. From this theme the lowly hollyhock was given the name by which it is known in the Southwest: Varas de San José, "St. Joseph's reeds."

The folk traditions in the Southwest have a religious cast, demonstrated most obviously in names, whether of mountain ranges, such as Sangre de Cristo; streams, such as Purgatorio; or persons, such as Dolores, Jesús, and María. The widespread use of religious names caused one Anglo-American traveler to remark:

The old adventurous Spaniards, if they did a little too often seek to square accounts with their neglected saints by giving their names to mountains, nevertheless had an eye to the resemblances of nature, and at least never perpetrated such hideous vulgarities as Hog-eye and Shirt-Tail Canyon.[6]

LAS POSADAS

The Christmas season in the Hispanic Southwest was never a one-day affair, either socially or religiously. It began on December 15 and continued through the Epiphany, January 6. An important folk presentation of the season was *Las Posadas (The Inns)*, which tells the story of Mary and Joseph and their unsuccessful effort to find lodging at one of the inns of Bethlehem. *Las Posadas* was more like a miracle play than a mystery play, because emphasis was placed on the devil's design to turn Joseph and Mary away from the inns.

Originally *Las Posadas* was presented on nine evenings, culminating on Christmas Eve. Gradually, the custom was modified, and the play was presented on any evening before Christmas. In California, where the December weather is benign, they celebrated all nine evenings, but in the mountain villages of New Mexico the participant's compromised by holding the *Posadas* celebration on Christmas Eve, stopping at nine different homes on the way to the manger.

As the singers stopped at a home, to which they were directed by a lighted candle in the window, the devil hid behind the door and answered the plea for lodging. The procession sang:

> ¿Quién dará posada a estos peregrinos
> Que vienen cansados de andar los caminos?
>
> Who will give lodging to these pilgrims
> Who are tired of traveling on the road?

The devil answered:

> Posada no damos ni podemos dar
> Que pueden ser ladrones que vienen a robar.
>
> We do not give lodging, for we cannot serve
> Those who may be thieves coming here to rob.

The interesting and traditional Spanish melody of *Las Posadas* is sung today throughout the Southwest and in Mexico by the folk and by urban residents as well, while the enactment of the devil's part seems forgotten. In neighboring Mexico a *posada* is celebrated as a social gathering accompanied by music, dancing, and cocktails. Even the orchestras at the nightclubs of Mexico City take part in it by ingeniously making the transition from a popular waltz into the music of *Las Posadas*. Unknowingly the guests continue dancing to the religious melody. It is done in such good taste that it does not detract from the spirit of Christmas; rather, it enhances it. Enjoyment and gaiety prevail over what ordinarily would be just another dance piece.

LOS PASTORES

The most widely diffused and popular folk play of the New Testament cycle is the Nativity play commonly known as *Los Pastores (The Shepherds)* or *La Pastorela*. Aside from the play's theme, a central event in Christian religious history, the characters and setting—shepherds in the hills watching their flocks by night—were familiar to the people of a region that was predominantly sheep-raising country. Neither the audience nor the participants had to stretch their imaginations to reenact the scene; indeed, often the actors were real-life sheepmen.

Although this play, like many others, was religious in nature, the village participants did not lose the opportunity to ad lib whenever possible. When the Devil, a leading character, tried to entice Gila the Shepherdess into eloping with the Hermit, he added a few bits of local gossip, much to the delight of the audience. The same was true of Bartolo, the lazy Shepherd whose name became synonymous with indolence.

The Devil is contrasted both in speech and in size with his nemesis, the Angel Michael. The role of Satan is usually played by a large actor who wields a wicked-looking saber and rants, threatens, and otherwise tries to appear as fierce as possible. His costume is elaborate, including moving jaws and a "serpent" for a tail. The Angel, on the other hand, is usually played by a young boy who is the essence of innocence and repeats his lines in a childish voice as he holds a small sword in his hand. The symbolism of this contrast is clearly seen as evil falls inexorably before good when the Angel places his victorious foot on the Devil's head and leads him out in chains.

The setting was as realistic as possible, to the point that live actors portrayed Joseph and Mary, and, whenever possible, a live baby portrayed the infant Jesus. Some villages boast lifelike Christ dolls that were imported from Germany and have been continuously used in the Nativity play for over 150 years. The symbolism of the ornate *bá-*

culos held by the shepherds and their folk concept of beauty are manifested by colored ribbon streamers attached to the staffs, small mirrors, Christmas decorations, and other colorful trinkets that elicit spontaneous cries of admiration: "¡Qué bonitos!"

Juan B. Rael, who made a thorough study of the diffusion of the shepherds' plays, discovered that they were written for the most part in Mexico and followed the path of Franciscan missionaries. In California a *pastorela* written by Padre Florencio of the Soledad mission was performed often, according to Bancroft, who found it in the Vallejo documents. This Nativity play was a great favorite. Pío Pico, a prominent Californio, played the part of Bato, the chief shepherd. One Jacinto Rodríguez took his performance so seriously that he used to go to the seashore to practice his part.[7]

Rael found several copies of the play in Los Angeles, Santa Clara, and Monterey, California, and discovered that most of them were versions of originals from Mexico. The language of these compositions was not the popular tongue used by Hispanic folk in the Southwest but the formal language of educated Spaniards.[8]

LOS REYES MAGOS

The sequence of the Christmas season continues with *Los Reyes Magos*, the play about the wise men who come to offer their gifts, while Herod tries to learn from them where to find the babe.[9] The authors of these plays, obviously intending them for folk audiences, did not fail to press a point wherever possible, taking occasional liberties with details or relying on their imaginations. The evil characters were strongly presented so that their contrast with the righteous would be more apparent. In the process they must have pleased their folk audiences, who usually had an uncomplicated concept of right and wrong. The language of the plays was hardly folk speech, strongly pointing to a cultured authorship. The unfamiliar language in the plays was sometimes transmitted imperfectly, resulting in some ludicrous lines, but the folk audiences already knew the plays by heart.

EL NINO PERDIDO

In the last play of the second cycle, *El Niño Perdido (The Lost Child)*, the twelve-year-old Jesus is pitted against *doctores de la ley judaica*, the doctors of Jewish law. In the play the wisdom of the child is properly demonstrated to reinforce belief in Christ as the Son of God. His mother, Mary, shows all the concern and love for her lost son that would be expected of a good and affectionate mother. The usual struggle of rich against poor is introduced in this play, by having the child stop at the portals of a *rico* who is enjoying a sumptuous meal, refuses to share any of it, and rebukes Jesus, although he admires the child's wisdom.

The religious lessons couched in the form of drama, designed originally to communicate with non-Spanish-speaking Indians, eventually became the theater of the folk in Mexico and throughout the Southwest, but the original intent to teach and indoctrinate was never completely lost.

LOS COMANCHES, A RELIGIOUS PLAY

As mentioned above, few of the religious plays were written by the folk of the Southwest. An interesting exception is a play entitled *Los Comanches*, which, because of its manner of presentation, could be termed a dance drama. This play is often confused with the eighteenth-century historical drama of the same name. The religious *Comanches* first appeared in north-central New Mexico about the turn of the century. It was composed, as a manuscript states, "recalling the Indian chief Victorio who attacked in 1880 and Nana in '81."[10] In the late 1920's and early 1930's it was presented in Arenales, a small settlement adjoining Albuquerque. It was also very popular in San Rafael, a small village on Highway 66 in western New Mexico.

According to informants who had the original manuscript, the events related in the play actually took place in San Rafael in the days when the Comanches were roving over the Southwest. The story is sung and danced in its entirety. All the members of the cast except those representing the Holy Family are dressed in full Indian costume. There is hardly any dialogue; the participants communicate through song and dance. They weave in snake-dance patterns and tell the story with unmistakable mimicry. At times it is difficult to tell whether it is an Indian dance or a religious play.

The struggle between Spanish settler and Indian in such plays is comparable with that of Christians and Moors depicted in the Spanish traditional drama *Los Moros*. *Los Comanches* relates in song and mimicry an Indian attack on a Spanish village that occurs while the Nativity play is being presented. The Indians kidnap the Child. The settlers pursue and overtake them, and, after bartering through song and dance, they buy back the Child for a blanket. The Indians become interested in the Spanish ceremony, which they had interrupted, and end by joining the settlers in the adoration at the manger with more exuberant dancing and loud singing by the Comanches. Again, the usual triumph of good over evil makes this performance a morality play combining Spanish and Indian tradition.

LOS MATACHINES, A DANCE DRAMA

It is remarkable how a region so isolated from the rest of the Spanish Empire could preserve cultural contacts that kept alive many traditions from the Peninsula by way of Mexico. One of the best examples of this continuity is *Los Matachines.* Originally it was a sword dance in which Moors and Christians took part. This dance drama of fifteenth-century Spain was performed in North America from the days of the Conquest and continues to be performed in connection with any church holiday. In Mexico City it is performed during the celebration of the Virgin, in Sonora and Chihuahua on the day of La Santa Cruz.

Mary Austin claimed that the bishop's miter worn by some of the dancers in *Los Matachines* in New Mexico was explained by the fact that the original dance was performed by the newly appointed Indian bishops in Mexico. The dance, she said, was purposely designed to take the place of former Aztec dances in honor of the goddess of fertility, whose cult was celebrated on the Hill of Tepeyac where the Virgin first appeared. It is a very interesting explanation that unfortunately was never documented.

Los Matachines is the same sword dance known in England in the Middle Ages as the Morris Dance and in Spain as Danzas de Espadas or Moros y Cristianos. It is likely that the dance was further dramatized in Mexico by the addition of such characters as El Monarca, representing Moctezuma, to give it significance for the Aztecs, and that the allegorical characters El Abuelo, El Torito, and La Malinche were representatives of the forces of evil against virtue, as in so many of the religious folk plays.

La Malinche, a historical personage known as Doña Marina in the retinue of Cortés, has become a legend associated with happenings with which she had no historical connection. In *Los Matachines*, she is a young bride, whose purity is indicated by her white veil. The horned Torito, representing worldly lust, tries to abduct her, but Abuelo, or Grandfather, holds him back with his long whip as the *matachines* gather around to prevent her abduction.

This dance drama was also performed by the Yaquis of the Southwest on the Day of Santa Cruz, but their interpretation was a combination of the Yaqui *pascola* dance with guitar accompaniment and untold quantities of mescal and tequila. The men did a circle dance with their arms over each other's shoulders, chanting as they performed a sidestep from sunup until sundown.

The presentation in New Mexico was more peninsular in that there was elaborate costuming, with definite dance steps done to musical accompaniment. There were eight to ten movements to the danced *Matachines*, each with a corresponding name. The opening was a vigorous polka called *la carrera*, followed by *la patada grande, el caracol, cambio de captitanes, la toreada, brincada de palmas, la cruz, la India,* and *la despedida.*

LOS COMANCHES, A HISTORICAL PLAY

The Comanche tribes moved west as their hunting grounds were gradually taken over by the westward-moving Anglo-American frontiersmen. Some historians believe that the Indians were also actuated by their desire to acquire horses in the Spanish Southwest. In their move west early in the eighteenth century the Comanches attacked both the Indians and the Spanish settlers in New Mexico. The struggle increased in scope and violence after the Comanches added the horse to their mode of warfare.

Not all contacts between the Comanches and the settlers were hostile. Both peoples were fond of trading, and they engaged in barter and trade, the Comanches offering the spoils of their raiding expeditions and the settlers the local products that the Indians wanted and needed. Horses, grain, pelts, blankets, and dried buffalo meat changed hands between Comanchero traders, as the New Mexicans and the Indian bands were called. But more often than not, the Comanches sought to supply their needs by force and stealth, particularly when they had the necessary manpower.

The struggles and the threats to the Spanish settlers continued with increasing intensity, until in 1778 the colonial government took steps to eliminate the Comanche barrier by sending an outstanding Indian fighter, Juan Bautista de Anza, the founder of San Francisco (according to Bolton), to take command of the province. In 1774, Carlos Fernández, an aged but wary Indian fighter, had pursued a large band of Comanches north of Santa Fe and, after inflicting heavy losses on the enemy, had recovered over a thousand horses in addition to other spoils. But this defeat did not lessen for long forays by the Comanches, led by their famous chief, Cuerno Verde (Green Horn, which he was not). The campaign, intensified by Fernández in 1774, and the methodical domination of the dangerous Indian leader by Anza in 1779, inspired a historical drama, which was written by an unknown participant on his return from the successful battle, which took place near the present site of Greenhorn, Colorado.

As with all traditional compositions, the author's name did not survive, but his epic drama, which he entitled *Los Comanches*, did. The play was usually performed in the northern section of the province of New Mexico, the region most intimately concerned with these nomadic Indians. In passing from one generation to another, the play suffered some losses; some lines were lost and others garbled. Nevertheless, the written play survived through the interest of copyists, who transcribed it into ledgers and notebooks, but by 1929 only three incomplete manuscripts were to be found.

In 1907 the well-known New Mexican folklorist and scholar Aurelio Espinosa edited a version of this play, which he obtained from a leading citizen of Santa Fe, Amado Chávez. The manuscript appeared in a daybook interspersed with such records as: "Today the bay mare had a black colt." "Today, the 25th of April, 1906, the masked cow had a strawberry roan bull." At the end of the manuscript appears the line: "This version was copied from another manuscript in 1864."

How many years after the battle of 1774 the play was written it is difficult to say, but the omission of Anza's name would indicate that it was written before his arrival in 1778. Yet the events dramatized toward the end of the play tell of the death of Cuerno Verde, who was killed in the battle led by Anza near Pike's Peak.

Many of the leaders of the Spanish army mentioned in the play are historical characters, as are also the various chiefs of the Comanche Nation. Carlos Fernández, Salvador Ribera, Toribio Ortiz, Miguel de la Peña, and others are historical leaders who participated in the Indian campaigns of the eighteenth century as commanders, captains, and sergeants. Cuerno Verde was well known, and his lesser chiefs, Cabeza Negra, Oso Pardo, and Tabaco Chupa Janchi may have actually been part of his enclave.

Los Comanches, unlike the religious plays, was staged in the open spaces, where a battle on horseback could be enacted, and the plains of Galisteo and the high mesas around Taos were favorite sites where both audiences and participants could enjoy the drama. Real Indians often took the parts of the Comanche braves, and as the battle that is the climax of the play opened, both sides became caught up in the action. When the summer tourists visiting Taos in 1929 witnessed the drama on the mesa between Taos village and Ranchos de Taos to the south, hundreds of warriors and soldiers took part on both sides. They presented such a realistic scene, to the accompaniment of rifle shots and arrows, that the visitors took cover, thinking that real warfare had broken out.

The plot of *Los Comanches* is simple. The Indians have drawn near and tried, unsuccessfully, to trade. They take two hostages, referred to as *Las Pecas*. In the open plain the Spaniards have set up their encampment, or *castillo*, while the Comanches camp directly across in their tipis. The various leaders advance from either camp to the "demilitarized zone" and from a safe distance make pronouncements and hurl threats at each other.

After the Spanish camp has been alerted to the arrival of the Comanches, the sentinels are set up, the Spanish standard goes up and the chief of the Comanche Nation, Cuerno Verde, advances to make his opening speech (103 lines in romance-foot meter):

Desde el oriente al poniente,	From the sunrise to the sunset,
Desde el sur al norte frío,	From the south to frigid north,
Suena el brillante clarín,	Blare my mighty battle clarions,
Y brilla el acero mío! . . .	And my steel brilliantly shines! . . .

He is answered by Carlos Fernández in equally heroic terms:

Aguarda, detén espera;	Bide your time, hold now and wait;
Que soy de tan noble brillo	I am of such noble mettle

| Que vengo sin que me llames | That I come without your call |
| A cuidar este castillo. | To defend my fort and castle.[11] |

Each Comanche chief advances and threatens to demolish the Spaniards, and each leader is answered in like coin until both sides run out of words and decide to fight. After a lively Indian war dance performed by the warriors, the Spaniards charge with their historic cry, "¡Santiago!" The play ends with the defeat of Cuerno Verde and the rout of his army.

Los Comanches was written by someone well informed on the history of Spanish military activities in the Southwest, someone who knew the Indian tribes and the men who commanded the garrison in Santa Fe. In addition, the author had an excellent command of heroic-sounding Spanish, which would be expected in a composition of this nature. The Spanish Empire was still strong in the Southwest when this play was written, as was proved by Anza's successes.

Los Comanches was intended to be presented in the open air, realistically, with the salty dust of the prairie, the smell of horseflesh, and the crack of the Spanish musket. The descendants of the original settlers who took part in the battle are reminded by this drama of the struggle of their ancestors to repel the mighty Comanches. The Spaniards never belittled the courage and valor of the Indian leaders, and other famous battles were the subjects of Spanish chroniclers and poets. In South America, Ercilla y Zúñiga wrote the long epic poem *La Araucana*, in which the Indian chiefs Colocolo and Caupolicán stand out more prominently than their Spanish conquerors.

It was therefore fitting that the long struggle between the Comanche Indians and the Spanish settlers in the Southwest should be recorded in a historical drama.

SPANISH AND MEXICAN COMEDIES

In New Mexico and Texas many comedies brought from Mexico during the nineteenth century continued to be presented regularly. In California troupes of players and *maromeros*, acrobats, also followed the well-traveled Camino Real to the pueblos of Los Angeles, San Diego, and Monterey, particularly during the unpopular governorship of Mariano Chico in 1836. The directors left some of their manuscripts behind, and the folk undertook to present them to audiences eager to be entertained. Some of the plays were written by well-known Mexican dramatists, but the folk were not concerned with authorship—they simply wanted to see a play. To the extent that the plays continued to be part of the secular-drama tradition, they were folk drama.

The list of these plays, known variously as *sainetes*, *comedias*, and *juegos*, is long, and they range from romantic dramas to one-act farces. *La Vuelta del Cruzado*, by Fernando Calderón, is a romantic period drama that became popular under the title *La Comedia de Hernán*, after the principal character in the play. *Una Lluvia de Ingleses (A Shower of Englishmen)* is a comedy based on mistaken identity comparable with *The Importance of Being Earnest*. Shorter skits, such as *El Gato*, *Don Patricio*, *Bonifacio*, and *Margarita Piojo*, were one-act farces that had disappeared from public view by World War I.

Singing has always been such an integral part of Spanish cultural tradition that it is not surprising to find in the Southwest an abundance of songs which have constantly increased since the arrival of the Spanish colonists at the end of the sixteenth century. These early settlers brought with them the songs that were current in their day. They continued to sing the old songs and also composed new ones, thus keeping alive the old repertoire and enlarging it in succeeding generations. From Texas to California ballads were sung and *canciones* were composed by village troubadours who, in the tradition of the bards of the Middle Ages, spoke of love, of suffering, of man's inhumanity to man, and of countless other themes of their everyday lives.

Throughout the past three centuries in the Southwest there has never been a dearth of versifiers and songsters to give expression to their feelings and those of others. As travelers moved from place to place, the songs of their land went with them, and when they returned home, they brought those they had learned in their travels. Thus was song kept alive and growing by people to whom music and song were so integral a part of their lives.[1]

THE SPANISH BALLAD

The oldest type of folk song known in the Southwest was the Spanish ballad, or *romance*, popular in Spain at the time of the Conquest. It was so well known, indeed, that when the conquistadors Portocarrero and Cortés found themselves in a difficult situation during the siege of Mexico, they alluded to it by quoting from the medieval ballad *Cata Francia Montesinos*. Throughout the New Spain of the sixteenth century the Spanish ballads continued their popularity and spread north with the population as far north as Colorado and west to California where they have been collected by folklorists for many decades. These compositions tell of forbidden love, of the eternal triangle, of kings' pages, of unfaithful wives, and of course, of shepherds and shepherdesses.

The most popular, or at least the most widespread, of the old ballads was *Delgadina*, the story of the young princess who repulsed the incestuous advances of her cruel father and suffered imprisonment in the tower of the castle rather than submit. When she was dying of thirst and called for a drink, the king had his servants take water to her in golden goblets, thinking that she was ready to capitulate. But when the cupbearers arrived, Delgadina was already dead. The colonials, who had undergone similar privations in the arid West, could not allow the ballad to end at this point. They satisfied their sense of justice by adding two more verses in which the ballad tells how Delgadina went to heaven to render an account to God, but her father went to hell and was in the custody of the *diablo mayor*.

Another ballad that gained considerable popularity told of the loves of Gerineldo, Charlemagne's page, and the princess of the court. The aggressive young princess suggests to the page that he visit her bedroom one evening, but the virtuous young man refuses, saying that she simply wants to tease

Próspero Baca, the bard from Bernalillo, New Mexico, whose *cuadernos* contained sixteenth-century Spanish ballads, as well as a wealth of songs and verses of his own composition.

234

him because he is a servant. She leaves her door ajar that night, hoping that the page will change his mind, and is not disappointed. The following morning the emperor calls for his page, but he does not answer. The royal sire picks up his sword and goes in search of the errant page, only to find him asleep in his daughter's bed. His first impulse is to strike the page dead with his sword, but he changes his mind when he realizes that he has raised the young man from childhood. With a royal gesture he lays his sword between them and leaves. They awaken to find that the king has paid them a visit. Again the Hispanic colonials could not allow such irregularities to occur in the palace, and improved their moral tone by adding two lines telling that the two young lovers were married: "Y allí se tomaron las manos como mujer y marido."

Southwestern folk had a very simple, straightforward sense of justice and morals. Some of the ballads inherited from Europe told of events based on the Spanish honor code, which was designed principally for courtly life, and sometimes offended the settlers' own code. For example, they tried ending the story of the wayward wife of the following ballad as many as three different ways to satisfy their own standards. The ballad was *Bernal Francés*, or *Don Bernardo el Francés*, in which the wife is having an affair with a French nobleman, and the husband, also a nobleman, finds it out.

In the dark cover of night the husband replaces the lover in the garden and makes ardent love to his wife, who mistakes her husband for her lover. According to the Spanish honor code, a man's honor could be avenged in such instances only by shedding blood, but the Southwesterners could not decide whose blood should be shed, and so they ended the ballad three different ways. In one the lover Bernal (Don Bernardo) is killed by the offended husband; in another one the unfaithful wife is killed; and in the third the husband kills the lover and then commits suicide so that the philandering wife will suffer the loss of both for the rest of her life.

To judge by the large number of original ballads and their variants still known in the Southwest, these traditional Spanish songs must have been very popular in colonial days. Melodies have changed, no doubt. Because the music was not written down until recently, it is impossible to ascertain whether the current tunes are the same ones sung by the colonials. Not too many historical ballads, of the sort that tell of knights and their experiences, have survived; most of the ones pre-

served by tradition are concerned with human relationships, religion, and children's songs and games. One fragment tells of Coronado's march through the Southwest in 1540, the only reference in the ballad repertoire about the Southwest's first conquistador.

The Spanish form of indirect address often used in folk songs was also used in ballads such as *Agraciada Golondrina* and *La Calandria*. In the first the lover writes to his sweetheart in a distant land. He gives the missive to a swallow, who takes the message to the girl. The bird returns on the third day with no written answer—only a verbal message telling the young man to console himself with the cage, because the bird has taken wing:

> Le di la carta tu dueña pero no te contestó;
> solamente me decía, y esta noticia te envió;
> Consuélate con la jaula que ya el pájaro voló.

In *La Calandria* a lark imprisoned in a golden cage promises a little sparrow that, if he helps her escape, she will marry him. The bird tears the cage wires and frees the lark. The ungrateful lark takes to the four winds and promptly forgets her promise. The sad and gallant sparrow sits in the open cage, reflecting on the fickleness of women. He philosophizes in the closing lines:

> Les encargo a mis amigos
> antes de acabar de hablar;
> Unos son los que las sacan,
> y otros las van a gozar.

> I should like to warn my friends
> before I end this discourse;
> Some come to rescue them,
> but others will enjoy them.

From Texas to California the Spanish settlers sang ballads on all religious occasions and topics: saint's days, Christmas, miracles, and praises to the Virgin. In New Mexico some of the best versions of these religious ballads were found by Aurelio Espinosa among the Indians of Isleta, south of Albuquerque. It is not surprising that religious poetry should be so prominent in the oral tradition of these people. Though professed Catholics, they did not have the advantages of regular church worship that settlers in the cities enjoyed. As a consequence, they had to preserve their culture in oral tradition.

Authors who write about the Penitentes often refer to "Penitente songs" when they hear them sing the *alabados*, but these religious ballads are known from New Mexico to Chile. They are written in traditional sixteen-syllable, assonated verse and usually narrate in verse an episode in the life of the religious character who is the subject.

THE BALLAD OF CORONADO

Coronado arrived in the Southwest in 1540, but tradition has been particularly silent about his exploits. A fragment of a ballad about him was recited by a Navajo in 1933, when she was over 110 years old. As a young girl Gertrudes S. de García was taken captive by Spaniards in one of the encounters between the colonials in New Mexico and the Navajos, and she remained until her death in the home of Don Silvestre Mirabal, one of the largest Spanish sheep raisers in western New Mexico. She eventually married and outlived her own children. When asked if she remembered any old songs, she sang a few bars of a song telling of Coronado's march, and then broke off, laughing, saying that she could no longer remember more of it. In Spanish, the only language she knew, she exclaimed: "Son, I am so old that my memory fails me." Attempts to have her try to sing more about Coronado provoked laughter and giggling. Finally she went back to plastering her adobe house, which she was getting ready for the coming village fiestas.

The verses she remembered, and the characteristic refrain of the traditional ballad, clearly indicated that whoever composed it must have been with the conqueror:

> Coronado se paseaba por toda la tierra 'fuera,
> Y no hubo quien le pisara el paso de su bandera.
>   Por aquí, por allí, que bueno va!
>   Por aquí, por allí, que bueno va!

Coronado had indeed roamed all over the land, and no one stopped the progress of his standard, as the two sixteen-syllable lines declare, but if there was a longer ballad telling of his feats, it is lost to tradition. Doña Gertrudes, already in her third childhood, could not stop laughing long enough to recall what may have been an interesting historical ballad of Spain's first official entry into the Southwest.

PASTORAL BALLADS

One of the best-known pastoral ballads sung in New Mexico and California since colonial days is *La Dama y el Pastor*, a short account of a wanton young lady and a fickle shepherd. The protagonist, to judge by his behavior, could have been a buffoon in the guise of a shepherd who ignored the artifice of love. Despite the young woman's entreaties and promises to the naïve shepherd, enticing him to spend a night and maybe three with her, he insists that he must return to sleep in the mountains, where he has his flock of sheep. In the end he thinks it over, changes his mind, and goes back to the lady, who, having been scorned once, turns him down saying:

> Llora tu soledad, que yo la lloré primero.

> Weep in your solitude, for I was the first to weep.

The shepherdess in *La Zagala* was sitting by a fountain, and the noise of the falling water covered the approach of an impetuous lover. He was more successful than the young man who insisted on going back to sleep with his flock. He picked wild flowers and offered them to her, sat by her, and, using the usual wiles, won his fair shepherdess, who in the end swore that her love had never surrendered to anyone else.

The most charming of the pastoral ballads is entitled *El Zagal*, or *The Shepherd*. Though no counterpart is known in Spain, the internal evidence definitely suggests a peninsular origin. The story, told in ten assonated sixteen-syllable verses, is short and to the point. A young man goes out with his flock one morning and meets a shepherdess he has never seen before:

> Salí una mañana al campo, mi rebaño a apacentar.

> I went to the fields one morning, my flock of sheep to tend.

When he asks her for a kiss, she promptly consents, provided he will pay for it in gold. He is very sorry, he tells her, that his gold is in his camel's saddlebags and his camel is in Fermán, a distant land. She counters mischievously, saying that her kisses are locked behind her teeth, and her mother has the key, but, unfortunately, she too was in the same distant land:

> Los besos que traigo en mis labios, mis dientes están
>   detrás;
> la boca donde los guardo cerrada con llave está.
> La llave tiene mi madre, mi madre está en Fermán.

> My teeth are behind the lips where I keep my kisses, sir;
> The mouth wherein I keep them is sealed with lock and
>   key
> My mother who holds the key is also down in Fermán.

Charles Lummis collected a ballad in California

that was well known not only in all the Southwest but in other stock-raising countries of Latin America. In New Mexico and California this ballad, telling the troubles and problems of a young cowboy, is generally known as *El Vaquero* or simply by the name of the unfortunate cowhand, *Nicolás*. Although the consequences are fatal, the ballad, in the true banter of the vaquero, makes light of the fact that the remedy suggested is a quick demise. Nicolás is madly in love with the *mayordomo's* young daughter, and when the former notices how sad the vaquero is, he inquires about his problem, promising that he will give him anything he asks for. Nicolás loses no time asking for a good mount, a saddle, and spurs. The *mayordomo* grants all his requests, but when he asks for the girl, he tells him that she already has a *dueño* and belongs to someone else. Nicolás threatens to jump over a cliff or shoot himself, to which the boss tells him to shoot straight and jump headfirst:

Y el mayordomo le dice: '¡De cabeza, Nicolás!'

EXAGGERATED ABSURDITIES

Another ballad theme, which in other parts of the Western world appears in prose, is the exaggerated absurdity. English author Samuel Foote wrote a unique absurdity in prose:

So she went into the garden to cut a cabbage-leaf to make an apple pie; at the same time a great she-bear, coming down the street, pops its head into the ship. 'What! No soap?' So he died, and she very imprudently married the barber.[2]

Throughout the Hispanic Southwest, these absurdities, written in eight-syllable verse, were called *mentiras*, "lies," and usually related impossible doings by members of the animal and insect worlds. One of them begins: "Ahora que estamos solitos, vamos a contar mentiras," "Now that we are alone, let's tell a few lies." They tell about a cow dragging a pine tree over a canyon road, a centipede and an ant making tamales, and all sorts of absurdities. In the ballad *El Piojo y la Liendre*, a nit and a louse decide to get married, but they lack everything. The entire barnyard provides all the necessary things for the banquet, but at the last moment they discover that they have no best man. The mouse gallantly volunteers for the role, but while the guests are passing the wine around, the cats break out and gobble up the best man:

Suéltanse los gatos y sóplanse el padrino.

Occasionally these compositions were written in the form of *coplas*, four-line stanzas of which there are thousands. One of the most commonly known is a quatrain that, roughly translated, tells about a blind man who is writing down what a mute is telling him. A deaf man is listening as he watches a paralytic cripple running around.

Un ciego estaba escribiendo
Lo que un mudo le decía,
Y un sordo estaba escuchando
Mientras un tullido corría.

CHILDREN'S BALLADS

The traditional ballads included also a good number of compositions that were sung to amuse children or that had a childlike quality of particular attraction to little people, who, with more retentive memories, preserved them from childhood and passed them on to their own children. In this never-ending cycle, ballads and songs were more likely to survive, because grownups have a tendency to refresh their memory by reminiscing. Since the so-called "children's songs" were passed on from adults to children, in a sense what we label children's songs are actually perpetuated by adults. Many ballads and songs used in singing games were strictly of Spanish peninsular provenience. In fact, most of these ballads are traceable directly to Spanish sources.

Don Gato is one of the most popular ballads, known since colonial days, and tells about an amorous cat:

Estaba señor don Gato
En silla de oro sentado
Con camisita de lino
Y zapatito bordado

As he sits on a gilded chair wearing a linen shirt and knitted boots, he hears about a very attractive she-cat who roams over the housetops. The impetuous Don Gato is so impatient that he jumps from the roof trying to reach his quarry, loses his footing, and lands on the ground with three broken ribs and a fractured foreleg. The young she-cats are so concerned that they dress in mourning while Don Gato lies in the hospital, but the mice celebrate by dressing in bright red.

This song must have been greatly amusing to children in colonial days, when oral entertainment was about the only kind they had. Fortunately the adults had a good store of songs, stories, and games for children. The ballad *Hilo de Oro*, known also as *Angel de Oro*, was a children's

Hispanic musical lore begins at an early age. Here two future troubadours are ready to play and sing at the drop of a peso.

Francia, do, re, mi," as well as "Malbrú se fué a la guerra," which is exactly the opening line of the French version: "Malbru s'en va t'en guerre." The children of the Southwest must have sung it lustily, because the melody was very singable. Countless other games of long standing served to strengthen Hispanic culture by enriching it with bonds of oral tradition.

THE TROUBADOURS

The folk song was an accepted form of communication that overcame the strict customs of families with marriageable daughters. In years past, when parents and male members of the family protected an unmarried girl from the onslaught of a young *pretendiente*, he had recourse to the village troubadour, who would compose a song for him to sing, or, if the hopeful young man could not sing, the troubadour would do the honors for him. Parents who objected to a young man's personal appearance at the home, even one with honorable intentions, would think highly of him when his thoughts were expressed in eight-syllable verse. Many songs originated in this fashion, and the

game played in a circle from which a player was chosen at the end of each stanza. Like many children's games, *Hilo de Oro* was sung as the participants skipped around the circle. Another well-known children's ballad was a game called *Escogiendo Novia*, *Choosing a Sweetheart*, which opened with the lines:

Yo soy la viudita del Conde Laurel
Que quiero casarme y no encuentro con quién.

I am the widow of Count Laurel
Who wants to get married and doesn't find anyone.

The ballad *Mambrú*, or *Membruno*, is widespread in western Europe and Hispanic America, and there are dozens of variants known by different names. In France it is called *Le Convoi de Malbrough*. It must be of French origin because some of the versions begin: "Un niño nació en

A pair of village folksinger-composers photographed in Arroyo Hondo, New Mexico, in 1932. These men sang *primera* and *segunda*, the folk close harmony of southwestern Hispanic troubadours.

Mountain children from Carnuel, a village in the Sandia Mountains near Albuquerque, play a traditional children's game dressed in colonial attire.

feelings expressed and the messages carried are as meaningful today as the day the songs were written.

At the *bailes*, which were never lacking in colonial days, an attractive young lady with many

A quartet of Hispano troubadours entertaining at a private fiesta in 1939. They later became professionals and went on tour.

suitors would not be offended when men vied with each other for her favors by reciting *bombas* to her while the dance was in progress. If a suitor was unable to write a good *copla*, he called on an always-present troubadour, who would oblige with a few lines in praise of the girl's many graces, for which he was amply rewarded by the hopeful swain. If the suitor was dancing with a special girl, he would shout to the bard as he danced by, "¡Estímela, trobador!" "Compliment her, troubadour!" By the time he came around again, dancing to the rhythm of a lively polka or *valse chiqueado*, the troubadour would have his lines ready to recite, much to the enjoyment of the girl and the amusement of the audience.

The village poet or troubadour was present wherever people congregated: at *bailes*, at *fiestas*, and also at taverns where the men were "muy alegres," according to oral accounts and "aficionados a la parranda," an old Hispanic way of saying that men were accustomed to going out on the town.

When the womenfolk were present, such a gathering was more respectful and sedate, and was called a *tertulia*. The *cantador*, or singing bard, was there, too, and was always invited to sing, because that was his occupation. Every village boasted of its own *poeta* or *cantador*—he was not a *cantor*; that title was reserved for the professionally trained singer. When the *patrón* of the village or pueblo arrived at a festivity, the *poeta* would greet him with a few verses of his own composition that were sure to please the village's most important citizen, and the troubadour's efforts were rewarded.

People in the Hispanic Southwest have always held the rhymed word in high regard, whether in song, *versos, coplas,* or even proverbs. Most of the last are in rhymed verse. The quality of these sayings is, on the whole, more expressive and effective than that of their counterparts in Spain. A village composer was considered an important member of society, a person who could be called on for a composition at a birthday, a fiesta, a wedding, or a funeral.

In the days of the overland trade to Chihuahua the hardships of wearisome travel with pack trains and *carretas* was made more bearable by the presence of the troubadour, who entertained each evening by the campfires. Every caravan boasted of a good bard who not only sang the songs the traders knew but also composed all sorts of humorous verse based on anecdotes and happenings along the trade routes. No one became offended when the itinerant troubadour made sport in verse of someone's weakness by singing appropriate *décimas* or *coplas.*

The more romantically inclined insisted on love songs that brought solace to their lonely hearts, for many of the young men accompanying the caravan were out to prove their mettle to win the hand of the girl they left behind.

It was also customary for the *mayordomos* along the Santa Fe Trail, when they met on the prairies, to issue a challenge to each other's troubadours for a song fest when they camped together for the night. Sometimes these singers of the trail would sit face to face until sunup, trying to outdo each other until their repertoires ran out.

Some of these southwestern troubadours of the past century became so well known that the old folks in New Mexico used to quote them with great familiarity: "As Chicoria used to say," or "Like El Viejo Vilmas once said," followed by some sage quotation attributed to a wise bard. The poet El Pelón was born in Pojoaque, north of Santa Fe, in 1844 and became a sheepherder to enjoy the solitude of the lonely range. Some of his manuscripts, written on rawhide, were found about

fifty years ago in a cave, but the contents were a bit "rare" for public consumption. His sense of humor more than compensated for his outspokenness and his themes, which were a bit risqué for the mores of the turn-of-the-century generation.

El Viejo Vilmas was greatly admired for his endurance and for his broad knowledge of ecclesiastical matters. One of the contests in which the old bard took part included troubadours known to tradition as Taveras, Cienfuegos, and Gracia. The challenge was made by the old veteran himself:

> Salga él que fuera prudente
> A trovar con la razón,
> Que él que es amante no teme
> Antes busca la ocasión.

> Let him come forth who so wishes
> To compose with wit and knowledge
> For he who is fond fears not;
> But seeks and enjoys the occasion.

The challenge did not fall on deaf ears, and the contest was on. They parried with wit and folk knowledge of theology and history, and, amid puns, plays on words, and facile versifying, all went down, vanquished by the more experienced Vilmas, who ended the contest with a challenge to all the poets to vie together against him:

> Ablanden bien sus gamuzas
> Y mírenlo bien perplejo
> Júntense todos los puetas
> Y cárguensele a este viejo.

> Get yourselves in fighting shape
> As you watch your vanquished friend.
> Get together, all you poets;
> Try to overcome this oldster.

THE *CORRIDO*

The folk were not content to sing only the traditional ballads of their original homeland, particularly when succeeding generations lost contact with courtly affairs, kings, palaces, and princes. Fortunately they had inherited the art of the troubadour along with a peninsular repertoire, and they composed new songs based on the life they led in a land that was now their own and added countless compositions to Spanish folk music.

A narrative form of ballad in eight-syllable verse was called the *romance corrido,* which was very popular in Andalucía, in southern Spain, where it may have originated. The verse form was brought to Mexico and thence to the Southwest toward the end of the eighteenth century. There it has continued to be one of the most popular verse forms in which the folk muse casts stories of love, crime, tragedy, flood, catastrophe, and particularly the deeds, heroic and unheroic, of men who invariably were mounted on spirited *caballos alazanes*, sorrel-colored horses. The chestnut, or dark sorrel, was the favorite horse of tradition. A proverb quoted among the folk praised the virtues of this horse:

> Caballo alazán tostado,
> antes muerto que cansado.
> A sorrel horse is sooner
> dead than tired.

A Hispanic hero running on foot would have been contrary to the equestrian tradition of the folk in the days before automobiles. Affairs of the heart— and their consequences—were often sung about such daring men as Insunza, who rode into a dance, swept up his lady love, and rode into the night:

> Insunza como valiente
> Del baile se la sacó

Scores of these folk knights of the saddle lived recklessly and dangerously, but usually their escapades ended, so the *corridos* say, with a knife thrust or gunfire. Macario Romero died on his horse as he fled from a posse after killing fourteen of his pursuers. Lucio was taken from a dance and stabbed four times. Guadalupe Rayos fought bravely until he ran out of ammunition but left the last shell for himself. And so the heroic *corridos* told tragedies of men and women who died violently.

Girls also died in the *corridos*, victims of the strange honor code by which folk heroes lived. It was an unpardonable breach of the man's code for a girl to turn down an invitation to dance. This was *desairar*, the reason why Juanita Alvarado and Rosita Alires died, the former in 1882 and the latter in 1885. It was customary for many *corridos* to begin with the date when the event took place:

> Año de mil ochocientos
> Ochenta y cinco al contado
> Hoy murió Rosita Alires,
> En el baile la mataron.
> T'was the year of eighteen hundred
> Eighty-five to be exact;
> Today died Rosita Alires,
> In a dance hall she was killed.

Other *corridos* have recorded in song floods that wiped out villages along the upper Río Grande and the story of a little boy who became lost in a blizzard while picking piñón and froze to death in the company of his faithful dog Fido, whose last effort before dying was a heroic attempt to protect his master.

During the early nineteenth century many of the village bards wrote *corridos*, but they were not *corridistas*, *corrido* composers, such as the ones who appeared in such profusion during the Mexican Revolution of 1910. In Texas and in New Mexico composers used the *corrido* form to tell of a tragedy or an important event, but they did not write *corridos* exclusively. In California, Mexican nationals wrote this ballad form as a continuation of their own tradition. Lately, however, the *corrido* has become the principal verse form of the Mexican Americans, the Chicanos, and activists who use it as a medium for protest. They take their cue from the *corridos* written about Mexican revolutionaries, such as Zapata and Pancho Villa, and write about the California *huelgas*, or strikes, life in prison, and other tragic subjects. But the heroic song is not as common today as it was a century ago.

VARIETY OF VERSE FORMS

In addition to the *corridos* and the *trovos*, or love ballads, there was another form of Spanish ballad called the *décima*. It was not popular with young people because of its lugubrious and difficult melodies. Eventually the melodies disappeared, and the *décima* became simply one more form of popular poetry. The poems were written in four ten-line stanzas introduced by a four-line quatrain, and were grouped into love, religious, *jocosas*, and *a lo divino décimas*. These compositions also had their origin in Spain, where they were called *espinelas*, and eventually arrived in the Southwest along with other traditional song forms.[3]

The folk-song tradition of the Southwest is varied and rich. When we include the *canción*, or lyric folk song of Spanish and Mexican provenience, the repertoire becomes endless. In addition to the ballads and songs, the unbroken singing and composing tradition of Hispanic peoples served to keep alive their folk-music heritage. The same tradition helped them keep the heritage alive and express more fully their own feelings, to tell their history in the New World more accurately than ballads about remote kings and princesses.

No other cultural group in the United States has had as long and varied a folk-singing tradition as the Hispanic folk of the Southwest. The *copla*, the four-line stanza with its distinctive wit, wisdom, or satire, was the essence of Spanish epigrammatic brevity. It also traveled unchanged to the far frontiers of the Spanish Empire, where it inspired thousands more, many of which became part of the Southwest's heritage. With a figure of speech born of the equestrian life in the region, a folk bard put a witticism in *copla* form and said:

> Nadie diga que es querido,
> aunque lo estén adorando.
> Que muchos en el estribo
> Se suelen quedar colgando.

> Let no one say he's truly loved,
> Though he may be seemingly adored.
> For many with foot in the stirrup
> Have been many times left hanging.

Whether the subject was love, hate, envy, sarcasm, or any other human emotion, there was always a *copla* to sum it up succinctly.

For melodic interest and popularity among all members of society, the *canción* superseded the *corrido*, the *décima*, and the old ballad. Varied and adaptable, the *canción* was composed as a verse form, and the melody was composed for it or was adapted from another song. It was terse and classical in the eighteenth century and thoroughly romantic in the next century and a half. In recent decades the songs have dealt with social and economic inequalities, as well as with the timeless affairs of the heart.

As noted earlier, many of the folk songs of the Southwest originated in Spain. The references to the Spanish court, the minor-key melodies, and the *danza* rhythm indicate a much more distant origin than songs about *mi rancho bonito* or *la ladera*. There is a note of nostalgia when a southwestern girl sings:

> El Rey de España
> me verá pasar
> con túnica blanca
> y corona de azahar.

> The king of Spain
> will watch me go by
> with a white wedding dress
> and orange-blossom crown.

A number of the songs, both the ranchero songs and those composed on Spanish models, convey their message by indirect address. A *canción* directs its message to a star, to a princess, or even to

University students serenading a coed singing "Princesita."

an inanimate object, but the girl who listens understands. She knows who is meant by *princesita* or *estrellita*.

The *cancioneros*, or song collections, published in Mexico, San Antonio, Los Angeles, and Santa Fe, have songs about the little mountain deer, *el venadito*, who comes down under the cover of night to drink. There is also the messenger bird, *pajarillo barranqueño*, whose mission is implied; and *la enredadera*, the morning-glory vine that frames the girl's window. The two classics of the Hispanic world, "La Paloma" and "La Golondrina," convey their messages in melody and words. For years the latter was the Hispano-Mexican counterpart of "After the Ball Is Over" at *bailes* in the Southwest. When the strains of *La Golondrina* were heard, everyone knew it was the last number.

In addition to the rich romantic repertoire of the Hispano Mexicans, there is a growing number of *corridos* whose composers speak of economic problems, social and political inequalities, and political heroes. Many of the published ballads are not set to music. The romantic *canciones* of Mexico, popular and semiclassical, however, continue strong on radio and television. Other effective instruments of transmission are the *mariachi* bands, which have become a part of the musical tradition of a southwestern population whose folk origin is alive and strong.[4]

FOLK DANCING

Folk singing and folk dancing, closely related forms of entertainment, have always been popular among Hispanic folk in the Southwest. The repertoire of folk dances has varied from the solo to the "mixer." Along the border, where there was closer contact with Mexican and European tradition, there were Spanish *jotas*, Basque *zorzicos*, sensual *zarabandas*, and *boleros*.

The dance tradition, which was taken up by the folk from formal society, filtered down across the centuries from the viceregal court in Mexico City to the villages, and some of these dances eventually found their way to the upper regions of the Southwest. The ceremonial *pavana* and the French *gavotte* were seldom danced outside the larger cities, but there were also lively folk dances, which the people of the Southwest preserved and danced regularly, even after they passed out of favor in Mexico.

A favorite Spanish dance was the fandango, which was so popular that an evening of dancing came to be known by the same name. Many early travelers in California spoke of the fandango (and thought it a bit suggestive and immoral), but it is difficult to say what specific dance they referred to, because many kinds of dances were danced at a *baile*. In the Southwest they had verses to accompany a fandango:

> Vente borracho conmigo,
> Yo te llevaré a tu cama.
> Prefiero más mi botella
> Que ir a ver mi dama.

> Come along with me, you tippler,
> And I will put you to bed.
> I much prefer a good bottle
> To a visit to my lady.

In addition to the *jotas*, *boleros*, and *fandangos*, other folk dances became "naturalized," so to speak, such as the *jarabe*, the *varsoviana*, the

Fiesta time in Durango, Colorado.

polka, the *schottishe* (known as the *chote* or *chotis*), and, of course, the waltz. The *jarabe* became a specialty in Mexico and eventually was formalized into what is called the hat dance. The *varsoviana* and the *cracoviana* were Polish dances, introduced during the time of Emperor Maximilian in Mexico. The latter was from a court dance known as the *krakoviat*, and the former was from the *warszowanka*, which was also known among the Anglo-American southwesterners as "Put Your Little Foot."

The waltz lent itself to all sorts of variations, as did the mazurka. The old-timers in Santa Fe, San Antonio, and southern Colorado can still remember when they danced *vals de los paños*, or "waltz of the handkerchief," and *vals despacio*, or "slow waltz," along with the *galopa*, a fast dance at the end. One of the favorite folk dances was *la cuna*, or "the cradle," performed by four couples joining hands and going through a series of intricate over-and-under movements, ending with all hands joined in the center in the form of a cradle. The music then changed tempo into a rocking rhythm as the dancers "rocked the cradle."

The French quadrilles were as popular in the Southwest as they were in other parts of the United States, but in California, New Mexico, and parts of Mexico, they used the last part known as *el cotillón* as a separate waltz. In New Mexico the name was corrupted to *el cutilio*. In addition to the confetti and serpentines used at particularly gay affairs, there was the *baile de cascarones*, a dance to which the young people brought confetti-filled eggshells and broke them on each other's heads during the dance. Usually the contents were perfumed so that the ladies would not mind confetti falling on their dresses. A variation occurred when a young man, bent on mischief, might put a few lice into the eggshell and then break it over an intended victim.

The party was usually enlivened when the *bastonero*, or dance leader, announced a *valse de la silla* or a *valse de la escoba*. This was a combination of musical chairs and other parlor games of the past century. A chair was placed at one end or in the middle of the dance floor. As a couple danced by the chair, the young lady sat in it and remained seated until her young man proffered a compliment in verse. All the young men came ready with good assortments of quatrains that they recited at the proper moment. If they were not poetically gifted, there was always a troubadour at the dance who would give them a quatrain or two for a consideration. This same dance was popular among the gauchos of Argentina, where it was known as the *chair polka*; the *vals de la escoba* was a scramble for partners. The men and women lined up separately, and an odd man began dancing with a broom. When a change was announced by the *bastonero*, the odd man dropped the broom and tried to get a girl in the scramble for partners. The dance continued until another formation was announced.

The audience always listened to spontaneous versifications with more than passing interest because they sometimes led to a contest. If the girl was popular, each admirer would choose a different troubadour to try to outdo his rival's compliment. This custom was common in California, where the girl's *pretendientes* shouted, "Bomba!" during the dance. The contest began with the two young men, and eventually ended with everyone taking sides and urging the favorite troubadour to better and more insinuating versifying. Coins began to shower around him, urging him to great-

er heights of poetic endeavor. If the contest became personal, it often closed with a donnybrook that was enjoyed by everyone and was considered a mark of a successful evening. "Este baile se acabó al estilo mexicano," wrote the village bard, "The dance ended in Mexican style."

These entertaining folk dances were arranged regularly to celebrate a happy occasion. Over the years the repertoire grew, with all sorts of regional dance creations: *el jilote*, "young corn"; *el vaquero*, "the cowboy"; *la Indita*, "the Indian maiden"; and many others, such as *el taleán*, *el rechumbé*, and *la camelia*, which are danced today by older people.

In California the number of dances and the frequency with which *bailes* and balls were held were even greater than in New Mexico and Texas. The records compiled by Bancroft list scores of folk and ballroom dances performed regularly in homes and at community affairs. The Indians at the missions were also encouraged to put on their own aboriginal dance feasts, which, according to historical records, were greatly enjoyed by the residents and visitors from the East.

A number of circumstances contributed to the popularity of dancing in California. There was more affluence in the population, and there was also more leisure in a society where most of the work was performed by mission-Indian labor. Food and wine were abundant, and the moderate climate enabled people to enjoy themselves for much of the year.

According to records left by J. Arnaz and Antonio F. Coronel, the Californios, like the Mexican-American folk in southwestern Texas, erected *ramadas*, roofed with green boughs, in front of their houses. These dance floors were enclosed on three sides with cotton *mantas*. The fourth side was left open but had a low picket fence to keep horsemen beyond the dance floor. The *caballeros* attending the dance sat on their horses behind the fence until they were ready to enter the ballroom, hat in hand, after removing their spurs.

The *bastonero* indicated the ladies who were dancing by taking them one by one for a short turn in the center of the dance floor. Those who were not dancing rose, took his hand, and were seated again. A *bastonero* regularly led the dances in the Southwest until after World War I. At most wedding dances and all formal balls the printed program identified the leader with a note: "Bastonero—Lazo azul." The blue ribbon was his badge of office.

Bancroft's list of accounts of California dances indicates a large variety of folk dances by such names as *cuando*, *queso*, *el malcriado*, and *La Vaquilla*, and numerous others, which mean everything from "the heifer" and "the gopher" to "cheese" and "bad boy." The music, played by an orchestra made up of guitars and violins, was known as *son*, or, simply, "tune." *Sones* are still danced to in Veracruz and Michoacán in Mexico.

In addition to the folk dances there were also more formal numbers, such as the *contradanza*, the *jota*, and the *cuadrilla*, imported from Mexico and Spain. They were often accompanied by singing troubadours, who enlivened the evening with their verses and *estribillos*.

HISPANIC FOLK DANCES TODAY

The Hispanic population today tends to follow the current national vogues in dancing. The folk dances of Hispanic tradition have become a spectator entertainment performed by those who have had special training. Many of the traditional folk dances once popular in northern New Mexican villages and in the mountain towns have been preserved through the efforts of the Santa Fe Folklore Society. On special occasions, such as the Santa Fe Fiesta, the Folklórica, as this society is usually called, presents such numbers as *la cuna*, and a variety of forms which the waltz has taken. Two of the most popular variations are *valse despacio* and the *vals de los paños*. The latter dance form is found throughout Latin America, though not always in waltz time. In the California fiestas, and particularly at the annual Santa Barbara Fiesta, there is a revival of both Spanish and Mexican folk dances, in addition to those of local invention.

In years past the traditional *varsoviana* was a must at the governor's inaugural ball. The University of New Mexico student body adopted it as the official university dance during the 1936 homecoming festivities. One reason for the continuing popularity of this folk dance may be its dual English and Spanish tradition.

Spanish and Mexican folk dances owe their survival in part to the effort of the dancing masters who teach them and to professional and amateur performers who present them at conventions, parties, and school programs and on such Mexican national holidays as Cinco de Mayo and Independence Day. Mela Sedilla Brewster taught Mexican and Spanish folk dances at the University of New

Mexico from the early 1930's until the mid-1940's. In 1938 she published *Mexican and New Mexican Folk Dances*, the first manual of traditional Spanish and Mexican folk dances in New Mexico. A second edition appeared in 1950.

In the late 1930's a young performer and dancing teacher in El Paso, known professionally as La Charrita, began a long career as entrepreneur and performer of Spanish and Mexican folk dances. She was featured with the Típica Orchestra, sponsored by the El Paso Chamber of Commerce, and also performed during the Texas Centennial at the Alamo in San Antonio.

When she moved to Albuquerque, La Charrita organized various dancing groups, who performed at conventions and festive gatherings in the city. During the Coronado Cuarto Centennial celebrations, she was appointed by the United States Coronado Exposition Commission to train groups of young people who presented the older forms of Spanish folk dances in the states where the Coronado *entrada* was enacted. After World War II she moved to Denver and was instrumental in reviving interest among the young folk of both cultures in learning Hispanic folk dances. Many of her well-trained students became teachers, and some of the gifted ones went to Spain for advanced training. On their return to the United States, these professionals made national reputations in their own right.

A dual tradition in folk dancing has evolved in all states of the Southwest, with the possible exception of Texas. The Hispanos tend toward the Spanish dance, while Mexicans along the border naturally are more inclined to continue their national dance tradition. With the renewed interest in Mexican culture since World War II various Mexican-American groups in the principal cities of the southwest have actively participated in ethnic dances. Many dancing masters, former members of the Ballet Folklórico of Mexico City, have been invited to teach old and new Mexican folk dances. As a result, there has been a flourishing of Mexican folk dancing among young people. Interest is heightened by regular appearances on television stations throughout the region of enthusiastic young people who might otherwise have neglected their traditions.

In California the motion-picture and television industry has been instrumental in helping intensify interest in both Spanish and Mexican folk dances. Another important influence has been the professional dancing troupes that tour the country

The Trujillos, brother and sister, dancing Spanish *bulerías* during an outdoor fiesta in Denver, Colorado. Photograph by José Gonçalves.

Young people in Denver, Colorado, cultivating their Hispanic folk-dance heritage as taught by their Spanish dancing teacher.

Jeannette Trujillo McDowell, one of La Charrita's outstanding students, in a Spanish *intermedio* at the Larimer Square Fiesta, Denver. Photograph by José Gonçalves.

Mexican dancers revive interest in Mexican folk dancing and help maintain authenticity in regional dancing.

Members of the Ballet Folklórico de Denver directed by Lu Liñan doing a folk dance from Michoacán, Mexico, one of the many Mexican dances taught by Agustín del Razo, of the Ballet Folklórico of Mexico City. Courtesy of Lu Liñan.

Some young Hispano professional women who keep up their folk-dance heritage as a hobby.

A Mexican *mariachi* band, Alma Jaliciense, at the Santa Fe Fiesta. The *mariachis* have replaced the all-string bands called *típicas* in Mexico. Photograph by Mark Nohl.

or perform regularly in a particular locality. José Greco and other gifted performers have been responsible for helping keep alive the folk-dancing tradition. The most noticeable transformation in the Spanish-Mexican folk dance is its transition from a performing art, so to speak, to a form of entertainment where the participants are the performers, though the number of performers has greatly increased in the past two decades.

Hand in hand with folk singing and folk dancing goes the popular *mariachi* orchestra, mentioned earlier, which during the past decades has become a *sine qua non* on local television shows in the Southwest, at *bailes*, at fiestas, and even in Catholic churches, where *mariachi* masses are presented. For important occasions, such as the Santa Fe Fiesta, *mariachi* bands come from Mexico to perform.

Today we usually associate arts and crafts with some form of hobby—not a full-time occupation but a leisure-time activity of busy people, a diversion from everyday work. To the Spanish colonials of the Southwest, however, a craft meant any useful skill that provided them with the necessities for field and home. When they first arrived, they had with them agricultural tools, implements, and all the paraphernalia needed in a pioneer civilization. They had also provided themselves (as shown by the inventories declared on their departure from Mexico) with the clothing, bedding, footgear, and arms they would need in the new land. The more affluent in the expedition brought along many of the luxuries to which they were accustomed in urban life. If such articles proved to be practical for pioneers, they served as models to be used when making replacements as the originals wore out. The supply lines, established shortly after the colonials settled in and around present Santa Fe, were not able to provide for all the needs of the colony, and before very long it became necessary for craftsmen to replenish goods worn out or lost to Indians.

EARLY CRAFTSMEN

Among the first settlers of the Southwest were a few craftsmen—carpenters, weavers, spinners, carders, and a few ironworkers and silversmiths. Most were farmers and stock raisers, with a sprinkling of men interested in mining.

A census report made in the jurisdiction of Albuquerque on October 22, 1790, indicates, by the classification of artisans, those crafts that had become established in the northern province. The fifty plazas and two pueblos included in the census included eighty-two weavers, twenty-two carders, fifteen spinners who were Indians or *mestizos*, thirteen carpenters, eleven tailors, five ironworkers, five shoemakers, and only two silversmiths. The small number of metalworkers indicates that two centuries after the colonization of New Mexico the lack of metals still limited the number of

craftsmen; the number of artisans engaged in the production of textiles was twenty times as large. Aside from the many and diversified uses for textiles in the home, the coarsely woven *jerga* was an important trade item taken to the Chihuahua fairs.

No mention is made of potters, basket makers, or cabinetmakers in this census, but that is explainable. The Indian slaves and household servants provided the Spanish families with all the necessary wares for cooking and serving food. Moreover, the more refined glazed pottery and *majolica* were imported from Mexico by those families who could afford such luxuries; hence no pottery was produced in the north. A glance at the many wills recorded in the province reveals articles that were treasured highly enough to be mentioned specifically. Such items as metal grills, serving and cooking spoons, kettles, dippers, and articles of clothing made from materials unobtainable in the provinces were included in all the wills.

In 1774, Margarita Martín listed in her will a *comal de fierro*, or iron grill, and a *cazo grande*, or kettle. These *cazos* continued in use not only in New Mexico but in Texas and California. They were large copper kettles, usually three feet in diameter across the rim and sloping inward to about two feet at the bottom, and were standard equipment for slaughtering hogs and making soap. The museum of the Santa Ynez Valley Historical Society has on display a *cazo* that belonged to one of the original rancheros of California.

In a land where Indian basket weaving was one of the oldest and most highly developed crafts, there was no need for Spanish artisans to take up the craft, particularly when they had Apache servants who could turn out useful and highly artistic basketry.

Cabinetmakers were not in demand because home furnishings were limited to cupboards, chests, and benches. The production of these articles was simply an extension of carpentry. The *ebanista*, or cabinetmaker, was an artisan who worked in ebony, as the name implies. The simple pieces of pine furniture for a colonial household did not demand the services of such a highly skilled artisan as an *ebanista*.

BAZAN WEAVERS

It is difficult to understand why General Jacobo Ugarte y Loyola, commandant of the internal provinces, asked for weavers to be sent to New Mexico in 1788 when the census listed eighty-two of them two years later. Despite this large number of craftsmen, their product continued to deteriorate, according to the governor of the province, and eventually (in 1805) the Bazán brothers, master weavers from Saltillo, Mexico, were sent to Santa Fe, where they taught the weaving art. Ignacio and Juan Bazán not only taught New Mexican weavers how to improve their craft but also brought looms for weaving cotton. Some art historians believe that cotton weaving dates from the arrival of the Bazáns. When Antonio Barreiro made an inspection tour of New Mexico in 1832, he too decried the condition of the weaving craft, declaring that the Indians turned out excellent woven materials but that the product of the New Mexicans was without merit. Although the Bazáns went to Santa Fe to teach, their influence spread to Chimayó, a village a few miles north of the capital. New Mexican weaving and *sarape* art have been identified as "Chimayó weaving."

LIMITED MATERIALS

A factor that limited craft production in the northern provinces was the materials available in the country. There were no hardwoods available for fine carving and cabinetmaking and no metals with which to trim chests, make fancy Spanish locks, and turn out wrought-iron articles characteristic of Hispanic craft. The little iron that was hauled by mule pack was used for such indispensable articles as axes, hoes, and knives.

The scarcity of building materials was also reflected in the architecture of the homes and public buildings of the early Southwest. Adobes and pine poles called *vigas* were not enough to erect the kinds of structures that are commonly found in cities farther south. Despite these drawbacks, the building artisans developed a style of housing that was adequate for the climate and the life they led. Thick adobe walls were a good insulation against the weather, and the *azoteas*, or dirt-topped roofs, in addition to serving as protection against cold and heat, were convenient places to dry vegetables for winter use.

House interiors were whitewashed with a thin lime or gypsum solution, to which some of the more practical-minded added a small amount of *engrudo*, a wheat-flour paste that kept the lime from rubbing off on contact. Many Anglo-American travelers commented on how their clothes were whitened after visiting a New Mexican home and touching the walls inadvertently.

SMALL DEMAND FOR CRAFT

Despite the limited materials available, the craftsmen could have devised ways of producing more elaborate and useful artifacts if there had been a demand for them. The simple living design of most colonials did not require much more than what they had. Houses were simple structures, designed for protection against the weather and hostile Indians. They had no separate sleeping quarters, and the single rooms of most family homes served all purposes. During the day a long built-in shelf along one wall served as a sofa where the family placed their folded bedclothes; they slept on the floor.

The larger homes had separate bedrooms with *camaltas—camas altas*, "high beds." For this reason the idiom used in the Southwest for making the bed was *alzar la cama*. Residents literally "lifted the bed" from the floor and placed the bedclothes on the sofa-shelf (the usual expression is *hacer la cama*, like the English "to make the bed").

Chairs and tables were not used from colonial days until the middle of the nineteenth century, when the Anglo-Americans arrived; until then families ate seated on the floor or on low stools. E. Boyd quoted Father Dominguez' inventory of the parish church in Santa Fe in 1776. In the inventory he described the lord governor's seat, a single armchair that belonged to the government.[1] The chair represented status and was used for important persons. Because there were no chairs, there was no need for a table in the modern sense. Those who could afford it had low coffee tables, or *bancas* (known elsewhere as *tarimillas*), which could be easily reached while sitting on the floor. Some have surmised that this manner of eating is reminiscent of the Arabs, who still continue the practice in parts of North Africa. Their influence in Spain, while it may not have established a new habit, may have given the Spaniards the idea that eating on the floor was practicable, particularly in a pioneer setting. The beautifully carved chairs and tables on the market today are modern furniture, combining the structural designs from eastern factories and later Spanish models from Mexico, embellished with Spanish-Indian design. Purists may object to combining several elements of art and craft, but this is truly a southwestern artistic creation from New Mexico, which has spread to all parts of the Southwest.

THE *RICOS*

One misleading concept, giving readers the impression of wealth and luxury on the frontier, derives from the adjective *rico*. It seems to give some people the idea that the *ricos* of New Mexico lived like the privileged individuals nearer the large colonial cities who had access to all the comforts of the day. *Hacendados* of colonial Mexico were usually called *hidalgos*, or higher nobility, who gathered at the viceregal court and indulged themselves in lavish living. In the Southwest, however, a man was considered *rico* who owned large flocks of sheep. His household differed from others in the colony mostly in the number of servants he had and in the size of his establishment. The same implements that served the common people were used in the larger household but were replaced more often. In addition, the "wealthier" colonist had a separate room for the craftsmen of the home, who turned out bedding, clothing, floor coverings, and other necessaries. Usually the craftsmen were skilled Indians.

HOUSEHOLD UTENSILS

In addition to the woven goods produced by Indians in the Spanish homes, the Indians provided other household utensils, as they did in Mexico. The cooking pots were called *ollas*, the same word used in Spain, and the receptacles for drinking water were called *tinajas*, known in Spain since Phoenician days and commonly used to transport olive oil. Not only was a *tinaja* a receptacle for water, but it was a convenient cooler in a land where evaporation was a blessing or a curse, depending on how it affected the people's lives. The clay *tinaja* was covered with gunnysack and was kept constantly moist, suspended from the rafters of the *portal* or hanging from a shade tree near the house, with an ever-present *jícara* or *jumate* for a drinking cup. The cup was made by cutting a nonedible gourd lengthwise and using

the narrow neck for a handle. In Spain the *jícara* is a chocolate cup, and the same name was extended to the Indian *jumate* in the New World. Both words are interchangeably used in the Southwest for the same kind of ladle.

The influence of Indian culture in the arts and crafts of the Southwest is almost negligible, despite the fact that Indian servants and slaves working in Spanish homes supplied the colonists with many implements. When Hispanos used Indian articles of wear or household utensils, they always referred to them as such or called them by their Indian name. Indian moccasins were always referred to as *teguas*, and other Indian-made articles were usually qualified by the adjective *indio*. Sometimes they used Indian articles temporarily until they could secure Spanish counterparts, but if the Indian product was more practical and serviceable, they did not hesitate to adopt it. It would be difficult even today to replace the Navajo saddle blanket with anything better, and so nearly every horseman who can afford it owns one.

Similarly, the Indians of the Southwest, as well as those in Mexico, adopted a number of Spanish articles for their own use. They have become identified with some Spanish products so completely that, for example, the casual observer will be heard to refer to the colonial clay ovens in the Río Grande Indian villages as "Indian ovens." In a true acculturated situation there is always a certain amount of exchange, though the dominant culture may be the principal donor. So much interest has been manifested in Indian ethnology during the past century that many Spanish practices and artifacts are ascribed an Indian origin.

COOKING UTENSILS

One of the reasons the pottery craft was of little consequence among the Spaniards is that the Indians provided them with all they needed. That did not include lacquered specimens, or anything approaching the quality of Talavera pottery of Puebla, Mexico, but it was adequate mainly for the simple cooking processes in the northern provinces. Foods were prepared in the fireplace or over an open *brasero* on a homemade grill called a *parra* or *parrilla*. The *parra* was particularly useful for broiling dried meat in winter, when fresh meat was less abundant.

The conical oven outside the house was very practical for baking, but the *comal* was much faster when the cook was preparing corn or wheat

A traditional Santa Clara, New Mexico, potter at work. These Indian artisans provided the early Spanish settlers with household utensils.

tortillas. The original *comal* was an oversized clay platter, which was usually placed over live coals. A few fortunate families also had metal *comales* they had brought from Mexico. This article is standard equipment today in campgrounds in the Rocky Mountains.

It is surprising not to find in northern New Mexico the Mexican *brasero* or *hornilla* built against the kitchen wall, where meals were prepared in colonial days. This stovelike adobe contrivance had two openings on top of each compartment, on the design of modern stove gas burners. It was open in front and fired with charcoal and had as many compartments as the family needed. In Mexico today, *braseros* are covered with tile and are normally used by poor people or in places where there is no electricity.

Old-timers in Cayoncito, near Las Vegas, New Mexico, remember having seen *braseros* in their youth, but in that part of the Southwest they were called *estufas*. In villages of southern Colorado they had something similar, called a *fogón*. The word *fogón* is commonly used in New Mexico for a fireplace. Like most country people, the colonists of the Southwest arose early, particularly the women who did the cooking. Their first chore was to bring the coals back to life with a palm-leaf fan or with a *fuelle*, a hand bellows. As the day began to break and dawn approached, they sang a song, "El Alba," "Dawning."

TOOLS

The simplicity of the tools used by the southwesterners extended to agricultural implements and to simple means of transportation. Though many kinds of plows were in use in Spain at the time of colonization, only a combination Extremadura-Andalusian kind of plow was introduced into the part of the New World extending from New Mexico to Chile. According to anthropologist George Foster, the reason for the choice was that this particular plow was simpler in construction and did not utilize much iron, an important consideration in colonial days. Foster sees this as formal culture in America, a guided acculturation to facilitate the complicated problem of settlement, rather than guidance purely by tradition.[2]

As the Spanish Empire pushed its frontiers northward, the tools that accompanied the expeditions became even more selective. As a result the outer fringes of settlement, such as northern New Mexico, had the least and simplest of everything. A visit to the state museum in Santa Fe reveals the utter simplicity of colonial crafts up to the Anglo-American period. Another item unknown in the Southwest was tile roofing, which the settlers could have used profitably.

LIVING HABITS

An important factor in the development of arts and crafts in any region is the demand arising from the diverse living habits of the population. Most of the southwestern settlements, with the exception of the Texas settlements along the present Mexican border and California, were composed of a relatively classless society. The government appointees and a few functionaries in the governor's office generally brought their own households and took their property with them when they returned to Mexico. Reference is made occasionally to some of the fine things that these people had in their homes, but there is no trace of the finery that they owned. The few wealthy families of the region had personal things sent to them over the trade routes from the south, but they also remained in their own households, as verified by the wills they wrote. But the wills list a sort of miscellany that does not add up to a complete wardrobe or to a household fully furnished the way the members of the upper classes outfitted themselves in the large cities of the south. Because the basic articles used in all households were uniform, there was never any great demand for a variety of artifacts that would challenge the creativity or imagination of the artisans.

California was an exception to this uniformity and simplicity, first, because there was a wide gulf between the landless poor and the wealthy rancheros, with thousands of acres and great herds of stock. Moreover, the Californios had access to some of the luxuries that were hard to come by in isolated regions of New Mexico and Texas. The maritime trade opened the way for the acquisition of a number of luxuries denied to land-locked settlers. The Manila galleon also brought to California fineries from the Far East. All these favorable circumstances enabled the California *ricos* to live better than the less fortunate laborers and helped create socioeconomic classes.

MONUMENTS OF SPANISH CIVILIZATION

The best index to any civilization is the monuments left behind. In the Southwest, except for the California, Texas, and Arizona missions, there is no evidence of a culture beyond a simple pastoral one. The missionaries were not true settlers, who remained in the country. They were itinerants, or they had definite missions to accomplish in a limited time. Most of them were well-trained men, often versed in architecture, who, with the help of Indian labor, were able to erect buildings patterned after the European churches but utilizing local building materials.

Had the settlers been as well trained, with a cultural background comparable with that of the churchmen, it is conceivable that they would have designed more elaborate living quarters and achieved greater artistic success. As it was, even the Palace of the Governors in Santa Fe was a simple structure much like the *finca* of a large rancho. The Art Museum a block away is made of exactly the same materials but utilizes a better planned and executed architectural and decorative design. This newer building clearly indicates the possibilities of artistic achievement with comparable materials and illustrates why the missionaries were able to turn out such edifices as the California missions and the cathedrals of northern Mexico, Arizona, and Texas.

Contemporary furniture in the style introduced by the Spanish colonials in New Mexico. The chairs and table are modern adaptations of the style, but the *trastero*, or cupboard, is more traditional.

WOODWORK

A few household artifacts from colonial days have been saved, and although there are not enough of them to get a complete picture of the range of craftsmanship, they indicate the simple life that the Hispanos led. An interesting piece of furniture was the *trastero*, a cupboard that probably had other uses than the storage of dishes. This style of furniture has been revived in Mexico in the Mediterranean furniture renaissance. It is much like

articles made by the colonials of the Southwest, except for the turned spindles on the doors and other niceties that trained artisans working with better woods were able to produce in Mexico. The *trasteros* from New Mexico were also made with two-leaf doors, but the relief designs were often fashioned from gypsum instead of being entirely carved.

Occasionally one sees a pine chest with the lion design of the Spanish province of León, the same design found today in Leonese rugs exported to

257

the United States. The one item seldom manufactured by the Hispanos was the *ropero*, or wardrobe, so much in evidence in Latin-American homes lacking a built-in closet. The folk, as well as the better-to-do, kept their clothes in *baúles*, storage chests similar to the "razor-back" trunks of the nineteenth century. In Spain and Mexico they stored clothes not in daily use in another chest called a *cofre* and hung the other articles in a *ropero* in much the same way that Americans did, until the closet was included in house plans. There are no indications that the *arca*, another kind of chest, was used in the Southwest. It was a strongbox in which valuables were kept; when the articles to be stored were large, colonials used a bigger chest called an *arcón*.

NOMENCLATURE OF ARTIFACTS

The names used today for a number of furniture items and implements reveal the uses made of certain pieces of furniture in years past and also explain why others were not known. New Mexicans today refer to a chair as a *silleta* rather than the usual name, *silla*. It comes from the word *sillete* or *silleta*, meaning a kind of footstool that was used in colonial days when there were no tables. Writers of the period tell us that people in the Southwest (and, for that matter, people in many parts of the world at that time) carried on many activities—eating, sewing, and visiting—seated on the floor. The *silletes* were used as coffee tables and also to sit on. When chairs came into general use, they were called *silletas*, and these craft pieces are known by that name today.

People in New Mexico refer to a tub as a *cajete*, instead of *tina*, using the Mexican name for bowl. The *cajetes*, or *tinas*, were made of barrel staves, and were used mostly for washing clothes. The word for bucket in New Mexico is *cubeta*, the name used in Spain for a wooden bucket, like the "old oaken bucket," but the name has been transferred to the modern metal bucket known in the Spanish-speaking world as *balde*.

Article names that have changed in other parts of the world indicate that some of the artifacts used by southwesterners continued to be identified by the names of articles to which they were accustomed. When horses and mules replaced oxen as dray animals, the colonials of northern New Mexico continued to use the nomenclature for farming implements associated with oxen. The breast yoke used with a wagon tongue pulled by a

team of horses was referred to as a *yugo*, instead of a *polea de pecho*, because it resembled the simple wooden yoke used with oxen before the advent of harnessed horses. In textiles this practice of adapting names is even more evident. The New Mexicans wove a coarse woolen fabric called *jerga*, used by the poorer people as clothing material but also used commonly as a floor covering. After regular carpets came into use, the New Mexicans continued to call them by the old name, *jerga*, and today this is the common name for machine-made carpets and rugs instead of the word *alfombra*, used elsewhere. A more finished material called *cuti* was also used for making clothes, and a garment made from this cloth, usually a coat, came to be known as *cute*, a variation of *cuti*. Some mistakenly believe that the word is a Hispanicization of the English "coat."

A peasant did not wear a coat in the modern sense, but he did wear a loosely fitting article like a slipover sweater called a *cotón*, which, when made from the heavy *jerga*, was a *cotón de jerga*. A folk story of the same name tells about a humble young man who worked at a palace; a princess fell in love with him despite his poverty, indicated by the coarse *cotón* he wore.

Government officials and other men of rank usually wore frock coats called *levas*, and if the coat was a heavy one, it was called a *leventón*. When full suits became the general dress, the colonials in the north referred to the coat as *leva* also, and *cute* was transferred to the overcoat. The words *sobretodo* and *abrigo* for an overcoat never came into popular use, nor did *saco*, the word for coat commonly used in Mexico.

The lacquer used by artisans to decorate smaller articrafts and figurines was known in colonial days, as it is today, as *maque*, from the Japanese *zumaque*, or sumac. In the absence of these lacquers the artisans used a homemade tempera prepared with the white of egg. But they referred to it also as *maque* and called the process *maquear*. By extension the same word was used for paint of any kind, including calcimine. Knowledge of these shifts in the use of words for different concepts can be valuable in determining the origin of some of the craft of the Southwest.

ARTS-AND-CRAFTS SURVEY

The revival of interest in arts and crafts began in the late 1920's. It was particularly strong during the Depression years, when it was thought that a revival of traditional crafts would enable many Hispanos to earn extra income or even gain full employment through using their traditional training. It was discovered, however, that there were not as many craftsmen as hoped, and so vocational programs at state and local levels were instituted, some of which were funded by federal grants.

In order to determine the economic status of arts and crafts, in 1934 the University of New Mexico sponsored a two-year statewide survey, funded by the Federal Emergency Relief Administration as Project No. S–Al–17.[3] Although the primary purpose of the study was not to trace the origin and development of the various crafts in the state, that phase was studied to determine the potential of arts and crafts as a full-time occupation for artisans and as supplementary employment during the difficult years of the Great Depression.

I directed the study as a member of the Hispanic Studies section of the university. The staff included eight field workers and five office assistants, including Cornelius Kuipers, a statistician well versed in Indian culture. Of the 865 artisans interviewed, 351 were Hispanos distributed in six principal crafts as follows: 66 woodworkers, 176 weavers, 10 tinworkers, 10 silversmiths, 10 leatherworkers, and 62 women who did needlework and spinning. The other 513 artisans were mostly Indians of the various pueblos and a few Anglo-Americans on the east side of the Rocky Mountains (in the Pecos Valley in New Mexico) and in Taos who were bootmakers and saddlemakers, with a scattering of weavers.

The Hispano craftsmen were clustered in the northern counties of the state, from Albuquerque to Taos and Raton. There were a few weavers around Socorro, seventy-five miles south of Albuquerque. The southern part of the state had no artisans to speak of; because of the longer growing season and better farmland most of the people were occupied in agriculture and related activities, and those classified as craftsmen were builders, carpenters, masons, and so on. The only craftsmen who were engaged in leather carving, woodcarving, and the like, were Mexican nationals working for well-established firms such as the Myers Company of El Paso.

The weaving craft, so important in colonial days during the Chihuahua and other trade fairs, seemed to have disappeared completely from the southern part of the region. In the north the craft had had a series of ups and down. In the course

of the survey it was discovered that the craft products of the Hispanos did not sell as readily as Indian artifacts. Most of the articles were sold to tourists as souvenirs or to local residents who had a historical interest in traditional crafts.

Mary Austin, and many other well-known writers and artists in Santa Fe, established the Native Market, where the arts and crafts could be encouraged and have a better outlet, but the public had not yet developed the taste for the handmade artifacts and traditional art of our present generation. Indian products had been on the market more consistently than the Spanish craft, so they sold better, and people had developed a stronger desire for the decorative value of Indian crafts.

Though the early 1930's were very difficult years, the annual turnover of all crafts in New Mexico alone was around two million dollars, and, as economic conditions improved, this figure began an upward trend. Today southwestern Spanish arts and crafts of all kinds are well-established industries.

SPINNING AND NEEDLEWORK

One of the oldest and most consistently practiced crafts in the Spanish Southwest was spinning. It was a very useful craft in prerailroad days, when such practical articles as socks were constantly in demand. Yarn spinning was the work of women and young girls, who must have been very active, to judge by the number of spinning bees held a century ago. Unlike the people of the eastern United States, the Hispanos of the Southwest did not use the spinning wheel. They preferred spinning with a *malacate*, or hand-twirled spindle, and they became so adept at this art that they could turn out sewing thread on one spinning.

The Native Market in Santa Fe tried to train the local artisans to use a spinning wheel propelled by a sewing-machine treadle, but the women found the device too complicated and went back to their hand-turned spindles. In addition to socks, a very popular product made from a loosely spun yarn was a fabric called *borrego* in southern New Mexico and along the Texas-Mexico border, where it was used almost exclusively as a bed cover. With the arrival of commercial products after the extension of the railroad to the Southwest, many of the domestically produced crafts made from homespun yarn were discontinued, except for those that provided an artistic outlet for women in particular.

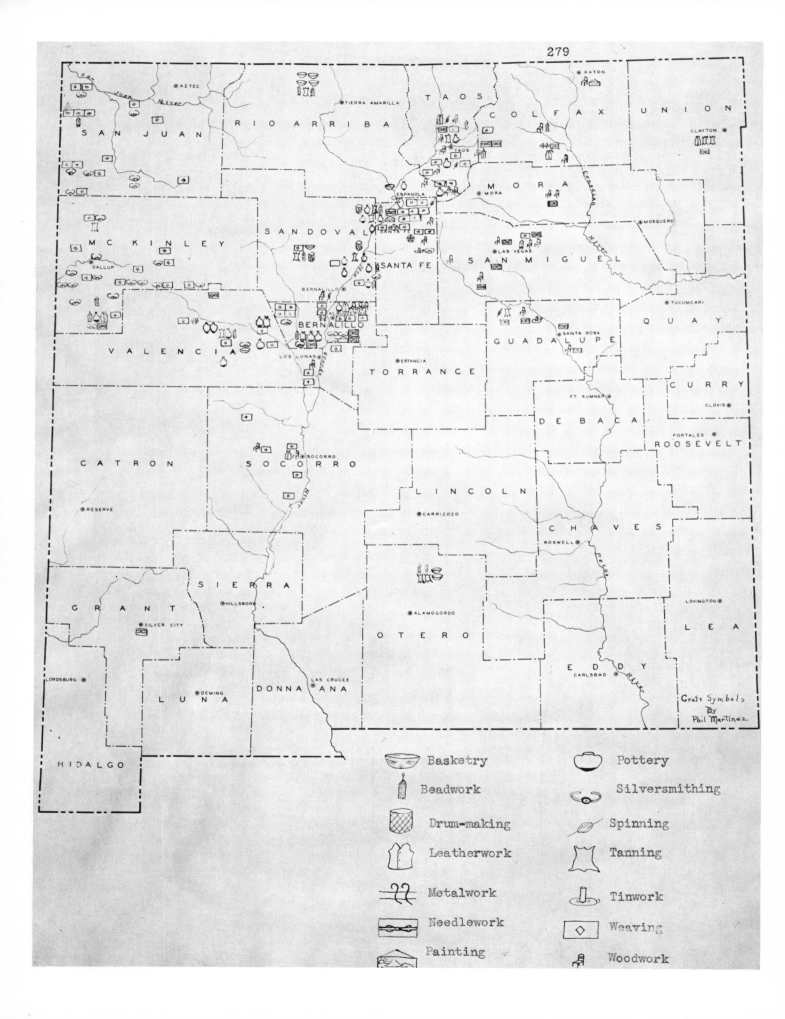

Craft Symbols
By
Phil Martinez

Basketry   Pottery

Beadwork   Silversmithing

Drum-making   Spinning

Leatherwork   Tanning

Metalwork   Tinwork

Needlework   Weaving

Painting   Woodwork

Such needlecrafts as the well-known Spanish *deshilado* continued as an artistic creation. This drawn work is in a way the opposite of embroidery, in that the solid material is made open by removing and separating the threads of the material into geometric patterns. It is an ornamental process used on linens, handkerchiefs, and sometimes in delicate articles of feminine wear, such as blouses. The art has never disappeared from the Southwest, particularly among the Mexicans in Texas and Arizona, although it has diminished with the lessening of leisure time and the introduction of other forms of diversion. Much of the *deshilado* in southwestern markets comes directly from Mexico, where it has been produced without interruption.

COLCHAS

Another form of needlework greatly cultivated in the Southwest is the embroideries used on bedspreads, or *colchas*. The foundation material for these *colchas* was either the homespun cotton *manta* or the woolen *sabanilla*, the latter being more versatile because of its weight and durability. Embroidered table covers and even small throw rugs were made for the home, but generally this kind of needlework was used for bedspreads.

It is not definitely known when the "*colcha* stitch," as some writers have called it, was first used in the Southwest, although it must be assumed that this craft was carried on along with other early forms of needlework. Wills of the past two centuries mention *colchas* among the articles inventoried, but they are not described, and so it is impossible to know how they were decorated. That women in the Southwest developed a stitch that was not employed in Spain would indicate a long history for the craft. Rebecca James gives a complete account of this unique ornamentation craft, which is still produced by the women of New Mexico.[4]

The *colcha* embroideries are generally realistic, representing landscapes, flowers, or saints. Lately, Penitente scenes have been embroidered by members of the confraternity, but they are uncommon. The artisans do not follow the Spanish custom of dividing their art according to Mohammedan and Christian cultures. In the Southwest there may appear a likeness of a saint with flower borders, symbols taken from nature, and other conventional designs in a Mohammedan pattern. There is a suggestion of arabesques in the way branches or vines are grouped along with beak-to-beak dove designs, but very seldom are the patterns purely geometric.

The two kinds of southwestern *colchas* are based on the manner in which the base material is covered. Some are solidly embroidered, giving a rug-like texture resembling high-quality commercially produced chenilles, except that the designs are entirely realistic. Other bedspreads are embroidered with border designs and a center pattern, with no attempt to cover the *colcha* solidly. This craft is more creative and artistic in that the artisan usually tries to give expression to some original religious or secular art form.

LEATHERWORK

The 1934 arts-and-crafts survey disclosed that the curing of hides and the production of leather craft among the Hispanos had almost become a lost art. Tanned hides and *gamuza*, as chamois is called in the Southwest, were usually bought or traded from the Indians, who have always cultivated this craft. Leather carving was almost exclusively the work of Mexican nationals. Hispanos later began to relearn the craft in vocational programs funded by the state or the federal government.

Brice H. Sewell, state supervisor of trade and industrial education in New Mexico, visited the leathercraft centers in Mazatlán, Mexico, in the 1930's and used much of the information he gained there in the state vocational training program. Most of the leather used in colonial days was prepared by Indian artisans working in Spanish homes. The demand for saddles, footgear, and harnesses was limited in colonial days, and the usual *talabartero*, or leatherworker, who plied his trade in Mexico did not flourish in the Southwest. In fact, the word itself is not commonly known among southwestern folk, except those living close to the Mexican border. Moreover, the *guarnicionero*, or harnessmaker, was not much in evidence, because most of the drayage was performed with oxen, who wore very little harness.

Rawhide was the common substitute in an arid

A map of New Mexico showing the concentration of traditional crafts in the north-central region where the original colonists settled.

country where buffalo hides were easily available. The same material went into footgear and saddles. The *charro* dandy of colonial Mexico demanded everything from fancy stirrups to *gualdrapa*, where a lady could be carried *a la grupa* to a party or an excursion. Such horse trappings were unknown in the Southwest. The only artisan who worked with leather in the Southwest was the *zapatero*, or shoemaker, and he had a limited clientele, because most people wore Indian moccasins, called *teguas*. In Albuquerque the Zamora family has a leather shop where traditional as well as modern products have been made for several generations. Zamora's *talabartería* is an active family enterprise with a long tradition of craftsmanship.

The leather-carving art, taken to Spain by the Moors, was introduced into the Southwest by the Spaniards and has taken root not only among the Hispanos and the Mexicans in Texas and New Mexico but also among the Anglo-Americans, who have modernized the tanning art and popularized all kinds of leather products, from saddles and boots to golf bags and women's handbags. The artwork in this leather, today called "southwestern," is in reality a direct development from the original Spanish craft. Many of the leather-carving establishments employ Mexican craftsmen for this work, for obvious reasons.

A leather article of wear that was very useful in the Southwest was the buffalo leather jacket, called the *cuera*. During the early land exploration of California many different kinds of soldier uniforms were worn. One detachment mentioned by the chroniclers was composed of *soldados de cuera*, soldiers equipped with thick leather jackets reinforced with additional layers of leather, strong enough to turn an Indian's arrow. These *cueras* eventually became plain jackets, except for the highly elaborate specimens with long fringes that are very much in demand among young Anglo-Americans, who purchase them in Mexico or in arts-and-crafts import stores in the United States.

The original *cuera* of Spanish days has gone through three stages in the Southwest. First it was a form of military armor, then an all-weather utility piece with handy thongs for fringe that the wearer could pull out when needed, and finally a sport coat for the man with a bent for frontier attire.

WEAVING

One of the important handcrafts in the Spanish Southwest has always been weaving because of its many practical applications. When commercial fabrics become readily available, however, weaving for the home experienced a sharp decline and caused artisans to turn their attention to handcrafted articles that were not available through commercial outlets. The transition to woven articles, other than blankets, occurred several years after the Anglo-American occupation of the Southwest but did not find general acceptance until the beginning of the current century. The best-known woven products in New Mexico, other than Indian blankets, continued to be those of the Chimayó weavers, who had been weaving blankets of all sizes and for varied uses since the early 1800's.

The art of weaving was carried on wherever the Spaniards settled. In San Gabriel, California, they wove *sarapes* and blankets after the Mexican fashion and also the coarse-woven colonial *jerga* that had so many domestic uses. Indians of that part of the Southwest were not as able weavers as those of the upper Río Grande. They were instructed by Spanish artisans until they learned the trade and became *gente de razón*. They were put in charge of Indians working in an *obraje*, or hand factory, and given the title *maestro*.

During the arts-and-crafts survey the village craft of Chimayó was studied in detail because of its commercial possibilities and its well-established name. The Depression years had reduced the demand for blankets and various other products that artisans were beginning to turn out. In 1934 there were 176 individuals engaged in the weaving craft, but less than 15 percent of them were engaged in it full-time. Most of them practiced the craft as a subsidiary occupation to farming. Shortly after the conquest of New Mexico the weaving craft was turned over to Indian slaves and house servants, who were soon turning out a product superior to that of the Spaniards, according to Spanish and Mexican chroniclers. The subsequent decline in Spanish weaving eventuated in the introduction of Mexican weaving teachers from Saltillo; as a result Chimayó and Santa Fe became the weaving centers of the far Southwest. In the 1930's very little weaving was done by Hispanos elsewhere. The vocational centers of Taos, Santa Fe, and other towns attempted to teach the weaving craft to other Hispanos in these areas as a rehabilitation medium, and awakened an interest in the craft, but Chimayó again emerged as the most active region in the state. Blankets made by artisans in the valley became popularly known as

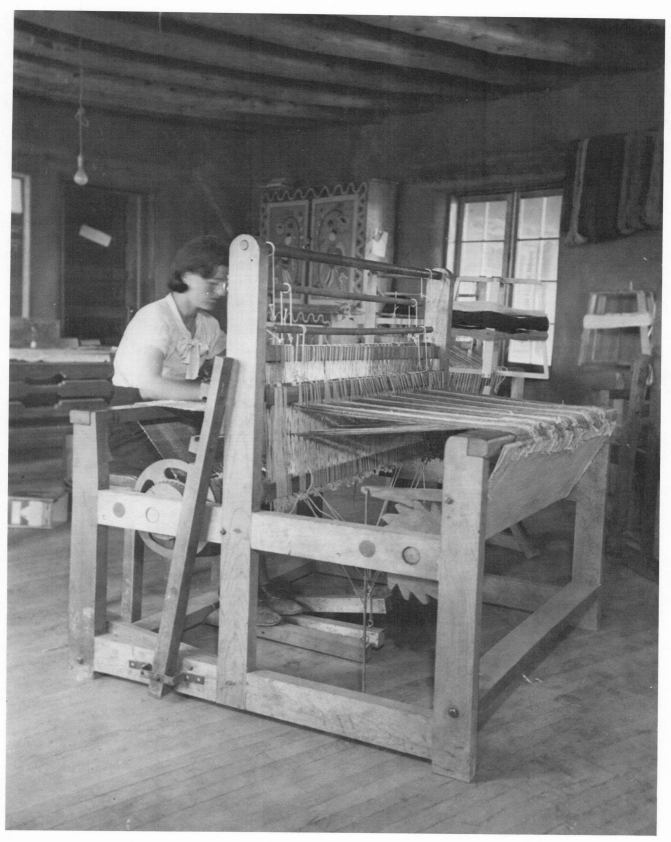

A Taos weaver using the horizontal Spanish loom. The Indians used vertical looms.

Spanish women in sixteenth-century dress visiting a Navajo weaver. Indian weavers were valuable assets in large colonial homes. Courtesy of Coronado Cuarto Centennial.

"Chimayó blankets." Harry P. Mera claimed that that was a misnomer, and he substituted the name "Río Grande blankets," to distinguish them from those woven by the Indians, according to E. Boyd.[5] The blankets are divided chronologically into four groups, beginning with the Saltillo imitations in the first quarter of the nineteenth century.

One factor that served to improve and increase the production of all Spanish craft in the Southwest, from needlework to woodwork and weaving, was the efforts by dealers and the diversified products that they eventually placed on the mar-

ket. From Chimayó blankets the craftsmen moved into handwoven ties, women's handbags, and sports coats. These products put new life into the craft, even if it did not improve the artistic value of it, in the opinion of many.

The dealers-and-employers section of the survey disclosed that craft-production increase was in direct ratio to the market outlets created by dealers and employers. Such firms brought the artisans into their own establishments and gave them greater incentive by paying them by the hour or by the piece. The dealers also placed the Chimayó

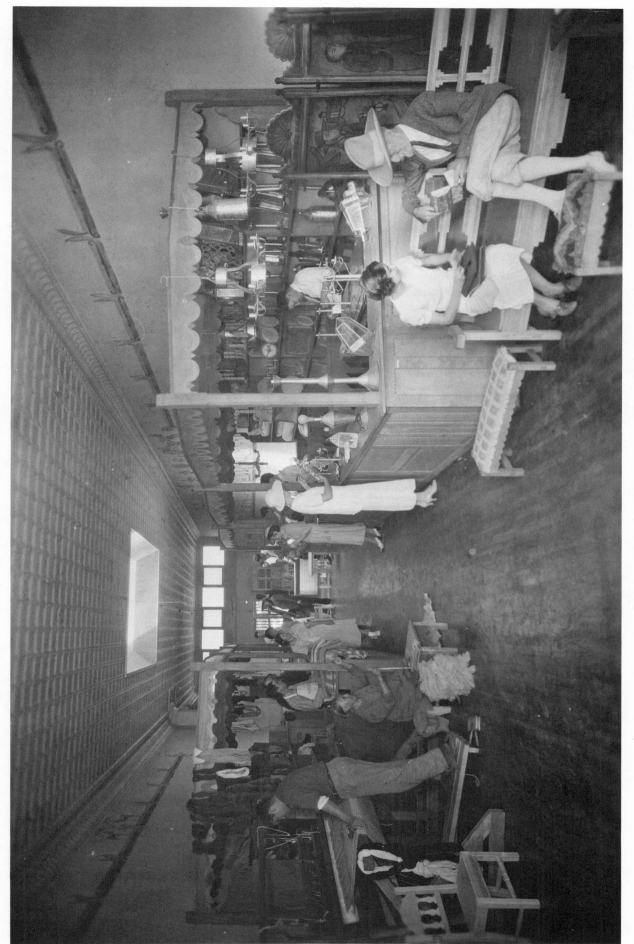

The Native Market in Santa Fe in the 1930's. The market featured handmade articles produced by local Hispano artisans.

weavers on consignment contracts, providing them with the yarn so that they had less investment to make and could count on a guaranteed income. This put the initiative on the businessmen, who sometimes tried to specify what products should be turned out, depending on the salability of the merchandise. They were not always as concerned with the artistic genuineness of the product as they were with selling it. Anglo-American business houses popularized the handcrafted products of the Hispanos in the Southwest and created, through extensive advertising and business know-how, a market that hitherto had not existed.

WOODCARVING AND FURNITURE MAKING

In woodcarving and furniture making the same results were achieved. Before the Depression years there was only a very limited market for colonial handmade furnishings, either in the home or in public buildings. They were sought largely by museums wanting them as representative of the history of the Southwest. La Villita in San Antonio, the Art Museum in Santa Fe, the County Courthouse in Santa Barbara, and the missions of Arizona and California had good examples of colonial articles, as did a few interested collectors.

Many of the WPA programs of the Depression turned to traditional arts and crafts and soon complete furnishings for public buildings and universities were being produced under contract. In a sense the renaissance of craft production began auspiciously at the top and then worked down to a popular level, but the results were economically salutary from Texas to California.

Architects also played an important part, designing Spanish colonial buildings that required the furnishings and decor consonant with the architecture. Indian design also was incorporated in the interior decoration of buildings. *Vigas*, or rafters, were installed in the Spanish fashion with elaborate corbels and lath ceilings, but the designs also included Indian adaptations that blended well with the Spanish pueblo buildings. The Southwest was doing in the early 1930's what had been done in Mexico since colonial days. The handcrafts of that country had always incorporated elements of Indian art, and in the Southwest they blended Indian art forms to produce what can properly be called southwestern Hispanic arts and crafts.

TINWORK

Part of the decoration used in house interiors in-

cluded an art form that began to flourish in the Southwest with the arrival of canned goods. Tinwork was not unknown in the Southwest, but, lacking the rolled leaf, the southwesterners had to obtain tin products from Mexico, where the tin craft has had a long history. When tin cans became available, the craftsmen in New Mexico particularly began to roll out the containers and pound them into serviceable candleholders, picture frames, and other articles. They followed the same punched-design technique, with occasional colors first of their own making and later obtained from commercial sources. In addition to providing artisans a new medium to work with, the tin cans were utilized, an admirable ecological and conservation practice. The craft was developed by later artisans, who provided not only picture frames and small items within the limitations of the tin size but large chandeliers for public buildings and homes in the larger cities. In 1934 there were only ten practicing tinworkers with an average of eight years in the craft and an average annual production of only four hundred dollars. There were indications even then, however, that this craft, while it could not support a large number of artisans, had a very promising future. Some authors, in commenting on tinwork, have indulged in speculation about the designs used by the Hispano artisans that have carried them far afield. Tinwork, like the other crafts of the Southwest, followed the same roads that led the southwesterners from Mexico. That the craft of the southwestern Hispanos is Spanish is not surprising; Spaniards introduced it in Mexico.

SPANISH ARTISANS

A few Spaniards went directly from Spain or from Mexico into the Southwest. Most of them were churchmen, whose art has been preserved in missions from Texas to California. E. Boyd has covered this Spanish-Mexican contribution in *Popular Arts of Colonial New Mexico*. The missionaries in all parts of the Southwest trained the converts in arts and crafts from the very first days of colonization. They, together with artisans provided by the crown, are responsible for 99 percent of Hispanic art forms known today in the Southwest.

The furniture craft that lately has had such a popular acceptance not only in New Mexico but elsewhere is different from the colonial furniture of Mexico. When the Mexicans speak of "colonial," they mean Spanish colonial of a more cultivated

A contemporary light fixture of traditional Spanish tinwork combined with glass. The design of the ceiling is also traditional. Courtesy of the Coronado Cuarto Centennial.

The chandelier and rafters are good examples of modern Spanish design. The *latía*, or lath, was used under the rafters in the center. The corbels in the back are a standard support in all mission architecture. Courtesy of Coronado Cuarto Centennial.

Craftsmen in Las Lunas, New Mexico, manufacturing the Spanish colonial furniture they have made for the past three and a half centuries.

nature, owned by the upper classes. In the Southwest the furnishings reflected the needs of a pioneer culture in a pastoral land with very limited media to work with. To call Southwestern craft "folk craft" does not detract from its artistic value and effectiveness.

Among the folk in Spain one finds almost exact duplicates of the articles designed and made in the Southwest. A chair copied from one made in Majorca, in white pine in the Southwest, is very little different except that the Spanish product will make a greater utilization of leather. The large brass nails with their utilitarian and decorative purposes are not commonly found in southwestern furniture, because this metal was not available to the artisan. But the massive design of

Hispanic furniture in the Southwest, the decorative carvings, and the general appearance, although constructed of different material, follows its Spanish antecedent, with a few variations that are the creative contribution of the artisan. One article that has changed very little from Spanish tradition is the door. The paneled construction is close to that of its ancestor, except for the wrought iron and brass decoration.

ICONOGRAPHIC FOLK ART

An art form in the Southwest that was produced mostly in New Mexico is the *santo*. Most writers agree about the artistic merit of *santos*, when speaking of those brought from Spain and Mexico.

Celso Gallegos, *santo* carver of Santa Fe, New Mexico.

During the research conducted in the 1934 survey, the field investigators tried to determine whether the representative art designs in New Mexico were used deliberately or were merely attempts at representation, limited by the artisan's art knowledge and his ability to implement it. A particularly realistic example of a carved *santo* was shown to some of the *santeros*, who invariably commented that it was the sort of work they would like to turn out but added, "Uno hace lo que puede," "One does the best one can." Obviously it was not a case of deliberately discarding perspective and anatomy. The same experiment was tried with needleworkers and other practitioners of folk art in an effort to determine whether the designs by New Mexican folk were a set form that some of the vocational centers were trying to impose on trainees as "the way New Mexican folk art should be."

The criticisms of Protestant Anglo-Americans, to whom any form of image veneration was anathema, cannot be expected to be objective; but when Mexican and Spanish churchmen also derided the folk art of the *santeros* and removed some of their products from church altars, one wonders what basis to use in evaluating religious folk art in the Southwest. In all the literature available on this subject the carefully documented study by José E. Espinosa is the most valuable and informative, particularly because, in addition to being a thorough scholar, the author is a New Mexican and a Roman Catholic. He is therefore in a better position to judge the intent of the folk artist when painting or carving a *santo*. In the forward to Espinosa's *Saints in the Valleys*, Fray Angélico Chávez also raises very interesting questions and explains some difficult problems. The oft-repeated statement that the *santero* concentrated his interest on the meaning of the image that he was painting or carving because of his sincere devotion and veneration of the saints was certainly sometimes true, but having watched a number of *santeros* working on consignment for a given sum, I find the claim somewhat exaggerated. No doubt the early *santeros* did try to externalize their deeply-felt spiritual convictions in their products, as Espinosa says. But for the serious critic, it is very difficult to be convinced that a carved representation that violates all the tenets of art is really more than an interesting folk artifact. This is probably why opinions vary so widely about the quality of the *santos* as art forms. In other crafts in which religion is not a factor, the public in general accepts

But in speaking of those that were produced by New Mexican folk carvers and *santo* makers, critics hold a considerable range of opinions, not only about their artistic worth. They also question the objective of the folk wood carver when he turned out a Santo Niño or a San Isidro from a cottonwood tree root. Most critics tend to overstate their position in order to make a point. An example is Boyd's statement that, "if the *santero* concentration of interest in the meaning of the image led him to discard perspective, anatomy, and the third dimension, it seems to have been deliberate and not merely due to incompetence."[6] This seems to imply that the folk *santero*, who had no artistic training or knowledge of anatomy, would have been capable of incorporating into his art, had he wished, all the elements of sculpture employed by the trained artist.

Cristo Rey Church in Santa Fe, New Mexico, the largest adobe church in the United States. It has the artistic features of colonial Spanish architecture. Photograph by Robert H. Martin Photography.

and indeed treasures many forms of folk art.[7]

Regardless of the differences of opinion, the fact remains that for over two centuries the southwestern artisan turned out at home different forms of religious art that, by its very continuity, indicates his perseverance in trying to express himself and his interest in the subject.

The religious art produced by southwestern artisans is divided into several categories, not all of which are exactly like the artifact originally so named. The *retablos*, which in English are called reredos or altar screens, were originally series of scenes with actual figurines, sometimes representing an event or telling a story, something like a diorama. In New Mexico a *retablo* may be a single picture painted on a board and placed behind the altar, or it may be composed of several sections and in varying sizes.

In her book Boyd includes complete tables of religious art, giving the location and a full description of each item. She also includes color plates of some of the outstanding altar screens, such as the one in the mission at Laguna Pueblo and *bultos* by such artists as Fray Andrés García, Bernardo

The altar screen at Cristo Rey Church in Santa Fe, the only stone reredos in the Southwest. It was built in 1761 by Antonio Marín del Valle and his wife, María Ygnacia Martínez de Ugarte, for the military chapel known as La Castrense. In 1859 it was transferred to St. Francis Church and later to its present location. It is sculptured in sandstone and measures eighteen by fourteen feet. Photograph by Robert H. Martin Photography.

Miera y Pacheco, and others. The *bulto* is usually a hand-carved figure of a saint made either in separate sections or in a single piece. Gypsum was used very extensively for bas-reliefs, probably because soft pine and cottonwood did not lend themselves to detailed carving.

The third form of religious art consisted of paintings on wood panels. Originally they were painted on animal hides, and this kind of *santo* drew considerable criticism from the church hierarchy in Mexico, who felt that a religious subject was desecrated when it was painted on an animal skin. As a result, many of the older paintings were taken from the churches and have become lost. Many critics believe that the *santos* painted on this medium had a greater artistic value.

Most of the best examples of religious art have found their way to museum collections throughout the Southwest, but a few good specimens are still in private hands and in mission churches. *Santeros* have become aware of the demand for their products and the high prices that they bring on the market. According to many critics, demand has lowered the artistic value of religious art, and if Espinosa's and Fray Chávez' criteria are applied to these purveyors of what was once a very personal artistic expression, it can be said that religious art is experiencing a decline today.

Enthusiasm for an art form alone is not likely to improve quality, unless different techniques are employed, which will enable the craftsman to fix better the abstraction in his mind when he begins his work. Despite all the rhetoric spent trying to bridge the gap between simple folk craft and creative art, there remains a repetitious sameness in the work of most *santeros*, and there is also a uniform appearance in many *santos* that are supposed to represent different persons. It appears that when a craftsman produces an object he has a tendency to repeat himself every time he attempts to create a different image. There are some variations, but a similarity results from use of the same techniques and also because *santeros*, by and large, are self-taught. Rather than being variants of the Spanish and Mexican models, the New Mexican *santos* are atrophied renditions that have declined over the years from lack of instruction. All students of iconography in the Southwest agree that the earlier forms are much superior to the present *santos*. George Mills believes that this distinctive Spanish-American art form ends in 1900.[8]

One of the reasons for the atrophied condition of iconography, particularly in New Mexico, is

that nine-tenths of the manufacturing methods of *santos bultos* consists not of carving but of simply paring down the cottonwood with a knife. This is whittling pure and simple, because the artisan cuts away from him in long strokes or toward him when putting on the finishing touches. Instead of carving in the strict sense of the word, the *santero* attempts to create a relief by the use of gypsum in modeling facial features, a technique akin to clay modeling.

Second, the *santero* expresses such body attitudes as sitting and reclining by attaching separate parts, such as arms or legs, with wire or leather strands to give them mobility. Comparable figures are carved from a solid piece of wood in South America and in Mexico and have carved facial features. Very seldom does one find joints attached separately except in *títeres*, or marionettes, used on the Day of the Dead.

Some of the best examples of religious art are found at the Central Bank in Ecuador. An eighteenth-century *mestizo* named Capiscara did a polychromed Virgin in wood similar to the one in a low-relief *retablo* by a *santero* of the same period in New Mexico.[9] It compares favorably with the Quiteño's Virgin, except for the latter's more intricately carved work. When Latin-American carvings are placed side by side with those of the same period in the Peninsula, it is difficult to determine the nationality of each specimen because they follow essentially the same technique, a technique that was not taught in New Mexico or if taught has been forgotten.

RELIGIOUS ARCHITECTURE

There developed over the Southwest two architectural designs in the construction of churches, designs that were governed by the building material available and by the long lines of communication, stretching 2000 miles to northern New Mexico. The periods of history during which the churches were built were also reflected in the façades and interiors of the structures. The simpler, more austere designs were predominantly used in New Mexico. The use of adobe for walls made it necessary to build much more massive walls than those of brick and mortar. That did not necessarily detract from the beauty of the churches. The church in Ranchos de Taos and the ruins of the one in Pecos are good examples of the utilization of local building materials. After the Anglo-American occupation, the use of tin and the substitution of

Ranchos de Taos Church, built in 1772 and unchanged except for periodic refurbishing with adobe. Photograph by José Gonçalves.

sharp spires for the traditional towers resulted in some less-artistic variations, such as the churches in Isleta and the one in Old Albuquerque.

In San Antonio the churches built in the eighteenth century were large because they also housed large craft centers. In California, where nature was more benign, it was possible to add landscaping that the churches of the arid Southwest could not have. California also had available wrought iron and materials brought by ship. The *atajos* of mules over the Camino Real could not carry large enough

quantities of building supplies to Santa Fe and the northern villages.

The early churches were in constant danger from hostile Indians, who burned down the structures from time to time. It usually happened that during rebuilding the style of the church, or at least of the front façade, was altered to suit the taste of the current administration. This practice continues to some extent today, though the only enemy today is the weather—and an occasional barbarous tourist.

San Felipe de Neri Church in Albuquerque, New Mexico, built around 1707 and occupied continuously for the longest period of any church in the Southwest. Photograph by José Gonçalves.

Isleta Pueblo Church in Isleta, New Mexico, as it looked in 1940. The Indians from this pueblo went down to Ysleta, Texas, near El Paso, during the Indian uprising of 1680 and founded the Ysleta church there. Courtesy of the Coronado Cuarto Centennial.

The preparation and preservation of food were domestic crafts that developed in the Southwest as soon as the settlers began producing their own foodstuffs. The Oñate Expedition brought with it livestock and staples. But during the first years of settlement in New Mexico, the colonists survived largely on provisions the Pueblo Indians shared with them. The preservation of supplies to be used the year round depended on the length of the growing season and the climate. The European practice of drying fruits was sometimes extended to vegetables, after the custom of the Indians. In California and in south Texas, where the growing season was much longer, there was less need to dehydrate foods, but in New Mexico, Arizona, and southwest Texas preservation by drying was a necessity. Eventually dehydration of fruits and vegetables became common, and various early-day dishes prepared from dried foods are still popular today.

DAIRY PRODUCTS

In the semiarid regions of the Southwest, where forage was limited, the settlers introduced goats as supplements to the few cattle. Goat's milk was used as a beverage in some households, but goat cheese was more extensively used in the rural villages and towns, particularly in Texas and New Mexico. Carnuel, a village ten miles east of Albuquerque on Highway 40, has a long-established tradition as a producer of excellent *queso de cabra*. The hilly country that surrounds the village lends itself to goat raising.

Hispanic folk in the Southwest have never been very selective in animal husbandry. Cattle were free to roam on the open range, where they were left to fend for themselves and to increase where there was abundant forage, as in south Texas and California. The milk from cows kept close to the home was utilized as food. Milk was used as a beverage or allowed to clabber and turned into *cuajada*, by straining the *suero*, or whey, and serving the curd. The cream was skimmed and churned into butter or used as a sour-cream spread. From the whey was prepared a finely textured cottage cheese called *requesón*, which was sometimes enriched by the addition of cream. Unlike *cuajada*, *requesón* was cooked like today's cottage cheese.

When there was an accumulation of sour milk, it was combined with a proportion of sweet milk, to which the juice of the wild *trompillo* or *tomatillo* (*Solanum elaegnifolimn* Cav.) was added as a substitute for rennet to curdle the milk to produce the clabber. This combination of ingredients was cooked in a deep pan and stirred until it was *en punto*, or ready to be pressed into small cakes while hot. *Asaderos*, as this "instant" cheese is called, was used in making *chile con queso*, a traditional dish that the late President Lyndon B. Johnson served at his inaugural banquet.

The folk also made use of colostrum, or *calostros*. Some families boiled the thick milk, which cows produce the first few days after parturition, and served it. Rural folk in some regions believed that colostrum was for the newborn calf and refused to milk a cow "come fresh" for the first week. Others refused it, believing that it was milk that had remained in the udders after the cows went dry and should therefore be cleaned out to make way for the fresh milk. The most highly prized milk was *leche de apoyo*, the "strippings" that a cow held back for her calf. When colonists had several milking cows, they reserved the *leche de apoyo* until there was enough to make a rich cheese known as *queso de apoyo*.

PUERCO, COCHINO, MARRANO, OR *CERDO*

Pork was known by four different names, depending on the region and the cultural background of the speaker. In New Mexico, *cochino* was the most common name for "pig"; and farther south along the Mexican border the porkers were called *marranos*. When speaking of hog meat, Mexicans normally used the term *carne de puerco*, but urban individuals who ate pork but never raised pigs used the more cultured term *cerdo*. Idiomatically, as in English, a person with low sanitary or moral standards was called *cochino;* if the person was really degraded, he was called *marrano.*

Regardless of the name by which it was known, the by-products from pork were almost identical all over the Southwest, and the manner in which various foods were preserved did not vary noticeably. The slaughtering of a pig specially fed for the occasion was usually referred to as *la matanza del cochino* or *del puerco,* depending on the region. In New Mexico and west Texas slaughtering took place in the fall. Friends and neighbors were invited after the "preliminaries" were over and the *chicharrones* or cracklings were ready to come out of the *cazo* where they were rendered. *Beneficiar un puerco* meant to make proper use of all the edible parts of the carcass. Blood sausage was known by the more poetic name *morcilla* and was prepared both sweet and salty, according to taste. The sweet variety was prepared with raisins, piñóns, or other nutmeats; and the *salada* was spiced with garlic and other herbs, but not chile. Another sausage made from pork, and sometimes from beef and pork, was the well-known *chorizo,* which today is produced by packing houses in the Southwest labeled "Mexican sausage" or simply "chorizo sausage."

The most popular product of pork was *chicharrones.* There were two varieties of this product, one of which has become Anglicized to some extent and is sometimes sold under the same Spanish name. The *chicharrones* could be a gourmet's dish when properly prepared. The *lonjas,* or thick strips of fat removed from the meat, were cut into small cubes and fried in *cazos.* The rendered fat was removed and poured into large cans. The cubes were pressed to release the fat, and removed to a large skillet, where they were browned further until they released most of the fat. If the host of the *matanza* was well versed in making *chicharrones,* he would add cream and salt as they browned. In preparation for the occasion a couple of *tortilleras,* or tortilla makers, had been summoned to pass out hot, fresh corn tortillas to the guests. They made *burritos* with the hot *chicharrones* and added a bit of Mexican sauce made from fresh tomatoes, green chile, and fine-cut onion spiced with garlic. That was the moment they were all waiting for. If the host knew how to prepare golden brown *chicharrones,* it was worth being invited to *la matanza del cochino.*

The second kind of *chicharrón* was made from the rind, after the fat was removed. The strips of fresh pork skin were cut into pieces two by three inches and baked in the oven, where they curled and burst under intense heat. These were called *chicharrones de vieja.* Today this kind of crackling is made from bacon rind, but the Hispanos did not make bacon, and very rarely did they cure hams. It is somewhat strange that pork was not prepared in this fashion for preservation, particularly since the Spaniards used it widely in the province of Estremadura, which sent so many *conquistadores* to the New World.

Pork, unlike beef, did not lend itself to drying, because the fat had a tendency to become rancid. To preserve it, the Hispanos, as well as the Mexicans throughout the Southwest, used a marinating process called *adobo.* Eventually this process gave rise to the well-known barbecued pork ribs. The marinating sauce was a mixture of vinegar, wine, garlic, red chile, and other spices in which ribs and pork loins were soaked for a week or ten days. The meat was hung out to dry and then stored indoors under proper ventilation to avoid molding. When used, the meat and ribs were usually grilled, *a la parilla,* and basted with the same sauce.

Other uses of pork included *queso de puerco,* or head cheese. In the preservation of all these foods no canning process was used. Therefore, such by-products as pig's feet had to be used fresh in a dish called *posole,* prepared with hominy and served like a stew. Fine-chopped green onions and oregano were served on a side dish.

DEHYDRATED FOODS

The dry, sunny climate of the Southwest was just right for dehydrating meats, vegetables, and fruits. Beef and buffalo meat were cut into thin strips called *charqui,* rendered by frontiersmen into "jerky," and hung out to dry. When the meat was dried, it was usually referred to as *carne seca.* This was one of the products that was taken to trade at the Chihuahua fair every year. It was also used as a sort of Indian pemmican; it was pounded on a *metate* into small particles and packed with red chile powder.

Housewives dehydrated surplus vegetables and fruits to store for winter. Tomatoes too ripe to market were halved and dried on the flat roofs of southwestern homes. Green ears of corn were parboiled, dried, husked, and stored like grain for winter use. This grain was called *chacales* in most of the Southwest, except in northern New Mexico, where it was known as *chicos.* When ready to serve, the dried corn was boiled back to life. Squash was cut into slices called *rueditas*, because they resembled "little wheels" when dry. Green beans were really "string beans" when they were parboiled and strung like beads with needle and thread. Vegetables so prepared took the place of the modern frozen or canned foods. Those wanting to prepare *chile pasado*, dried green chile, roasted the peppers on the stove, peeled them, and hung them by the stems in bunches to dry. When it was time to use the chiles, the cook simply immersed them in boiling water or added them to whatever dish she was preparing. The red chile variety, so well known today, had the same origin; that is, it was dehydrated red chile put up in *ristras*, or strings; it dried in the fall and could be kept indefinitely.

Dried fruits were not a unique product; the practice of drying ripe fruit was well known to all Europeans. The only difference was in the name used for this product. In Spanish the name *orejón* is applied to dried peaches, but in the Southwest the Hispano Mexicans included all fruits in this category and even spoke of *orejón de tomate*. One of the dried fruits often mentioned by the first Anglo-Americans was dried grape clusters, or raisins, called *pasas*, which they enjoyed in El Paso and in California. The Indians of New Mexico and Colorado dried wild plums, and the Hispanic settlers followed suit, picking wild fruits and drying them without removing the pits.

FOOD PREPARATION

Like all other pioneer people, the Hispanos of colonial days had to use their ingenuity to utilize the staples available and the quantity of food on hand. Their Mediterranean-Mexican forebears had provided them with simple food dishes made palatable by the addition of spices, in which chile in various forms was an important ingredient. The menu of southwestern Hispanos became very early a combination of Indian, Mexican, and Spanish dishes. The Indian foods were adapted to a more European taste and became the basis for much of the Mexican fare served today in restaurants. Some of the more complicated foods, such as *tamales* and *enchiladas*, were not daily fare, because it took a good deal of time to prepare them.

One Spanish dish that the southwesterners never lost was soup—not just a simple variety, but one prepared with different kinds of meat, vegetables, spices, and the omnipresent *garbanzo*. The name for this dish varied according to the region, and even in families. In northern Mexico and California it was known either as *caldo* or *cocido*, while in the northern part of the New Mexican colony and into southern Colorado it kept the old Spanish name *puchero*. Beef, pork, and chicken were generally the meats used, depending on what was available; the more affluent used all three kinds of meat, producing a typical *cocido madrileño*. The generic name for soup was *caldo*, but in the Southwest and in northern Mexico, a variation of the Spanish *sopa*, meaning soup, was applied to rice, spaghetti, or even beans. It meant that the rice was "soupy," hence *sopa de arroz*, *sopa de fideo*, and many others. On the other hand, if there were meat, potatoes, and other leftovers, the lady of the house prepared a *caldillo* by adding fresh green coriander leaves, diced onions, and stock. Unlike *sopa*, this dish was a true variety of soup or *caldo*, prepared without the long *cocido* process.

Mutton and goat were two meats enjoyed throughout the Southwest long before the arrival of the Anglo-American frontiersmen. In the pastoral culture sheep were readily available for food. Mutton has always been highly regarded by Englishmen as well as by Spaniards, but the Anglo-Americans evidently lost the taste for mutton. It was therefore strange to read comments by travelers that no one could prepare this meat like the New Mexicans. Mutton is without a doubt a meat equal to the best fish, according to the Spanish proverb:

> De la mar el mero;
> de la tierra el carnero.
>
> Bass from the sea,
> and mutton from the land.

Mutton chops were usually cooked with rice, but the back was prepared in an *olla*, or deep stewing pot, and flavored with red chile pods and other spices. This was the ordinary *estofado* cooked in the fireplace. The *asado*, or roast, was common on winter days, when the meat was grilled in the fireplace.

The most common *asado* in the Southwest, particularly along the Mexican border and in early California, was *cabrito asado*, a roast made from a very young goat spiced with garlic. This dish is still served in restaurants and private clubs in northern Mexico but is seldom seen on menus in New Mexico. Many dishes prepared by Hispanic people combined several ingredients, a practical method for stretching food when there were no great quantities of each staple. The "catalyst" generally used was chile in various forms. A small amount of meat combined with potatoes and other leftovers could be turned into a very tasty *caldillo* or *guiso* by the addition of a bit of garlic and liberal portions of chile, either red or green, depending on the season. They soon discovered that ground or diced meat would produce an unusual dish when combined with a thick sauce of red chile, properly flavored with garlic, *cominos*, and oregano. If the chile peppers were too hot, they softened the *picante* with tomatoes. The housewife knew that a good sauce of roasted green peppers, fresh tomatoes, and diced green onion could make up for any deficiencies in the meal put on the table.

One of the most versatile staples in the Hispanic Southwest was corn. Many of the dishes made from it were derived from Indian culture, but the Hispanos and the Mexicans expanded the preparation of corn by combining it with other ingredients. In addition to plain corn on and off the cob, hominy, and corn bread, *maíz* was used in other ways. When the New Mexicans' larder was low, they could prepare *chaquegüe*, a form of Indian corn mush, which in the South is called grits. Parched corn was ground into a meal called *pinole*, used as a cereal by adding brown sugar, a bit of cinnamon and clove, and serving it with milk. It was also made into a drink called *atole de pinole*, which took the place of coffee. *Pinole* flour was boiled and sweetened into a light gruellike drink to which milk was added when available. *Atole* was the standard drink of those who could not afford coffee or chocolate. The simpler *atole* was made from the *masa* used for making *tortillas*. This corn dough was cooked in water to a thin consistency or it was boiled in milk and sweetened. *Atole blanco*, the simplest to make, was the poor people's drink throughout all of New Spain and the Southwest.

Chacales, dried, parboiled corn on the cob, was cooked with any meat available to produce a very good combination. *Menudo*, made from beef viscera, was cooked with corn, to produce a very tasty dish that was particularly in demand for the morning-after-the-night-before. Another variation of the same was *posole*, except that it was preferably made with pig's knuckles. When all these corn foods are added to *torillas*, *tacos*, *enchiladas*, *chalupas*, *tostadas*, and *tamales*, it can be easily understood why corn became so important to the Hispano Mexicans.

The settlers who came to the Southwest after the end of the sixteenth century had already been introduced to various forms of Indian cooking in the Mexican plateau, but the adaptations made later in Mexico were not known to them after they became isolated in the northern provinces of the empire. For this reason the Hispano Mexicans relied largely on traditional Spanish cooking, except for a few items such as corn *tortillas* and *chaquegüe*, which the northern Indians made.

Wheat *tortillas* replaced the corn product in Hispanic homes in northern Mexico and most of the Southwest. It was considerably easier and faster for the housewife to prepare the biscuitlike dough and roll it out than to go through the long process of making *nixtamal* by parboiling corn with lime and then washing it five times before grinding it over a backbreaking *metate*. After the *masa* or dough was prepared, she still had the laborious work of patting out each individual *tortilla* cake between her hands and baking them over the griddle. With wheat *tortillas* she could have bread on the table in a matter of minutes.

In homes that had Indian servants, the corn *tortillas* continued to be made, because the *molienda*, or grinding, was common work for Indian women. Cornbread was prepared in a number of variations; the dough was mixed with pork *chicharrones* and baked in the conical ovens outside the house. It provided a good variety for the home. They could also make *sopaipillas*, a fried bread for which New Mexico has earned a deserved reputation. This Spanish confection was well known in the sixteenth century, to judge by the reference made to it in one of Lope de Vega's plays: "Que vengan las sopaipas." The Southwest added the diminutive *illas* from which the modern name derives.

Another variation of this fried bread was the more sophisticated cruller called *buñuelo*, prepared with egg batter, spiced with cinnamon and clove, and served in early days with a thin grape jelly called *arrope*. Both the *buñuelo* and the jelly are Spanish products known all over the Hispanic world. In the absence of grape jelly, a plain brown-sugar syrup called *piloncillo* in northern New Mexico and *panocha* elsewhere in the Southwest, was used. In the north another dish by the latter name was prepared from ground sprouted wheat molded into cakes and baked, or it was served as a thick gruel with sugar and milk. Another product made from wheat flour was the *bizcochito*, still served on holidays through the Southwest but particularly in New Mexico and Chihuahua. It is a small fat cookie sprinkled with sugar and cinnamon and served with chocolate, coffee, or wine, depending on the season.

Many of the dishes that the Hispano Mexicans of the past century prepared are now served in only a few of the more traditional households, where they still enjoy a *pipían de pollo*. This dish was once one of the specialties of the Southwest. *Pipían* was a sauce made with almonds and served over chicken or other roasted meats. Another favorite in the ranchos of Texas was *barbacoa*, a side of beef, pork, or mutton, prepared in a way the early Spaniards learned from the Indians of the Caribbean and the Central American coast. Like many Mexican dishes common today, it was an adaptation that was practical for feeding large crowds. True *barbacoa* is not prepared with bottled sauce and bottled smoke to give the impression that the meat has been roasted in a pit. Originally the Indians wrapped the meat in banana leaves and buried it in a pit, after heating several large rocks that held the heat to roast the carcass. The Anglo-Texans have been instrumental in keeping this traditional dish by preparing from time to time an old fashioned pit barbecue with all the sauce and trimmings.

The food that today is called "Mexican" attained popularity gradually through a combining of elements of Indian and Spanish cooking. Basically such dishes as *tamales* and *enchiladas* were transformations of simple Indian dishes. The cheese and onions and the oil for frying the *tortillas* in preparing *enchiladas* are Spanish adaptations of the Aztec *chilaquiles*. When other variations are prepared with breast of chicken and toasted almonds, Mexican cooks are combining ingredients that Moctezuma never tasted or heard of. The same may be said about the *tamal*, one of the most elaborate Mexican dishes, second only to *mole poblano*, when *tamales* are made from scratch at home.

ANGLO FRONTIERSMEN'S ENDORSEMENT

It is not surprising that Anglo-American frontiersmen, traveling across mountains and deserts, should find Hispanic food in the Southwest so appetizing after living off the land when their bacon and flour gave out. Pike spoke glowingly of both the food and the way it was served when he was a guest of the Spanish government at the Palace of the Governors in Santa Fe. He made this entry in his diary:

> We then sat down to dinner which consisted of various dishes, excellent wine, and to crown all, we were waited on by half a dozen of those beautiful girls, who like Hebe at the feast of the gods, converted our wine into nectar, and with their ambrosial breath shed incense on our cups.[1]

Josiah Gregg, too, while not as poetic as the young lieutenant, praised the qualities of the dried fruits produced in El Paso Valley and other foodstuffs, which he found unusually good. The well-spiced food served by Hispano-Mexican settlers on occasion must have been a welcome change from the bland foods that the newcomers had lived on for months at a time.

STORAGE

Families who wished to enjoy fresh fruits and vegetables after the harvest season built an outdoor earth-covered bin called an *almárcigo*, from the Spanish *almáciga*, or plant nursery. They also used the name *bodega*, not only for a wine cellar but also for a storage of produce. An *almárcigo* was built by digging a three-foot-deep trench near the back of the house. A gabled framework of juniper or cottonwood poles extending to the ground was built over it and roofed with tied bunches of small branches, reeds, or any other available material. In the hot, sandy country of west Texas and southern New Mexico they used a straight-stemmed plant called *cachanilla*, usually found growing up to five feet tall along the lower ends of *arroyos*. Over this storage-bin roof they shoveled about a foot of earth to insulate it from the cold. It had an entrance at one end, also covered with earth when not in use. The last growth of green tomatoes, potatoes, sweet potatoes, all varieties of root vegetables, melons, and a species of winter watermelon called *chilacayote* were stored in the *almárcigo*. Until the innovation of modern food-preservation facilities, the southwesterners combined traditional practices of European origin, a few Indian borrowings, and their own ingenuity to survive.

Anyone who has lived in the Southwest, where Hispanic and Anglo-American cultures meet, is aware of the differences between the two civilizations. But simply because they are not alike in every respect does not mean that they are totally different. Aside from the Indians, who were already there when the first Europeans arrived, the Spaniards and their culture should not be entirely strange to Anglo-Americans, who also originated in Europe. Social scientists have explored the nature of Hispanic culture in the Southwest; over the past century and a half historians, travelers, and traders have made many observations that, if not always accurate, at least indicate how apparent these cultural contrasts are, even to the casual observer. It does not follow, however, that all differences are mutually antagonistic simply because they are at variance with what people believe to be the norm. In fact, many find complementary features in this variety of customs, values, and attitudes that make life more interesting and enjoyable. The interest is often heightened by the realization that the southwesterners, whether Indian or Spanish, antedate the Europeans of the eastern seaboard by a considerable period of time and as a result give the country a strong sense of belonging.

CULTURAL DIFFERENCES

Many cultural differences between Hispanic and Anglo-American peoples are implicit in the conceptual content of the languages spoken by the two civilizations, and their value systems stem from a long series of historical circumstances to which the culture bearers accommodate themselves. The history of these two empire builders of the New World does not begin in North America, although that is the arena where they eventually met. The cultural differences that have resulted in a lack of complete mutuality and harmony stem from their European heritage; those differences were discernible before either culture set foot on the North American continent.

English culture was basically insular, geographically and ideologically, more integrated as a whole, except for theological differences, and was zealous to maintain its racial "purity." Spanish culture, on the other hand, was peninsular, a geographical circumstance that made it a catchall for Mediterranean, central European, and North African peoples over a period of twenty-five centuries. The composite nature of the population produced a marked regionalism that prevented close integration, except for religion, and led to a very strong sense of individualism. These differences were reflected in the colonizing of both countries. The English maintained their insularity and, in the main, isolated themselves from the Indians physically and culturally, with the result that the latter were pushed aside, and eventually confined on reservations. The Spaniards, with strong notions about *pureza de sangre*, or purity of blood, among the nobility, were not collectively adverse to adding one more strain to their racial makeup by assimilating the aborigines, through the instrumentality of the *encomienda*, the *repartimiento*, and other more personal means. Hernán Cortés led the way by siring the first *mestizo* in North America, and the rest of the conquistadors followed suit with prolific results. The ultimate products of these two colonizing enterprises meet today in the Southwest and become polarized when trying to reconcile their ancestral backgrounds and several centuries of life in the Western Hemisphere.

Many basic cultural configurations underlie the behavior patterns of these two American peoples. Anglo-American culture was guided by an absolutist morality at the onset, that is, a culture wherein all dominant values were considered identical for all, regardless of time and place. Such values as justice, charity, and honesty were considered the superior order for all men and were governed largely by biblical tenets that were later embodied in the United States Constitution. The Spaniards brought with them a more relativistic viewpoint, seeing fewer moral implications in

tesy is spontaneous. One is never haunted by the guilty question, "Did I say or do the right thing?" after having met someone of particular interest and importance.

There is no "right or wrong" way of doing in Hispanic social behavior, any more than there are "right or wrong" answers. In Spanish a person gives a correct or an incorrect answer, and in society one hears someone say that another person is *muy correcto*, meaning in English, that he does the right thing. The Anglo-American is concerned about doing the right or the wrong thing, as much as he is about feeling good or feeling bad. In Spanish one renders the expression, "You are right," by simply saying "Tiene usted razón"; "You are reasonable." Instead of feeling "bad," one feels ill, and instead of feeling "good," one feels well. The fact that the Spanish always use "ill" and "well" instead of the American "good" and "bad" leads one to conjecture whether this choice of vocabulary is a residue of the Puritan ethic.

The contrast of Hispanic and Anglo-American customs is also noticeable in such a simple act as offering a person a drink or a beverage. In Spanish the guest or invitee is asked to accept or turn down the offer when asked "¿Gusta usted?" "Would you *like* to have a drink?" In English one is more likely to say, "Have a drink," implying that the standard thing to do is to have a drink. To ask a person if he wants to have a drink seems to imply that he will be offered one only if he wants one, in which case it is a courtesy, as well as an accommodation. That both Anglo-Americans and Hispanos drink does not vitiate the fact that in Spanish one is invited to make an individual choice while in English the other is almost expected to accept one.

At the expense of belaboring the inherent implications of language, it may be reasonable to say that behavior patterns are circumscribed, to a larger extent than we often realize, by cultural limitations imposed by the language one speaks. It is difficult to say whether the word concept precedes the action or attitude, but some anthropological linguists believe that man's freedom extends no further than the limits set by the language he speaks. Peter Farb says that, linguistically speaking, man is not born free, because he inherits a language filled with quaint sayings, archaisms, ponderous grammar, and fixed ways of expression that may shackle his thoughts. "Language," he adds, "becomes man's shaper of ideas rather than simply his tool for reporting ideas."[2]

According to Sapir, man does not live in the midst of the whole world, but only in a part of it, the part that his language lets him know. "He is," says Sapir, "very much at the mercy of the particular language which has become the medium of expression of his group."[3] The real world is to a large extent unconsciously built on the language habits of the group, and the worlds in which different societies live are distinct worlds, not merely the same world with different labels attached. The world of Hispanic peoples tends to be much more individualized, and the language carries with it individual implications of which a person may or may not be aware.

Often an expression of courtesy is a mere gesture that need not come to fruition as a completed action. When one admires an object in someone else's possession, the owner may offer it by saying, "It is yours," and the person returns the compliment by answering, "It is already in better hands." Again, in English the courteous thing to say to a guest is, "Make yourself at home," while the Spanish expression is, "This is your home." The idea behind each expression is the same, but the expressions differ.

At times a feeling may be conveyed by an incorrect expression, as it was by an American Methodist bishop attending a conference in Mexico before the revolution. As he rounded the corner of a busy street, he collided with an Indian woman vendor who was carrying a large basket of fresh bread balanced on her head. They landed on the sidewalk, surrounded by sundry varieties of Mexican sweet rolls. The bishop tried to think of something that would express his regret to the vendor, and he summoned a very expressive "¡Muchas gracias!" delivered in his best clerical tones. The Indian woman became amused when she realized the foreign clergyman's dilemma and then accepted his thanks with a very courteous, "¡De nada, señor cura!" "Not at all, Mr. Curate." A person accustomed to courtesy, she understood his intent and gave him the proper answer to his incorrect expression in such a manner that it made the bishop feel that she had understood.

Unfortunately many urban Hispanos in the Southwest have forgotten the courtesy that Anglo-Americans noticed among their forebears. In some small villages and mountain towns, where vestiges of old Hispanic culture still cling, people cultivate the amenities of old. A guest in a Taos home played over and over a record of a song that he particularly liked. When he left, the family packed the record in his traveling bag with a note saying that they hoped he would continue to enjoy it at home. The rector of the University of Zaragoza in Spain noticed how much his guest from the United States enjoyed some *jotas* being played over a loudspeaker in a music store. When the visitor departed, there was a package at the desk with a note expressing the wish that he would enjoy the *jotas* after a "bon voyage." From a university president in Spain to a Hispano villager in New Mexico there is a considerable distance, but it is greatly shortened when both respond to the same heritage. A practical-minded Anglo-American might have sent a check to the record company, asking that the selection admired by his friend be mailed directly to him.

CHARITY AND PHILANTHROPY

Another cultural contrast in the Southwest may be observed in the varying ways the cultures share part of their material substance with the less fortunate members of society. The Anglo-American usually contributes regularly to all sorts of eleemosynary societies and institutions, some of which solicit funds from door to door with a highly organized system of drive captains or neighborhood supervisors. He also endows foundations, research centers, and scientific laboratories. This kind of giving is philanthropy, a form of contribution that to a Hispano seems too impersonal. He prefers to bestow his contribution directly on the recipient, where he can personally see the person he is helping; this is an act of charity. Because of this there are beggars all over the Hispanic world, whose personal appeals and supplications appear to an Anglo-American as a survival of the *patrón* mentality.

Spanish writer Díaz Plaja has observed this trait in Spain, and so it is logical to find it also among southwestern Hispanos, whose culture is largely derived from colonial days. Says Díaz Plaja:

It is true that organizing committees to help those whom fortune has disinherited would require a capacity for collective action which the Spaniard doesn't possess, but show any citizen of the peninsula or its islands an unfortunate man and he is likely to go to his assistance, however poor he may be himself.[4]

The Hispanos of the Southwest contribute sparingly to such organizations as United Way or Red Cross; in contrast to the practice of Anglo-American society, they are considered lacking in civic-mindedness. Only those who have become acculturated to Anglo-American life participate to the same extent as everyone else. There are, in fact, very few foundations created and endowed by Hispanic people, anywhere. On the other hand, the Spaniards say that if half of Spain were wealthy, the other half would be beggars. Personal solicitation is not countenanced by Anglo-American society, unless it is done for a benevolent organization, a church, or a civic enterprise. (Some very clever individuals, aware of American philanthropic practices, do not resort to outright begging but "collect" for whatever institutions or cause they ingeniously invent, and often they do well until the law catches up with them.)

BEING AND DOING

Another source of cultural contrast lies in the difference between *being* and *doing*. Back in 1938, I referred to this as "the right to do" and "the right to be"; since then the classifications of "action culture" and "being culture" have become popular among anthropologists. An action-conditioned Anglo-American cannot fully enjoy leisure, because, even when he takes a vacation, he takes along a lot of unfinished business to keep him busy while he is "doing nothing." The pleasure of doing nothing does not apply so aptly to an Anglo-American as it does to a Hispano, who can say, when asked what he is doing, that he is merely *veriwelleando;* that is, he does very well while doing nothing.

Americanos are usually so engrossed with doing that they go to the dogs in their leisure time. In contrast with Hispanos, they claim that "an idle mind is the devil's workshop." This conditioning begins early among young people, who, the minute they find themselves idle, call their friends on the phone and propose, "Let's do something!" Hispanos with that much time on their hands, and a comparable amount of economic resources, do not find it necessary to invent anything just for the sake of doing something. If they must do something, they prefer to do what comes natural to young people, and that does not have to be invented.

Doing and being present a number of interesting contrasts. Even when he is trying to be individualistic, the Anglo-American achieves it by the things he does. When the young Anglo-Amer-

Hispanos *veriwelleando,* "doing very well doing nothing."

ican generation decided to "be themselves," as they called it, to get away from the standardization of the establishment, they let their hair grow, wore odds and ends for clothing, and even went barefooted. They ended up doing the same things and simply created another stereotype. The freedom enjoyed by the individuality of being rather than doing makes it unnecessary for Hispanos to attempt to be different, and their similarity lies in that they are all different, except when they become acculturated to "hippyism."

The sense of being leads to another complicated form of individuality, which in Spanish is called *amor propio.* It is usually misunderstood and translated as "self-love" and characterized as false pride. The pride of being one's self is an innate pride in being simply a member of the human race, with no economic or social considerations; consequently a Hispano cannot put it in his pocket and forget it. The freedom of being oneself, without conforming to the image of the group, naturally leads to an extreme sense of individualism, which, when allowed to run its full course, turns into personalism, a very common occurrence in Latin-American *caudillos* and not unknown to Mexican-American or Chicano leaders in the Southwest.

This exaltation of the self puzzles Anglo-Americans considerably and sometimes leads into misunderstandings and even fatal confrontations. *The right to be* may be a survival of the old Spanish honor code, by which a man's soul, the essense of his being, cannot be compromised under any circumstances. The peasant Pedro Crespo in Calderón's *Alcalde de Zalamea* refuses to com-

promise his personal honor—even for his king— because "honor is the patrimony of the soul, and the soul belongs to God." *Amor propio* is used in Hispanic society as an instrument for strengthening character and not necessarily as a justification for unbridled reaction. The latter is called *desmande,* or lawlessness, and vitiates *amor propio.*

It has taken years of national social strife to bring Anglo-Americans to the point of at least tolerating the idea that a man has the right to be black, Mexican, Oriental, or whatever, without being subject to exclusion and discrimination. An interesting contrast is provided by the Spaniards, who deprive less fortunate members of society of the *right to do* but insist that the *right to be* gives them a measure of freedom that is worth more. Spanish essayist Julio Camba once wrote:

Isn't Spanish liberty worth a hundredfold? There may not be freedom of speech, but there exists a freedom of being. One is allowed to be what he pleases: Russian, Australian, or Chinese; be sad or jovial, ingenious or stupid, elegant or careless, blond or brunette. [5]

The same contrast occurs when inquiries are made in English in an attempt to determine a person's source of pride. The question is asked, "What has he *done* to be so proud?" Pride is based on what a person does, on accomplishment, in a doing culture. Another question asked among club ladies when appraising an absent member is, "What does her husband *do?*" In a doing culture that is important. But in a being culture one simply asks, "Who *is* her husband?" and the implicit meaning is an inquiry into the worthiness of the person, which is not necessarily based on what he does. Again, when an Anglo-American introduces himself to a person of importance, he will give his name and indicate what he does by way of identification. He is Mr. So-and-So, manager or president of Such-and-Such. In Spanish, this would sound ludicrous, and to attempt it would be awkward.

An interesting experiment was conducted in 1963 by a team of psychologists from the University of Guadalajara and the University of Michigan with seventy-four upper-middle-class students from each university. It was a semantic differential method for measuring ways of resolving interpersonal conflict in the two cultures. Individualism and personalism were found to be central values in the Mexican students. This was explained by saying that, for a Mexican, his own value as a person was derived from his awareness that he is unique and in his being, not, as in the view of the Anglo-Americans, because of concrete accomplishments. Therefore, the Mexican is more disturbed by a criticism of his *being* than by any criticism of an *action* that manifests learned skills. Efficiency and accomplishment are derived char-acteristics that do not affect worthiness in the Mexican, whereas in the American worthiness is equated with success, a value of highest priority in American culture. In other words, the study revealed a marked contrast between the value of being and the value of doing, one of the many contrasts between Hispanic and Anglo-American cultures.[6]

Hispanic people in the Southwest have experienced three distinct periods of change and development over the last 375 years, and they are now in the midst of a very fractionated and controversial fourth one. When the current period has run its course, the end result may determine the nature of this culture and the place that it will occupy in American society. This consideration is essential, regardless of the direction eventually taken, because all the persons concerned will still be residents and citizens of the United States.

The first stage of Hispanic culture began with the arrival of Don Juan de Oñate and his settling expedition in 1598 and continued, except for the interlude of the Indian revolt of 1680, relatively unchanged until Mexican independence in 1821. During this period of two and a quarter centuries the culture that was to prevail among southwestern Hispano Mexicans became well established. The ethnic pattern was the same then, except for the proportions of the various components and the names by which they were known. There were few Spaniards, many more *criollos*, the usual preponderance of *mestizos*, and Indians in varying degrees of Hispanicization. The rest were Indians who lived in the various pueblos and a number of tribes who led a seminomadic existence. By the end of the first period the original area of settlement had extended through other expeditions to the California coast, to Texas, and to Arizona. Except for adaptations required by climate, geography, and by the presence or absence of basic natural resources, the Hispanos followed the traditional customs and folkways uniformly known throughout the Southwest.

The second period was violently ushered in by the long struggle for independence from Spain, after which the original Hispanic culture began to acquire regional characteristics. After 1821 some of the outlying provinces like New Mexico began to feel the influence of Anglo-American culture with the arrival of trappers and traders, who were allowed greater latitude under the Mexican regime. It was the beginning of an influence that was to

produce many changes in the long-established Hispanic civilization and eventually to engulf it. In Texas the change that took place was more than a gradual influence. First was the arrival of large numbers of Anglo-American families at the invitation of the Spanish government. These families became permanent residents, who beckoned to others, who followed into that part of the Southwest throughout the Mexican period. When Texas became a separate nation, with a different cultural tradition, unsympathetic to the one under which the region had been settled, Hispanic culture was not only influenced but replaced or separated as a minority culture. The original settlers, now known as Mexicans, were pushed into the background in a coexistence in which they had very little participation.

In California the cultural development of the original settlers was conditioned by their late arrival in the Southwest, by the benign nature of the climate, and by the clerical state set up by the Franciscans who established the missions. The unorganized aborigines, although not very coopera-

Concha Ortíz y Pino of the prominent New Mexican cattle-raising family in Spanish dress at the Santa Fe Fiesta in 1936. She is a direct descendant of Pedro Bautista Pino, New Mexican delegate to the Spanish Cortes in 1812.

tive, were less troublesome than the roaming Navajos, Comanches, and Apaches of other parts of the Southwest. The settlers on the West Coast were not happy about the neglect of their welfare during the Spanish regime and even less so under the Mexican government that followed independence. They adopted the name Californio largely to disassociate themselves from a virtual colonial status. The secularization of the missions by the Mexican government furnished hundreds of Californios with land and cattle with which to establish more ranchos, thus increasing what was already a semilanded aristocracy of cattlemen, who led a different existence from that of their confreres in New Mexico and Texas. It was inevitable that, as products of a caste society, the Californios, too, should develop distinctions based on wealth rather than on no-longer-existent titles of nobility. The former convicts and other undesirables sent into the region by the Mexican government and the freeing of Indians and laborers helped establish a class system. The various classes were referred to as Mexicans, *cholos*, and rancheros, the last being the privileged group around which developed a culture somewhat romantically called the halcyon days of California. By contrast with the rest of the population, the rancheros did live a life of affluence and leisure, but their natural gaiety and proclivity for enjoyment may have given the mistaken impression that they were totally idle and lived in a virtual paradise.

In New Mexico the period from 1821 to 1848 was one of gradual engulfment, first by the trappers and merchants and eventually by the confusion created with last-minute land grants by which property changed hands rapidly, sometimes without the full knowledge of those directly affected. There were no Alamo incidents, no rancheros with fertile lands to be coveted, and no gold rushes to arouse the greed of the so-called argonauts, hungrier for gold than any conquistador ever was. The Santa Fe Trail brought from the East not only men and women but a good amount of material culture, which was incorporated into the region's Hispanic way of life, changing habits of long standing and accustoming people to a number of innovations that modified their culture, in the long run, considerably more than in other parts of the Southwest.

During the third period, officially initiated after Anglo-American occupation, Hispanic culture not only became modified by the presence of another civilization but was replaced in sectors of greater contact, where it became incidental in the very land in which not long before it had been dominant. The large portion of the older population of the Southwest receded into a folk culture, now referred to derisively as "Mexican," because this label represented the people who had been defeated in war. Many of the distinctions that had separated *ricos* and *patrones* from the ordinary folk lost almost all significance. The differences now were based on skin pigmentation and degree of affluence. Many Hispano Mexicans became Anglicized, sent their children to eastern schools, and participated in the new life with some degree of success, but the bulk of the population did not fare so well. In time even the vestiges of Hispanic folk culture receded into the background, into small villages and towns away from the growing centers of population. Eventually these hidden byways of New Mexico became oases of traditional lore, which years later were sought by folklorists and students of history.

One of the factors that served to preserve this folk culture was the lack of industrialization in the state. It continued its pastoral and agricultural economy until the early 1920's. Hispanic culture was preserved or modified by the acceptance or rejection that it experienced in Anglo-American circles. As the two cultures became acclimated to each other, tolerance or acceptance gradually increased on both sides. Anglo-American color consciousness, and the accompanying discriminatory practices based on pigmentation, however, continued to plague the residents and drove the Hispanos to defensive moves by which they circumvented this insidious Anglo-American attitude. A greater emphasis was placed on their Spanish background by ascribing racial origins and cultural labels harking back to the conquistadors or to Spain itself. It has already been pointed out how Mexican food, among other things, was referred to as "Spanish" to avoid a designation that might not be acceptable.

The fourth phase of what may be considered the current development began to take shape at the beginning of the twentieth century, when many cultured Anglo-Americans went to the Southwest, seeking something more than land, mineral wealth, or industrial possibilities. These people were artists, writers, and students of antiquities and culture, who settled in those sections of New Mexico where Hispanic culture had not been totally uprooted. Historians began to discover and interpret old documents and records of

292

significant events. Artists looked for natural beauty in the region, which until then had gone unheeded. Writers wrote interesting factual accounts and fictional works, some of which became great literature, using as characters and setting the same people and country that had been condemned and submerged in prejudice by their predecessors. Hispanic culture began to regain some of its lost ground in the new interpretations given by Anglo-American writers.

But the event that was most instrumental in bringing about the current phase of development was World War II. The returning servicemen were more acculturated to American life and, at the same time, were more conscious of the role that they were supposed to play in the new society. The G.I. Bill gave them further opportunities to improve their situation, and many took advantage of it. As the enthusiasm and euphoria of victory died down, much of the old Anglo-American pattern began to manifest itself, but this time the Hispano Mexicans did not shrug their shoulders and accept conditions simply because they existed. The traditional fatalism of which so many spoke before the war had been replaced by a questioning of the status quo. They could not be told not to rock the boat, because the boat was already being rocked by the new Anglo-American generation, who had become disenchanted with the materialism of their forebears. The Hispanic population saw a change that expressed their own feelings also. They took heart and joined in the cultural upheaval, which, like all sudden upheavals, uprooted much that was good along with the evils that they were trying to rectify.

As the fourth phase began to take definite form, the Hispano Mexicans formulated their demands. In New Mexico they wanted a return of the lands that they had lost through the manipulation of land grants. Others demanded proportionate participation in public life and in politics. The extremists eschewed everything Anglo-American and demanded their own system of education, their own teachers, and their own schools. They even demanded the right to be un-American. In the colleges and universities new curricula, Chicano studies and Mexican-American studies, were offered. Before long, groups with differing philosophies were forming in all parts of the Southwest, including La Raza Unida, Sons of Moctezuma, Children of Aztlán, El Quinto Sol, La Alianza, and scores of other exotically named organizations. The labels they used to identify themselves were also in dispute, because there was no consensus on a single name that would include all the differing concepts of self-identity.

In spite of many individual differences, a good deal of headway has been made since the Hispanos, the Mexican Americans, and the Chicanos began campaigning. Many of the programs instituted in the universities and in the neighborhoods where these dissatisfied members of American society live have achieved, among other things, a consciousness that a culture that has undergone so many changes is now eager to participate in the whole spectrum of American culture, not as a tolerated minority but as an integral part, on a par with the whole.

In some parts of the Southwest less negative actions taking the form of protest and confrontations incur the ill will of the dominant culture. But in California, in New Mexico, and in parts of Texas the end results have proved that, given the proper training and equal opportunity, the same proportion of Hispanos can become useful producers in American society. Now that society is committed to improving the lot of Hispanic people, there is little need of protesting to the point of defeat, because nothing can undermine the effectiveness of a movement more than failures of the few who insist on making extreme demands that are never granted. Moreover, the pendulum of Anglo-American society tends to swing from one extreme to the other. At present, there is a commitment to help and cooperate, but, should the pendulum begin to swing in the opposite direction, all the progress made in the last few decades will begin a downward trend.

It seems quite clear that the direction this fourth phase ultimately takes will depend on two important factors: first, the consensus reached by all Spanish speakers regarding their self-identity, whether it be Hispano, Mexican, or Chicano. These terms will have to be sharply defined so that there will be no fear of recrimination because of the choice made by any group or individual. Thus far most Chicanos disavow anyone who does not want to be classified by their designation, and most Hispanos are definitely unwilling to be represented by the Chicano movement. Second, the manner in which all can be integrated with American society, in order to live in concord without abandoning their entire cultural heritage, must be defined. Otherwise the struggle will continue unabated and unsolved. "Entire" is used advisedly, because it is not conceivable that any modern culture is so completely adequate today that it cannot be profitably modified. Some of the better-informed and more practical-minded leaders of the current movement are already advocating moderation, saying that there is no place for extreme individualism and that, if they are to accomplish their objectives, they must work together. A good deal of belligerence and rejection still exists in some vocal individuals, who are unfortunately becoming more like the traditional *caudillos* than enlightened leaders. On the other hand, some very sober voices are making themselves heard; if given support, they will help work out the two elements necessary for the success of the present upheaval and channel it in productive, useful directions.

The voices of the Hispanos, the Mexican Americans, and the Chicanos can be heard through the scores of periodicals, newspapers, and journals published by different segments of the population. Every month new books, monographs, and articles appear, ranging from scholarly studies by university faculty members to earthy offerings by members of the folk who want to be heard. The messages of the latter express varying degrees of protest and rejection of Anglo-American practices, which they believe are inimical to their progress and best interests. The labels chosen to designate each group become banners and slogans used in combating the ills that have plagued them for generations. Some of the labels are not easily defined. For example, too much time and effort are dissipated in trying to explain to everyone's satisfaction, including the Anglo-Americans', the origin and real meaning of Chicano. Many of the Hispanic people feel that someone is trying to hang a monicker on them that they cannot accept. Others believe that the Chicano group had its birth 4,000 years ago and that the name is therefore a respectable one for the members of the present movement. Those who have an academic bent define the Chicano in ethnic and cultural terms. The difficulty with labels in a controversial field is that they tend to alienate many who are sympathetic to the movement but do not wish to have any particular label applied to them. The question that arises is, Are labels that important?

All members of the current movement share certain ideological characteristics, whether they call themselves Hispanos, Mexican Americans, or Chicanos. They are not content with their present lot, and they are eager to do something about it.

The manner in which they propose to accomplish this becomes a point of contention that divides and diminishes their effectiveness. The Hispanos, the descendants of the original settlers, want what everyone else wants but without a return to an aboriginal past. They are strongly attached to their Spanish ancestral culture and wish to have it reinforced and recognized. Anglo-Americans find it easier to integrate a European culture, which has such deep roots in the Southwest; Hispanos have a shorter distance to travel for the same reason. Mexican Americans, whose label implies a combination of two cultures, are prone to emphasize their Mexican heritage, but this does not mean that they eschew all forms of Spanish culture, because they are products of a civilization that has cultivated the Spanish language, institutions, and traditions. The distinctive personality that the original Spanish culture has acquired is Mexican: hence their insistence on preserving this Hispano-Mexican culture as part of their heritage. The Chicanos go a step further, removing themselves from their Spanish background, and refusing to accept the Anglo-American civilization by which they are surrounded. They reject both Anglo and Spanish culture, proclaim a mythical "Aztlán" origin, and insist on having their own educational system, their own schools if possible, and their own teachers, because they feel themselves exploited by both Anglo-Americans and Spanish civilizations. A complete separation rather than an integration is their ideal.

It is conceivable that before long someone will make an inventory of the cultural content that they wish to preserve from their Hispano-Mexican heritage and the Anglo-American elements that they wish to incorporate in their eventual integration. Some have already become assimilated by natural biological processes, so that the degree of each culture that they preserve is purely a matter of individual choice. Those who have become acculturated have developed a set of values by which they determine the cultural practices from either culture that they consider essential to their happiness. Many leaders fall into this category; that is, they personally have no problems to speak of, but they see and understand the problems that confront the rest of the large Spanish-speaking population.

A glance at the Hispano-Mexican range, from the Middle West to the California coast and the Gulf of Mexico, reveals that this movement is moving on all fronts simultaneously. That is one

Governor Jerry Apodaca of New Mexico, a typical successful Hispanic man of the Southwest.

Julian Nava, Ph.D. Harvard, 1955, president of the Los Angeles Board of Education, 1970 and 1976; professor of history at California State University, Northridge, and the author of many books.

Senator Dennis Chavez of New Mexico, a distinguished member of an old Hispano family. He made a worthy contribution to the nation in the field of politics without sacrificing the dignity of his own heritage.

Gilberto Espinosa, a New Mexico attorney who has earned an enviable reputation as a scholarly historian. He is a member of a large family of scholars who have distinguished themselves in some of the nation's leading universities.

source of its strength. There are leaders in the labor camps and labor unions, in the educational institutions from kindergarten to graduate school, in housing, in industry with its equal-opportunity campaigns, and in sports and entertainment. The success lies in the satisfaction achieved by participants who feel a sense of accomplishment where a generation ago they felt frustration. Observers note that the tapping of Hispanic human resources has brought to light manifestations of excellence in many fields that hitherto were undiscovered. The "new" Hispanic people now tend to compete in the open market, rather than among themselves, where they achieve only a false sense of accomplishment. At one time many Hispanic intellectuals and scholars leaned so heavily on the guidance of well-meaning Anglo-Americans that they were reluctant to venture on their own. Today's intellectuals are relying on their own resources and are discovering that the genius of accomplishment is not limited to any one group. Today this confidence tends to be contentious, but as it matures, it will acquire the mellowing that comes with age and experience. When enough of these intellectuals, potential industrial leaders and future government officials take their respective places in American society, there will be no need for labels. The fourth phase will be a fait accompli.

NOTES

Chapter 1

1. UNESCO, *Recuento de Vocabulario Español*, p. 668.

2. Miguel León-Portilla, *Aztec Thought and Culture*, p. 61.

Chapter 2

1. The Coronado Monument stands on the excavated ruins of Tiguex, the Indian village where the murals described by Castañeda, the chronicler of the expedition, were found. For a long time there was some question about the location of the village, because, when the river changed its channel, it left the village on the opposite side. This is mentioned by Castañeda.

2. W. Owen, *A New and Universal Collection of Voyages and Travels Consisting of the Most Esteemed Relations Which Have Been Hitherto Published in All Languages, Containing Every Thing Remarkable in the Various Parts of the Known World*, Vol. 2, pp. 410–11. The quotation is taken from Chapter X of this rare book, whose chapter heading reads: "A Brief History of the Discoveries, Settlements, and Conquests Made by the French in America, Extracted Chiefly from Their Own Authors."

3. The Moors entered the Peninsula through the Straits of Gibraltar in A.D. 711 and overthrew the Spanish Goths and King Roderick. For over 780 years the Spaniards fought the Moors intermittently. They took the last Moorish stronghold, Granada, in 1492 after a decisive battle. After the final victory Queen Isabella saw her way clear to underwrite Columbus' voyage. The armies of the Spanish reconquest were transferred to the newly discovered land with very little additional training, because they had been on a war footing for so long. The expeditions of the Spaniards were manned by soldiers, unlike those of the English, whose settlements were established by civilians. This fact alone colors the colonization of both countries: the Spaniards, an army of explorers and conquerors; the English, a community of working families.

Chapter 3

1. George H. Hammond, *Don Juan de Oñate: Colonizer of New Mexico, 1595–1628*. "The offer was to take two sets of bellows for the mines that might be found." In the Salazar inspection six bellows were declared: "On this day the governor declared six pairs of bellows, with iron pipes, for use in mines or blacksmithing."

2. *Ibid.*, p. 421, quoting a translation from *Patronato*, legajo 22 of the *Archivo General de Indias*, "The Assays of the Ores from Mohoqui," which reads in part: "A soldier named Miguel Montero gave this witness a rock weighing about half a pound which he assayed after having mixed it with quicksilver for eight days; it produced six *adarmes* of silver. After being pressed it produced twelve ounces, more or less, for each *quintal* of ore."

3. It is logical to assume that prospecting was carried on by some of the colonials before the Revolt of 1680, although there is no historical record of profitable exploitation. Stuart A. Northrop states, in *Minerals of New Mexico*, that "gold was mined in *la Mina de La Tierra* in the Cerrillos district, . . . and several mines near Picuris Pueblo were registered before Governor Don Joachín Codallos y Robal." The assumption that the retreating Spaniards left mines behind in 1680 is given some credence in that a mine known as Nuestra Señora de Los Reyes de Linares was reopened in 1713 in the Sierra de San Lázaro, now known as Old Placer Mountains.

4. Jessie Bromilow Bailey, *Diego de Vargas and the Reconquest of New Mexico*, pp. 208–209. During the inspection trip of the province of New Mexico made by De Vargas' *maese de campo*, Luis Granillo, he repeatedly mentions the size of the haciendas. The one belonging to Miguel Luján was said to be just large enough for one family. Some had enough land for two families but for the most part a family held a *suerte*, a single cultivated piece of land.

5. Hammond, *op. cit.*, p. 50. In the contract for the pacification and conquest that Oñate signed on September 25, 1595, he specifically requested: "Further, the said conquerors and settlers shall be informed of the favors granted them and their descendants and successors by his majesty in ordinance 99, by which they are named *hidalgos* or an established lineage, so that they may enjoy all these honors and privileges; and they shall have the right to do everything that hidalgos and caballeros in the Kingdom of Castile may do, according to the traditions, laws, and customs of Castile, in conformity with the said ordinance."

6. L. S. M. Curtin, *Healing Herbs of the Upper Río Grande*, p. 154. Although the title of Curtin's book indicates that it deals specifically with the healing herbs of the upper Río Grande, most of the information given in her excellent study is applicable to the entire Southwest with very minor variations. It is the best publication to date on the pharmacopoeia of southwestern folk, well documented and illustrated with photographs of many of the plants mentioned in the book.

Chapter 4

1. Hammond, *op. cit.*, p. 355.
2. Edgar Lee Hewett, *Ancient Life in the American Southwest*, p. 70.
3. Omer C. Stewart, "Peyotism: A Modern Indian Religion," *Gadfly*, October 18, 1963, pp. 3–4.
4. Richard L. Nostrand, "The Hispanic-American Borderland: Delimitation of an American Culture Region," *Annals of the American Geographical Association*, December, 1970, p. 4: "Drawing upon both Spanish and Indian beliefs, the Catholicism of the Hispanic population, like that of the Mexican in Mexico, is mainly folk Catholicism permeated with unorthodox beliefs and superstitions."
5. Dabney Otis Collins, in "Escalante's Trail, or Plunder Road of the West," *Brand Book of the Denver Westerner*, Vol. 21, p. 357, quotes J. H. Lyman, who in 1841 reported that the price of slaves in New Mexico varied according to the condition and age of each Indian between $50 and $100 for ten- to fifteen-year-olds. Ten years later the price was $100 for boys and $150 to $200 for girls. According to an Indian preacher named Joseph Williams, the New Mexicans bought the better-looking Indian women for "wives" from Antoine Roubideaux's trading post on the Uinta River in eastern Utah.
6. Tomás Rivera, a merchant *patrón* of Ranchos de Taos, New Mexico, in the 1920's, had two household servants whom visitors took to be members of the Hispanic community in the village because of their speech and general appearance. Rivera explained that the women were full-blood Indians who had come to serve in his home when they were young girls and had grown up in his household, where they became like members of the family.
7. The best account of the Comancheros is given by Paul I. Wellman in the historical preface to his novel *Comancheros*.

Chapter 5

1. Arthur L. Campa, *Spanish Folk Poetry in New Mexico*, p. 18. Apolinario Almanzares was bought from the Comanches by the residents of Las Vegas, New Mexico, when he was a young boy. The Indians used him as a jockey to race their horses when they went to New Mexico on trading expeditions. The Spanish residents, noticing his light complexion, traded a blanket for the boy, and he took the name of the family who ransomed him. After he grew up, he became a well-known troubadour in northern New Mexico. He died at the age of ninety-eight.

Chapter 6

1. Ruth Murray Underhill, *Social Organization of the Papago Indians*.
2. Arthur L. Campa, *Treasure of the Sangre de Cristos*, p. 34. The Spaniards called the place where they found the nuggets Arizonac from two words of the Pima dialect, *ari*, "few," and *zoni*, "springs." Whether from the Spanish Arizonac or from the Pima dialect, this semiarid state is aptly named Few Springs, or Arizona.
3. Sidney B. Brinkerhoff, Introduction to Yjinio Aguirre, "The Last of the Dons," *Journal of Arizona History*, Vol. 10, No. 4 (Winter, 1969), pp. 239–54.
4. Odie B. Faulk, *Arizona: A Short History*, p. 174.
5. Frank Lockwood, *Pioneer Days in Arizona*, p. 335.

Chapter 7

1. Bancroft, *Works*, Vol. 18, p. 60.
2. John W. Caughey, *California: A Remarkable State's Life History*, p. 24.
3. Bancroft, *Works*, Vol. 26, p. 53.
4. Walter A. Starr, "Drake Landed in San Francisco Bay in 1579: The Testimony of the Plate of Brass," *California Historical Society Quarterly*, Vol. 41 (1962).
5. Herbert Eugene Bolton, *Spanish Explorations in the Southwest*, p. 91.
6. Caughey, *op. cit.*, p. 35.
7. Bancroft, *Works*, Vol. 23, p. 603.

Chapter 9

1. Richard Henry Dana, *Two Years Before the Mast*, p. 81.
2. James Clyman, *American Frontiersman, 1792–1881: His Own Reminiscences and Diaries*.

Chapter 10

1. Bancroft, *Works*, Vol. 23, p. 576.
2. Alfonso Teja Zabre, *History of Mexico*, p. 171: "In 1549 prospecting work was carried out at San Bernabé, near Guanajuato, by driving a tunnel or gallery along a vein and men thus began to know practically what is the structure of a 'mother lode.' And as it happened that the miners of the Spanish colony earned for themselves an almost magical reputation in the art of divining the courses of veins of silver.

"After that came Bartolomé de Medina's invention, which was an original discovery on his part, although there are reasons for supposing that the system of mercury amalgamation was known a few years before in Italy, thanks to Biringuccio or to some German miners.

"The Sonoran miners who came to California passed this know-how on to the Anglo-Americans."

3. Leonard Pitt, *The Decline of the Californios*, pp. 181–91.

4. Manuel Ruiz, Jr., *Mexican American Legal Heritage in the Southwest*, p. 23.

Chapter 11

1. Warren A. Beck, *New Mexico: A History of Four Centuries*, p. 105. Beck gives a colored picture of the "mountain men" when he says that they were "typical of those who had steadily pushed the fringes of civilization"; there was already a civilization in the West.

2. John Francis Bannon, *The Spanish Borderland Frontier, 1731–1821*, p. 230.

3. *Ibid.*, p. 231.

4. Richard N. Ellis, *New Mexico: Past and Present*, p. 107: "Another branch of the American economy which the Mexican trade stimulated was the mule-breeding industry, especially in Missouri, where it reached a celebrated preeminence. As early as 1823, some four hundred jacks, jennets, and mules were brought to Missouri by returning caravan; in 1824, over six hundred; in 1827, eight hundred; and in 1832, thirteen hundred." Although jacks were purchased in various states of Mexico, the Sonoran was more sought after because of his size. When bred to American mares, he produced a larger and stronger mule than the usual Spanish mule.

5. Glenn R. Vernam, *Man on Horseback*, p. 8.

6. Letter of July 1, 1843, to Consul Manuel Alvarez in Santa Fe by Charles Bent, quoted by Harold H. Dunham in "Sidelights on Santa Fe Traders," *The Westerners Brandbook*, p. 277.

7. Milton W. Callon, "The Merchant Colonists of New Mexico," in *Brand Book of the Denver Westerners*, Vol. 21, p. 6.

8. Arthur L. Campa, "Piñon as an Economic and Social Factor," *New Mexico Business Review*, October, 1932, pp. 20–30.

Chapter 12

1. Gregory Razran, "Ethnic Dislike & Stereotypes: A Laboratory Study," *Journal of Abnormal Psychology*, Vol. 45 (1950), pp. 7–27.

2. James Knox Polk, *Polk: The Diary of a President*, ed. Allan Nevins, p. 106.

3. William Watts Hart Davis, *El Gringo, or New Mexico and Her People*, p. 85. Young Davis was overly impressed with his own importance and often judged prematurely what he saw in New Mexico. As he became acquainted with the people of the territory, he quali-

fied his original judgments and became more objective.

4. Bannon, *op. cit.*, p. 6.

5. Lansing B. Bloom, "New Mexico Under Mexican Administration," *Old Santa Fe*, Vol. 1, No. 3 (January, 1914), p. 260. Bloom cites a letter to the Secretary of State of Mexico of April 14, 1832, from Don José Agustín Escudero, a citizen of Chihuahua.

6. Manuel Gamio, *Aspects of Mexican Civilization*, p. 105.

7. David J. Weber, *The Taos Trappers: The Fur Trade in the Far Southwest, 1540–1846*, p. 104, quoting Governor José de Urquidi to the Minister of Foreign Relations (of Mexico), May 13, 1825.

8. *Ibid.*, p. 79.

9. John J. Bodine, "A Tri-ethnic Trap: The Spanish Americans in Taos," in *Spanish Speaking People of the United States*, p. 147.

10. Beck, *op. cit.*, p. 117.

11. Bloom, *op. cit.*, p. 172.

12. Davis, *op. cit.*, p. 29.

Chapter 13

1. Leo Grebler, Joan Moore, and Ralph Guzman, *The Mexican American People*, p. 6.

2. Alfred Barnaby Thomas, *After Coronado*, p. 5.

3. Bolton, *op. cit.*, p. 20.

4. *Ibid.*, p. 25.

5. J. Manuel Espinosa, "Journal of the Vargas Expedition to Colorado," *Colorado Magazine*, Vol. 16, No. 3 (May, 1939), pp. 81–89.

6. Thomas, *op. cit.*, p. 69.

7. Noel M. Loomis and Abraham Nasatir, *Pedro Vial and the Roads to Santa Fe*, p. 431.

Chapter 14

1. Ralph Carr, "The Sangre de Cristo Grant," *Brand Book*, Vol. 3, No. 7 (July, 1947).

2. Bancroft, *Works*, Vol. 5, p. 427.

Chapter 15

1. Morris F. Taylor, *Trinidad, Colorado Territory*, p. 214. Some of the information regarding Trinidad comes from this well-researched publication.

2. Dewitt C. Peters, *The Life and Adventures of Kit Carson*, p. 493.

3. Ralph C. Taylor, *Colorado South of the Border*, p. 134.

Chapter 16

1. On the corner of Alameda Boulevard and Valdespino Road, about ten miles southeast of El Paso, a state monument marks the approximate location of the original San Antonio de Senecú Mission of 1682. It lists the names Governor Don Antonio de Otermín

and Father Francisco Ayeta, who founded the mission for the Piro and Tompiro Indians.

2. According to Armando Ortiz, program and sales manager of the Tigua Trading and Reservation Center in Ysleta, Texas, the scattered members of the Tigua tribe were brought together by Colmenero and a couple of other old tribe members who were the legitimate members of the tribe. There are about five hundred survivors who are said to be Tiguas in Ysleta, although they look no different from the Mexican inhabitants of the region. With the help of the state they erected a large building in southwestern-Indian style, where they now have a large display of Indian arts and crafts for sale. They do not wear the traditional costumes of the Tiguas because they have not worn that style of clothing for generations. They have revived weaving, pottery, and other crafts characteristic of the Tiguas and have added silver jewelry manufacturing of Navajo and Zuñi style.

3. C. L. Sonnichsen, *Pass of the North*, p. 46.

4. Josiah Gregg, *Commerce of the Prairies*, ed., Max Moorhead, p. 313. "It is from El Paso [now Juárez] that Chihuahua is chiefly supplied with fruits, and liquors, which are transported on mules or in carretas. The fruits, as well fresh as in dried state are thus carried to distant markets."

5. Cleofas Calleros, *El Paso Then and Now*, p. 168.

Chapter 17

1. Fritz Leo Hoffman, "Martín de Alarcón and the Founding of San Antonio, Texas," in Robert C. Cotner and Carlos E. Castañeda, eds., *Essays in Mexican History*, p. 30.

2. Herbert Eugene Bolton, *Texas in the Middle of the Eighteenth Century*, p. 2.

3. Florence Johnson Scott, "Spanish Colonization in the Lower Río Grande, 1747–1767," in *Essays in Mexican History*, p. 5.

4. W. Eugene Hollon, *The Southwest, Old and New*, p. 107.

5. José Vasconcelos, *Breve Historia de México*, p. 345.

6. Otis N. Singletary, *The Mexican War*, p. 145.

7. General Winfield Scott, *Memoirs*.

8. Stanley Walker, *Texas*, p. 120.

Chapter 18

1. Aniceto Aramoni, "Machismo," *Psychology Today*, January, 1972, pp. 69–72. This Mexican psychoanalyst traces the roots of *machismo* into the dark, sexual depths of violence and hatred. According to him, it is the epitome of "the fundamental problem of any person who is trying to emerge from a profound symbiosis; that is, the machista is impelled to dominate others in order to deny his own weakness. It is an ill-fated drama wherein the man, painfully attached to

his mother, his sisters and the Virgin, seeks their exclusive admiration and worship." The author adds that *machismo* is a disturbed, uniquely Mexican answer to the universal quest of individuation.

Chapter 19

1. [*Thomas*] *De Quincey's Writings*, Vol. 8, *Christianity, Paganism, and Superstition*, p. 533.

2. H. M. Wiltse, "Some Mountain Superstitions of the South," *Journal of American Folklore*, Vol. 12, No. 45, p. 132.

3. Juan Rodríguez Freile, "El Carnero," in Anderson-Imbert and Florit, eds., *Literatura Hispano-Americana*, p. 90.

4. Arthur L. Campa, "Some Herbs and Plants of Early California," *Western Folklore*, Vol. 9, No. 4 (October, 1950), pp. 338–47.

Chapter 20

1. Alfred Bates, *The Drama*, p. 80.

Chapter 22

1. Aurelio M. Espinosa, *Studies in New Mexican Spanish*, University of New Mexico Bulletin, Language Series, Vol. 1, No. 2 (December, 1909).

2. Eleanor Adams and France V. Scholes, *Books in New Mexico*, reprint, *New Mexico Historical Review*, July, 1942.

Chapter 23

1. Bancroft, *Works*, Vol. 17, p. 127.

2. Arthur L. Campa, *Spanish Religious Folktheatre of the Spanish Southwest (First Cycle)*.

3. Carlos E. Castañeda, "The First American Play," *Catholic World*, January, 1932, pp. 429–37.

4. Campa, *Spanish Religious Folktheatre of the Spanish Southwest (First Cycle)*.

5. Arthur L. Campa, *Spanish Religious Folktheatre in the Southwest (Second Cycle)*.

6. Stephen Powers, *Afoot and Alone: A Walk from Sea to Sea*, p. 85.

7. Bancroft, *Works*, Vol. 34, p. 429.

8. Juan B. Rael, *The Sources of the Mexican Shepherds' Play*.

9. Campa, *Spanish Religious Folktheatre in the Southwest (Second Cycle)*, p. 55.

10. Arthur L. Campa, *Los Comanches: A New Mexican Folk Drama*, University of New Mexico Bulletin, Modern Language Series, Vol. 7, No. 1 (April 1, 1942), p. 43.

11. Gilberto Espinosa, "Los Comanches," *New Mexico Quarterly*, May, 1931, pp. 130–42.

Chapter 24

1. Campa, *Spanish Folk Poetry in New Mexico*.
2. Marcel Gautier, "De quelques jeux," *Revue Hispanique*, Vol. 33 (1915), p. 384.
3. The word *espinela* derives from the late-sixteenth-century Spanish poet Vicente Espinel, who wrote very popular ten-line stanzas. However, Gregorio Silvestre wrote forty-four-line poems like those of the composers of the Southwest and many nations of Latin America almost a century before Espinel.
4. A recent (1975) song collection of the lower Río Grande is Américo Paredes' *A Texas-Mexican Cancionero: Folksongs of the Lower Border*. It contains a representative collection of colonial ballads, *corridos*, and romantic songs. The musical notation and an English translation accompany the selections.

Chapter 25

1. E. Boyd, *Popular Arts of Colonial New Mexico*, p. 51.
2. George M. Foster, *Culture and Conquest, America's Spanish Heritage*, p. 54.
3. Arthur L. Campa and Cornelius C. Kuipers, "Arts and Crafts in New Mexico: A Survey of the Present Status of Handicrafts in New Mexico" (unpublished manuscript of a survey made under the Federal Emergency Relief Administration, begun in 1934 and con-cluded in 1936 under the National Youth Administration).
4. Rebecca James, *Embroideries: The Colcha Stitch*.
5. Boyd, *op. cit.*, p. 187,
6. *Ibid.*, p. 37.
7. José E. Espinosa, *Saints in the Valleys*.
8. George Mills, *The People of the Saints*, p. 62.
9. *Ibid.*, p. 83.

Chapter 26

1. Zebulon Montgomery Pike, *The Journals of Zebulon Montgomery Pike*, ed. Donald Jackson, Vol. 1, p. 401.

Chapter 27

1. Fernando Díaz-Plaja, *The Spaniard and the Seven Deadly Sins*, trans. Inderwick Palmer, p. 158.
2. Peter Farb, *Man's Rise to Civilization*, p. 235.
3. E. Sapir, "The Status of Linguistics as a Science," in *Language: Selected Writings in Language, Culture, and Personality*, pp. 207–14.
4. Díaz-Plaja, *op. cit.*, p. 152.
5. Julio Camba, *La Rana Viajera*, p. 27.
6. Noel McGinn Bruck, Ernest Harburg, and Gerald Ginsburg, "Diferencias entre mexicanos y norte-americanos en su relación a conflicto inter-personal," *Revista mexicana de psicología*, Vol. 1, No. 2 (November, 1963), pp. 109–22.

BIBLIOGRAPHY

BOOKS

Adams, Eleanor, and Scholes, France V., *Books in New Mexico*. Reprint, *New Mexico Historical Review*, July, 1942.

Bailey, Jessie Bromilow. *Diego de Vargas and the Reconquest of New Mexico*. Albuquerque: University of New Mexico Press, 1940.

Bancroft, Hubert Howe. *Works*. Vols. 17, 18, 23, 26, 34. San Francisco, 1886–90.

Bannon, John Francis. *The Spanish Borderland Frontier, 1713–1821*. New York: Holt, Rinehart and Winston, 1970.

Barreiro, Antonio. *Ojeada sobre Nuevo México*. Ed. Lansing Bloom. *Historical Society of New Mexico Publications in History*, Vol. 5 (March, 1928).

Bates, Alfred. *The Drama*. Vol. 3. London: Athenian Society, 1903.

Beck, Warren A. *New Mexico: A History of Four Centuries*. Norman: University of Oklahoma Press, 1962.

Benedict, Ruth. *Patterns of Culture*. Boston and New York: Houghton-Mifflin Company, 1934.

Bentley, Harold W. *A Dictionary of Spanish Terms in English*. New York: Columbia University Press, 1932.

Bodine, John J. "A Tri-ethnic Trap: The Spanish Americans in Taos." In *Spanish Speaking People of the United States*. American Ethnological Society, Annual Meeting, 1968. Distributed by University of Washington Press, Seattle, 1969.

Bolton, Herbert Eugene. *Spanish Explorations in the Southwest*. New York: Barnes and Noble, reprint, 1967.

———. *Texas in the Middle of the Eighteenth Century*. Austin, 1962.

Boyd, E. *Popular Arts of Colonial New Mexico*. Santa Fe, N. Mex.: Museum of International Art, 1974.

Brenner, Anita. *Idols Behind Altars*. New York: Payson & Clarke, 1929.

Calleros, Cleofas. *El Paso Then and Now*. El Paso: American Printing Company, 1954.

Camba, Julio. *La Rana Viajera*. New York: Heath, 1928.

Campa, Arthur L. *Los Comanches: A New Mexican Folk Drama*. University of New Mexico Bulletin, Modern Language Series, Vol. 7, No. 1 (April 1, 1942).

———. *Spanish Folk Poetry in New Mexico*. Albuquerque: University of New Mexico Press, 1946.

———. *Spanish Religious Folktheatre of the Spanish Southwest (First Cycle)*. University of New Mexico Bulletin, Modern Language Series, Vol. 5, No. 1 (February 15, 1934).

———. *Spanish Religious Folktheatre in the Southwest (Second Cycle)*. University of New Mexico Bulletin, Modern Language Series, Vol. 6, No. 2 (June 15, 1934).

———. *Treasure of the Sangre de Cristos*. Norman: University of Oklahoma Press, 1963.

Caughey, John W. *California: A Remarkable State's Life History*. Englewood Cliffs, N.J.: Prentice-Hall, 1970.

Clyman, James. *American Frontiersman, 1792–1881: His Own Reminiscences and Diaries*. Ed. Charles Camp. San Francisco, 1928.

Curtin, L. S. M. *Healing Herbs of the Upper Río Grande*. Santa Fe, N. Mex.: Laboratory of Anthropology, 1947.

Dana, Richard Henry. *Two Years Before the Mast*. New York: Heritage, 1947.

Davis, William Watts Hart. *El Gringo, or New Mexico and Her People*. Santa Fe, N. Mex.: Rydal, 1938.

[*Thomas*] De Quincey's Writings. Vol. 8. *Christianity, Paganism, and Superstition*. New York: Houghton-Mifflin, 1877.

Díaz-Plaja, Fernando. *The Spaniard and the Seven Deadly Sins*. Trans. Inderwick Palmer. New York: Scribner's, 1967.

Doobs, Leonard W. *Becoming More Civiliaed*. New Haven: Yale University Press, 1960.

Edmondson, Munro S. *Los Manitos: A Study of Institutional Values*. New Orleans: Middle American Research Institute, Tulane University, 1957.

Ellis, Richard N. *New Mexico: Past and Present*. Albuquerque: University of New Mexico Press, 1971.

Espinosa, Aurelio M. *Studies in New Mexican Spanish*. University of New Mexico Bulletin, Language Series. Vol. 1, No. 2 (December, 1909).

Espinosa, Carmen. *Shawls, Crinolines, Filigree: The Dress and Adornment of the Women in New Mexico, 1739–1900*. El Paso: Texas Western Press, 1970.

Espinosa, José E. *Saints in the Valleys*. Fwd. Fray Angélico Chávez. Albuquerque: University of New Mexico Press, 1967.

Ezell, Paul H. *The Hispanic Acculturation of the Gila River Pimas*. American Anthropological Association, Memoir 90. Vol. 63, No. 5, Pt. 2 (October, 1961).

Farb, Peter. *Man's Rise to Civilization*. New York: Dutton, 1968.

Faulk, Odie B. *Arizona: A Short History*. Norman: University of Oklahoma Press, 1970.

Foster, George M. *Culture and Conquest: America's Spanish Heritage*. Chicago: Quadrangle, 1960.

Gamio, Manuel. *Aspects of Mexican Civilization*. Chicago: University of Chicago Press, 1926.

Grebler, Leo, Moore, Joan, and Guzman, Ralph. *The Mexican American People*. New York: Free Press, 1970.

Gregg, Josiah. *Commerce of the Prairies*. Ed. Max L. Moorhead. Norman: University of Oklahoma Press, 1954.

Hammond, George H. *Don Juan de Oñate: Colonizer of New Mexico, 1595–1628*. Albuquerque: University of New Mexico Press, 1953.

Hewett, Edgar Lee. *Ancient Life in the American Southwest*. Indianapolis: Bobbs-Merrill, 1930.

Hoffman, Fritz Leo. "Martín de Alarcón and the Founding of San Antonio, Texas." In Robert C. Cotner and Carlos E. Castañeda, eds. *Essays in Mexican History*. Westport, Conn.: Greenwood Press, 1972, p. 30.

Hollon, W. Eugene. *The Southwest, Old and New*. Lincoln: University of Nebraska Press, 1968.

James, Rebecca. *Embroideries: The Colcha Stitch*. Santa Fe, N. Mex.: Museum of International Folk Art, 1963.

Jiménez, A. *Picardía Mexicana*. Mexico City: Libro Mex Editores, 1960.

León-Portilla, Miguel. *Aztec Thought and Culture*. Trans. Jack Emory Davis. Norman: University of Oklahoma Press, 1963.

Lockwood, Frank. *Pioneer Days in Arizona*. New York: Macmillan, 1932.

———. *Pioneer Portraits*. Tucson: University of Arizona Press, 1968.

Loomis, Noel M., and Nasatir, Abraham. *Pedro Vial and the Roads to Santa Fe*. Norman: University of Oklahoma Press, 1967.

Lowrie, Samuel Harmon. *Culture Conflict in Texas, 1821–1835*. New York: Columbia University Press, 1932.

Mills, George. *The People of the Saints*. Colorado Springs, Colo.: Fine Arts Center.

Northrop, Stuart A. *Minerals of New Mexico*. Albuquerque: University of New Mexico Press, 1944.

Owen, W. *A New and Universal Collection of Voyages and Travels Consisting of the Most Esteemed Relations Which Have Been Hitherto Published in All Languages, Containing Every Thing Remarkable in the Various Parts of the Known World*. Vol. 2. London: Printed for W. Owen, at Homer's Head, in Fleet Street, 1775.

Paredes, Américo. *A Texas-Mexican Cancionero: Folksongs of the Lower Border*. Urbana: University of Illinois Press, 1976.

Peters, Dewitt, C. *The Life and Adventures of Kit Carson*. Hartford, Conn.: Dustin, Gilman, 1874.

Pike, Zebulon Montgomery. *The Journals of Zebulon Montgomery Pike*. Ed. Donald Jackson. Vol. 1. Norman: University of Oklahoma Press, 1966.

Pitt, Leonard. *The Decline of the Californios*. Berkeley: University of California Press, 1970.

Polk, James Knox. *Polk: The Diary of a President*. Ed. Allan Nevins. New York: Longmans, Green, 1929.

Powers, Stephen. *Afoot and Alone: A Walk From Sea to Sea*. Hartford, Conn.: Columbia Book, 1872.

Rael, Juan B. *The Sources of the Mexican Shepherds' Play*. Guadalajara, Mexico: Librería La Joyita, 1965.

Robinson, Cecil. *With the Ears of Strangers: The Mexican in American Literature*. Tucson: University of Arizona Press, 1963.

Rodríguez Freile, Juan. "El Carnero." In Enrique Anderson-Imbert and Eugenio Flores, eds. *Literatura Hispano-Americana*. New York: Holt, Rinehart and Winston, 1960, p. 90.

Rubel, Arthur J. *Across the Tracks: Mexican-Americans in a Texas City*. Austin: University of Texas Press, 1966.

Ruiz, Manuel, Jr. *Mexican American Legal Heritage in the Southwest*. Los Angeles: Published by the author, 1972.

Scott, Florence Johnson. "Spanish Colonization in the Lower Río Grande, 1747–1767." In Robert C. Cotner and Carlos E. Castañeda, eds. *Essays in Mexican History*. Westport, Conn.: Greenwood Press, 1970, p. 30.

Scott, General Winfield. *Memoirs*. 2 vols. New York: Sheldon Publishers, 1864.

Sigüenza y Góngora, Carlos de. *Mercurio Volante*. Ed. Irving Albert Leonard. Los Angeles: Quivira Society, 1932.

Singletary, Otis N. *The Mexican War*. Chicago: University of Chicago Press, 1960.

Sonnichsen, C. L. *Pass of the North*. El Paso: Texas Western Press, 1968.

Taylor, Morris F. *Trinidad, Colorado Territory*. Pueblo, Colo.: O'Brien Printing & Stationery Co., 1966.

Taylor, Ralph C. *Colorado South of the Border*. Denver: Sage Books, 1963.

Teja Zabre, Alfonso. *History of Mexico*. Mexico City: Ediciones Botas, 1948.

Thomas, Alfred Barnaby. *After Coronado*. Norman: University of Oklahoma Press, 1935.

———. *Forgotten Frontiers*. Norman: University of Oklahoma Press, 1932.

Underhill, Ruth Murray. *The Navajos*. Norman: University of Oklahoma Press, 1956.

———. *Social Organization of the Papago Indians*. New York: AMS Press, reprint, 1969.

UNESCO. *Recuento de Vocabulario Espanol*. Vol. 1. Río Piedras: University of Puerto Rico, 1952.

Vasconcelos, José. *Breve Historia de México*. Madrid: Ediciones de Cultura Hispanica, 1952.

Vernam, Glenn R. *Man on Horseback*. New York: Harper & Row, 1964.

Walker, Stanley. *Texas*. New York: Viking, 1962.

Weber, David J. *The Taos Trappers: The Fur Trade in the Far Southwest, 1540–1846*. Norman: University of Oklahoma Press, 1968.

Wellman, Paul I. *Comancheros*. New York: Doubleday, 1952.

ARTICLES

Aramoni, Aniceto. "Machismo," *Psychology Today*, January, 1972, pp. 69–72.

Bloom, Lansing B. "New Mexico Under Mexican Administration," *Old Santa Fe*, Vol. 1, No. 3 (January, 1914), p. 260.

Bruck, Noel McGinn, Harburg, Ernest, and Ginsburg, Gerald. "Diferencias entre mexicanos y norteamericanos en su relación a conflicto inter-personal," *Revista mexicana de psicología*, Vol. 1, No. 2 (November, 1963), pp. 109–22.

Callon, Milton W. "The Merchant Colonists of New Mexico." In *Brand Book of the Denver Westerners*. Vol. 21. Ed. Arthur L. Campa. Boulder, Colo.: Johnson, 1966, p. 6.

Campa, Arthur L. "El Héroe Popular Norteamericano," *Revista Hispánica Moderna*, Vol. 34, Nos. 3–4 (July–October, 1968), pp. 558–63.

———. "Piñon as an Economic and Social Factor," *New Mexico Business Review*, October, 1932, pp. 20–30.

———. "Some Herbs and Plants of Early California," *Western Folklore*, Vol. 9, No. 4 (October, 1950), pp. 338–47.

Carr, Ralph. "The Sangre de Cristo Grant," *Brand Book*, Vol. 3, No. 7 (July, 1947).

Castañeda, Carlos E. "The First American Play," *Catholic World*, January, 1932, pp. 429–37.

Collins, Dabney Otis. "Escalante's Trail, or Plunder Road of the West," *Brand Book of the Denver Westerners*. Vol. 21. Ed. Arthur L. Campa. Boulder, Colo.: Johnson, 1966, p. 357.

Dunham, Harold H. "The Four-Fold Heritage of New Mexican Records," *The Denver Westerners Monthly Roundup*, Vol. 23, Nos. 8, 9 (September, 1967).

———. "Sidelights of Santa Fe Traders." In *The Westerners Brandbook*. Denver: University of Denver Press, 1950.

Espinosa, Gilberto. "Los Comanches," *New Mexico Quarterly*, May, 1931, pp. 130–42.

Espinosa, J. Manuel. "Journal of the Vargas Expedition to Colorado," *Colorado Magazine*, Vol. 16, No. 3 (May, 1939), pp. 81–89.

Garcia, Rudy. *Denver Post*, May 2, 1972.

Gautier, Marcel. "De quelques jeux," *Revue Hispanique*, Vol. 33 (1915), p. 384.

Nostrand, Richard L. "The Hispanic-American Borderland: Delimitation of an American Culture Region," *Annals of the American Geographical Association*, December, 1970.

Razran, Gregory. "Ethnic Dislike and Stereotypes: A Laboratory Study," *Journal of Abnormal Psychology*, Vol. 45 (1950), pp. 7–27.

Sapir, E. "The Status of Linguistics as a Science." In *Language: Selected Writings in Language, Culture, and Personality*. Berkeley: University of California Press, 1963, pp. 207–14.

Scholes, France V. "Civil Government and Society in New Mexico in the Seventeenth Century," *New Mexico Historical Review*, Vol. 1 (April, 1935), p. 97.

Starr, Walter. "Drake Landed in San Francisco Bay in 1579: The Testimony of the Plate of Brass," *Calinia Historical Society Quarterly*, Vol. 41 (1962).

Stewart, Omer C. "Peyotism: A Modern Indian Religion," *Gadfly*, October 18, 1963, pp. 3–4.

Wiltse, H. M. "Some Mountain Superstitions of the South," *Journal of American Folklore*, Vol. 12, No. 45, p. 132.

UNPUBLISHED MANUSCRIPTS

Campa, Arthur L., and Kuipers, Cornelius C. "Arts and Crafts in New Mexico: A Survey of the Present Status of Handicrafts in New Mexico." Funded by the Federal Emergency Relief Administration and housed at the University of New Mexico. Begun in October, 1934, as Project No. S–Al–17 and concluded under subsidiary Project No. Y–4–8–8 of the National Youth Administration, in June, 1936.

Hill, Shirley Witt. "Migration into San Juan Indian Pueblo, 1726–1968." Unpublished doctoral dissertation, University of New Mexico, 1969.

ADDITIONAL SUGGESTED READINGS

BOOKS

American Ethnological Society. *Spanish Speaking People in the United States.* Annual Meeting, 1968. Distributed by University of Washington Press, Seattle, 1969.

Boas, Franz. *Race, Language, and Culture.* New York: Free Press, 1940.

Bogardus, Emory Stephen. *The Mexican American in the United States.* New York: Arno, 1970.

Burma, John. "The Civil Rights Situation of Mexican Americans and Spanish Americans." In Jitsuichi Masuoka and Preston Valien, eds. *Race Relations: Problems and Theory.* Chapel Hill: University of North Carolina Press, 1961.

Burns, Walter Noble. *The Robin Hood of El Dorado: The Saga of Joaquin Murrieta.* New York: Coward-McCann, 1932.

Buschlen, John Preston. *Senor [Eugenio] Plummer: The Life and Laughter of an Old Californian.* Los Angeles: Times Mirror Press, 1942.

Calleros, Cleofas. *El Paso Then and Now.* El Paso: American Printing Company, 1954.

————, and Graham, Marjorie. *Queen of the Missions: Our Lady of Guadalupe.* El Paso: American Printing Company, 1952.

Calvin, Ross. *Sky Determines: An Interpretation of the Southwest.* Albuquerque: University of New Mexico Press, 1965.

Campa, Arthur L. "Culture Patterns of the Spanish Speaking Community." In J. Edward Moseley, ed. *Spanish Speaking People of the Southwest.* Dallas: Council of Spanish American Work, 1966, pp. 20–36.

————. "Individualism in Hispanic Society." In J. Edward Moseley, ed. *Spanish Speaking People of the Southwest.* Dallas: Council of Spanish American Work, 1966, pp. 11–20.

Carrillo, Leo. *The California I Love.* Englewood Cliffs, N.J.: Prentice-Hall, 1961.

Céliz, Francisco. *Diary of the Alarcón Expedition into Texas, 1718–1719.* Los Angeles: Quivira Society, 1935.

Chávez, Fray Angélico. *Origins of New Mexico Families in the Spanish Colonial Period. Part 1. The Seventeenth (1598–1693) Century. Part 2. The Eighteenth (1693–1821) Century.* Albuquerque: Historical Society of New Mexico, 1954.

Darley, the Rev. A. M. *The Passionists of the Southwest.* Pueblo, Colo., 1893.

Dedera, Don and Robles, Bob. *Goodbye, García, Adíos.* Flagstaff, Ariz.: Northland Press, 1976.

Demaris, Ovid. *Poso del Mundo: Inside the Mexican-American Border, from Tijuana to Matamoros.* Boston: Little, Brown, 1970.

Dobie, J. Frank. *Coronado's Children: Tales of Lost Mines and Buried Treasures of the Southwest.* Dallas: Southwest Press, 1930.

————. *Puro Mexicano.* Publication 12. Austin: Texas Folklore Society, 1935.

Dobyns, Henry F. *Spanish Colonial Tucson: A Demographic History.* Tucson: University of Arizona Press, 1976.

Duffus, R. L. *The Santa Fe Trail.* New York: Longmans, Green, 1930.

Duncan, Otis Durant. *The Southwest: A Cultural Area in Evaluation.* Stillwater, Okla.: Redland Press, 1960.

Dundes, Alan. *Every Man His Way: Readings in Cultural Anthropology.* Englewood Cliffs, N.J.: Prentice-Hall, 1968.

Evans, Max. *Long John of Taos.* Los Angeles: Westernlore Press, 1959.

Faulk, Odie B. *Land of Many Frontiers: A History of the American Southwest.* New York: Oxford University Press, 1968.

Fisher, Reginald Gilbert. *Sacred Paintings on Skin.* Santa Fe, N. Mex.: Museum of New Mexico, 1944.

Folmer, Henri. *Franco-Spanish Rivalry in North America, 1542–1763.* San Francisco, 1953.

Forbes, Jack. *Apache, Navaho, and Spaniard.* Norman: University of Oklahoma Press, 1960.

Galarza, Ernesto. *Mexican-Americans in the Southwest.* Santa Barbara, Calif.: McNally and Loftin, 1969.

Gamio, Manuel. *The Life Story of the Mexican Immigrant: Autobiographic Documents Collected by Manuel Gamio.* Intro. Paul S. Taylor. Berkeley: University of California Press; New York: Dover, 1971.

Garber, Paul Neff. *The Gadsden Treaty.* Gloucester, Mass.: Peter Smith, 1959.

Garrett, Julia Kathryn. *Green Flag over Texas: A Story of the Last Years of Spain in Texas.* New York and Dallas: Cordova Press, 1939.

Gerald, Rex E. *Spanish Presidios of the Late Eighteenth Century in Northern New Spain.* Santa Fe, N. Mex.: Museum of New Mexico Press, 1968.

Gillin, John. "Modern Cultural Development and Synthesis in Latin America." In *Acculturation in the Americas*. Ed. Sol Tax. Chicago: University of Chicago Press, 1952.

Gonzáles, Nancie L. *The Spanish Americans of New Mexico: A Distinctive Heritage*. Advance Report 9, Mexican-American Study Project. University of California, Los Angeles, 1967.

Grant, Blanche C. *When Old Trails Were New: The Story of Taos*. New York, 1934.

Hackett, Charles Wilson. *Revolt of the Pueblo Indians of New Mexico and Otermin's Attempted Reconquest, 1680–82*. Albuquerque: University of New Mexico Press, 1942.

Hallenbeck, Clove. *Land of the Conquistadores*. Caldwell, Idaho: Caxton Printers, 1950.

Hammond, George Peter. *Narratives of the Coronado Expedition, 1540–42*. Albuquerque: University of New Mexico Press, 1940.

Herscovits, Melville J. *Acculturation: The Study of Contact Culture*. New York: J J. Augustin, 1938.

Howard, John R. *Awakening Minorities: American Indians, Mexican-Americans, Puerto Ricans*. Chicago: Aldine, 1970.

Hughes, Anne Eugenia. *The Beginning of Spanish Settlement in El Paso District*. Berkeley: University of California Press, 1914.

Inman, Henry. *Stories of the Old Santa Fe Trail*. Kansas City: Millet & Hundson, 1881.

Keleher, W. A. *The Fabulous Frontier*. Albuquerque: University of New Mexico Press, 1963 (originally published in 1945).

Kessell, John L. *Friars, Soldiers, and Reformers: Hispanic Arizona and the Sonora Mission Frontier*. Tucson: University of Arizona Press, 1976.

Kibbe, Pauline. *Latin Americans in Texas*. Albuquerque: University of New Mexico Press, 1946.

Kino, Eusebio Francisco. *Kino's Historical Memoir of Pimeria Alta: A Contemporary Account of the Beginnings of California, Sonora, and Arizona*. Cleveland: Arthur H. Clark, 1919.

Kluckhohn, Florence R., and Strodbeck, Fred L. *Variations in Value Orientations*. New York: Harper, 1961.

Kubler, George. *The Religious Architecture of New Mexico in the Colonial Period and Since the American Occupation*. Colorado Springs, Colo.: Taylor Museum, 1940.

Lafora, Nicolás de. *The Frontiers of New Spain: Nicolás Lafora's Description, 1766–1768*. Berkeley: Quivira Society, 1958.

Leonard, Irving A., ed. *The Mercurio Volante of Don Carlos de Singüenza y Góngora*. Los Angeles: Quivira Society, 1932.

Linton, Ralph. *The Cultural Background of Personality*. Englewood Cliffs, N.J.: Prentice-Hall, 1945.

Locke, Alain, and Stern, Bernard J., eds. "Predicament of Minorities." In Committee on Workshops, Progressive Education Association. *When Peoples Meet*. Camden, N.J.: Haddon, 1942.

Lummis, Charles Fletcher. *Some Strange Corners of Our Country: The Wonderland of the Southwest*. New York: Century, 1906.

———. *Spanish Songs of Old California*. Los Angeles, 1923.

McKittrick, Myrtle M. *Vallejo, Son of California*. Portland, Oreg.: Bindford and Mort, 1944.

Madsen, William. *Mexican Americans in South Texas*. New York: Holt, Rinehart and Winston, 1964.

Magoffin, Susan Shelby. *Down the Santa Fe Trail and into Mexico: The Diary of Susan Shelby Magoffin*. Ed. Stella M. Drumm. New Haven: Yale University Press, 1962 (originally published in 1926).

Marco da Nizza, Padre. *The Journey of Fray Marcos de Niza*. Dallas: University Press, 1949.

Mead, Margaret, ed. "The Spanish Americans in New Mexico, U.S.A." In *Cultural Patterns and Technological Change*. Paris: UNESCO, 1953.

Meier, Matt S., and Rivera, Feliciano. *The Chicanos: A History of Mexican Americans*. New York: Hill and Wang, 1974.

———, and ———, eds. *Readings on La Raza: The Twentieth Century*. New York: Hill and Wang, 1974.

Moorhead, Max L. *The Apache Frontier: Jacobo Ugarte and Spanish-Indian Relations in Northern New Spain, 1769–1791*. Norman: University of Oklahoma Press, 1968.

Moquin, Wayne. *A Documentary of the Mexican-Americans*. New York: Praeger, 1971.

Mora, Jo. *Californios: The Saga of the Hard-riding Vaqueros*. Garden City, N.Y.: Doubleday, 1949.

Morfi, Juan Agustín. *History of Texas, 1673–1779*. Albuquerque, N. Mex.: Quivira Society, 1935.

Otero, Miguel Antonio. *My Life on the Frontier*. 2 vols. New York: Press of the Pioneers, 1935–39.

Otero, Nina. *Old Spain in Our Southwest*. New York: Harcourt, Brace, 1936.

Peixoto, Ernest Clifford. *Our Hispanic Southwest*. New York: Scribner's, 1916.

Pérez Rosales, Vicente. *California Adventure*. Trans. Edwin S. Morby and Arturo Torres Rioseco. San Francisco: Book Club of California, 1947.

Pike, Zebulon Montgomery. *The Southwestern Expedition of Zebulon Pike*. Chicago: Donneley & Sons, 1925.

Pino, Pedro Bautista. *Three New Mexico Chronicles: The Esposición of Don Pedro Bautista Pino, 1812; The Ojeada of Lic. Antonio Barreiro, 1832; and the Additions of José Agustín de Escudero, 1849*. Albuquerque, N. Mex.: Quivira Society, 1942.

Powell, Donald W. *The Peralta Grant: James Addison Reavis and the Barony of Arizona*. Norman: University of Oklahoma Press, 1960.

Prieto, Alejandro. *Historia geográfica y estadística del estado de Tamaulipas*. Mexico City, 1873.

Robinson, W. W. *Land in California: The Story of Mis-*

sion Lands, Ranchos, Squatters, Mining Claims, Railroad Grants, Land Scrip, Homesteads. Berkeley: University of California Press, 1948.

Romano-V, Octavio Ignacio. *Voices: Readings from El Grito, A Journal of Contemporary Mexican-American Thought, 1967–1971*. Berkeley, Calif.: Sol Publications, 1971.

Ross, Stanley R., ed. *Views Across the Border: The United States and Mexico*. Albuquerque: University of New Mexico Press, 1977.

Sánchez, George I. *Forgotten People: A Study of New Mexicans*. Albuquerque: University of New Mexico Press, 1940.

Saunders, Lyle. *Cultural Difference and Medical Care: The Case of the Spanish-speaking People in the Southwest*. New York: Russell Sage Foundation, 1954.

———. *A Guide to Materials Bearing on Cultural Relations in New Mexico*. Albuquerque: University of New Mexico Press, 1944.

Shannon, Lyle W. "The Study of Migrants as Members of Social Systems." In *Spanish Speaking People of the United States*. American Ethnological Society, Annual Meeting, 1968. Distributed by the University of Washington Press, Seattle, 1969.

Sigüenza y Góngora, Carlos de. *The Mercurio Volante of Don Carlos de Sigüenza y Góngora: An Account of the First Expedition of Don Diego de Vargas Into New Mexico in 1692*. Los Angeles: Quivira Society, 1932.

Simmons, Marc. *Spanish Government in New Mexico*. Albuquerque: University of New Mexico Press, 1968.

Simmons, Ozzie G. "Anglo-Americans and Mexican-Americans: The Pattern of Inter-Group Relations." In J. Edward Moseley, ed. *Spanish-speaking People of the Southwest*. Dallas: Council of Spanish American Work, 1966, pp. 54–85.

Stark, Richard B. *Music of the Spanish Folk Plays in New Mexico*. Santa Fe: Museum of New Mexico Press, 1969.

Swadesh, Frances L. "The Alianza Movement: Catalyst for Social Change in New Mexico." In *To See Ourselves: Anthropology and Modern Social Issues*. Glenview, Ill.: Scott, Foresman, 1973, pp. 96–103.

Tebbel, John Willlam. *South by Southwest: The Mexican American and His Heritage*. New York: Doubleday, 1969.

Ulibarrí, Horacio. *The Effect of Cultural Differences in the Education of Spanish-Americans*. Albuquerque: University of New Mexico Press, 1958.

Villagrá, Gaspar Pérez de. *A History of New Mexico*. Chicago: Rio Grande Press, 1962.

Waddel, Jack O. "From Dissonance to Consonance and Back Again: Mexican-Americans and Correctional Processes in a Southwest City." In *Spanish Speaking People of the United States*. American Ethnological Society, Annual Meeting, 1968. Distributed by University of Washington Press, Seattle, 1969.

Wagner, Nathaniel N. *Chicanos: Social and Psychological Perspective*. St. Louis: C. V. Mosby, 1971.

Zavala, Adina de. *History and Legends of the Alamo and Other Missions in and Around San Antonio*. San Antonio, Texas, 1917.

Zea, Leopoldo. *The Latin American Mind*. Trans. James H. Abbott and Lowell Dunham. Norman: University of Oklahoma Press, 1963.

ARTICLES

Aguirre, Yjinio F. "Echoes of the Conquistadores: Stock Raising in Spanish-Mexican Times," *Journal of Arizona History*, Vol. 16, No. 3 (Autumn, 1975), pp. 267–86.

———. "The Last of the Dons," *Journal of Arizona History*, Vol. 10, No. 4 (Winter, 1969), pp. 239–56.

Broom, Leonard, and Kitsuse, John I. "The Validation of Acculturation: A Condition to Ethnic Assimilation," *American Anthropologist*, Vol. 57 (February, 1955), pp. 44–59.

Campa, Arthur L. "Language Barriers in Intercultural Relations," *Journal of Communication*, November, 1951, pp. 1–10.

Chávez, Fray Angélico. "The Penitentes of New Mexico," *New Mexico Historical Reivew*, Vol. 29, No. 2 (April, 1954), p. 111.

Dunham, Harold H. "New Mexico Land Grants with Special Reference to the Title Papers of the Maxwell Grant," *New Mexico Historical Review*, Vol. 3 (January, 1955).

Escobar, Rómulo. "Memorias del Paso del Norte," *Boletín de la Sociedad Chihuahuense de Estudios Históricos*, Vol. 6 (October–November, 1946), pp. 61–62.

Espinosa, J. Manuel. "The Legend of Sierra Azul," *New Mexico Historical Review*, Vol. 9 (April, 1934), pp. 113–58.

Forbes, Jack D. "Race and Color in Mexican-American Problems," *Journal of Human Relations*, Vol. 16 (First Quarter, 1968), pp. 55–68.

Foster, George M. "Cofradía and Compadrazgo in Spain and Spanish-America," *Southwest Journal of Anthropology*, Spring, 1953, pp. 1–28.

———. "Relationships Between Spanish and Spanish-American Folk Medicine," *Journal of American Folklore*, Vol. 66 (1953), pp. 201–47.

———. "What is Folk Culture?" *American Anthropologist*, April-June, 1953, pp. 159–73.

Gipson, Rosemary. "The Mexican Performers: Pioneer Theatre Artists in Tucson," *Journal of Arizona History*, Vol. 13, No. 4 (Winter, 1972), pp. 235–53.

Graf, Leroy P. "Colonizing Projects in Texas South of the Nueces, 1820–1845," *Southwestern Historical Quarterly*, Vol. 50 (April, 1947), pp. 431–49.

Hackett, Charles W. "Retreat of the Spaniards from New Mexico in 1680, and the Beginnings of El Paso," Part 1, *Southwestern Historical Quarterly*, Vol. 16 (October, 1912); Part 2, Vol. 16 (December, 1912).

Haley, J. Evetts. "The Comanchero Trade," *Southwestern Historical Quarterly*, Vol. 38 (January, 1935).

Hammond, George P. "Oñate Marauder?" *New Mexico Historical Review*, Vol. 10 (October, 1935), pp. 249–70.

Jones, Robert C. "Ethnic Family Patterns: The Mexican Family in the U.S.," *American Journal of Sociology*, May, 1948, pp. 450–52.

Lange, Yvonne. "Lithography, an Agent of Technological Change in Religious Folk Art: A Thesis," *Western Folklore*, Vol. 33 (January, 1974), pp. 51–64.

Lewis, Oscar. "Urbanization Without Breakdown: A Case Study," *Scientific Monthly*, Vol. 80 (July, 1952), pp. 31–41.

Lieberson, Stanley. "A Societal Theory of Race and Ethnic Relations," *American Sociological Review*, Vol. 26 (1961), pp. 902–10.

Linton, Ralph. "Nativistic Movements," *American Anthropologist*, Vol. 45, No. 2 (April, 1943), pp. 230–40.

Lugo, José del Carmen. "Life of a Rancher," *Historical Society of California Quarterly*, Vol. 32 (September, 1950), pp. 185–236.

McConville, James Edward. "El Paso–Ciudad Juárez: A Focus of Inter-American Culture," *New Mexico Historical Review*, Vol. 40 (July, 1965), pp. 233–47.

Maloney, Thomas. "Factionalism and Futility: A Case Study of Political and Economic Reforms in New Mexico." In *Spanish Speaking People of the United States*. American Ethnological Society, Annual Meeting, 1968. Distributed by University of Washington Press, Seattle, 1969.

Marshall, C. E. "The Birth of the Mestizo in New Spain," *Hispanic American Historical Review*, May, 1939, pp. 161–84.

Michaelson, Mike. "Can a Root Doctor Actually Put a Hex on, or Is It All a Great Put-on?" *Today's Health*, 1972, p. 39.

Mintz, Sidney, and Wolf, Eric R. "An Analysis of Ritu-al Co-Parenthood (Compadrazgo)," *Southwestern Journal of Anthropology*, Vol. 6, No. 4 (Winter, 1950), pp. 341–69.

Moorhead, Max L. "Spanish Transportation in the Southwest, 1540–1846," *New Mexico Historical Review*, Vol. 32 (April, 1957).

"On Mexican Folk Medicine," *Journal of the American Anthropological Association*, Vol. 72, No. 1 (February, 1970).

Redfield, Robert. "The Folk Society," *American Journal of Sociology*, Vol. 52, No. 4 (January, 1947), pp. 292–308.

Romano-V., Ignacio Octavio. "Donship in Mexican-American Community in Texas," *American Anthropologist*, Vol. 62 (December, 1960), pp. 966–76.

Rubel, Arthur J. "Concepts of Disease in Mexican-American Culture," *American Anthropologist*, Vol. 62, No. 5 (October, 1960), pp. 795–814.

Samora, Julián, and Larson, Richard. "Rural Families in an Urban Setting: A Study of Persistence and Change," *Journal of Human Relations*, Vol. 9, No. 4 (1961), pp. 493–503.

Scholes, France V. "Church and State in New Mexico," *New Mexico Historical Review*, Vols. 11, 12 (1936–37).

Scott, Florence Johnson. "Customs and Superstitions Among Texas-Mexicans," *Publications of the Texas Folklore Society*, Vol. 2 (1923), pp. 75–85.

Smith, Ralph. "Mexican and Anglo-Saxon Traffic in Scalps, Slaves, and Livestock, 1835–1841," *West Texas Historical Association Yearbook*, Vol. 36 (October, 1960), pp. 98–115.

Valdez, Daniel, and Pino, Tom. "Who Are the Hispanos?" *Denver Post*, August 19, 1968.

Weeks, O. Douglas. "The League of United Latin-American Citizens: A Texas-Mexican Civic Organization," *Southwestern Political and Social Science Quarterly*, Vol. 10 (December, 1929), pp. 257–79.

INDEX